About this Book

This volume is the product of a mutually enriching collaboration between Indigenous leaders, other social activists and scholars from a wide range of disciplines. It explores what is happening today to Indigenous peoples as they are inevitably enmeshed in the remorseless expansion of the modern economy and development, subject to the pressures of the marketplace and government. It is particularly timely, given the growing criticism of free-market capitalism, and of development.

The volume assembles a rich diversity of statements, case studies of specific struggles and situations, and wider thematic explorations. All start from the fact that Indigenous peoples are actors, not victims. The accounts come primarily from North America, and particularly the Cree, the Haudenosaunee (Iroquois) and Chippewa–Ojibwe peoples who straddle the US/Canadian border. There are also studies of Indigenous peoples from South America, and even from the former Soviet Union.

The intellectual focus is on the complex relationships that develop between Indigenous peoples, civil society and the environment in the context of market- and state-mandated development. The volume shows how the boundaries between Indigenous peoples' organizations, civil society, the state, markets, development and the environment are ambiguous and constantly changing. It is this fact that lies at the heart of the political possibility of local agency, but also, ironically, of the possibility of undermining it.

The volume seeks to capture these complex, power-laden, often contradictory features of Indigenous agency and relationships. It shows how peoples do not just resist or react to the pressures of market and state, but also sustain 'life projects' of their own which embody local history and incorporate visions and strategies for enhancing their social and economic ways of living and their relationships to state and markets.

The Editors

Mario Blaser is an Argentinian–Canadian anthropologist who has worked and collaborated on a variety of endeavours undertaken by the Yshiro people since 1991. His scholarly work focuses on exploring the epistemological and political possibilities of non-modern ways of knowing.

Harvey A. Feit is Professor of Anthropology at McMaster University, Ontario. He was an adviser to the Grand Council of the Crees during their 1972–78 treaty process. His research is on how Cree epistemology shapes conservation practices and how these inform political relationships.

Glenn McRae is an applied anthropologist who has worked extensively throughout the United States, India, South Africa, Southeast Asia and Latin America as an environmental consultant. He has a Ph.D. from the Union Institute and University, and teaches at the University of Vermont.

In the Way of Development

Indigenous Peoples, Life Projects and Globalization

EDITED BY MARIO BLASER,

HARVEY A. FEIT AND GLENN McRAE

ZED BOOKS
London & New York

in association with

International Development Research Centre

Ottawa · Cairo · Dakar · Montevideo · Nairobi · New Delhi · Singapore

In the Way of Development was first published in 2004 by
Zed Books Ltd, 7 Cynthia Street, London N1 9JF, UK,
and Room 400, 175 Fifth Avenue, New York, NY 10010, USA

in association with the International Development Research Centre,
Box 8500, Ottawa ON, Canada K1G 3H9
info@idrc.ca/www.idrc.ca

www.zedbooks.co.uk

Designed and typeset in Monotype Bembo by Illuminati, Grosmont
Cover designed by Andrew Corbett
Printed and bound by Gutenberg Press, Malta

Distributed in the USA exclusively by Palgrave Macmillan, a division of
St Martin's Press, LLC, 175 Fifth Avenue, New York, NY 10010

A catalogue record for this book is available from the British Library
Library of Congress Cataloging-in-Publication Data available

Zed ISBN 1 84277 192 2 (Hb)
Zed ISBN 1 84277 193 0 (Pb)

IDRC ISBN 1 55250 004 7

Contents

Acknowledgements

We have benefited from the contributions of many colleagues and participants, to whom we owe much for the development of this project. Jasmin Habib of Wilfred Laurier University has been an extraordinary and generous colleague, who has shaped the conceptualization and implementation of this project throughout. Peter Harries-Jones also provided advice and critical insights throughout all phases of publication, and helped to make this a better book. Many Haudenosaunee people from the Six Nations helped to host the meetings that led to this volume and contributed to the participants' understandings of Indigenous teachings. The late Chief Longboat played a central role in the development of this project. He co-organized the meetings at McMaster University and on the Six Nations lands. He gave a keynote lecture, provided an overview and synthesis of the results of the meetings, and encouraged the development of this volume. Clan Mother Gloria Thomas, Tom Deer, Dawn Martin-Hill, Bev Jacobs and Linda Staats all helped to host and shape the meetings. An extraordinary group of high school students from the Six Nations also attended and entered into discussions eloquently and memorably. Pehuenche Lonko Antolin Curriao from Chile and Alberto Santa Cruz from Paraguay brought Indigenous perspectives from South America, along with Bruno Barras and Aldisson Anguita Mariqueo, who have each contributed to this volume.

In the final stages of editing, the chapter manuscripts were read critically and discussed in depth by the graduate students in our seminar at McMaster in the fall of 2002, and they offered us stimulating and often challenging advice: Alisa Kincaid, Jennifer Levy, Jennifer Mallory, Linda Scarangella, Jennifer Selby and Ben Stride-Darnley. We also benefited from the comments and advice of upper-year undergraduate seminar readers in Anthropology 4AE3.

We have been aided throughout by the exceptional work and continuing advice of numerous professionals, assistants and volunteers. William Coleman of McMaster, Jasmin Habib and Colin Scott served as rapporteurs at the meetings. Others who helped with the meetings were: Kathleen Buddle-Crowe, Patricia Austin, Theresa McCarthy, Saul Rich, Beth Finnis, Beth Barber and the McMaster First Nations Student Association. During our contributors' meeting and conference our Spanish-speaking contributors had the benefit of three days of continuous translation thanks to the extraordinary generosity of Professors John Browning, Nibaldo Galleguillos and George Sorger, and especially Ping-Mei Law, of McMaster and their students. The chapters submitted in Spanish, by Bruno Barras and Aldisson Anguita Mariqueo, were translated into English by Mario Blaser. At the editing stage we have been aided by the professional advice and services of Kenneth Blackwell, Caroline Kinsley, Amanda White and Candida Hadley. We have also benefited from the fine map-making skills of Glenn Garner. It has been a pleasure to work with the editors and production team at Zed Books, Lucy Morton and Robin Gable at Illuminati, and staff at IDRC.

The editors also wish to acknowledge the financial support of: the Social Sciences and Humanities Research Council of Canada (SSHRC) for research grants and a research conference grant to Harvey Feit; the International Development Research Council of Canada (IDRC), the Grand Council of the Cree (Eeyou Astchee) and the United Nations University for helping to fund travel for non-academic Indigenous participants; Environment Canada; and the McMaster University programmes in Indigenous Studies, Peace Studies and Engineering and Society, the Institute on Environment and Health, and especially the Department of Anthropology for administrative and assistantship support as well as financial contributions. Critical funding from the International Network on Water, Environment and Health (INWEH) of the United Nations University made it possible to complete the manuscript preparations.

To the Memory of
Haudenosaunee Chief Harvey Longboat,
1936–2001

1

Indigenous Peoples and Development Processes: New Terrains of Struggle

MARIO BLASER, HARVEY A. FEIT

AND GLENN McRAE

In the last three decades Indigenous peoples' struggles to keep control of their lives and lands have moved from being of concern only to themselves, and some specialists and specialized bureaucracies, to being issues of wide public awareness and debate in many sectors of society. Indigenous peoples' struggles are now carried on within complex transnational networks and alliances that traverse the boundaries between the state, markets and civil society, including the environmentalist and human rights movements. International forums such as the United Nations have become important sites in these networks, but major transnational organizations like the UN and the World Bank must themselves now have policies in place and access to expertise on Indigenous peoples in order to carry out many of their projects. Nearly every time the constitution of a nation-state is rewritten today, a major debate develops about how to include some form of recognition of Indigenous rights. Transnational corporations have to grapple with laws, norms and regulations that complicate their operations when these affect Indigenous peoples. These examples are but a few indications of the dramatically transformed terrains in which Indigenous peoples carry on their lives and their struggles today. Much has changed. But much has not changed.

This book provides the reader with a diverse series of analyses, strategic assessments, examples and reflections on Indigenous peoples' agency and struggles in the face of development projects carried out on these changing terrains. Many of the changes in the arenas in which Indigenous peoples carry on their struggles have been reshaped in these last decades by the initiatives of Indigenous peoples themselves. But much of the terrain has also been dramatically reshaped by others, through the changing roles of the nation-state and of NGOs, the growing importance of transnational corporations and global flows of capital, the expansion of media networks, and the rise of the environmentalist and human rights movements. These changes have altered Indigenous peoples' strategies of struggle to survive and to retain the autonomy they still exercise. We argue, however, that Indigenous peoples' agency and their alliances with wider movements themselves can have, and sometimes have had, transformative effects on the emergence of alternative structures of governance[1] that are not rooted in globalizing development.

The chapters in this book present diverse insights into these developments. The editors have invited chapters from Indigenous leaders and Indigenous and non-Indigenous activists and scholars in the conviction that emerging issues can be best explored and understood by working through a set of differing perspectives and literary forms. The forms range from declarations, to histories, comparative analyses, theoretical explorations and analytical case studies, to practitioners' handbooks.

The 'mix' of authors is also an important feature of the book because their perspectives and experiences are rarely brought together. Rather they tend to be seen either as mutually exclusive (even antagonistic), or as representing diverse 'levels' on a scale of knowledge. We reject models that put local/ traditional knowledge and global/scientific knowledge on opposing extremes of a scale of accuracy and, therefore, authority. It is within a framework of openness to dialogue and emerging understandings that we seek to explore the themes of this book.

The theme of Indigenous peoples' agency in the context of the changing terrains in which development processes take place is explored in many of the chapters of this book as a counterpoint between 'life projects' and 'development projects'. The two introductory chapters serve the parallel aims of providing the contexts for the chapters that follow, and contributing to an emerging conceptual framework for understanding and acting in these new terrains. This introduction contextualizes the changes in the terrains of Indigenous action over recent decades, and provides a preview of each chapter in the volume. The other introductory chapter, by Mario Blaser, sets out the idea and practice of Indigenous life projects as a key to under-standing and rethinking Indigenous agency in the midst of these changing contexts. It explores how Indigenous projects are linked to those terrains but also how Indigenous life projects differ from the dominant and more common ideas and practices of development and development projects. That chapter also provides an account of the structure of the volume in terms of its thematic sections.

Our sense as editors is that many readers of this volume will come to it with familiarity with one or more of the areas of these changes. But because we think that there has been only limited overlap between the literatures and venues devoted to Indigenous issues and those focused on development, we assume that many readers will not be familiar with the recent developments in all of the fields involved, and that most will not be familiar with the growing connections between them. This introduction was, therefore, conceived of as an overview of recent trends in, and the interconnections among, the areas of Indigenous rights, human rights, sustainable development, civil society and globalization. Our aim is not to review each area comprehensively, but to draw out how the changes in each of these areas impact and are impacted by Indigenous peoples. Indeed, we think that Indigenous peoples and issues have become key links among these terrains of knowledge and struggle.

Terrains of Subordination and Survival

Indigenous lives and life projects have never been pursued in a vacuum; they can only be pursued amidst other projects. If the relations between different projects were more or less symmetrical, the broad cultural values and the visions of both Indigenous peoples and developers would each find some point of mutual accommodation. As a few chapters in this volume show, when conditions of a relative balance of power occurred the treaties made between Indigenous peoples and newcomers have embodied the cultural underpinnings of both groups, as in the Two-Row Wampum discussed by Deborah McGregor and by Mary Arquette, Maxine Cole and the Akwesasne Task Force on the Environment.

Yet once the newcomers secured their dominion over Indigenous peoples – by resettlement with the aid of depredations caused by the spread of disease, military conquest, or incremental dispossession – they refused to recognize the latter's conceptions of right and the pursuit of their life projects, justifying this on the basis that Indigenous societies and cultures were primitive and undeveloped (Asch 2000). In this new situation of asymmetry, the colonizers have repeatedly imposed their cultural forms on relations with Indigenous peoples. Thus, under the 'custody' of the nation-states, Indigenous lands and resources, and even their children, have been susceptible to seizure either in the name of the greater good, for an abstract 'all', or for their own presumed benefit. These actions assume the colonizers' conceptions of the correct relationships that must prevail among humans, as individuals and groups, and between human and non-human entities, or roughly what is called 'nature'.

In the international system of sovereign states those Indigenous spokespersons who have again and again called attention to these abuses have gone mostly unheard (Wilmer 1993: 2–3). Further, even when abuses were attended to, the basic storyline of development was not doubted. As the International Labor Organization Convention 107 of 1957 expressed it:

Considering that there exist in various independent countries indigenous and other tribal and semi-tribal populations which are not yet integrated into the national community and whose social, economic or cultural situation hinders them from benefiting fully from the rights and advantages enjoyed by other elements of the population ... [g]overnments shall have the primary responsibility for developing co-ordinated and systematic action for the protection of the populations concerned and their progressive integration into the life of their respective countries [although] recourse to force or coercion as a means of promoting the integration of these populations into the national community shall be excluded. (ILO 1957)

Thus Indigenous peoples continually find themselves subordinated within the nation-state and international system. This implies that, for the most part, their struggles to pursue their own life projects take place in a field dominated by Western 'cultural underpinnings', including the central idea of development (see Stavenhagen 1996; Tully 2000).

In contrast, the visions embodied by Indigenous life projects entail a relationship between equals and an end to the subordination of Indigenous peoples. Thus, attention to the field of power relations in which they operate is among the central considerations of life projects. This attention to relationships and power informs the strategies through which Indigenous organizations struggle to end the subordination of their life projects and to pursue their unhindered realization. Central to their strategies has been the mobilization of Indigenous peoples for recognition of their rights. When we speak of rights, we are speaking of more than legal issues. We are talking more broadly of the life projects that embody visions of the world and the future, and of the inherent right to pursue one's own life.

As a consequence of the subordination of Indigenous peoples, their life projects have had to be furthered through the cracks left open, by unexpected events and the passage of time, in the oppressors' own discourses and legal expressions of rights. By having to speak the 'language' of the dominant group, the broad cultural underpinnings of Indigenous peoples' struggles have often been obscured, and their political significance has gone unaddressed by most analysts. This volume is part of a growing and diverse literature that seeks to reduce that omission.

From the 1960s onwards, and in connection with both the civil rights and decolonization struggles occurring around the world, subordinated groups, including Indigenous peoples, began to call more effective attention to the contradictions between the standards of human rights proclaimed by nation-states and international standards, and the actual way in which these were imposed on or ignored for Indigenous peoples (see Brysk 2000; Messer 1993; Niezen 2003; Wilmer 1993; Wright 1988). In the process they contributed to the erosion among nation-state authorities, and the public more generally, of unselfconscious confidence in dominant Western values, including the ideas of development.

In order to provide a background picture of how these transformations took place, what new political terrains they have shaped, and how Indigenous peoples pursue their life projects in them, we will examine several areas on which key changes have occurred. In the next section of this chapter we provide a brief overview of the processes through which Indigenous rights emerged in the context of development and the connections of these processes with environmental issues. In the following section we focus on the contemporary political terrains that have been partly shaped by these processes and discuss Indigenous peoples' organizational adaptations and strategies to pursue their life projects in the new terrains.

In reviewing the changes of recent decades we also set out to build some additional bridges between the domains of Indigenous rights as a specialization and critical development work, because these connections have often not been considered central to social analysis and action.

Indigenous Rights and Development

As indicated by the fragment from ILO Convention 107, the broader agenda of development included human rights to the extent that 'integration' of Indigenous peoples was supposedly aimed, in part, at extending to them some socio-economic human rights, or 'second-generation rights' (Messer 1993: 222). However, in pointing out that force had to be excluded as an instrument of integration, the convention underscored the contradiction between the goal of recognizing human rights and the way in which development was often being delivered.

When, in the late 1960s and early 1970s, the international human rights network began to take shape, some organizations – like the Anti-Slavery Society, the International Work Group on Indigenous Affairs (IWGIA), Survival International and Cultural Survival – focused specifically on the abuses committed against Indigenous peoples (see Martinez Cobo 1986; Wilmer 1993: 141). These organizations were at odds with dominant ideas in governmental circles because they asserted that respect for cultural differences was a viable alternative to integrationist development. Over time they developed active collaborations with ongoing efforts by Indigenous peoples to organize and make their voices heard in international arenas. For Indigenous peoples, this was a means to improve their situation in the national contexts where they lived (see Bodley 1988; Sanders 1977; Davis 1977; Wright 1988).

In the 1970s the proliferation of Indigenous advocacy and Indigenous organizations closely matched the internal expansion of many nation-states as they initiated grand schemes of development affecting resources and Indigenous peoples in 'peripheral areas', including, among others, agrarian reform, agricultural colonization, green revolution schemes, road building, dams, mining, and oil exploration and production (Sanders 1973; Wilmer 1993).

Indigenous peoples in Latin America, for example, responded to the developmentalist wave of the 1960s and 1970s by trying to stop it, or trying to direct some of its policies and programmes to their own benefit. The last strategy was used particularly in the context of agrarian reforms initiated by nation-states, and it involved the reshaping of previous relationships between Indigenous and non-Indigenous organizations and movements in each national context. In the Andean regions of countries like Bolivia, Ecuador and Peru, as well as in Guatemala and Mexico, Indigenous peoples created unions, political parties or cooperatives that, until the 1980s, did not articulate their demands in terms of their Indigenous identity; rather they tended to identify themselves as peasant organizations (see Yashar 1998; Albó 1999). In contrast, the organizations that emerged to challenge the threats of encroachment and destruction posed by the expansion of the states and markets into areas that had remained mostly outside their reach adopted a more decidedly international stance, without disregarding national alliances but stressing their ethnic identity (Ramos 1998; Maybury Lewis 1999; Brysk 2000).

The early organizations emerged with the support of non-Indigenous institutions, particularly sectors of the Catholic Church influenced by liberation theology. As Indigenous organizations grew they developed connections with each other. They obtained leverage through the international human rights network, whose main strategy consisted of lobbying donor countries and multilateral organizations to make development aid conditional upon the recipient countries' record of human rights (Sanders 1977: 25–6; Tomasevski 1993: 84–5; Keck and Sikkink 1998: 102–3). However, this support was not universal, and, in contrast to those organizations which specialized in Indigenous issues, the wider human rights network did not see development aimed at integrating Indigenous peoples into the national society as a human rights violation. Thus the ability of Indigenous organizations to call on human rights groups to further Indigenous life projects was limited (Brysk 1994, 1996). As long as a 'developing' state followed the model of the developed countries and avoided the most flagrant violations of human rights in executing its projects, its integrationist development agenda remained legitimate.

Through the 1980s Indigenous movements in Latin America actively participated in the wider processes of democratization that swept through the region (see Diaz Polanco 1997; Van Cott 1994; Ramos 1998; Horst 1998; Warren 1998). Thus, the idea of respect for Indigenous peoples' cultural differences began to expand, at least as rhetoric, into the policymaking of development donors, governments, international institutions and even markets (see Assies et al. 2000; Brysk 2000; Van Cott 2000). In the 1990s, several Latin American countries began state reforms. Although these reforms took shape in a wider context informed by neoliberal agendas such as the liberalization of trade, downsizing of the state, and decentralization of its operations, they opened the door for groups with specific interests to fight for inclusion in this process. This was the case with Indigenous rights, which were incorporated in a number of new national constitutions that emerged from these processes of state reform (see Yashar 1998; Van Cott 2000; Sieder 2002).

In North America the expansion of resource and social development projects in the 1960s and 1970s also gave impetus to rapid Indigenous mobilizations, led in some cases by Indigenous peoples in formerly remote or isolated areas who were now experiencing development projects on a new scale. In the post-Second World War boom years the growing affluence of significant sectors of North American societies led to a growing awareness of poverty, the failures of development and civil rights abuses for other sectors of the population and in some regions of the nation. The growing demands, and wider public awareness and support, for redressing these 'inequalities' focused on integrationist projects for economic development of black and urban poor communities and Indigenous urban and rural people. This wave of organizing and public support, and government efforts at co-optation, facilitated the emergence of new Indigenous organizations at regional and national levels in each country as governments needed and sought representatives with whom to consult on the development of policies and programmes for Indigenous peoples. This entire process was still envisaged within the framework of externally driven development projects. The new Indigenous organizations that survived from this period developed into more autonomous voices and actors, although for a long time some saw such development as the only avenue of escape from the history of colonial administration.

In the 1970s and 1980s breakthroughs in the national legal recognition of Indigenous rights transformed the arenas of action in the USA, Canada and Australia. Court cases brought by Indigenous peoples gained new recognition for Aboriginal rights based in part on legal anomalies and residues of the history of their recognition, and in part on challenging the courts to reread the provisions in earlier treaties both as binding documents and in the light of ideas of the period and testimonies about how they were presented, explained and negotiated with Indigenous signatories. In this light, legal provisions often affirmed and allocated access to resources, lands and aspects of self-government and sovereignty, and courts recognized that in new ways (Asch 1997; Harring 2002). In the USA and Canada treaty recognition expanded, and emerged alongside the first legal recognitions in Canada and Australia that Indigenous rights still existed generally over the land where they had not been dealt with by treaty. Once these legal changes began, they were also given impetus by the massive capital now being mobilized for resource developments in isolated regions of the continent and the corporate and investor needs that there be legal clarity and assurances about rights to lands and resources to protect investments.

These developments dramatically shifted attention from socio-economic deprivation to legal rights and governance claims, which had the effect of making Indigenous issues into questions of national importance for the first time in a century or more in these countries. The legal changes decisively moved the focus to the problems of recognizing plurality (Asch 1984; Tully 1995). These processes were paralleled by opportunities for Indigenous action under legislation assuring public involvement in environmental decision-making and the recognition of religious rights and freedoms.

The subsequent three decades have seen a plethora of legal developments, and setbacks, and growing and challenging assertions from Indigenous peoples that recognition of their rights does not mean recognition defined solely by the structures of colonial and national law, but of their own systems of customary law, governance, tenure and resource uses, and 'ways of life' or life projects (Lyons and Mohawk 1992; Alfred 1999; Harring 2002). In recent years, the continuing resource developments on Indigenous lands despite recognitions of legal rights, the growing conservatism and declining sympathies of a public that itself feels less secure in its affluence under neoliberal changes, and the continuing gap between the living standards of Indigenous peoples and other North Americans have led to a new urgency and recognition by many Indigenous communities that they need to participate in some forms of development (RCAP 1996). The patterns of that participation have, as yet, not become clear (but see Russell (Chapter 8), Coon Come (Chapter 9), Craik (Chapter 10) and Scott (Chapter 7) in this volume for exploratory initiatives).

Indigenous claims have in general been increasingly expressed through international initiatives and alliances aimed at pressuring national governments; through the development of Indigenous rights forums and draft conventions; through environmental alliances; and through a burgeoning public recognition of Indigenous arts and media. The latter have become a successful sector of North American, European and Australian consumer culture, albeit with mixed effects (Conklin and Graham 1995; Niezen 2003; Povinelli 1993, 2002).

Until the late 1980s, the most common response of multilateral development institutions and states to the contradictions between the growing pressures on them to uphold the rights of Indigenous peoples and the way in which development was carried out was the promotion of measures to mitigate the impacts produced by development (see Tomasevski 1993: 67–8; Davis 1993; Deruyttere 1997; Burger 1998; Swepston 1998; Kreimer 1998; Sanders 1998). However, through the 1970s the contradiction was increasingly clear, and this helped to open a crack in the so-far solid confidence that progress justified almost everything. This crack was widened with the consolidation in the 1980s of the transnational environmentalist movement. With this, the idea that Indigenous peoples have the right to sustain their own life projects received new impetus.

Ecological Differences

We will discuss here neither the antecedents nor the details of the last wave of environmentalism that arose almost parallel with the international Indigenous movement and that was consolidated during the 1980s.[2] Our focus is on how development was transformed by this movement and, in turn, how this transformation affected the struggles of Indigenous peoples to further their life projects.

By the mid-1980s, when environmental activism was booming, it was clear that a new form of relation between developmental and environmental concerns had to be worked out. Different positions about what the new relation should be were proliferating and becoming more visible as different organizations, institutions and movements established connections with each other. Just to mention a few, these positions included radical environmentalism arguing for the total subordination of human activity to natural cycles; environmental-justice movements and eco-socialists putting social inequalities at the top of the environmental agenda; peasants and Indigenous peoples mobilized against the privatization of their lands and resources; and ecological modernization advocating technical fixes for environmental problems (see Taylor 1995; Painter and Durham 1995; Hajer 1995; Collinson 1997; Esteva and Prakash 1998; Parajuli 1998). The result of these debates was the incorporation of environmental concerns into developmental agendas, and of developmental concerns into environmental agendas, by way of the concept of 'sustainable development'. Popularized by the report *Our Common Future* (World Commission on the Environment and Development [WCED] 1987), the ambiguities in the concept of sustainable development made it a useful tool for those pursuing agendas across interfaces connecting organizations and movements with radically different views (Ekins 1993; Worster 1993; Adams 1995).

Sustainable development and its environmental underpinnings contributed to widening the cracks through which Indigenous peoples' life projects could be pursued. Moreover, it strengthened Indigenous peoples' leverage in their dealing with development agendas promoted by state and markets. In the midst of heightened 'environmental awareness' (Lanthier and Olivier 1999), the trope of 'endangered forest, endangered people'[3] provided Indigenous peoples and their advocates not only with a way to frame integrationist development as inherently abusive of their universal human rights, but also with a platform to build the argument that Indigenous societies and cultures are a critical resource in the global search for sustainability because of their traditional environmental knowledge (TEK). Thus, as the sustainable use of the environment became the stated goal of several development institutions, Indigenous peoples came to be seen as worth preserving along with nature. With a synergistic effect, these developments were paralleled by the Indigenous peoples' participation in the democratization movements that, as mentioned before, swept through Latin America during the 1980s.

One could say that with the UN's *Agenda 21*, which provided the framework within which the nation-states should pursue the sustainable development of their societies into the twenty-first century, a reconfigured perception of Indigenous peoples was officially sanctioned by governments and development institutions. In this perspective 'indigenous peoples are given central focus *because of* rather than *in spite of* their cultural differences' (Ellen and Harris 2000: 13, stress in the original; see also Conklin 1997). For example, Chapter 26 of *Agenda 21* states that,

> In view of the interrelationship between the natural environment and its sustainable development and the cultural, social, economic and physical well-being of indigenous people, national and international efforts to implement environmentally sound and sustainable development should recognize, accommodate, promote and strengthen the role of indigenous people and their communities. (UNCED 1992)

The focus on the environment is important to Indigenous peoples in part because it provides a narrative anchor by which their concerns with survival can be articulated with non-Indigenous peoples' concerns for survival. In many cases development projects promoted by states and corporations on Indigenous territories have important environmental impacts that reach well beyond local settings. Thus, the potential exists for Indigenous peoples to gather support on the basis that the threat to their territories and survival constitutes a threat or a loss to people located elsewhere and a responsibility on the part of those whose lifestyles would benefit from the resources being extracted. The connections between these concerns are often constructed through alliances between Indigenous organizations and urban-based NGOs which may translate Indigenous concerns into a language of environmentalist symbols that are meaningful for the public whose support is vital. The problem is that these translations often involve important distortions of

Indigenous perspectives that eventually resurface and often create feelings of betrayal between former allies.

Guha and Martinez-Alier (1997) point out what they call the fundamental difference between 'the ecology of affluence and the environmentalism of the poor'. The dominant thrust of environmental movements and NGOs among relatively affluent urbanites has been the preservation of wilderness and protection and respect for other species. By contrast, the environmentalism of peasants and Indigenous peoples is often wrapped up in the problems of subsistence (see also Taylor 1995; Esteva and Prakash 1998). Because of the subordinated positions in which Indigenous peoples find themselves, it is usual for this second form of environmental concern to be translated into the first form. This pattern also occurs among those non-Indigenous allies who were more inclined to accept the idea of sustainable development than environmental preservation, but who nevertheless retain for themselves the authority to define what it means. Such alliances are bound to end in disappointment, for they disregard the fact that Indigenous communities oppose large-scale developments and programmes that imply the erosion or takeover of their subsistence base and territories, yet at the same time they seek to promote their own life projects. This usually entails resource-use projects that Indigenous communities envisage will improve the economic and social conditions under which they live but that can be entirely unacceptable to former allies.

Sustainable Development, Civil Society and Globalization

The role of Indigenous peoples and the environment is not the only feature that has changed in the new official visions of 'sustainable development'. Now organizations of civil society and not state governments are seen as the most appropriate instruments to achieve the sustainability of an economic development whose main motor is the market (see Peet and Watts 1996). In relation to the previous view of development, this refurbished version shows important differences. Development is no longer the responsibility of the state; rather, the state sets the wider framework, the market must be its motor, and civil society would give it direction (Rist 1997: 223–6). These transformations of development discourses and practices are part and parcel of wider processes often referred to as globalization. These processes, characterized by the increasing circulation of peoples, ideas and commodities, prompt the emergence of organizational forms that are intended to control, adapt and tap into those circulations. Thus, many of the functions held by the nation-state are transferred upwards to supranational institutions and common markets through economic and political integration, downwards to regions and communities through political and administrative decentralization, and sideways to NGOs and the private sector through 'democratization' and privatization. As Rose (1996) points out, the state is increasingly 'de-governmentalized' and the practices of government 'de-statized'. The significance of these changes goes beyond any diminution in the role of the state, or shifts in the balance of power between the state, on the one hand, and market and civil society, on the other. Rather the meaning of these changes is that the boundaries of these domains get increasingly blurred (Alvarez et al. 1998; Wood 1997; Pearce 1997; Barry et al. 1996).

In the discourses of development this blurring of boundaries is underplayed, or rather it is interpreted as democratization because of the expansion of civil society. This view serves very well the development strategy that has become dominant in governmental and multilateral institutions. This strategy, based on neoliberal economics and liberal political theory (Edwards and Hulme 1996b), assigns to the state the role of a legislator and guarantor of the rules that allow the market to operate unhindered on a transnational and global scale. The assigned role for the market is to generate the wealth with which development can be built. The task of making development 'human' (see UNDP 1990: 10) − that is, to input other values than economic efficiency − has been increasingly assigned to organizations from civil society, or NGOs. This is because NGOs are perceived as well suited to provide the services that states abandon as structural adjustment advances, and to set limits to state abuse and inefficiency and provide a vehicle for more democratic participation through civil society (Hudock 1999; Eade 2000; Edwards and Hulme 1996a; Hulme and Edwards 1997).

The centrality that NGOs have acquired in development agendas has been shaped not only by forces coming from governmental and multilateral development institutions but also by pressures from grassroots movements resisting or trying to modify the development agendas promoted by states and markets. Often there is a coalescing into formal organizations, including NGOs of distinct social movements, such as those that resent the human, social and environmental consequences of development agendas, those that seek to incorporate their concerns into the development agendas, and those that want to further alternative life projects (see Geddicks 1993; Taylor 1995; Collinson 1997; Esteva and Prakash 1998). In searching for leverage to accomplish their purposes, NGOs have tended to establish links with each other and with governmental and multilateral institutions (see Keck and Sikkink 1998; Fox and Brown 1998; Alvarez et al. 1998).

In turn, the development industry and governments in many countries have realized that they cannot negotiate with the vast number of local communities and groups. Thus, since the late 1980s, they have begun to rely on NGOs to communicate, consult and implement programmes. In this context, most organizations of the so-called civil society have ended up performing hybrid functions, serving multiple purposes and shaping, along with state and market organizations, a complex transnational network through which the life projects of Indigenous and other groups and the different agendas of development are struggled over (see Fisher 1997; Bellier and Legros 2001).

Indigenous peoples have had to keep pace with these complex changes. Thus they make use of a wide spectrum of strategies and organizational possibilities adapted to the evolving terrain in which their struggles take place. A detailed description of these organizational forms and strategies would exceed the scope of the volume, yet we think it useful to highlight some general patterns that can be extracted from the pertinent literature, specially those patterns that are relevant to understanding the cases discussed here.[4]

Indigenous and Non-Indigenous Organizations

To understand the organizational forms adopted by Indigenous peoples' movements, it helps to consider the relationships between these movements and the degree of control and input that Indigenous peoples have in the political and judicial processes that affect them – in other words, to what extent they can further their claims through political parties, unions and/or other organizational forms with direct access to decision-making processes within the state and/or by recourse to a relatively independent judicial system.[5] Another illuminating dimension is the relationship between organizational forms and the demographic weight that Indigenous peoples have in the total population of a nation-state. Focusing on these dimensions we suggest that:

- In national contexts where Indigenous movements have relatively high levels of control and input in the political process, and their demographic weight is nationally or regionally important, Indigenous concerns can achieve expression in practically the whole spectrum of organizational forms from political parties to NGOs, and from local forms of government to unions. This obtains in varying degrees, but the paradigmatic case is Bolivia, where in 1993 the president and vice-president of the Republic emerged from a coalition of Indigenous movements and a political party. To a lesser extent Ecuador and some regions in Mexico fit this scenario.
- Where high demographic weight is associated with low control and input to the political and judiciary process, it usually occurs because participation is blocked by the use or threat of violence. These are highly explosive con-

texts where armed struggles are a likely occurrence with the consequent formation of guerrilla-type organizations, although this does not mean that other forms of organizations will not be present. The paradigmatic cases here are Guatemala and Chiapas in Mexico.

- In contexts where control and input are relatively high but demographic weight is low, organizational forms usually include, with varying levels of sovereignty and autonomy, some state-recognized form of tribal government, or Indigenous governments that exercise sovereignty over restricted territories, or de facto ethnically controlled regional governments within a national structure. The Kuna in Panama, the Miskito in Nicaragua, the larger self-governing tribes in the USA and the Inuit of Nunavut in Canada are examples of these possibilities.
- In contexts in which Indigenous movements have relatively low control and input and little demographic weight, what we commonly find is the presence of NGOs that may perform governmental functions in parallel or conjunction with established local Indigenous sources of authority.

Most cases in this volume fall into the last two categories. In these categories, complex forms of organization can develop and also be transformed into other types. Usually the invasion of governmental authority and development projects into local settings requires the creation of a forum that the interlopers can negotiate with and understand. Thus where local systems of organization cannot provide such forums, or established local governments are not recognized as such by dominant institutions, the state or private sector takes over essential functions such as the administration of justice and control over common resources, among others. This has happened to most Indigenous peoples throughout the world in varying degrees.

However, Indigenous peoples have often succeeded in creating NGOs that provide both an institutional interface with outside pressures and a forum in which the language of the state and development industry can be translated for the local community, and vice versa. Now, these forms of organization can coexist with already established or 'traditional' sources of authority and government, or they can eventually evolve into such. In any case, these organizations may administer community funds, start businesses, serve as a forum for negotiations among the communities' members themselves and with provincial and national governments, carry out local governance functions, and engage in international diplomacy and litigation.

Local NGOs can provide a deliberative buffer between communities and outsiders (developers or other NGOs and social movements), often to the frustration of non-Indigenous NGOs and governmental units seeking quick decisions. This intermediary position opens up great opportunity to sustain and protect local processes, but also to create misinterpretations or even abuse. This is ingrained in the nature of local NGOs, for they are generally controlled by a small group of people who act as representatives of a whole community, a community which might not operate according to the expectations of state representative politics. In addition, to the extent that these organizations are not clearly established as legitimate authorities, they are vulnerable to attacks by interested external parties who may claim that they do not represent the interests of the communities and therefore disregard them as valid political interlocutors. This is a common tactic by governments and private interests when the agendas put forward by local organizations collide with their interests.

In summary, Indigenous organizations could be analysed as part of civil society, yet many of them take on governance functions. In many cases they even become entrepreneurial, taking on functions usually relegated to the marketplace. Moreover, Indigenous administrative structures and service organizations are, on occasion, tied to state structures for funding and legal legitimacy, which in turn makes them partly accountable to the state. Nevertheless, they may also be held accountable to other sources of authority deriving from established 'traditional' institutions, such as hereditary chieftaincies or elders, or in relation to locally held moral values and notions of legitimacy. Thus, Indigenous organizations are inside and outside both civil society and the state and markets. But this positioning, as several chapters show, fits quite well with contemporary processes that make it difficult to sustain the distinction between civil society, state and market.

Indigenous and Non-Indigenous Strategies

There is also a relationship between the degree of control and input that Indigenous peoples have in a nation-state's political and judicial processes and the dominant orientation that emerges in patterns of alliance-making, lobbying and support gathering. In varying degrees, the greater the control and input, the more the strategic orientation of Indigenous movements is inward towards the national context. In the Americas, inward orientations are observed mostly in contexts in which Indigenous peoples' participation in the political process is not severely or specifically blocked, or where some degree of sovereignty and self-determination, recognized through treaty rights and other binding agreements, are enforced or can be plausibly contested on grounds of non-enforcement. In North America a dominant inward strategic orientation has also been connected to the modest effect that pressures and lobbying via external third parties can have in so-called First World states' political and judiciary processes, although it can be important in specific instances.

The 'boomerang strategy' (Keck and Sikkink 1998: 12–13) of using international political arenas to influence national decision-making is most common in contexts where control and input by Indigenous peoples in the political and judiciary process are more restricted and where armed struggle is clearly not a viable option.[6] The boomerang strategy can be aimed at stopping or modifying particular development projects or promoting wider policy and legal changes to attain Indigenous peoples' rights. However, as we hinted above, Third World states are usually more vulnerable than First World states to these kinds of strategies because in most cases they need the latter's political and financial support (also channelled through multilateral financial institutions) to advance development projects. These First World states, in turn, often do not have too much to lose, and sometimes have something to gain, by submitting to the demands of environmental and human rights lobbying groups, since they can claim credit for trying to improve conditions in the Third World.

Private corporations undertaking mega-development projects in Third or First World countries are even more shielded than First World states against this strategy, since private financing institutions do not necessarily subscribe to or enforce the norms officially accepted by public institutions regarding Indigenous peoples' rights.[7] Moreover, as Johnston and Garcia-Downing point out in this volume (Chapter 13), lack of accountability becomes the norm as the privatization of development financing expands.

A corollary of this is that Indigenous peoples facing mega-development projects are left in a very weakened position – they can count less and less on the boomerang strategy and often do not have recourse to a relatively independent judicial system. But even if a relatively independent judicial system exists, it is an alternative only to the extent that Indigenous peoples have the economic means to make use of it. And even in that case, the legal alternative is besieged by traps and counterproductive results for Indigenous movements. All of this indicates the need to follow a multi-pronged strategy of lobbying, alliance making, appealing to courts, and public campaigns.

Yet the feasibility of a multi-pronged strategy that includes alliances with other social movements and NGOs as well as public campaigns is highly dependent on the existence of clearly delimited and visible rallying points of common interest. Such can be the case in the impending construction of a dam or mine (see Coon Come, Craik, and Gedicks and Grossman, Chapters 9, 10 and 11 in this volume) or the destruction in a short period of time of a vast expanse of forest, as in the Amazon. The problem is that the most common situation for Indigenous peoples is the one described in this volume by Anguita Mariqueo (Chapter 12), where pressures over their territories and resources are more or less continuous, consistent with a wider logic of economic development, but not necessarily connected through a master plan promoted by states or corporations. In these circumstances Indigenous movements only have recourse to the more general norms about human rights, environmental sustainability and cultural diversity that, while recognized to some extent by the public and in official documents, are often ambiguous. Even when they are unambiguous, their enforcement by the state and other international institutions is faltering, to say the least. These circumstances often generate inward-directed violence and sometimes – as a strategy of last resort to seize the attention of the national and international public about impending environmental and social catastrophes – violent uprisings in the communities.

Chapter Previews and Conclusions

In the shifting terrain of rapidly changing structures of governance throughout the world today, the opportunities for alliances across social movements have become more numerous. Indigenous peoples further their life projects by engaging themselves with and against governments and corporate interests while connecting themselves into networks of exchange and solidarity with other groups and communities in their region, country or across the globe.

These movements have the potential, through these alliances, to disrupt emerging structures of governance, as several of the papers in this volume show. For example, Glenn McRae shows (Chapter 7) how the interaction between Vermonters and James Bay Crees, during the latter's campaign to stop a hydroelectric mega-development in Quebec, set in motion processes that led some Vermont activists to see their state in a new light and to undertake to transform the very structures through which Vermonters govern themselves. He shows that the forms of 'grassroots transnationalism' that emerge around this kind of campaign serve to stimulate and strengthen the communities that enter into contact, while they maintain their distinctiveness. These kinds of effects of Indigenous alliances have not been previously explored to our knowledge, and they expose the unexpected results and possibilities of Indigenous movements and alliances. Brian Craik (Chapter 10) looks at these connections from another perspective, that of the Crees' strategists and Cree leadership. He discusses the complex issues and decisions that the Cree leadership had to face, having to wage campaigns that responded, at the same time, to immediate opportunities, long-term goals, community demands, and allies' expectations. His is an insider's view into how some contemporary Indigenous organizations operate and forge connections that strengthen them while enhancing the autonomy of their allies.

The strengthening of connections and the transformation of networks is also a point addressed by Al Gedicks and Zoltán Grossman's chapter (11) on the anti-mining coalition that emerged from a very unlikely terrain. In the 1980s Indigenous and non-Indigenous communities in northern Wisconsin were often antagonistic to each other over the use of natural resources and treaty rights. Yet in the 1990s the threat that mining operations posed to the same regional resources led these communities into unexpected alliances, which emerged not only from recognizing new common concerns, but from the utility of treaty and Native Americans' rights for protecting regional resources for all. As a result, the authors argue, the whole idea of who are outsiders and who are insiders has radically reshaped identities in ways that strengthen local and regional connections in the face of mobile capital. This resonates with Pramod Parajuli's chapter (14) on the formation of 'ecological ethnicities'. Parajuli argues that the ravages of transnational capital itself produce the commonalities that connect ecological ethnicities across their differences: they are all dependent on the local resources from which mobile capital incessantly dispossesses them. As the Zapata- and Gandhi-inspired movements in Mexico and India show, in their struggles to sustain the basis of their livelihood and their ways of living, ecological ethnicities strive for a form of autonomy that alters relations of power and questions: 'what is power, what is governance and what are other possible roles of state, civil society and communities?'

Barbara Rose Johnston and Carmen Garcia-Downing (Chapter 13) discuss a different aspect of translocal connections. In their case, the connections under focus are those between a struggling Indigenous people, the Pehuenche of Chile, and human rights organizations, international professional associations, and development institutions. They show the possibilities and the limitations that these kinds of connections have for stopping human rights abuses in the context of mega-developments. Aldisson Anguita Mariqueo's chapter (12) shows that, in the same national context, mega-developments are just part of a general historical and contemporary pattern of development that, because it proceeds through apparently unconnected operations, is not always recognized as a systematic abuse of Indigenous peoples' human rights.

Chief Matthew Coon Come describes (Chapter 9) a very similar pattern in a different national context, Canada. He forcefully argues that since colonial times, Canada and Quebec have consistently disregarded the Indigenous peoples' and his own James Bay Cree nation's interests and way of life as unworthy of attention when they dispose of land and resources in Cree territory. Thus he argues that the Crees not only seek to survive mega-developments, they struggle to share equitably in the benefits of their lands, through their distinctive ways of life and ways of relating to the land, and he argues that this is founded on their determination to establish their rights of self-governance and self-determination. In her contribution (Chapter 18), Dawn Martin-Hill provides an intimate and powerful portrayal of the human

dimension of rights abuses. The testimonies she shares show the abusive exer-
cises of power and the suffering they create, and how they are hidden by the
abstract arguments of government and media. She shows what Lubicon Cree
and particularly Lubicon women have to endure in the face of development,
and yet how their struggles continue in the midst of their suffering.

Colin Scott argues in his chapter (17) that in contemporary politics
contested rights are at the core of structural reform vis-à-vis Aboriginal
peoples. His chapter maps the contours of conflicting political discourses on
Aboriginal entitlements and scrutinizes the assumptions that underlie policy
prescriptions. He shows that these assumptions are rooted in long-standing
European notions of civilization and progress, race, freedom and equality.
He explores the effects of these notions on ideologies of state governance,
property and market organization, and their impact on different options for
Aboriginal self-determination and development.

For Peter Harries-Jones (Chapter 16), the ability to control their own
forms of development is critical for Indigenous peoples' life-politics. He
argues that the life-politics of Indigenous traditions counter a 'wild globalization' that is completely out of step with ecological cycles. He explores
conceptual bridges that may both help science to understand and grapple
with globalization in ecological terms, and establish connections between
these scientific efforts and those that Indigenous peoples pursue through
the traditional knowledge embodied in their life-politics. The connection
between science and Indigenous traditional environmental knowledge, in
the context of sustainable development, is the focus of Deborah McGregor's
chapter (5). She shows that the ways TEK is conceptualized and used within
dominant Western settings undermines its insights into the reasons for the
environmental crisis, and its possible resolution. Turning from thinking of
TEK as knowledge to exploring it as an ongoing way of living, she shows
how TEK addresses power asymmetries between Indigenous and non-indigenous peoples. As long as this is unrecognized in TEK research and
implementation, the uses of TEK in science and policymaking constitute
another form of colonialism that cannot but reinforce the current crises of
the environment.

The profound connections, from the standpoint of an Indigenous epistemology and ontology, that exist between the domination of one group of
people by another and environmental degradation, are convincingly demonstrated by Mary Arquettte, Maxine Cole and the Akwesasne Task Force on
the Environment (ATFE). In Chapter 19 they show how the Haudenosaunee
(Iroquois) conceive the whole of Creation as being a web of interconnections
and responsibilities that cannot be interrupted without perilous consequences.
Thus, the imposition of development and the disruption brought to the relations and responsibilities that the Mohawk of Akwesasne sustained with their

environment have had devastating consequences for the whole of Creation. In order to reverse this process they propose that relations and responsibilities be given their proper respect. Harvey Feit's chapter (6) follows this line of argument by tracing the connections that many James Bay Crees see between ways of relating to non-humans and ways of relating to humans. In his analysis, Feit shifts the usual focus in studies of Indigenous peoples' relations to the environment by exploring how Cree ways of understanding relations to animals extend into the political actions of Cree leaders. In this way he interprets Crees' actions that, in the midst of struggles around development, appear to be in contradiction with their claims of attachment to the land, when in reality they are the most consummate example of this attachment.

In his statement (Chapter 3), Yshiro leader Bruno Barras aptly describes how governments, private interests and NGOs in Paraguay constantly make assumptions about the Yshiro's needs and thus carry on with their own agendas of development, always claiming that it is for the Yshiro's benefit. Against this the Yshiro counterpose their life projects, which are nothing less than being able to carry on with their own lives in a way that is meaningful and purposeful for them. For this, Barras says, the Yshiro need to be heard on their own, not through the voices of non-Indigenous NGOs or the government. In the following chapter (4), Mario Blaser discusses the context in which this plea for removing intermediaries makes sense. He shows how the idea of life projects took the form of a pan-Yshiro organization that is trying to regain for the Yshiro the authority to define themselves and their projects. Blaser shows that Indigenous peoples must engage with opponents and self-proclaimed allies, both of whom operate with dominant images of indigenousness that set the terms of debates about Yshiro futures. Thus, the Yshiro are compelled to cut across these debates in order to open up spaces for their own life projects.

Petra Rethmann focuses (Chapter 15) on a similar kind of attempt by Native activists in the Chukotka peninsula in the Russian Far East who search for ways to create political initiatives that are meaningful to the region's Indigenous peoples. She argues that these attempts involve the creation of 'fields of attraction' that are articulated in relation to several layers of history and against the grain of contemporary governmental and capitalist discourses of development in the region. Wendy Russell also discusses (Chapter 8) multiple layers of history that operate as a mnemonic tool to interrogate received notions of economic development for the Cree of Fort Albany in Canada. The memory of the people and history inscribed in the landscape of the settlement exposes the colonial policies that are the continuing context of present imbalances between this community and the mainstream industrial economy. The Cree discourses politicize the poverty of the community today and serve as keys in planning for self-sufficiency by building on the community's entrepreneurial traditions to restructure their relationships with regional economic, social and administrative networks.

As a consequence of their pursuits of these life projects, and almost as a side effect of them, we suggest that these kinds of Indigenous movements imply a reshaping of current structures of governance. These chapters highlight the question and the possibilities: might Indigenous peoples, and other counter-hegemonic movements, generate alternatives to the structures of governance furthered by development under its new guise as globalization?

Notes

1. By 'governance' we refer to the complex of practices, discourses and institutions by means of which human populations and the processes of 'nature' are conducted according to certain ends that themselves are informed by specific values and visions of the world.
2. For the antecedents of the environmental movement, see Grove 1995, Judd 2000, and Guha and Martinez-Alier 1997. For details of the consolidation of the environmental movement in the 1980s, see Keck and Sikkink 1998.
3. We take the phrase from the title of an article by Peter Brosius 1997 on environmentalists' representations of Indigenous knowledge.
4. Some sources in English focusing on different national contexts are Albó 1999; Maybury-Lewis 1999; Van Cott 1994; Diaz Polanco 1997; Warren 1998; Warren and Jackson 2002; Ramos 1998; Gutierrez 1999; Assies et al. 2000; Niezen 2003; Alfred 1999; RCAP 1996; Bellier and Legros 2001. The literature trying to provide a coherent picture of the transnational dimension of Indigenous movements is still scarce. For the most relevant examples see Wilmer 1993, Brysk 2000, and Niezen 2003.
5. By a relatively independent judicial system we mean not only that interference and intrusion by other state institutions in the judicial process is limited but also that even in cases where this is the case, the judicial system itself responds to culturally specific understandings of justice. Thus, it can never be impartial and independent in relation to Indigenous conceptions of justice.
6. The 'boomerang strategy' consists in Indigenous peoples allying themselves with other interested parties (most often environmental and human rights movements) who can reach and lobby external financing institutions or governments so that these exert pressures on national governments.
7. By 'norms' we mean values that are usually codified as laws, covenants, policy frameworks, operational directives, etc.

References

Adams, W.M. (1995) 'Green development theory? Environmentalism and sustainable development', in J. Crush (ed.), *Power of Development*, London: Routledge, pp. 87–99.

Albó, X. (1999) 'Andean people in the twentieth century', in F. Salomon and S. Schwartz (eds), *The Cambridge History of the Native Peoples of the Americas*, vol. 3: *South America – Part 2*, Cambridge: Cambridge University Press, pp. 765–869.

Alfred, T. (1999) *Peace, Power, Righteousness: An Indigenous Manifesto*, Oxford: Oxford University Press.

Alvarez, S.E., E. Dagnino and A. Escobar (eds) (1998) *Cultures of Politics Politics of Cultures: Re-visioning Latin American Social Movements*, Boulder, CO: Westview Press.

Asch, M. (1984) *Home and Native Land: Aboriginal Rights and the Canadian Constitution*, Toronto: Methuen.

—— (1997) *Aboriginal and Treaty Rights in Canada*, Vancouver: UBC Press.

—— (2000) 'First Nations and the derivation of Canada's underlying title: comparing perspectives on legal ideology', in C. Cook and J. Lindau (eds), *Aboriginal Rights and Self-Government: The Canadian and Mexican Experience in North American Perspective*, Montreal: McGill-Queen's University Press, pp. 148–67.

Assies, W., G. van der Haar, and A. Hoekema (eds) (2000) *The Challenge of Diversity: Indigenous Peoples and Reform of the State in Latin America*, Amsterdam: Thela Thesis.

Barry, A., T. Osborne and N. Rose (eds) (1996) *Foucault and Political Reason: Liberalism, Neo-Liberalism and Rationalities of Government*, Chicago: University of Chicago Press.

Bellier, Irene and Dominique Legros (eds) (2001) 'Mondialisation et stratégies politiques autochtones', *Recherches amérindiennes au Québec*, vol. 31, no. 3.

Bodley, J.H. (1988) *Tribal Peoples and Development Issues: A Global Overview*, Mountain View, CA: Mayfield.

Brosius, J.P. (1997) 'Endangered forest, endangered people: environmentalist representations of Indigenous knowledge', *Human Ecology*, vol. 25, no. 1, pp. 47–69.

Brysk, A. (1994) 'Acting globally: Indian rights and international politics in Latin America', in D. Van Cott (ed.), *Indigenous Peoples and Democracy in Latin America*, New York: St Martin's Press, pp. 29–51.

—— (1996) 'Turning weakness into strength: the internationalization of Indian rights', *Latin American Perspectives*, vol. 23, no. 2, pp. 38–57.

—— (2000) *From Tribal Village to Global Village: Indian Rights and International Relations in Latin America*, Stanford: Stanford University Press.

Burger, J. (1998) 'Indigenous peoples and the United Nations', in Cohen C. Price (ed.), *The Human Rights of Indigenous Peoples*, Ardsley, FL: Transnational, pp. 3–16.

Collinson, H. (ed.) (1997) *Green Guerrillas: Environmental Conflicts and Initiatives in Latin America and the Caribbean*, Montreal: Black Rose Books.

Conklin, B.A. (1997) 'Body paint, feathers, and VCRs: aesthetics and authenticity in Amazonian activism', *American Ethnologist*, vol. 24, no. 4, pp. 711–37.

—— and L.R. Graham (1995) 'The shifting middle ground: Amazonian Indians and eco-politics', *American Anthropologist*, vol. 97, no. 4, pp. 695–710.

Davis, S.H. (1977) *Victims of the Miracle: Development and the Indians of Brazil*, Cambridge: Cambridge University Press.

—— (1993) 'The World Bank and Indigenous peoples', Washington, DC: World Bank, at www.worldbank.org/html/extdr/thematic.htm (and choose Indigenous Peoples and then Resources).

Deruyttere, A. (1997) *El Banco Interamericano de Desarrollo y los pueblos indígenas*, Documento de Trabajo: Unidad de Pueblos Indígenas y Desarrollo Comunitario, Washington, DC: Banco Interamericano de Desarrollo, Departamento de Desarrollo Sostenible.

Diaz Polanco, H. (1997) *Indigenous Peoples in Latin America: The Quest for Self-Determination*, Boulder, CO: Westview Press.

Eade, D. (ed.) (2000) *Development, NGOs and Civil Society: A Development in Practice Reader*, Oxford: Oxfam.

Edwards, M. and D. Hulme (1996a) *Beyond the Magic Bullet: NGO Performance and Accountability in the Post-Cold War World*, West Hartford, CT: Kumarian Press.

———— (1996b) 'Too close for comfort: the impact of official aid on nongovernmental organizations', *World Development*, vol. 24, no. 6, pp. 961–73.

Ekins, P. (1993) 'Making development sustainable', in W. Sachs (ed.), *Global Ecology: A New Arena of Political Conflict*, London: Zed Books, pp. 91–103.

Ellen, R. and H. Harris (2000) 'Introduction', in R. Ellen, P. Parkes and A. Bicker (eds), *Indigenous Environmental Knowledge and Its Transformations*, Amsterdam: Hardwood, pp. 1–33.

Esteva, G. and M. Prakash (1998) *Grassroots Post-modernism: Remaking the Soil of Cultures*, London: Zed Books.

Fisher, W. (1997) 'Doing good? The politics and antipolitics of NGO practices', *Annual Review of Anthropology* 26, pp. 439–64.

Fox, J. and David Brown (eds) (1998) *The Struggle for Accountability: The World Bank, NGOs, and Grassroots Movements*, Cambridge, MA: MIT Press.

Geddicks, A. (1993) *The New Resource Wars*. Boston: South End Press.

Grove, R.H. (1995) *Green Imperialism: Colonial Expansion, Tropical Island Edens and the Origin of Environmentalism, 1600–1860*, Cambridge: Cambridge University Press.

Guha, R. and J. Martinez-Alier (1997) *Varieties of Environmentalism: Essays North and South*, London: Earthscan.

Gutierrez, N. (1999) *Nationalist Myths and Ethnic Identities: Indigenous Intellectuals and the Mexican State*, Lincoln: University of Nebraska Press.

Hajer, M. (1995) *The Politics of Environmental Discourse: Ecological Modernization and the Policy Process*, Oxford: Oxford University Press.

Harring, Sidney L. (2002) 'Indian law, sovereignty, and state law: native people and the law', in Philip L. Deloria and Neal Salisbury (eds), *A Companion to American Indian History*, Oxford: Blackwell, pp. 441–59.

Horst, Rene (1998) 'Authoritarianism, Indigenous resistance and religious missions: Paraguay, 1958–1992', Ph.D. thesis, Department of History, Indiana University.

Hudock, A. (1999) *NGOs and Civil Society: Democracy by Proxy?* Cambridge: Polity Press.

Hulme, D. and M. Edwards (eds) (1997) *NGOs, States and Donors: Too Close for Comfort?* New York: St Martin's Press.

International Labour Organization (ILO) (1957) *International Labour Organization Convention (no. 107) concerning the Protection and Integration of Indigenous and Other Tribal and Semi-Tribal Populations in Independent Countries*, New York: United Nations Treaty Series.

Judd, R. (2000) *Common Lands, Common People: The Origins of Conservation in Northern New England*, Cambridge, MA: Harvard University Press.

Keck, M. and K. Sikkink (1998) *Activists beyond Borders: Advocacy Networks in International Politics*, Ithaca: Cornell University Press.

Kreimer, O. (1998) 'The future inter-American declaration on the rights of Indigenous peoples: a challenge for the Americas', in Cohen C. Price (ed.), *The Human Rights of Indigenous Peoples*, Ardsley, FL: Transnational, pp. 63–72.

Lanthier, I. and L. Olivier (1999) 'The construction of environmental "awareness"', in E. Darier (ed.), *Discourses of the Environment*, Oxford: Blackwell, pp. 63–78.

Lyons, Oren and John Mohawk (eds) (1992) *Exiled in the Land of the Free: Democracy, Indian Nations, and the U.S. Constitution*, Santa Fe: Clear Light.

Martinez Cobo, J. (1986) *Study of the Problem of Discrimination against Indigenous Populations*, New York: United Nations.

Maybury-Lewis, D. (1999) 'Lowland peoples of the twentieth century', in F. Salomon and S. Schwartz (eds), *The Cambridge History of the Native Peoples of the Americas*, vol. 3: *South America – Part 2*, Cambridge: Cambridge University Press, pp. 872–938.

Messer, E. (1993) 'Anthropology and human rights', *Annual Review of Anthropology*, vol. 22, no. 221–49.

Niezen, R. (2003) *The Origins of Indigenism: Human Rights and the Politics of Identity*, Berkeley: University of California Press.

Painter, M. and W.H. Durham (eds) (1995) *The Social Causes of Environmental Destruction in Latin America*, Ann Arbor: University of Michigan Press.

Parajuli, P. (1998) 'Beyond capitalized nature: ecological ethnicity as an arena of conflict in the regime of globalization', *Ecumene*, vol. 5, no. 2, pp. 186–217.

Pearce, J. (1997) 'Between co-option and irrelevance? Latin American NGOs in the 1990s', in D. Hulme and M. Edwards (eds), *NGOs, States and Donors: Too Close for Comfort?* New York: St Martin's Press, pp. 257–74.

Peet, R. and M. Watts (1996) 'Liberation ecology: development, sustainability, and environment in an age of market triumphalism', in M. Watts and R. Peet (eds), *Liberation Ecologies: Environment, Development Social Movements*, London: Routledge, pp. 1–45.

Povinelli, Elizabeth A. (1994) *Labor's Lot: The Power, History, and Culture of Aboriginal Action*, Chicago: University of Chicago Press.

——— (2002) *The Cunning of Recognition*, Durham, NC: Duke University Press.

Ramos, A.R. (1998) *Indigenism: Ethnic Politics in Brazil*, Madison: University of Wisconsin Press.

Rist, G. (1997) *The History of Development: From Western Origins to Global Faith*, London: Zed Books.

Rose, N. (1996) 'Governing "advanced" liberal democracies', in A. Barry, T. Osborne and N. Rose (eds), *Foucault and Political Reason: Liberalism, Neo-Liberalism and Rationalities of Government*, Chicago: University of Chicago Press, pp. 37–64.

RCAP (Royal Commission on Aboriginal Peoples) (1996) *Report of the Royal Commission on Aboriginal Peoples*, 5 vols., Ottawa: Royal Commission on Aboriginal Peoples. Also on CD-ROM (1997) *For Seven Generations*, Ottawa: Libraxus.

Sanders, D. (1973) 'Native people in areas of internal national expansion: Indians and Inuit in Canada', *IWGIA Document* 14.

——— (1977) 'The formation of the World Council of Indigenous Peoples', *IWGIA Document* 29.

——— (1998) 'The legacy of Deskaheh: Indigenous peoples as international actors', in Cohen C. Price (ed.), *The Human Rights of Indigenous Peoples*, Ardsley, FL: Transnational, pp. 73–88.

Sieder, R. (ed.) (2002) *Multiculturalism in Latin America: Indigenous Rights, Diversity and Democracy*, New York: Palgrave Macmillan.

Stavenhagen, R. (1996) 'Indigenous rights: some conceptual problems', in E. Jelin and E. Hershberg (eds), *Constructing Democracy: Human Rights, Citizenship, and Society in Latin America*, Boulder, CO: Westview Press, pp. 141–59.

Swepston, L. (1998) 'The Indigenous and tribal peoples convention (no. 169): Eight years after adoption', in Cohen C. Price (ed.), *The Human Rights of Indigenous Peoples*, Ardsley, FL: Transnational, pp. 17–36.

Taylor, B. (ed.) (1995) *Ecological Resistance Movements: The Global Emergence of Radical and Popular Environmentalism*, Buffalo: SUNY Press.

Tomasevski, K. (1993) *Development Aid and Human Rights Revisited*, New York: Pinter.

Tully, James (1995) *Strange Multiplicity. Constitutionalism in an Age of Diversity*, Cambridge: Cambridge University Press.

——— (2000) 'A just relationship between Aboriginal and non-Aboriginal peoples of Canada', in C. Cook and J. Lindau (eds), *Aboriginal Rights and Self-Government: The*

Canadian and Mexican Experience in North American Perspective, Montreal: McGill-Queen's University Press, pp. 39–71.

UNCED (United Nations Conference on Environment and Development) (1992) *Agenda 21: Programme of Action for Sustainable Development – Rio Declaration on Environment and Development – Statement of Forest Principles – the Final Text of Agreements … United Nations Conference on Environment and Development*, New York: United Nations Department of Public Information.

UNDP (United Nations Development Programme) (1990) *Human Development Report*, Oxford: Oxford University Press.

Van Cott, D. (2000) *The Friendly Liquidation of the Past: The Politics of Diversity in Latin America*, Pittsburgh: University of Pittsburgh Press.

—— (ed.) (1994) *Indigenous Peoples and Democracy in Latin America*, New York: St Martin's Press.

Warren, Kay B. (1998) *Indigenous Movements and Their Critics: Pan-Maya Activism in Guatemala*, Princeton: Princeton University Press.

—— and J. Jackson (eds) (2002) *Indigenous Movements, Self-Representation and the State in Latin America*, Austin: University of Texas Press.

WCED (World Commission on Environment and Development) (1987) *Our Common Future*, Oxford: Oxford University Press.

Wilmer, F. (1993) *The Indigenous Voice in World Politics*, Newbury Park, CA: Sage Publications.

Wood, G. (1997) 'States without citizens: the problem of the franchise state', in D. Hulme and M. Edwards (eds), *NGOs, States and Donors: Too Close for Comfort?* New York: St Martin's Press, pp. 79–92.

Worster, D. (1993) 'The shaky ground of sustainability', in W. Sachs (ed.), *Global Ecology: A New Arena of Political Conflict*, London: Zed Books, pp. 132–45.

Wright, R.M. (1988) 'Anthropological presuppositions of Indigenous advocacy', *Annual Review of Anthropology* 17, pp. 365–90.

Yashar, D. (1998) 'Indigenous movements and democracy in Latin America', *Comparative Politics*, vol. 31, no. 1, pp. 23–43.

2

Life Projects:
Indigenous Peoples' Agency
and Development

MARIO BLASER

This volume explores the relations between Indigenous peoples and development in the context of the rapid changes in civil society, the environment and globalization.[1] It does this in part by focusing on the ways development, state and markets are reshaping Indigenous communities and movements. But the editors assert that Indigenous communities do not just resist development, do not just react to state and market; they also sustain 'life projects'.[2] Life projects are embedded in local histories; they encompass visions of the world and the future that are distinct from those embodied by projects promoted by state and markets. Life projects diverge from development in their attention to the uniqueness of people's experiences of place and self and their rejection of visions that claim to be universal. Thus, life projects are premissed on densely and uniquely woven 'threads' of landscapes, memories, expectations and desires. Contributors to the volume try to capture these complex, substantive, power-laden, and sometimes contradictory features of Indigenous peoples' agency. Granted, in most chapters Indigenous peoples' struggles against development projects are the key element in the storyline. Yet I think that this is because, more often than not, development is in the way of life projects. One of the aims of our book is to contribute to an understanding of what these life projects are about, how they are furthered in spite of having development blocking their ways, and what they offer in terms of alternative paths to Indigenous futures.

As indicated in the previous chapter, the theme of Indigenous peoples' agency in the context of the changing terrains in which development processes take place is explored in many of the chapters of this book as a counterpoint between 'life projects' and 'development projects'. The editors see three key moments that need to be examined in this counterpoint: (a) the contrasts between Indigenous peoples' life projects as place-based perspectives and the universalist visions that justify and shape development projects; (b) how Indigenous peoples pursue their life projects against those development projects being done at their expense and in the context of emerging structures of governance and subordination; and (c) how, in spite of Indigenous peoples' willingness to share land and resources with other users, development projects are unwilling to recognize and seek to obscure coexistence.

These moments provide the thematic focus of each of the three sections in which the volume is organized: Visions, Strategies, Invitations. I take up each of these themes in more detail after I discuss why the editors find it is critical to focus on the interface between Indigenous peoples' life projects and development.

Development and Life Projects

The ideas of development and of indigenousness have a long and intimate historical relation. It was the conceptual and legal-political problems that followed the discovery of hitherto unknown other humans in the 'New World' that helped set in motion the reconceptualization by Western Europeans of where and who they were and how they fit in time and history. In part because of their discovery of peoples and places not foreseen in medieval world-views or biblical and ancient sources, Western Europeans began to imagine themselves and their societies as distinctive agents in a progressive history (Elliot 1970; Dussel 1995). They came over time to see their own being as the result of development, 'the active principle according to which new and higher stages of human society might emerge out of old and more simple ones: the driving motive in human history' (Ferguson 1997: 153; see also Fabian 1983; Rist 1997: 25–46).

At the basis of this active principle that divided the human world into two (developed or modern, and underdeveloped or traditional) there was a third conceptual term, nature, which provided the ground, or departure point, of humankind's voyage towards a secular paradise located at some point in the future. Paradoxically, advances on the voyage of progress were marked by the distance, implied by the dominion of humankind over nature, between society and nature. The more nature was mastered, the less humankind was dependent on nature, and the further humankind moved in the line of progress. With this background, and to the extent that Indigenous peoples were located closer to nature than the modern West, the dynamics of progress justified the treatment of the 'Natives', along with nature, as objects of domination. But where a common humanity with the 'backward' other was recognized by the 'developed' West, whether out of necessity as in the case where Indigenous peoples were allies, or out of adopting a self-serving tutelage, this situation of dominion was reshaped by the avowed aim of bringing the Indigenous other closer to the vanguard of progress and its supposed benefits. This basic storyline formed the core of several succeeding discourses and practices of dominant Western-educated elites about Indigenous peoples in many and diverse settings.

By the late twentieth century the social and environmental consequences of this conceptualization of continuous development began to erode the dream of unending progress and confidence in the mastery of nature by 'modern man'. As a response, new and mutually contesting ways of conceiving relations among humans and between humans and nature have emerged, producing transformations in the eroding idea of development. These changes are ongoing in the midst, and partly as a result, of the continuing and ever-expanding incorporation of lands, resources, territories and peoples into the effective dominion of nation-states and global markets.

The editors believe that most development practices have furthered, and still further, the transformation of relatively autonomous and self-governing communities, which over the years have carefully developed an intimate re-lationship with their lands, into dependent communities easier to subordinate to transnational markets and nation-states. Yet, while Indigenous communities have opposed many of these development agendas, their agendas are themselves emergent, rather than a reaction to other agencies. That is to say, their life projects are socio-cultural in the broadest sense rather than narrowly strategic. Their life projects are also place-based but not limited to the local.

In contrast, development promoted by market or state-backed agents, with its claims to political necessities, the greater good and market demands in the context of globalization, appears to be disengaged from place conditions. Development as a practice and discourse embodies the European Enlightenment's implicit project of making specific local world-views and values, those broadly described as modern and Western European, into universals. As a successor to imperialism and colonialism, development has extended the reach of those local world-views and values far beyond the place in which they took shape. I think that pointing out the place-basedness of development is critical to understanding how life projects are situated in relation to development. A place-based perspective provides a fruitful standpoint from which one can understand life projects, become more open and receptive to their visions, and refuse the Enlightenment pretence of universalism. I believe that this pretence is fulfilled when the world-views and values of modernity that are promoted by development are taken to be disembedded from place, made entirely abstract and equated ultimately with 'the global'. Thus, situating life projects in contrast to development requires a discussion of place and how it is related to the politics and epistemology implicit in the ideas of local and global.

Like Escobar (2001: 152), I understand place as 'the experience of, and from, a particular location with some sense of boundaries, grounds, and links to everyday practices'. I am also aware, with Escobar, that this experience is emergent and not a given. A previously implicit understanding of place, in anthropology and other disciplines, as a given and natural locus from which senses of community and identity derive, has been recently displaced by more complex understandings which conceive place as a process, as 'embodied practices that shape identities', in part through resistance to changing 'strategies of power' (see Gupta and Ferguson 1997). This perspective on place-making stresses the point that the immediate experiences of place and identity are inevitably constituted within larger sets of spatial relations.

Doreen Massey (1999: 18) has argued that place can be fruitfully seen as a knot made of a particular mix of threads (i.e. links and connections), 'including local relations "within" the place and those many connections which stretch way beyond it'. I would add that, as the chapters by Russell, Rethmann, McGregor and Feit in this volume show, the links and connections that make place do extend not only spatially but also temporally, as previous 'mixtures of threads' are part of the genealogical make-up of contemporary constitutions of place. These chapters also remind us that place is 'grounded'; that is, place is an emergent of the specific everyday engagement of specific peoples with specific landscapes, environments or 'natures' (see Dirlik 2001: 21; Escobar 2001: 6). Thus I will talk, for ease of presentation, of two kinds of 'threads' shaping place: vertical threads will refer to those links and connections that ground place in specific histories and landscapes; horizontal threads will refer to trans-place linkages in a spatial sense. Within the mutually constitutive relations between these vertical (history/'nature') and horizontal (trans-location) threads the specificity of places arises, thus contributing the elements with which people delineate their more or less stable but always porous boundaries that distinguish them from other lands and other peoples.

Within this brief discussion of the meaning of place, I can advance the argument that both development and life projects are place-based; that is, both are broadly socio-cultural praxes emerging from specific mixes of horizontal and vertical threads. What distinguishes them is the relative importance that each gives to horizontal and vertical linkages and what consequences these visions have for place-making. The chapters in the first section of the volume address the intersections of life projects and development projects, and their consequences, for these different visions.

Visions: The Particularity of Life Projects

Although it entails much simplification, let us say that development, as an expression of modernity, emerged from the addition to the vertical and horizontal links that made up medieval Europe, of horizontal links that were entirely unprecedented.[3] The new horizontal links connected the emergence of modern Western Europe with the fate of another place, the New World, thus modifying the previous mix of threads. Yet the emergence of modernity has been marked by a persistent blindness to connections and hybridity not only between nature and society (Latour 1993) but also between the vertical and horizontal threads that make up place. The 'moderns' have imagined themselves and their place as pure and self-contained, as if the vertical links that made up the modern West were independent from the horizontal links that connected it to other places (see Blaut 1993).

The severing of vertical from horizontal threads allowed the moderns to raise this most disjointed sense of place to the status of a universal, and then, following another separation, concentrate on the horizontal threads to the point of neglecting the vertical threads. Thus modernity, a particular place project (see Dirlik 2001: 36), became a project of making other places whose only grounding threads extend horizontally to modernity itself.

Yshiro leader Bruno Barras clearly expresses in his chapter how life projects cut across this self-centred universalist project. In effect, he describes his people's life project as being about the possibility of their defining the direction they want to take in life, on the basis of their awareness and knowledge of their own place in the world. The subsequent chapter by Mario Blaser provides further arguments showing that a central feature of Yshiro life projects is to cut across the imposition of universalist criteria. This feature contrasts sharply with the focus of development on applying general rules (ideas of indigenousness, for example) regardless of the specificity of a particular place.

Wendy Russell's chapter highlights how development embodies the focus on 'horizontal threads'. Indeed, the development programmes proposed to the Cree people of Fort Albany are concerned more with replicating models applied in other places than with attending to the specificity of this particular place. However, as she also shows, the universalist pretension of modernity (i.e. its fostering of self-centred horizontal threads) has not done away with vertical threads. On the contrary, everywhere, as in Fort Albany, people permanently connect newly emerging horizontal threads to their history and relation to the landscape, discovering and rediscovering 'their own approach to life'. Russell shows that, to the extent that this approach to life is disregarded by the forces of development, a process of fast-paced and highly dysfunctional efforts to achieve accommodation between vertical and horizontal threads is set in motion, which generates endless new programmes and blueprints for development.

Precisely because development, as a project that privileges horizontal threads, is hegemonic, other place-based projects appear, by contrast, as favouring the vertical threads making up places, identities and traditions. This is because, in the face of relentless attacks – through colonization, assimilation and development – aimed at suppressing the vertical threads shaping their sense of place and identity, life projects are devoted in large part to permanently rebuilding and strengthening those vertical threads. But the appearance of a central focus on vertical threads also responds to the fact that the pursuit of life projects takes place in a field of power still dominated by the modern conception of separations (i.e. the disjunction of vertical and horizontal threads). Thus, in many cases Indigenous peoples find themselves in the situation of having to authorize their life projects in a very modern fashion as 'authentically Indigenous' – that is, as if they emerged solely from vertical threads. Yet, given that some groups and organizations truly embrace this tendency to favour vertical threads, it is necessary to distinguish such place-based projects from both development projects and life projects. In effect, although they might be opposed to development, I do not see projects based on the primacy of vertical threads as life projects. Rather, in so far as they assume the same disjunction of vertical and horizontal threads as development does, these projects appear to us as the reverse image of the former.

The particularity of life projects, then, resides in their constant awareness that place and identity arise from the mutually constitutive nature of vertical and horizontal threads. Mohawk scholar Taiaiake Alfred clearly states this point when he argues that to accept the dichotomies of the European world-view (including the distinction of Whites from Natives, which is another way of talking of places) as fixed and essential not only goes against traditional Native beliefs but also fosters the continuation of the status quo (Alfred 1999: 20). In her contribution to the volume, Anishnaabeg scholar Deborah McGregor points out that traditional indigenous knowledge, which is critical to Indigenous identity-making, emerges not only from a history of engagement with the landscape (the vertical threads) but also from the struggles that Indigenous peoples sustain with the newcomers (the horizontal threads). She argues that framing Indigenous peoples and their knowledge within the dichotomous terms of modernity amounts to losing the richness and complexity of their life projects, including their ingrained criticism of power asymmetries and the possibilities they can offer for the survival of 'Creation'.

In short, the awareness of the complex, non-dichotomous but mutually constitutive connections between one's own self/place and others grounds the common trait that allows us to distinguish life projects from other place-based projects. This common trait is the centrality of coexistence in their formulation. I will explore this point below.

Although life projects are one possibility among others, we must recognize that the field of power in which they must be furthered is nowadays dominated by one kind of placed-based project: development/modernity. The hegemony of development/modernity as a particular 'regional discursive formation' (Peet and Watts 1996: 16) means that the relations in the field are usually expressed in terms of binary oppositions in which development appears as the opposite to place-based, just as abstract is opposed to concrete, universal to particular and global to local.[4] These binary oppositions, and particularly the last one, tend to obliterate the complexity of threads and the dynamics involved in place-making and, thus, make it hard to understand what life projects are about and how they are produced and advanced. This can be examined in more detail.

Global/Local, the Politics of Scale and Hybrid Networks

In a recent work, Arif Dirlik (2001: 24) pointed out that, given the 'hegemony of the modernist marginalization of places', one of the first tasks in disentangling the relationship of the local to the global involves the realization that the global is place-based as well. Building on Latour's idea that the terms 'local' and 'global' offer points of view on hybrid networks that are neither local nor global, Dirlik suggests the term 'glocal' to capture the double process of localization of the global and globalization of the local. He argues that, given their hybrid nature, glocalities (i.e. places) must be compared in relation to the differences that arise between them from power asymmetries. As he puts it: 'phenomena are all both local and global, but … they are not all local and global in the same way' (Dirlik 2001: 30). This way of conceiving the differences between related and mutually modifying places in a network is very useful because it connects power and scale: to talk about the globalization of something implies the power of that thing to stretch out across space (see Swyngedouw 1997: 142). However, Dirlik insists on seeing the hybrid character of glocalities as emerging from binary oppositions between the subordinated local and the hegemonic local (i.e. development), which in virtue of its hegemony becomes global (see Dirlik 2001: 40). I believe that his and other analysts' focus on binary relations obscures the complexity of place-making processes and the particularity of life projects in relation to other place-based projects.

Conceiving glocalities/places as the product of binary oppositions leads Dirlik to conceptualize 'place as project' in terms of a repudiation of development and as a defence of places against the encroachment of capital and states. This defence of place can succeed only by forging new forms of 'supra-place relationships' through a 'reorganization of space from below' (Dirlik 2001: 37–9; see also Appadurai 2000, 2002; Harvey 1996). Dirlik foresees that this reorganization of space may arise only to the extent that place can conceive itself as different and opposed to the globalism of modernity. Esteva and Prakash's (1998: 13) description of grassroots initiatives, which they see as challenging the global project, is a good example of this. In effect, in trying to give voice to these movements, the authors affirm that they 'are autonomously organized by "the people" themselves … both independent from and antagonistic to the state [which plays the role of agent for the global]'. Yet one could point out the hybridity of those grassroots move-ments, in the sense that they are not only related to institutions that promote globalism by opposition but also through collaboration, 'spaces of truce' and areas of unwilling mutual reinforcement. Dirlik might dismiss this argument because talking of hybridity in this sense might mean not recognizing 'the continued importance of essentialized identities in politics' and, thus, defusing the claims to alternative hybridities that are not driven by developmentalism (Dirlik 2001: 40). In other words, while these movements might be hybrids of 'global modernity' and local places, their claims of being 'pure' are central to their capacity to produce projects that are different from development. Yet I believe that by conceiving of places mostly in opposition to the globalism of modernity, these authors end up presenting a picture in which it is hard to think of the former as not being already overdetermined by the latter.

This is not a minor issue. In a recent discussion a group of anthropolo-gists addressed the dilemma presented to those who are engaged in critical analysis but are also sympathetic towards Indigenous peoples' struggles for environmental rights, self-determination and justice (see Brosius 1999). Is it complicity with the status quo to speak of the complexity behind what may appear or be presented as homogenous fronts and 'pure' agendas that are confronting each other? My own position is that showing how the terrain is much more than a struggle between two forces, and contesting the very assumptions that make it necessary to present struggles on these terms, are part of what life projects do. This is clearly demonstrated in my chapter below, where I show how the Yshiro leaders face a discursive field in which the struggle is not only against the encroachment of state and capitalist development but also against the encroachment of projects promoted by Yshiro supporters. The latter limit the Yshiro's 'essentially different' identity to their (assumed) hunter–gatherer traditions (vertical threads). This example highlights how life projects involve, to a large extent, the transformation of power asymmetries that would position Indigenous peoples between mutually exclusive alternatives defined by others.

Analytical and political perspectives that rely on binaries hide from sight the fact that even though modernity constitutes an ever-present horizontal thread in the make-up of contemporary places, it is not the only one.[5] If different places have different but nevertheless existing capacities to stretch out across space (i.e. to globalize), there is no reason to assume that the hybrid character of a place/project will emerge from its interaction with only one other place/project, even if the latter is hegemonic (i.e. stretches out the furthest). This calls for a clarification of what is meant by globalization and other related terms. If, as Escobar (2001: 150) argues, the 'local and the global are scales, processes, or even levels of analysis, but certainly not places', and we agree that places globalize when they stretch out, then we should not be talking of places as in relation to a single 'global'. On the other hand, if we are talking of the global as the specifically modern way of stretching out by colonizing other places, then we should not be using globalization to refer to phenomena like the Zapatistas stretching out through the Internet (see Dirlik 2001: 27), since they do not seek the control of other places. Not even the qualification of 'grassroots globalization' helps the matter, for either it is a platitude (all stretching out is done from a place, if that is what the term 'grassroots' implies), or it glosses over the variety of stretchings out of non-hegemonic projects.

It is precisely the difference between forms of stretching out that must be added to power differentials and scales in order to clarify the specificity of life projects. Consider the example of the James Bay Cree campaign in Vermont, discussed by Glenn McRae in this volume. McRae argues that the Crees looked for the support of Vermonters in their campaign against the Great Whale hydroelectric mega-development project, not chiefly by inviting them to embrace the Crees' cause ('we are all Cree'), but by prompting Vermonters to consider their own situation in relation to the problem that the Crees brought to their attention. In other words, the Crees 'stretched out', not through 'colonizing' Vermont but by redirecting Vermonters' attention to the connections between their own self-images, traditions and landscapes (all vertical threads) and to the relations Vermont sustained with other places, as in its imports of energy (horizontal threads). I would argue that this way of stretching out reflects the Crees' (and other Indigenous life projects') awareness that promoting a balance of horizontal and vertical threads elsewhere is the only way to achieve balance in one's own place. How Cree hunters cannot conceive of a balanced and sustainable relation with animals (what I have been calling vertical threads) by cutting connections (i.e. by not communicating) with the non-Cree is very eloquent in this regard (see Feit, Chapter 6).

As I mentioned above, the commonality across life projects is not their opposition to development but their focus on having a meaningful degree of control over (or, what is the same, having some degree of control over the meaning of) life as being-placed-in-the-world. This understanding requires careful attention to both horizontal and vertical threads. The beauty and the promise of life projects is that they trace a possible path towards the idea of unity in diversity. Indeed, what unites them is a focus on reaching a balance in the complex mix that produces places, yet the whole idea of balance depends on accepting that each place is, and must remain, unique. Because of this uniqueness life projects do not simply oppose development. It is true that, in trying to reach a balance between the horizontal and vertical threads constituting places, they stand in the way of development. In this sense, life projects consistently work to thwart the universalist pretensions of development. Yet because this is not necessarily the goal of life projects, they can on occasion strategically incorporate opportunities and openings offered by development.

Strategies: Networks and Grey Areas

There is opposition to development and the universalist pretensions of modernity, but I see this opposition as contingent, and thus I think that analyses dichotomizing the field of power in which life projects unfold are of little help. Instead of focusing on identifying 'globalization from below' (Appadurai 2000), 'oppositional networks' (Harcourt and Escobar 2001: 12), or 'binary oppositions' (Dirlik 2001), I find it critical to focus on the grey areas, those points in the networks connecting place-based projects in which there is not only opposition but mutual reinforcement, unwilling collaborations, turning points, indifference or sympathy. I also find it critical to recognize that these networks involve much more than two kinds of place-based project. Even when development and life projects might be the focus of our interests, we must keep in mind that sometimes their mutual relations are mediated by other place-based projects that do not respond to either of them. Thus most chapters in Part II refer, at least implicitly, to place-based projects that are neither life projects nor development, yet that often play a role in how the mutual relations of life projects and development are played out.

As discussed in the previous chapter, the chapters in Part II show that Indigenous peoples engage in a variety of alliances and partnerships with movements and organizations that have their own agendas and visions. These partners may range from environmental NGOs to neighbouring non-Indigenous communities and from professional associations to provincial governments. These alliances are central for Indigenous peoples' struggles. Barbara Rose Johnston and Carmen Garcia-Downing's chapter shows how transnational networks of environmentalists, human rights advocates and a professional association were mobilized to pressure the World Bank into addressing the violation of human rights suffered by the Pehuenche–Mapuche communities of Chile in the construction of a dam. But the chapter also shows that there are innumerable interfaces in the networks that connect these kinds of alliances and development institutions, and that these grey areas of connection can be used to create the appearance that something is being done while the development projects in question proceed. Moreover, as Brian Craik hints at in his chapter, in many such alliances the life projects of Indigenous peoples might be subordinated to the projects of their more powerful allies.

The case of the broad anti-mining coalition in Wisconsin analysed by Al Gedicks and Zoltán Grossman, and the James Bay Cree campaign against hydroelectric development analysed by Brian Craik, stand out because of their uniqueness: in these cases the Indigenous peoples involved have had a *relatively* high level of control over the direction of their struggle. These cases show what can be achieved when the appropriate conditions are in place. However, this situation is not enjoyed by the majority of Indigenous peoples. Thus the fact that Indigenous peoples promote their life projects in a hostile context and from a subordinated position must be borne in mind when evaluating the performance of their organizations in the complex transnational networks where struggles around development take place.

With the exception of a few relatively isolated instances, most contemporary Indigenous peoples are moving not from acceptable to bad conditions, but from bad to worse conditions. Of course, Indigenous peoples resist development projects that worsen their situations, but their life projects are not about resisting development; they are about the opportunity to live those life projects. Yet, as I said before, most chapters of the volume show Indigenous peoples struggling against or confronting different development projects.

Life projects are pursued as an uphill battle where the dominant values of development and evolutionary progress not only block their way but also continually subordinate them. As Brian Craik's chapter shows, the strength achieved through organized resistance to development projects sometimes creates rare opportunities to further those life projects that have been consistently blocked by the dominant society. The paradox of being in a subordinate position is that these situations sometimes afford opportunities, because they provide something to bargain with: the capacity of Indigenous peoples to block (perhaps only temporarily) a project from some sector of the dominant society. Thus, Indigenous peoples' struggles against development often involve much more than resistance.

For many non-Indigenous observers and allies, the situation appears in a different light. Many urban-based NGO allies start from a position in which resistance to a particular development project constitutes an attempt to maintain a previous status quo. Thus, their interest is very circumscribed, and a campaign is for them a win or lose game. Of course, this means that there are not many other connected issues that can be offered to such NGOs for negotiation. In contrast, Indigenous organizations cannot disregard offers to negotiate. In part, this is because – as former Assembly of First Nations National Chief Matthew Coon Come shows in his chapter on Canada – negotiations have something to offer when contrasted to development that is presented to them as a *fait accompli*, as usually is the case. It is also because – as Mapuche activist Aldisson Anguita Mariqueo shows in his chapter about development in Chile – a refusal of leaders or Indigenous organizations to negotiate may mean that governments or corporations bypass them and engage in one-to-one negotiations with community members. In contexts where attempts at organizing are only beginning or the leadership opportunities are very limited, this tactic can be highly successful, with deleterious consequences for the whole of the community. Finally, resistance to a project is seldom an end in itself. Rather, it is usually framed within the wider perspective of pursuing life projects. Thus, a deal offered to Indigenous peoples can be seen as an advance if it allows them to further some aspects of their life projects and improves their capacity to negotiate new openings for themselves.

How should we characterize such recurring strategies? In a recent article, Arjun Appadurai (2002) argues that facing the fact that today more than half the world's population lives in severe poverty, a variety of visions of emancipation and equity have begun to circulate that are at odds with ideas of development associated with the nation-state. Among the diversity of grassroots social movements that uphold these visions, Appadurai distinguishes those that follow a politics of partnership – that is, 'a politics of accommodation, negotiation, and long-term pressure [applied to states, markets and international organizations] rather than confrontation or threats of political reprisal' (2002: 29). The political horizon of these grassroots movements is, through alliances, to gain long-term capacity in order to transform their circumstances; thus they have to display a 'politics of patience' in order that the urgency of the problems assailing them does not take over and lead to their being overcome by their more powerful partners' interests (Appadurai 2002: 29–30). At a very deep level, Appadurai argues, these movements and their politics are shaping globalization from below (2002: 23). However, he says, although they provide some glimpses into a more democratic future, it is still to be seen whether the ethos and purpose of these local democratic projects can contain the ravages of development and the increasing mobility of capital that it fosters.

Invitations: Coexistence and the Politics of Resilience

The idea of a politics of partnership, its visions (i.e. political horizon), its prospects in the face of development and globalization, is an excellent entry point to discuss the topics addressed by contributors to Part III. Although many Indigenous life projects embody visions that assume the desirability and inherent possibility of their coexistence with other (human and non-human) users of land and resources, these 'invitations' to coexist are not readily accepted by states and other interested parties. Nevertheless, their searching for ways to enhance dialogue and mutual understanding is part of putting their own visions into practice rather than a means to an end. Thus, another peculiarity of Indigenous peoples' life projects is that they embody a politics of partnership whose political horizon or vision is not situated in the future. This peculiarity, which is based on ontologies radically different from the Western ontology of modernity, implies that life projects must be lived even when the surrounding conditions are profoundly unpropitious.

In his chapter Pramod Parajuli argues that peasants and Indigenous peoples, who depend on the maintenance and regeneration of ecosystems for their livelihood, constitute a barrier to the motion of global capital. Having to ensure the 'symbiotic connection between the human collectivities and the non-human collectivities', they stand in the way of development. Yet, as I argued above, and as Petra Rethmann shows in her chapter on the 'dreams' of Native activists in the Russian Far East, development stands in the way of life projects to the extent that it impedes the fulfilment of their embodied visions of a good and meaningful life. Because these visions are in many cases informed by ontologies and conceptions of self and place that differ from those that inform development, I argue that a politics of patience does not appropriately describe the ethos I see in life projects. A politics of patience might well have a longer temporal horizon than development projects, as Appadurai asserts, but nevertheless it still conjures up images of a final goal and of instrumental reason that resemble modernist tropes and their ontology of object/subject. Perhaps this is related to the fact that the movement analysed by Appadurai comprised urban poor, whose leaders were 'secularist in outlook' (Appadurai 2002). In any case, I surmise that while Indigenous organizations certainly have goals to which, on occasion, they subordinate their means, the politics of life projects are not goal-oriented and thus cannot be described as a politics of patience.

I see life projects as a politics and epistemology of resilience that assume relations, flows and openendedness as their ontological ground. There is a growing literature that has shown how Indigenous non-dualist ontologies open up an 'intellectual landscape … in which states and substances are replaced by processes and relations' (Descola and Palsson 1996: 12; also the contributors to Descola and Palsson 1996; Ingold 2000). These ontologies are embodied in conduct but are also often codified in stories and prayers. The chapter by Mary Arquette, Maxine Cole and the Akwesasne Task Force on the Environment (ATFE) provides us with good examples. The ethos that informs the stories and the prayers reproduced in this chapter (and the ontologies of which they are a part) does not envisage the value of partnership and coexistence in relation to an ulterior purpose but as the conditions of life itself.

An important body of literature has been devoted to how the lived experience embodied in these kinds of stories is conducive, in practice, to the regeneration of ecosystems upon which Indigenous peoples depend (see Grim 2001; Ingold 2000). In his chapter, Peter Harries-Jones discusses how these embodied traditions constitute forms of 'life-politics' that are in direct opposition to 'wild globalization'. These life-politics, which are attuned to the cycles of recursion (regeneration) of the environment, actively try to bring disturbances caused by human action within a range that can be absorbed within those cycles. Harries-Jones sees the concept of resilience as a promising bridge between these life-politics and the science of ecology. I also find the concept very appropriate for describing the politics of life projects.

The concept of resilience is connected to the central characteristics of the epistemologies and politics of life projects. According to Harries-Jones, the concept 'embodies inherent unpredictability and unknown outcomes of interactions between ecosystems and the human societies'; thus it refers to 'the conservation of the ability to respond to change'. I argue that, in contrast to modern epistemology and politics, unpredictability and unknown outcomes of interactions are taken as ontological conditions in the epistemologies and politics of life projects. Before I discuss this in detail it is convenient to point out that modern epistemology and politics are based on an ontological dualism that resolves the tension between its two terms in some form of synthesis (temporary as it might be). In practice, if not in theory, this synthesis is sought through the control of one of the terms of the dualist relation by the other. In political terms this leads to domination of the self over the other; in epistemological terms, this leads to the dominance of the knower over the known and, thus, of uncertainty about the status of the known.[6]

Amidst their enormous variety, Indigenous ontologies (at least in the Americas) seem in accord on the futility and/or danger of trying to control others. For example, in Arquette Cole and ATFE's chapter this is clarified by the idea that the different entities that populate the universe are 'nations', each with its own responsibilities to Creation, and that interfering with those responsibilities has catastrophic effects. Similarly, Yshiro mythology stresses the interconnectedness of everything that populates the universe, yet it also underscores that maintaining the universe as it is known depends on keeping the uniqueness of their own entities (Cordeu 1989a, 1989b, 1990, 1991a, 1991b, 1992a, 1992b). James Bay Cree cosmology sets human lives and animals in a world of persons bound by relationships of reciprocity and respect, a way of relating that Cree hunters extend even to those who deny respect to others, for to do otherwise because one insists one knows better is to reduce further the fabric of relationships that is the world itself. Knowledge in these ontological conditions cannot even be intended to be absolute. Knowledge is knowledge in context; it is relative. Given that one cannot have certainty about the results of interacting with others (humans and non-humans), the most sensible way of relating to others is always to try to conserve the ability to respond to change – in other words, to follow a politics of resilience.[7]

Life projects are about living a purposeful and meaningful life. In this sense, their political horizons cannot be located in the future, just as living in the present cannot be put on hold in pursuit of a future goal. Being forced to do that means a slow death, as Dawn Martin-Hill's chapter on the Lubicon women shows. Life projects have no political horizon; they *are* the political horizon. They are not points of arrival, utopian places, narratives of salvation or returns to paradise. They are the very action of maintaining openendedness as a politics of resilience. That is why, as Parajuli and Harries-Jones point out, Indigenous movements seek autonomy and self-management. These constitute the best conditions in which to live life projects. However, as Harvey Feit forcefully argues in his chapter, this does not mean that, when these conditions do not obtain, life projects can be put on hold; they have to be lived even in the face of their denial.

Coexisting with Denial

Indigenous peoples' politics of partnership have in some cases borne fruit, and there has been some recognition that Indigenous ways of conceiving relations among humans, and between humans and non-humans, deserve more attention. Throughout the 1990s constitutional reforms in Latin America and Canada recognized the rights of Indigenous peoples to maintain and foster their own ways of life (see Van Cott 2000; Sieder 2002; Lindau and Cook 2000). However, as Colin Scott argues in his chapter on Aboriginal rights and development in the Canadian North, this recognition is more rhetoric than practice. Indeed, the recognition of Indigenous life projects is in practice blocked by entrenched visions of development and social progress as 'evolutionary inevitabilities'. Governmental decision-making is led by these visions as if they were not anchored in cultural values and political actions that are not universal in character and that, therefore, should be tested on the ground of experience. On the contrary, these visions are taken to be grounded in a reality that can be known with increasing certainty; thus, errors can be fixed and 'done better' the next time, but the visions and goals do not need to be revised.

Dawn Martin-Hill's contribution lets us look into what development is as an experience for the Lubicon Cree women. Hers is a painful yet powerful reminder of the ravages of development. The suffering expressed by the Lubicon women is like the suffering caused by the loss of a loved one: one might eventually heal and learn to live with the loss, but one cannot 'fix it'.[8] Yet Martin-Hill is not just telling us a story; she performs her way of knowing and writing as a process that brings into sharp focus the importance of relationships, of responsibility and the costs of not honouring them. Knowing in this way is a life project that is carried out even in the midst of denial and suffering. As she expresses it, 'the fact that we are here continuing to do what we do is testimony to our strength, *resilience* and beauty as Indigenous women ... who hang in there no matter what.'

The ontologies that ground the politics of resilience of life projects demand a sense of responsibility that 'denies closure; the actions, connections, and intentions are not causal but obscure ceremonies' (Vizenor 1995: 675). It was to this kind of responsibility that Latour (1993: 41–2) referred when he argued that while the moderns have concentrated on purifying what exists as either nature or culture, thereby embracing a realist epistemology and becoming blind to the total effect of their operations, the wrongly called 'pre-moderns' have concentrated on the whole extent of relations: 'It is [the recognition] of the impossibility of changing the social order without modifying the natural order – and vice versa – that has obliged the pre-moderns to exercise the greatest prudence.' This prudence and the sense of responsibility attached to it cannot be delegated to abstract bureaucracies; it cannot be disregarded because other partners who share the world with us deny the connections that hold the universe together. This kind of prudence and responsibility have to be sustained no matter what.

How can life projects, their politics of resilience and their sense of responsibility towards Creation be fostered in the face of development and 'wild globalization'? The contributions to this volume show some examples of how Indigenous peoples are doing it. They also make explicit the meanings and broadly cultural foundations of life projects. In the chapter by Mary Arquette, Maxine Cole and the ATFE there is an invitation to the New York Power Agency to join the Mohawk of Akwesasne in their life project 'as we reflect and then proceed as partners in the restoration of balance and harmony in the world that we now share'. The editors believe that the answer to the question posed above is to accept these kinds of invitations to dialogue and coexistence. This implies not only a change in policymaking but also a change in the ways in which non-Indigenous peoples and institutions produce knowledge. The editors hope that in preparing this volume we have taken a step in this direction.

Notes

1. In this Introduction and in the context of the cases discussed in this volume, I use the term 'Indigenous peoples' to refer to 'the descendants of the people who occupied a given territory when it was invaded, conquered, or colonized by a foreign power or population' (Stavenhagen 1996: 148–9). Thus, some of our arguments may not apply to other Indigenous peoples living in countries where, like many in Africa and Asia, ruling groups are not necessarily the descendants of colonizing populations.

2. The term is introduced in the volume by one of our Indigenous contributors but seems to be gaining currency among grassroots activists in several places (cf. Escobar 1995: 212).

3. In this Introduction I use 'development' and 'modernity' as synonyms.

4. Peet and Watts (1996: 16) define a regional discursive formation as the modes of thought, logics and themes, but also the silences and repressions, that run through the discursive history of a particular region.

5. The tendency to think of hybridity in terms of the outcome of reproduction from two original stocks is just one of the several problems that besiege the use of hybrid as a metaphor (see Dirlik 2001: 26–30). Another one is that if it is not in contrast to a 'pure' state the term 'hybrid' is meaningless by itself. Given that hardly anybody claims the 'purity' of any phenomenon nowadays, I find the term 'hybrid' more confusing than helpful, precisely because it permanently brings back, even as a shadow, the idea of purity.

6. For a thorough discussion of the dynamics of this ontology in the relations between Europeans and Indigenous peoples of the Americas, see Dussel 1995. See Plumwood 1993 for a discussion of Cartesian dualism as an ontology of control and domination of nature, and Apfel-Marglin 1996 for a discussion of Cartesianism in relation to development.

7. In certain contexts, such as environmental movements, resilience might be seen as a goal, something that must be achieved. In the context of Indigenous peoples' life projects, I see resilience as a self-performing ethos. I discuss the issue further below.

8. The attitudes of governments, corporations and part of the non-Indigenous public that 'know' that these processes are inevitable can only be considered sadistic when, faced with their 'errors' that cannot be fixed, they feel that there is no reason to stop development. This is like telling someone who has lost a child that, since the child cannot be brought back, he or she should not mind losing any remaining children.

References

Alfred, T. (1999) *Peace, Power, Righteousness: An Indigenous Manifesto*, Oxford: Oxford University Press.

Apfel-Marglin F. (1996) 'Introduction: rationality and the world', in F. Apfel-Marglin and S.

Marglin (eds), *Decolonizing Knowledge: From Development to Dialogue*, Oxford: Clarendon Press, pp. 1–39.

Appadurai, A. (2000) 'Grassroots globalization and the research imagination', *Public Culture*, vol. 12, no. 1, pp. 1–19.

—— (2002) 'Deep democracy: urban governmentality and the horizon of politics', *Public Culture*, vol. 14, no. 1, pp. 21–47.

Blaut, J. M. (1993) *The Colonizer's Model of the World: Geographical Diffusionism and Eurocentric History*, New York: Guilford Press.

Brosius, J.P. (ed.) (1999) *Ethnographic Presence: Environmentalism, Indigenous Rights and Transnational Cultural Critique*, Newark, NJ: Gordon & Breach.

Cordeu, E. (1989a) 'Aishtuwente. Las ideas de deidad en la religiosidad chamacoco (Parte I)', *Suplemento Antropologico*, vol. 24, no. 1, pp. 7–77.

—— (1989b) 'Aishtuwente. Las ideas de deidad en la religiosidad chamacoco (Parte II)', *Suplemento Antropologico*, vol. 24, no. 2, pp. 51–85.

—— (1990) 'Aishtuwente. Las ideas de deidad en la religiosidad chamacoco (Parte III)', *Suplemento Antropologico*, vol. 25, no. 1, pp. 119–211.

—— (1991a) 'Aishtuwente. Las ideas de deidad en la religiosidad chamacoco (Parte III Cont.)', *Suplemento Antropologico*, vol. 26, no. 1, pp. 85–166.

—— (1991b) 'Aishtuwente. Las ideas de deidad en la religiosidad chamacoco (Parte IV)', *Suplemento Antropologico*, vol. 26, no. 2, pp. 145–233.

—— (1992a) 'Aishtuwente. Las ideas de deidad en la religiosidad chamacoco (Part V Cont. y Parte VI)', *Suplemento Antropologico*, vol. 27, no. 2, pp. 167–301.

—— (1992b) 'Aishtuwente. Las ideas de deidad en la religiosidad chamacoco (Parte V)', *Suplemento Antropologico*, vol. 27, no. 1, pp. 187–294.

Descola, P. and G. Palsson (eds) (1996) *Nature and Society: Anthropological Perspectives*, London: Routledge.

Dirlik A. (2001) 'Place-based imagination: globalism and the politics of place', in R. Prazniak and A. Dirlik (eds), *Places and Politics in the Age of Globalization*, New York: Rowman & Littlefield, pp. 15–51.

Dussel, E. (1995) *The Invention of the Americas: Eclipse of 'the Other' and the Myth of Modernity*, New York: Continuum.

Elliott, J.H. (1970) *The Old World and the New – 1492–1650*, Cambridge: Cambridge University Press.

Escobar, A. (1995) *Encountering Development: The Making and Unmaking of the Third World*, Princeton: Princeton University Press.

—— (2001) 'Culture sits in places: reflections on globalism and subaltern strategies of localization', *Political Geography* 20, pp. 139–74.

Esteva, G. and M. Prakash (1998) *Grassroots Post-modernism: Remaking the Soil of Cultures*, London: Zed Books.

Fabian, J. (1983) *Time and the Other: How Anthropology Makes Its Object*, New York: Columbia University Press.

Ferguson J. (1997) 'Anthropology and its evil twin: "development" in the constitution of a discipline', in F. Cooper and R. Packard (eds), *International Development and the Social Sciences: Essays on the History and Politics of Knowledge*, Berkeley: University of California Press, pp. 150–75.

Grim, J. (ed.) (2001) *Indigenous Traditions and Ecology*, Cambridge, MA: Harvard Divinity School.

Gupta, A. and J. Ferguson (1997) 'Culture, power, place: ethnography at the end of an era', in A. Gupta and J. Ferguson (eds), *Culture, Power, Place: Explorations in Critical Anthropology*, Durham, NC: Duke University Press, pp. 1–29.

Harcourt, W. and A. Escobar (2001) 'Lead article: women and the politics of place', *Development*, vol. 45, no. 1, pp. 7–14.

Harvey, D. (1996) *Justice, Nature and the Geography of Difference*, Oxford: Blackwell.

Ingold, T. (2000) *The Perception of the Environment: Essays in Livelihood, Dwelling and Skill*, London: Routledge.

Latour, B. (1993) *We Have Never Been Moderns*, Cambridge, MA: Harvard University Press.

Lindau J. and C. Cook (2000) 'One continent, contrasting styles: the Canadian experience in North American perspective', in C. Cook and J. Lindau (eds), *Aboriginal Rights and Self-Government: The Canadian and Mexican Experience in North American Perspective*, Montreal: McGill-Queen's University Press, pp. 3–36.

Massey D. (1999) 'Imagining globalization: power-geometries of time–space', in A. Brah, M. Hickman and M. Mac an Ghaill (eds), *Global Futures: Migration, Environment and Globalization*, New York: St. Martin's Press, pp. 27–44.

Peet R. and M. Watts (1996) 'Liberation ecology: development, sustainability, and environment in an age of market triumphalism', in M. Watts and R. Peet (eds), *Liberation Ecologies: Environment, Development and Social Movements*, London: Routledge, pp. 1–45.

Plumwood, V. (1993) *Feminism and the Mastery of Nature*, London: Routledge.

Rist, G. (1997) *The History of Development: From Western Origins to Global Faith*, London: Zed Books.

Sieder, R. ed. (2002) *Multiculturalism in Latin America: Indigenous Rights, Diversity and Democracy*, New York: Palgrave Macmillan.

Stavenhagen, R. (1996) 'Indigenous rights: some conceptual problems', in E. Jelin and E. Hershberg (eds), *Constructing Democracy: Human Rights, Citizenship, and Society in Latin America*, Boulder: Westview Press, pp. 141–59.

Swyngedouw E. (1997) 'Neither global nor local: "glocalization" and the politics of scale', in K.R. Cox (ed.), *Spaces of Globalization: Reasserting the Power of the Local*, New York: Guilford Press, pp. 137–66.

UNCED (United Nations Conference on Environment and Development) (1992) Agenda 21: Programme of Action for Sustainable Development – Rio Declaration on Environment and Development – Statement of Forest Principles – the Final Text of Agreements … United Nations Conference on Environment and Development, New York: United Nations Department of Public Information.

Van Cott, D. (2000) *The Friendly Liquidation of the Past: The Politics of Diversity in Latin America*, Pittsburgh: University of Pittsburgh Press.

Vizenor, G. (1995) 'Authored animals: creature tropes in Native American fiction', *Social Research*, vol. 62, no. 3, pp. 661–83.

PART I

Visions:
Life Projects, Representations and Conflicts

3

Life Projects: Development Our Way

BRUNO BARRAS

Bruno Barras is a leader of the Yshiro–Ebitoso people of the Paraguayan Chaco. He has participated in numerous organizations searching to improve the living conditions and political situation of his people in particular, and of Paraguay's Indigenous peoples in general.

I want to introduce you to our idea and vision of development, and to show why I propose a 'life project' instead of development projects to solve the problems of our people. I must begin, and I do not intend to offend anybody, with the arrival of the so-called 'discoverers' and what this event meant to us. Upon their arrival, they justified their deeds by saying that they came to civilize us. I wonder, what did they mean by 'civilization'? In our understanding and experience, civilization means the dispossession of our lands, the demise of our culture and the attempt to make White people out of us. We had our stories, our knowledge, our ways of organizing, our ways of praying and our ways of mapping our territories. But none of that was of importance to the Whites. They made their written words and their maps the only valid ones. Thus we lost our territories, and the younger generations were turned away from the ways of our ancestors. The colonizers completely disregarded our realities and asserted their own views of us. For example, they believed that they had arrived in India and called us Indians, when actually they had arrived in what is today called Latin America. In Paraguay, to this day, when ordinary citizens speak of Indigenous peoples they refer only to the Guaranis. Yet there are sixteen different ethnic groups, with their own languages and cultures. What about them? As you can see, from the beginning our relations with the Whites have been based on mistaken ideas and lack of knowledge of Indigenous peoples' realities.

Here our topic is 'development'. I wonder, what does 'development' mean? For us, it is the same as what we have seen in the Americas for the last

511 years. We do not see any significant change in the forms in which the offspring of the colonizers relate to us. After 511 years of 'civilization', in Paraguay there is not one university-educated Indigenous individual. After 511 years of 'civilization', we are still not allowed to speak for ourselves. In the Paraguayan parliament there is a commission on human rights that speaks in our name. Here, as in most institutions that are supposed to be in charge of our affairs, we do not have a voice or a vote in the decisions that are taken. I wonder, is it that we are mute? Who better than Indigenous peoples to defend our rights? What would be properly respectful is that we, Indigenous peoples, become the protagonists of our own future instead of having someone else speak on our behalf. Any other way of doing things diminishes us.

In Paraguay there is the Instituto Nacional del Indígena (INDI), which is the governmental institution in charge of furthering the development of Indigenous communities. We believe that it is time for us to control this institution. It is necessary that institutions in charge of Indigenous affairs be managed by Indigenous peoples. Many non-Indigenous people are in agreement with this idea, and many others are in strong disagreement. We wonder, why are there some who refuse to grant us control of this governmental institution? The answer is that with Indigenous participation it would be harder for corrupt functionaries to do their business. For example, a few years ago the government appointed, as INDI's head, a person about whose honesty Indigenous leaders had expressed serious concerns. We, Indigenous leaders, said that we did not want any more thieves in INDI. We took risks putting signs in front of INDI's building. We said that we were mourning. We were not mistaken in our distrust. The head of INDI, who was given the position by the president of the Republic for past political favours and who had no knowledge whatsoever of our realities and cultures, filled his pockets and now is on the run from justice. This kind of corruption still intervenes every time that we want to design and advance our own agendas for the future of our peoples. This is not acceptable.

There are others – private businessmen – who come to our communities offering diverse 'development projects'. It never fails that these projects will be based on the use of our natural resources. For example, a factory to process palm-sprouts was opened in the area where I come from. Nobody asked us anything, and that is how the destruction of the palm forest began. Palms are very important to us. We use them as food, as medicine for hepatitis and parasites, and as material for our houses. But here a businessman shows up wanting to cut down every single palm in our forest just for the palm hearts. We, the leaders, got together and calculated that the 600 guaranis (US$0.25) that would be paid for each sprout did not begin to cover the total value of the palm trees in terms of food, medicine, construction materials and handicrafts. Without palm trees we have no reserve of food, no medicine, no houses. We decided not to give away a single tree. This factory failed, thanks to the decision of the Indigenous leaders, who were able to foresee the consequences of the communities giving away their trees.

But it is not always like this. Unfortunately, there are situations in which community members do not want to listen to the advice of their leaders. Instead they listen to the NGOs. This situation leads many communities to commit enormous errors in following the advice of outsiders who do not understand our realities. The problem is that most NGOs treat us as if we are babies still drinking from feeding bottles. They speak for us and design projects for us. Most times they are the main beneficiaries of the projects 'for the communities'. In Paraguay there are hundreds of NGOs who, by obtaining the compliance of some Indigenous individuals, believe that they possess the right to decide on behalf of entire Indigenous communities. In other cases, not even acceptance by a few is required for advancing what outsiders view as solutions to our problems.

I have seen this with my own eyes. Once, an NGO came to our community. The NGO had designed a project without ever asking us what we wanted. When funding for the project was granted by an international donor, the NGO sent a musicologist to oversee the project. What we needed badly at that time was an agronomist, for the Yshiro-Ebitoso had been hunters, gatherers and fishers. We do not know how to plant very well, what seasons correspond to each crop, and so forth. We asked that this NGO send us an agronomist, but there is always this attitude of not listening to our voice. They sent us a musicologist, as if in our poverty what we need is just to go on singing. 'An agronomist, not a musicologist, is what we need', we said to them. 'Yes, yes. Sure, sure', they said but later on sent us a veterinarian. He was probably a friend of the NGO's director. We do not have animals! This is shameful. The projects never work out well because those who organize and direct them will not listen to us.

Something similar happens with the ecologists, which is very interesting, too. Nature is always being taken care of by Indigenous peoples. The environment is handled by our expert shamans. These are professionals, like astronomers, who observe the cosmos and its movements. They know what is going to happen in nature – the coming of the seasons, the behaviour of the rain, the coming and going of droughts, whether the animals will appear or whether they will hide. The shamans' school is the forest. In the past, our children were taught in the forest. They were taught not to damage the trees or burn the forest. Our ancestors knew that otherwise nature would curse them. Nowadays, the ecologists show up with their new preoccupation for the environment and wanting to create national parks and biological reserves without allowing a place for Indigenous peoples to live. They want to prohibit us from using the forest as we have always done. Is not this also a dispossession of our lands? They change the name, but for us it is just another word for the attempt to use our lands. The best they offer us is to be guardians in their parks. What is this? It is shameful.

Governments make their agreements for financing projects to do this or that with our lands, and nobody asks us what we think. It has always been this way. When in the early 1980s, during Stroessner's dictatorship, Indigenous peoples mobilized to create a national organization, we were deemed communists. We did not even know what a communist was. They just said that to silence our voice. They did not care what we had to say. But we fought until we obtained recognition of our existence and our rights to the land. I fought nine years to obtain property titles for my community. Bureaucrats and ranchers showed me papers and more papers to demonstrate that our lands were privately owned. I did not care because in that land our grandparents are buried. They showed me papers. I showed them bones. When I received the titles to our lands, the bureaucrats and ranchers who had laughed at me asked, 'How did you obtain the land?' 'With the bones of my ancestors', I replied.

The younger generations of our people are becoming more aware of our dispossession. When they want to move around our territory and cannot, they see that we must confront these problems. We are intent on recovering our ancestors' values. But for this to work, we have to make the Whites understand our values. Without understanding there is no communication. Without communication there is no mutual respect. We are simply asking for this: let us respect each other. We are really tired of things being done to us without ever being asked our opinion. This is at the root of our problems. We do not want anybody to speak for us.

We ask international donors to find mechanisms for direct consultation. We ask them to create mechanisms for making sure that funding requested by an NGO, on behalf of Indigenous communities, really reaches those communities. Those mechanisms must include the participation of Indigenous peoples in the administration of the funding. We are not children who need tutors to perform their duties. There are many among us who are perfectly able to take positions of responsibility in the management of programmes to further our peoples' quality of life.

I know that there are many potential donors who are sympathetic to our plight. We merely want them to avoid the perils and mistakes of funding projects that lead nowhere and only mean a waste of resources that never reach the communities. Be aware that in our country there are hundreds of projects that are made by someone sitting at a desk without having a hint of what is going on in the communities. Nevertheless, many of these projects obtain funding to pay big salaries to their personnel. The only thing these

NGOs do is pay a quick visit to the communities, distribute some food and medicine, and, as soon as they can, take their plane back to the city. Then they prepare a report for the donors saying that the project is working fine. But the project goes wrong, very wrong. And when the fact that it has gone wrong cannot be denied any longer, Indigenous peoples are blamed. 'They do not want to work', the 'professionals' say. The professionals have nothing to worry about. After all, they are left with the savings from their salaries and their four-wheel-drive vehicles while we are left as poor as ever and with our two legs.

For these reasons we are proposing what I call a life project. I call it that because our plans and projects are oriented to achieving autonomy in deciding our own future. We do not want somebody else taking us by the hand to lead us wherever they want to go. We want to advance our own projects so that what is done in the communities has continuity and so that the knowledge and skills brought by the technicians we hire will be transmitted to our youth. We are searching for ways to unite all our com-munities under one organization. We are trying to recover the way of our ancestors in organizing our communities. Who better than ourselves to do this and to fight for and defend our territories?

For us to carry on this life project we need the respectful support of donors and financing institutions from the North. We need them to con-sult Indigenous leaders and listen to them. The leaders know their peoples and, due to their participation in meetings and conferences, know what is going on at the national and international levels. I cannot find a stronger way of expressing the urgent need for direct contact between donors and Indigenous leaders to avoid the waste of resources and to remove the mistrust of Indigenous peoples' capacity to manage their own lives. If you want to know what we need and what we want, if you have meetings to discuss our situation, please, I ask you to contact our communities. Invite us directly, not the NGOs who say they represent us. Otherwise you will be playing their game, you will be empowering them and silencing us. Then they will always believe that they are our parents. Please do not do this any longer.

4

'Way of Life' or 'Who Decides': Development, Paraguayan Indigenism and the Yshiro People's Life Projects

MARIO BLASER

In community development projects it is standard procedure to call upon expert advice in order to obtain the most accurate picture of the target population and their needs. Such needs might include services, the effective exercise of granted rights, relief aid, reparations, impact assessment and the like. When these kinds of development projects target a particular Indigenous group, it is often the case that their needs are defined in advance as the needs of (generic) Indigenous peoples. Although specific projects may use participatory methodologies to establish what are the needs of a given Indigenous group, usually these projects have their objectives already defined in relation to wider policy frameworks. It is precisely through the objectives set up in policy frameworks, ranging from the operative plan of a development project to constitutional rights, that the needs of more or less generic Indigenous peoples are implicitly defined.

At this level of generality, the needs of Indigenous peoples are defined in association with dominant images of 'indigenousness'. A couple of simplistic examples will illustrate the point. If indigenousness is viewed as a state of backwardness, Indigenous peoples' needs might be taken to be progress guided by those who are more advanced, as the rhetoric of the civilizing mission and its successor, development, has it. Conversely, if indigenousness is conceived of as a state of harmony with nature, Indigenous peoples' needs might include the conservation of their cultures, as some versions of sustainable development would argue. If we discard conspiracy theories, it is admissible to assert that while these concepts of indigenousness are functional for certain interests, they are produced in complex interactions and struggles involving experts, activists, governments, interest groups and Indigenous peoples themselves.

Dominant understandings of indigenousness, which shape global standards of public credibility, conflate authenticity with objectification (Hornborg 1994). In other words, authentic indigenousness is conflated with objective and observable traits (from clothing to behaviours) that conform to the dominant definitions of what it is to be Indigenous. Given that Indigenous peoples' struggles to empower themselves 'are occurring in a global political space in which claims to authenticity are a critical dimension of legitimacy' (Brosius 1999a: 181), it is often the case that Indigenous peoples and their supporters have to resort to the same set of dominant images of indigenousness that states, interest groups and experts use to advance their own agendas. In Paraguay, for example, non-Indigenous supporters promote the rights of Indigenous peoples, including rights to land and specific forms of development, by using a definition of indigenousness that includes traits such as harmonious relations with nature and generosity with neighbours. An association of powerful landowners uses the same definition of indigenousness to argue that the current policy framework addressing Indigenous peoples' development (particularly the laws pertaining to their land rights) is flawed and must be changed. Their argument is simple: contemporary Indigenous peoples in Paraguay do not display these defining traits of indigenousness; therefore they are not authentically Indigenous. Non-Indigenous supporters also use the label of 'inauthentic' to refer to those Indigenous individuals who pursue economic and political goals that do not conform to their definitions of indigenousness.

In academic circles, the politics of representing and self-representing indigenousness and their consequences have been hotly debated during most of the last decade. These debates shed light on the entrapments posed by a politics of representation in which standardized images of indigenousness function as indexes of authenticity and legitimacy (see Jackson 1995; Mato 1996; Rogers 1996; Friedman 1996; Conklin 1997). However, these debates seem to have had little impact among those who design, implement or resist development agendas targeted at Indigenous peoples. Recognizing that Indigenous peoples' movements use standardized images of indigenousness to empower themselves in the face of encroaching agendas of development, scholarly debates have recently begun to reflect on the political impact that academics' critiques of these images may have on those movements (see contributors to Brosius 1999b). Friedman (1996: 568), for example, has argued that, 'If we are to make a critique of identity politics, our energy should be focused not on debates about authenticity but on the repudiation of endless analysis of discourse which neutralizes the struggles against the real structures of power in the capitalist world system.' Yet discourses and practices which are structured around notions of authenticity are very much part of the real structures of power in which Indigenous peoples are immersed.

In this chapter I will focus on how the leaders of the Yshiro peoples face material/discursive structures of power that are shaped by competing visions of development *for* the Indigenous peoples of the Chaco region of Paraguay. These visions of development, which are promoted by competing Paraguayan indigenist institutions and organizations,[1] draw inspiration from dominant notions of authentic indigenousness. I will argue that the life projects of which Yshiro leader Bruno Barras speaks in this volume are always in the making, and thus do not fit within the ready-made definitions of indigenousness that supporters and detractors of Indigenous peoples use to justify their visions of development. Moreover, life projects are to a large extent aimed at transforming the structures of power that constrain Indigenous peoples to act and live according to criteria of indigenousness that have no regard for their own ways of conceiving themselves and their being-in-the-world.

Primitivists, Ethnocidals and 'Way of Life'

In Paraguay, indigenist organizations and institutions provide expert advice, lobby the government, and promote policies affecting Indigenous peoples on the basis of their conceptions of indigenousness and the needs associated with them. The material and symbolic field in which indigenist institutions operate is traversed by tensions and antagonisms. The last two decades in particular have seen two distinct opposing sectors emerge. The line that both separates and connects the sectors is a notion of indigenousness associated with a hunting and gathering way of life. Authentic Indigenous peoples of the Chaco region of Paraguay are supposed to display certain traits that are typical of hunter–gatherers. These traits were identified by anthropologists who, in the mid-1980s, attempted to account for the failures of development projects based on the promotion of agricultural practices among Indigenous communities of the Chaco. Two of the most important traits are the moral ecology and the moral economy of hunter–gatherers.

According to the anthropologist Von Bremen (1987), Indigenous peoples of the Chaco display the moral ecology of hunter–gatherers since they live in harmony with nature and gather whatever nature has already produced without transforming it. Thus, development projects have failed because they have tried to transform people who do not transform nature (hunter–gatherers) into people who do transform it (agriculturalists). According to the anthropologist John Renshaw (1989, 1996), the moral economy of hunter–gatherers is revealed by the Indigenous peoples' maintenance of mechanisms of 'generalized reciprocity' that determine their 'cultural preference' for wage labour. This author argues that pressures on individuals to share with their group imply that activities with immediate returns – such as hunting and gathering, but in current contexts particularly wage labour – are preferred over activities with deferred returns, such as agriculture. Consequently, development projects have failed because they have assumed the wrong economic motivation among Indigenous peoples and have tried to incorporate them in activities that interfere with their search for immediate returns.

I will not discuss here the various problems that exist in the attribution of these traits of indigenousness to Indigenous peoples of the Chaco. Rather I will point out their success in providing criteria that have become the standard by which the justification or rejection of policies for the Indigenous peoples is evaluated. Indeed, it is hard to find indigenists who do not use these descriptions, either to justify or to discredit proposed or implemented policies (see, for example, Fritz 1993; ARP 1994; Rojas 1996; Delport 1998).[2] The wide adoption of these criteria is due in part to their simplicity and the aura of scientific anthropological truth, which make them attractive to semi-professional and amateur anthropologists who shape the field of Paraguayan indigenism. However, as we will see, a more fundamental reason for their success is that these criteria serve diverse purposes, sometimes mutually antagonistic.

Yet why has the definition of indigenousness based on the assumed moral economy and moral ecology of hunter–gatherers divided indigenist institutions in Paraguay? Because Article 64 of the Paraguayan Constitution of 1992 makes the way of life of an Indigenous community a criterion that must be taken into account in calculating the amount of land that the state is obliged to give it. This article grants Indigenous communities the right to own 'lands enough, in size and quality, to assure the preservation and development of their idiosyncratic [*peculiar* in the original Spanish] way of life' (CNP 1992).

Introducing the 'way of life' criterion into the equation for determining the actual amount of land that would be due to specific Indigenous communities of the Chaco region made the question of whether these peoples are still hunter–gatherers an issue hotly debated by indigenists. In this context, one would expect that the very definition of hunter–gatherer would be highly contentious, but this is not the case. Instead, the debates have centred on the 'developmental stage' of contemporary Indigenous peoples of the Chaco and whether this developmental stage requires special treatment regarding land tenure. Debate has been cast, by opposing indigenist sides, in terms of the alternatives of committing ethnocide or of being committed to primitivism. One sector of indigenism labels as 'primitivists' another sector that argues that Indigenous peoples of the Chaco are still hunter–gatherers and accuses the primitivists of opposing economic development. Correspondingly, those who argue that hunting–gathering is a stage of the past and that the people who inhabit the Chaco are no longer hunter–gatherers, are labelled 'ethnocidals'. The ethnocidals are accused by the primitivists of promoting a form of development that is unsustainable either for humans or for nature.

The labels of 'primitivist' and 'ethnocidal' make a caricature of the underlying visions of development advanced by those located at the opposing extremes of the indigenist arch, misrepresenting important nuances on each side.[3] The labels 'conservative' and 'radical' seem more appropriate for distinguishing one sector from the other since they make reference to visions of development, and their underlying land needs, that each side sees as more adapted to contemporary Indigenous peoples. Thus conservatives argue that development must be pursued as usual, without touching the current structure of land tenure. In contrast, the radical sector proposes models of development that entail a profound reform of that structure.[4] In what follows I will present a brief picture of the most important institutional actors within the field of indigenism. I will deal in depth with the institutions that have direct relations with the Yshiro people. I will begin by briefly discussing an organization, Asociación Rural del Paraguay (ARP), that has no direct relationship with the Yshiro but is the key actor in shaping the national policies that affect them.[5]

The Conservative Indigenists

ARP, the landowners' powerful national organization, got involved in the Paraguayan indigenist field in order to counter the threat of land expropriation deriving from the Indigenous peoples' land claims (Kidd 1995: 71–5). An ARP document argues that Indigenous peoples of the Chaco are either no longer hunter–gatherers (ARP 1994: 114, 138, 142–205) or are actively seeking to move away from that condition (ARP 1994: 113, 303–5). The authors cite the depredation of natural resources committed by Indigenous peoples in lands already granted to them as an example of the loss of their indigenousness. In other words, these peoples no longer display the Indigenous trait of moral ecology. In addition to being based on a mistaken evaluation of their developmental stage, ARP's report maintains that the policy of allowing large-scale and geographically specific land claims threatens Paraguay's economic development by frightening away investors (see Carisimo Pfannl 2000). Instead, ARP argues, development could be furthered if the state and NGOs supporting Indigenous peoples buy them the lands freely offered in the marketplace.

An institution that has direct relevance for the Yshiro people is Instituto Paraguayo del Indígena (INDI), the state institution in charge of Indigenous affairs. One of the purposes of INDI's creation in the mid-1970s was to oversee the activities of indigenist institutions that had become suspect under General Stroessner's regime (Susnik and Chase-Sardi 1995: 327–9; Blaser 1997: 98–101).[6] Under normal operations, INDI's proactive policies towards Indigenous communities can hardly be distinguished from those of beneficent institutions such as the Red Cross, Caritas or the Salvation Army.[7] However, given that INDI is the institution in charge of processing the legal recognition of Indigenous communities and their leaders, its position goes beyond beneficence, for it functions as a gatekeeper between the Indigenous peoples and the bureaucracy, both governmental and nongovernmental. Without INDI's recognition little can be done when dealing with other state institutions and many national and international NGOs. Furthermore, contacts within the institution provide the most direct access to a network of beneficent organizations serving Paraguay and whose resources are critical for Indigenous communities and their leaders. Since INDI was created, the governing Colorado Party has used it as a tool to root structures of patronage deep into Indigenous communities.

INDI is supposed to be the state institution in charge of enforcing the law and constitutional articles that protect and promote the Indigenous peoples' rights to their way of life. However, INDI's actual policies are constrained within the limits set by the state's aim of integrating, within the terms dictated by the dominant groups (including the landowners), all the resources of the country to the market economy. For this reason, to the extent that the Indigenous peoples are seen as hunter–gatherers needing large tracts of land, a contradiction arises between their formal rights and the actual policies of the institution. Thus, it is not surprising that in 1999 a president of this institution stated in her inaugural speech that

> Our current world works on the basis of a very sophisticated technology. If we do not make this technology reach Indigenous peoples they will be condemned to poverty. But we have to give them the alternative to choose between living in their traditions or living in the current world. (Pane 1999)

It is clear that the Indigenous peoples face the alternatives of changing their traditions (those 'unsophisticated' economic systems such as hunting and gathering) or living in poverty. Although, given its deplorable budgetary state, INDI can do little to direct that change, it can and does put obstacles in the way of other projects that go against the main aim of the state. I will return to this.

Proyecto de Desarrollo Sustentable del Chaco Paraguayo (Prodechaco) is a programme of cooperation between the European Union (EU) and the Paraguayan government and is the last indigenist actor I am going to discuss from the conservative side. If the definition of Indigenous peoples of the Chaco in the objectives and policy framework of the documents creating the project had been followed, Prodechaco should have been located on the radical side of the arch. The original documents described Indigenous peoples of the Chaco as being 'still today essentially forest dwellers' (SETA 1992: A1–1). The original aim of the programme, stated in early versions of the project proposal, was to 'preserve the way of life of the Indigenous populations [and] to protect the forest and the environment of the Chaco region' (EC 1994). These objectives were and are in line with several existing and developing EU policy instruments on sustainable development and Indigenous peoples (for an overview, see Fiering and Prouveur 1999). In spite of these characteristics, Prodechaco found insuperable obstacles to promoting effective projects of sustainable development based on the notion of the Indigenous peoples of the Chaco as hunter–gatherers. Indeed, Prodechaco has implemented its stated objectives only to the extent allowed by the more immediate interests of the actors involved in the execution of the project. Thus, the overarching interests of the EU, the Paraguayan government and Prodechaco staff set the limits within which Prodechaco effectively promotes the 'preservation of the [assumed] way of life of Indigenous populations'. Let us take a closer look at these interests.

According to some analysts – and the way Prodechaco has been handled confirms this – the EU's aid towards Latin America is secondary or instrumental to other interests such as trade and investment promotion (see Freres 2000: 64). The Paraguayan state, in turn, has shown a remarkable resistance to carrying out serious land reform for the benefit of the Indigenous peoples (see Stunnenberg 1993). Finally, Prodechaco staff had concrete economic interests in avoiding conflicts that may have ended in the termination of the project and their contracts. Changes that were later introduced to Prodechaco's objectives make it evident that these interests were incompatible with a vision of development based on the view of the Indigenous peoples as still hunter–gatherers. For example, in early drafts of the project proposal it was held that hunting–gathering was a way of life that, so long as it was performed within large territories, fitted the environmental conditions of the Chaco (EC 1994). In later documents, by contrast, hunting–gathering was deemed to fit present conditions no longer because of population growth. Consequently, the objectives of the project changed from the preservation of the Indigenous peoples' way of life to 'their incorporation into civilization' (see Prodechaco 1998a).

Obviously, the EU's bureaucrats in charge of this project and the company that won the bid to execute it were not interested in risking their immediate interests by antagonizing the Paraguayan government in its own area of interest. Nevertheless, the EU's institutions and their projects are to some extent accountable in terms of their written policies.[8] Thus, while Prodechaco avoided directly addressing the controversial issue of hunting and gathering – and the associated land tenure issue – it did not give up its claim that the project was profoundly committed to help the Indigenous peoples find their own path for development. However, Prodechaco's collaboration with the Indigenous peoples systematically avoided undertakings that could touch disputes over land tenure and tended to focus on agriculture and the acquisition of work skills (see Prodechaco 1998b and 1999).

The Radical Indigenists

The positions of radical indigenists on the Indigenous peoples and their development are closely connected to the issue of their representation, both in the sense of how they are imagined and in the sense of who speaks for them. While the dominant representation of the Indigenous peoples as hunter–gatherers is embraced by some radical indigenists out of conviction, others accept it in part as a strategy to harness national and international public support for land claims. In any case, predicated characteristics of hunter–gatherers are at the core of the radical indigenists' justifications of their actions. This is evident when the issue of 'who speaks for' the Indigenous peoples is addressed. For a variety of reasons radical NGOs claim a virtual monopoly on the 'legitimate' representation of Indigenous peoples and the decisions made regarding their future. The arguments are that the Indigenous peoples see them as their legitimate leaders, as one indigenist told me, that the Indigenous peoples lack knowledge of non-Indigenous institutions, and even that the Indigenous peoples' innocence makes them 'easy targets' for corrupted and corrupting characters.

It would be incorrect to assume that these justifications are intentionally self-serving. Rather, they are the logical consequence of how radical NGOs see the Indigenous peoples and the complex stakes they have in those representations. This is clear in an editorial note on the 'last sighting' of the 'forest Totobiegosode people' published in *Suplemento Antropológico*, Paraguay's anthropological journal:[9]

> [The Totobiegosode's] traditional life style in harmony with nature, which feeds and shelters them, represents, perhaps, the desire for freedom, for essence, for solidarity which probably all of us cultivate in the deepest secret corner of our lives. [Their case] represents in the continent, and in the world, a way of life which is on its way to extinction. Let us save it! (CEADUC 1997)

The images of freedom, essence and solidarity constitute a powerful mobilizing force without which, for many indigenists, there would be no reason to support the Indigenous peoples' struggles. Indeed, as one indigenist told me when I questioned the portrayal of Indigenous peoples as 'essentially' different from non-Indigenous people: 'If they are not different [in an essential way] from us, why should we struggle for special rights to be granted to them?'

On the radical side of Paraguayan indigenism, the dominant understanding is that to be Indigenous is to be essentially different and that this difference is embodied in traits of hunter–gatherer societies such as living in harmony with nature, equality, solidarity and the like. These traits might be more or less hidden because of the influence of non-Indigenous peoples but, nevertheless, they are always there, ready to be 'saved from extinction'. The radical indigenists envision that the way to save the traits of indigenousness (and thereby save the Indigenous peoples) is through development projects that promote sustainable ways of living. This implies granting the Indigenous peoples lands large enough for them to make use of natural resources without depleting them (Grünberg 1997).

We have seen that different indigenist institutions produce or shape their visions of development, directly or indirectly, in relation to the assumed characteristics of the hunter–gatherers. These characteristics determine whether Indigenous peoples of the Chaco deserve or require one form of development or another. It is clear that, for diverse reasons, the conservative side is averse to any important change in the land tenure structure of the Chaco. Thus their policies, in the best of cases, tend only to provide outlets for the 'social steam' produced by the permanent structural adjustment to which Indigenous communities in the Chaco have been subjected since the end of the nineteenth century. From the radical perspective, the problems faced by Indigenous peoples can only be solved through a policy of land granting that implies profound changes in the land tenure structure. Thus the radicals' main strategy has been mostly directed to support or, in some cases, to lead land claims. The common ground for this debate is provided by the traits that define 'authentic indigenousness'. Yet in this debate the voices of the Indigenous peoples appear as a mere chorus for the leading voices of the indigenists. As we will see in the next section, it is precisely this silencing of their voices that is at the centre of the Yshiro's preoccupations.

Facing Material/Discursive Structures of Power

During 1999 the Yshiro leaders joined their five communities under the organizational umbrella of Unión de las Comunidades Indígenas de la Nación Yshir (UCINY) (see Blaser 2003 for an ethnographic analysis of this process). As we will see, the discourses and actions undertaken by the Yshiro leaders with the aim of creating UCINY show that 'life projects' are not comparable to the different visions of development that indigenists struggle about. Since the first meeting, when leaders began to discuss the creation of the organization, the issue of the representation of the Indigenous peoples was at centre stage. However, the discussions were not about the relative accuracy of the Yshiro being represented either as hunter–gatherers or as no longer hunter–gatherers. Nor were the discussions about the relative advantages of the visions of development emerging from those representations. Instead the discussions were about who claimed to represent the Yshiro and the effects on their communities of having non-Yshiro speak for them. This does not mean that land tenure, poverty, lack of economic opportunities and declining natural resources were not discussed. Rather they were considered issues amenable to solution only to the extent that the central issue of who represents and, ultimately who decides, was tackled first. Let us see these discussions in more detail.[10]

Life Projects and Who Decides

During the discussions, it was pointed out several times that divisions within the communities were at the root of the problems faced by the Yshiro people today. This was underlined by comparing the cohesion existing among the 'ancient Yshiro' and the disorganization, individualism and lack of a unified agenda reigning within the communities today. For example, one of the leaders said:

Our problem is that we have abandoned our ancestors' way; we do not follow our customs. For that reason we have this problem of each one pulling on its own direction.... The [non-Indigenous] Paraguayans know very well we are divided and take advantage of it and disrespect us.

The leaders gave several examples of how the divisions in the communities are taken advantage of by non-Indigenous peoples. One example was the proliferation of indigenist NGOs that gather signatures from individuals in the communities in order to ask for funding that never reaches the communities:

Indigenists ask [for funding] on behalf of Indigenous peoples but do not let Indigenous peoples manage those funds. The Paraguayans ask for funding on our behalf but never let the leaders know exactly what they get. They eat all of it. If we get organized, we will manage those resources, because we know better what we need and what happens in our communities.

However, the leaders were also aware that the problems with indigenists go beyond some cases of bad faith and corruption:

Of course, there are many [White] people with good will. Nevertheless we have to be conscious that when somebody provides you with economic resources, like it or not, you have to respond to that provider. We all depend on somebody else, but when you depend on a *patron* you cannot resist them. Because that's the system of the Whites, if you do not obey them they cut 'the stream'. [You wonder] what the stream is? Economic support. If UCINY is the organization that will defend us against our *yamaho* [adversary], the *maro* [Paraguayan Whites], then its leaders must be free to oppose them; they must have no *patrones*.

As the last two quotations indicate, the leaders were clearly aware that the asymmetrical relations that the Indigenous peoples sustain with indigenists were not something that could be overcome by good will. The last quotation, in particular, shows that the leaders saw the pressures and demands that indigenists exercise over them as systemic, ingrained in the very structure of the field in which they interact with each other. One of the leaders pointed out that

Many [indigenist] organizations, when helping Indigenous peoples, are the same as the politicians and the churches: they help you and then they want you to do as they want…. We should not fall in the trap of UCINY being economically sustained by any [Paraguayan] organization because once this happens our organization will have no strength to criticize.

Even when indigenists have good intentions, lacking control over organizational resources means that the Indigenous peoples lack control over decision-making and therefore are constrained to accept the viewpoints of their supporters. Thus, seeing that the unequal structure of power in which they were immersed had emerged in part from the indigenists' monopoly in representing the Indigenous peoples, the leaders saw regaining command over their representation as a possible way to escape this structure: 'We do not want intermediaries, we want our organization to manage our affairs…. Our ancestors have their voices; if we do not have our organization our voices cannot be heard.' Yet the leaders were aware that regaining control over their representation would not be unopposed. A leader recommended that 'It is very important that we communicate with each other [because] Paraguayans are liars and want us to fight each other so that they can do their deeds undisturbed.' Another leader warned that

Our organization will be attacked not only by the Paraguayans but also by some of our brothers. I know my people very well. I know one by one those who like to criticize their brothers who are working for their communities. The Whites will support this kind of person so that they can create misunderstandings and confusion in our communities.

As one of the more experienced leaders eloquently expressed it, to promote community well-being and the recovery of traditional territories, the leaders would have to 'seal off' the extremely permeable boundaries of their communities in order to make them speak with one voice.

When the *intipohr* [wild boar] stick together the hunter cannot get his prey. He will wait for the *intipohra* that is detached from its group and then he will get his prey. In the same way when an *Yshir* is detached from our union he or she can be tamed by an external political influence to undermine our organization. For these reasons our organization has to watch out for its people, to avoid these traps. If we stick together as the *intipohr*, brave against the dogs, the hunter [the politician] is not going to get any of us alone.... We will sanction those that promote indifference towards our organization and those who speak with the authorities [the government] without having authority because they will be break-ing the principles of our union.... The objective of this organization is to further the well-being of our people. You know that misery gets worse year after year and we cannot fight against it because we are divided.... We know this land is ours but how are we going to prove it if the Whites get away with claiming their words are the only truth? ... Once the Whites have taken possession of our lands we do not have the right to go across their fences to secure our subsistence.... It is our dream that through this organization we are going to recover our ter-ritory, and we are not going to rest until we do it. [But] as we are a minority, and divided, non-Indigenous peoples dominate us at their whim.... Now we are closer to that great day in which we will create this organization. We are going to terminate individualism, and when outsiders intend to fool us we will force them to deal with our organization, because it will be through our organization that decisions will be made.

As is evident from this passage, the leaders saw the possibility of improv-ing the situation of the Yshiro communities by making UCINY their only representative. In this sense, they showed an understanding of an aspect of the politics of representation that dominates the indigenist field – that is, the idea that an organization is representative when it is *authorized* to speak for those whom it represents. But they also understood that to be author-ized to speak for the Yshiro, UCINY would have to speak in specific ways that suited the indigenist institutions' visions of the Indigenous peoples and their developmental needs. It is here that, in order to alter 'who decides', the leaders had to struggle with the indigenists' debates over the Indigenous peoples' ways of life.

Representing Ways of Life

The first practical problem faced by the Yshiro leaders was to find the material resources for the meetings necessary to create their organization. The leaders sought, and quickly obtained, from Prodechaco material support for the meetings. Moreover, this institution also offered radios for communication between communities, expert advice, and the promise to back up 'productive projects' proposed by the nascent organization. Prodechaco's enthusiastic embrace of UCINY as a legitimate interlocutor was in part due to the fact that the Yshiro leaders carefully avoided bringing to the forefront UCINY's long-term objective of recovering the Yshiro's traditional territory. Downplaying this, the leaders requested support, giving Prodechaco the opportunity of demonstrating its commitment to participation and grassroots organizational strengthening, and to its abiding by the objectives set up by the EU's policy without antagonizing the Paraguayan government on any sensitive issue.[11]

INDI is another important actor in UCINY's progress towards its consolidation as the legitimate representative of the Yshiro nation. The authority invested in INDI to recognize leaders and communities legally means that it can erode at the base any attempt to construct intercommunal representations. The leaders' aim was to obtain INDI's recognition of UCINY as the only valid representative of the Yshiro. They wrote a letter to the president of the institution claiming for UCINY the exclusive right to represent the Yshiro people in several matters, including land claims and the adjudication of legal leadership. The leaders argued that having UCINY as the only Yshiro interlocutor would speed up INDI's administrative procedures and thus would contribute to the 'development of the communities'.[12] INDI's response to UCINY's request was ambivalent. On the one hand, its president was inclined to accept the idea since UCINY could relieve the pressures that Indigenous individuals exert on the staff and the coffers of the institution. On the other hand, to accept UCINY as the only interlocutor meant to give up the remote control that INDI has within the communities through the formal recognition of leaders. That is, if UCINY were the only interlocutor, it would become the gatekeeper to the communities and this, in turn, would undermine the basis on which the governing Colorado Party's political-clientelistic apparatus rests. Facing this dilemma, the official attitude was to go halfway: an internal memorandum was circulated calling to the attention of INDI's staff the fact that UCINY had asked that no aid be granted to Yshiro individuals without its authorization. However, no mention was made as to how INDI's staff should respond to this request. The memorandum also made no mention of the most critical areas in which UCINY had requested exclusive rights to represent the Yshiro, the recognition of leaders and land claims (see INDI 1999).

Almost at the same time that dealings with INDI were being carried out, the leaders began to establish contacts with diverse indigenist NGOs. The general objective was to undermine the material base for independent 'wannabe' leaders. It was thought that by obtaining exclusivity in the intermediation of NGOs and the communities, UCINY could neutralize those people who, through their individual agendas, erode the basis for a unified leadership. A more specific purpose was to obtain legal advice and basic organizational support such as access to telecommunications in the capital city, Asunción.

The reactions of radical NGOs to UCINY were generally positive, though, in many cases, doubts as to the representativeness of the leaders were expressed. For example, one NGO staff member expressed doubts about the leaders because they had contacts throughout the spectrum of Paraguayan indigenism, showing that the leaders had learned 'too well how to hunt and gather projects'. This meant that they could garner too much power and destabilize the egalitarianism of the communities. To avoid this situation, it was argued, indigenists had to limit their support to raising leaders in spite of the fact that, as several indigenists put it, to operate in the Paraguayan indigenist-political field, Indigenous leaders need 'godfathers'. Thus this radical NGO's staff member demanded that, in exchange for his support, the leaders avoid relations with certain organizations labelled ethnocidal. The leaders did not respond directly to this demand, but afterwards carefully avoided mentioning meetings and activities with conservative indigenists like Prodechaco.

In general, the reactions of indigenist institutions to UCINY were ambivalent. The question that was always lurking in this ambivalence was whether UCINY would represent the Yshiro in a way that contested the visions of development promoted by either sector of Paraguayan indigenism. Given that the Yshiro leaders avoided taking a position along these lines, UCINY was seen by indigenist organizations as both an opportunity to further some of their visions and as a possible threat to themselves.

From the conservative side of the spectrum, it is not surprising to find ambivalence towards anything that might challenge the status quo. Indeed, it is their support that, although limited, is surprising. It was the Yshiro leaders' careful use of their knowledge of where institutions like Prodechaco and INDI stood that made dealings with this side of the spectrum relatively fruitful. Of course, such relations required trade-offs and a low profile regarding sensitive issues, but this was a condition imposed by the structure of a field also shaped by the radical indigenists.

While the conservatives' ambivalence is not surprising, the same cannot be said of the radical indigenists who supposedly are very much in support of empowering the Indigenous peoples. I believe that the ambivalence of this sector is related in part to the strong attachment that they have towards their images of authentic indigenousness or, as Ramos (1998: 267–83) calls it, the 'hyper-real Indian' (see also Conklin and Graham 1997). As in the case described by Ramos, the Indigenous leaders are expected by radical indigenists to be 'pure', without the tricks or tactics of manipulation used by non-Indigenous politicians. The ideal leader, according to these models, is one who is not involved in Paraguayan politics, who 'remains in the forest', and

whose leadership is based on supposed hunter–gatherer values. This is a leader
who will always need the mediation of non-Indigenous NGOs to deal with
the rest of the world. Thus, the political skills displayed by the Yshiro leaders,
even when seen by radical indigenists as stemming from hunting–gathering
skills, appeared as a possible index of inauthenticity to the extent that they
seem to alter the egalitarianism of hunter–gatherer societies.

In short, the ambivalence reflected in the indigenist institutions' responses
to UCINY reveal that the Yshiro leaders' struggle to gain command over
representation, and over who decides in what ways they must live, cut across
the indigenists' debates over their way of life. In this sense, the occurrences I
have discussed make it evident that life projects are not alternative blueprints
for organizing human societies and their relations to nature. Rather, I would
argue, life projects are about opening up spaces and creating the conditions
for dreaming one's own life.

Dreaming One's Own Life

The dominant debate about Indigenous peoples in Paraguay has centred on
whether or not they are hunter–gatherers. The radical indigenists seem to
have found an apparently powerful imagery to rally public support for land
claims. Some radical indigenists would argue, in private, that in spite of its
shortcomings the hunter–gatherer argument is necessary because it is the
only one that will allow large tracts of forest to be saved from destruction
for the use of future generations of Indigenous peoples. They argue that the
Indigenous peoples are currently not aware of the threat to their future, or
are so enmeshed in the problems of daily survival that they are not able to
see the significance of the struggles led by the radical indigenists. But even
in this case, taking the lead on behalf of the Indigenous peoples does not
guarantee that the land claimed, if it is ever obtained, will survive destruction and be there for future generations. The attachment and responsibilities
towards the land and the environment which radical indigenists automatically
ascribe to Indigenous peoples of the Chaco are rooted in concrete experience, and thus are necessarily transformed by history. The colonization of
the Chaco has meant great displacement of communities from their former
territories. This has had an enormous impact on the way in which the
younger generations, especially, feel attached to the land. Such attachments
can only be reinforced in the younger generations if they are thoroughly
involved in the struggle to recover their land.

In any case, the radical indigenists' trust in the hunter–gatherer storyline
has provided the conservative indigenists with a dead horse that is easy to
beat. Indeed, the terrain on which debates about the Indigenous peoples'

future has been situated not only imposes constraints on Indigenous peoples' capacity to further their life projects but is of dubious benefit for their land claims. Justifications of land claims that rely on the hunter–gatherer storyline are easily contested since the idealized images of the Indigenous peoples used in public campaigns are, as a radical NGO staff member confided to me, 'not verifiable in real conditions'. The subtle and not so subtle pressures that non-Indigenous supporters exert on Indigenous leaders to make them fit those images of 'indigenousness' estrange many Indigenous leaders from the radical indigenists and their strategies. This is readily used by the conservative side to wrest legitimacy from the objectives that the radical side stands for (see ARP 1994; Stahl 1993: 39). The result is the subordination of the Indigenous peoples to non-Indigenous supporters and very little land being obtained.

Debates about who the Indigenous peoples really are, and consequently what form of development they need, lose sight of the fact that communities are always complex, emergent processes. This is most evident when Indigenous peoples' actions do not fit established (although often mutually contradictory) notions of indigenousness. This automatically sets the analysis of these actions in the Manichaean dichotomy of authentic versus inauthentic, seriously constraining the ways in which the Indigenous peoples can form their own conceptions of themselves and their being-in-the-world. Life projects, as exemplified by the Yshiro case, are aimed at transforming those constraints by shifting the core of the debate that produces them.

For clarity's sake, let me distinguish the hard core of the debates over authentic indigenousness from their shell. By shell I refer to the obviously interested objectifications of the Indigenous peoples (either as backward savages needing development, or as noble savages functional to sustainable development) that are aimed at justifying more powerful actors' visions of development. I will not dwell on this kind of rhetorical operation because it is easy to expose such objectifications. In contrast, the hard core is more difficult to deal with, because it is the principle by which the visions of development imposed on the Indigenous peoples and their lands are continually generated. This generative principle is the profoundly ingrained notion of 'true knowledge' that grounds those visions. As long as indigenists of any persuasion do not question this notion, it is unlikely that they will engage the Indigenous peoples as subjects with the right to dream their own futures.

When the Yshiro leaders, through their life project, strive to be addressed directly and to manoeuvre carefully between various visions of indigenousness held by the indigenists, they are trying to lay the groundwork for a different sort of material/discursive field – a field that avoids the traps of the debates over authentic indigenousness by taking at its core the issue of who decides. It is important to keep in mind that life projects do not emerge with ready-made answers from a supposed 'pure' indigenousness standing against some of the blueprints for global development. Rather, life projects are an attempt to shift attention from the definitions of indigenousness used by the blueprints of development towards the idea that decision-making must be in the hands of those who are going to be affected by the decisions.

While Indigenous life projects certainly have roots reaching into the (hi)stories that precede conquest and colonization, they are also thoroughly historical, attentive to immediate political conditions and always in the making. As McGregor points out in this volume, Indigenous traditions include the experience of dealing with colonialism. This, I believe, is an experience that cannot be disregarded in the common struggle to make Indigenous and non-Indigenous life projects viable in the midst of very unfavourable material/discursive structures of power.

Notes

This work owes much to the honesty and openness of several people working in the Paraguayan indigenist field. I hope they will take my critique of indigenism with the constructive spirit that inspires it. My gratitude goes to Stephen Kidd, Mirta Pereyra, Rodro Villagra, Serafina Alvarez, Jorge Vera and Verena Regehr, with a special note of thanks to Ursula Regehr, with whom I began discussions of the ideas presented here. The welcoming and generous attitude of the Yshiro leaders, who made me part of the experience of taking UCINY out of the realm of daydreaming, is something I will never forget. I am grateful, therefore, to Bruno Barras and his family, Teresa and Gaspar Payá, Candido and Maria Martinez, Marciano Barboza, Zulma Franco, Julio Baez, Justino and Nidia Mallero, Don Sanchez, Feliciano Rodriguez, Babi Ozuna and Alejo Barras. I want also to thank my partner, Amanda White, for her untiring intellectual and human support. The opinions reflected in this chapter are solely the responsibility of the author. The Social Sciences and Humanities Research Council of Canada, the International Development Research Centre of Canada, the Organization of American States and the School of Graduate Studies at McMaster University generously funded the research on which this chapter is based.

1. The term 'indigenist' is very different from 'Indigenous'. The former refers broadly to non-Indigenous institutions and individuals that promote practices and policies that target Indigenous peoples (Diaz-Polanco 1997: 23).
2. From a Marxist framework, Gordillo (1993) has thoroughly criticized the arguments, pointing out their lack of factual grounds, their interpretive weaknesses and their internal contradictions.
3. The ethnocidal side is supposed to intend the total integration and assimilation of Indigenous peoples into a mass of indistinguishable rural poor. The primitivist side is supposed to conceive for the Indigenous peoples a future of being anthropological exhibits.
4. The structure of Paraguayan Chaco land tenure is characterized by the ownership of huge tracts of lands by a few landowners. In recent years these lands have begun to be parcelled up and sold to feed the demands of an expanding agricultural frontier. See Pastore 1972 for a study of land tenure structure in Paraguay.

5. Several small NGOs, which could be located all along the arch, are not mentioned because they do not develop their own policies; rather, they follow the lines traced by the institutions mentioned here.

6. The Stroessner regime lasted almost thirty-five years (1954–89), making it the most durable autocratic regime of South America.

7. I refer to normal operations because from 1995 to 1998 the Paraguayan government allocated nearly US$45 million to buy lands for the Indigenous peoples. During this period several partnerships were formed among landowners, 'false' Indigenous leaders and INDI's bureaucrats to profit from the land claims. Stephen Kidd (1998) has shown that most lands purchased during this period were not claimed by any real community, that the prices paid for some lands were up to 700 per cent above market prices, and that the lands were of poor quality.

8. In fact Prodechaco was, almost from the beginning, strongly criticized and endured a well-organized lobby of radical NGOs allied with European NGOs. The main point of the criticism was that Prodechaco did not take into account in its execution that Indigenous peoples of the Chaco had a hunter–gatherer way of life. This, the radical indigenists argued, revealed that the word 'sustainable' was just a token in the project (Meliá 1997; Lackner 1998).

9. The Totobiegosode are a subgroup of the Ayoreode. They came into permanent contact with non-Indigenous peoples in the 1960s. A group of Totobiegosode was 'hunted down' and brought into a New Tribes Mission in 1986, raising a public uproar (see Escobar 1989; Perasso 1988). Another small group has been spotted several times, but it actively avoids contact.

10. What follows are extracts from transcriptions of meetings recorded by the author between April and September 1999. The discussions were carried on in the Yshir language, and I tape-recorded them. Later, with the assistance of Yshiro interpreters, I transcribed the tapes and translated them into Spanish. In translating the speeches from Spanish to English I have favoured the intended meaning over a literal translation. The names of the speakers have been omitted to protect their privacy.

11. A dispute over hunting rights between UCINY and the Sub-Ministry of Natural Resources soon made clear that land claims were not the only controversial issue in Paraguay. The dispute, which originated in a project financed by Prodechaco, showed that this institution would not stand up to the Paraguayan government on any issue; at least where the consequences of avoiding confrontation were understood to be immediately threatening to the survival of the project. Although I cannot enter into the details here, let me point out that in the controversy over hunting rights, Prodechaco sided with UCINY because otherwise it might have had to face an antagonistic Paraguayan–European environmental lobby in addition to the indigenist lobby. See several notes signed by Roque Gonzales Vera and published in the Paraguayan newspaper *ABC* between 2 April and 6 August 2000 for a version of this controversy.

12. Letter dated 10 December 1999 from UCINY to INDI's president. Copy in the possession of the author.

References

ARP (Asociación Rural del Paraguay) (1994) *Tierras del Chaco para Indígenas y Campesinos.* Manuscript filed in Biblioteca Pablo VI, Universidad Catolica de Asunción.

Blaser, Mario (1997) 'The Chamacoco endurance: global politics in the local village (Paraguay 1890s–1990s)', M.A. thesis, Carleton University, Ottawa.

———— (2003) 'Governmentalities and authorized imaginations: a (non-modern) story about Indians, nature and development', Ph.D. dissertation, Department of Anthropology, McMaster University, Hamilton.

Brosius, Peter (1999a) 'On the practice of transnational cultural critique', *Identities*, vol. 6, nos 2–3, pp. 179–200.

———— (ed.) (1999b) *Ethnographic Presence: Environmentalism, Indigenous Rights and Transnational Cultural Critique*, Newark: Gordon & Breach.

Carisimo Pfannl, Robert (2000) 'A ineversionistas productores paraguayos, compatriotas indígenas y extranjeros', *Diario Última Hora*, 12 October, p. 8.

CEADUC (Centro de Estudios Antropológicos de la Universidad Católica) (1997) 'Editorial: La aparición de los silvícolas totobiegosode', *Suplemento Antropológico*, vol. 32, nos 1–2, pp. 2–3.

CNP (Constitución Nacional de Paraguay) (1992) Capitulo V de los Pueblos Indígenas.

Conklin, Beth (1997) 'Body paint, feathers, and VCRs: aesthetics and authenticity in Amazonian activism', *American Ethnologist*, vol. 24, no. 4, pp. 711–37.

———— and Laura Graham (1997) 'The shifting middle ground: Amazonian Indians and eco-politics', *American Anthropologist*, vol. 97, no. 4, pp. 695–710.

Diaz-Polanco, Hector (1997) *Indigenous Peoples in Latin America: The Quest for Self-Determination*, Boulder, CO: Westview Press.

Delport, Josef (1998) 'Los indígenas angaité en las estancias', *Suplemento Antropológico*, vol. 33, nos 1–2, pp. 235–73.

EC (European Commission) (1994) 'Proposal for a financing decision'. Unpublished internal communication dated May 1994, South America Unit, Brussels. Copy in possession of the author.

———— (1998) 'Working document on the support for Indigenous peoples in the development cooperation of the community and the member states'. Document SEC (1998) 773 final.

Escobar, T. (1989) 'Ethnocide: mission accomplished', *IWGIA Document* 64.

Fiering, Birgitte and Sylvie Prouveur (1999) 'Consultation and participation play a key part in policy development: dossier indigenous peoples', *The Courier* 173, pp. 34–6.

Freres, Christian (2000) 'The European Union as a global "civilian power": development cooperation in EU–Latin American relations', *Journal of Interamerican Studies and World Affairs*, vol. 42, no. 2, pp. 63–85.

Friedman, Jonathan (1996) 'The politics of de-authentification: escaping from identity, a commentary on "Beyond Authenticity" by Mark Rogers', *Identities*, vol. 3, nos 1–2, pp. 127–36.

Fritz, Miguel (1993) 'La changa: opción de los indígenas nivaclé de Campo Loa', *Suplemento Antropológico*, vol. 28, nos 1–2, pp. 43–106.

Gordillo, Gaston (1993) 'La actual dinámica económica de los cazadores-recolectores del gran Chaco y los deseos imaginarios del esencialismo', *Publicar*, vol. 2, no. 3, pp. 73–96.

Grünberg, Georg (1997) 'El Chaco sustentable y possible', *Acción* 171, pp. 5–8.

Hornborg, A. (1994) 'Environmentalism, ethnicity and sacred places: reflections on modernity, discourse and power', *Canadian Review of Sociology and Anthropology*, vol. 31, no. 3, pp. 245–67.

INDI (Instituto Nacional del Indígena) (1999). Copy of internal memorandum, in possession of the author.

Jackson, Jean (1995) 'Culture, genuine and spurious: the politics of Indianness in the Vaupes, Colombia', *American Ethnologist*, vol. 22, no. 1, pp. 3–27.

Kidd, Stephen (1995) 'Land, politics and benevolent shamanism: the Enxet Indians in a democratic Paraguay', *Journal of Latin American Studies* 27, pp. 43–75.

———— (1998) 'Report on the European Union's project for the sustainable development of the Paraguayan Chaco', Centre for Indigenous American Studies and Exchange, University of St Andrews.

Lackner, Thomas (1998) 'Comparación de la situación de las tierras indígenas con los resultados de prodechaco', *Proyecto de Consolidación Socio-Ambiental del Chaco Paraguayo (PCSA)*, Asunción: Asociación Indigenista del Paraguay.

Mato, Daniel (1996) 'On the theory, epistemology and politics of the social construction of "cultural identities" in the age of globalization: introductory remarks to ongoing debates', *Identities*, vol. 3, nos 1–2, pp. 61–72.

Meliá, Bartolomeu (1997) 'La cuestión del Chaco: antecedentes de un caso', *Acción* 171, pp. 16–19.

Pane, Leni (1999) Inaugural speech, Radio Pai Puku (Filadephia), 16 October.

Pastore, Carlos (1972) *La lucha por la tierra en el Paraguay*, Montevideo: Editorial Antequera.

Perasso, J. (1998) *Cronicas de cacerias Humanas: La Tragedia Ayoreo,* Asuncion: El Lector.

Prodechaco (1998a) 'Convenio de financiación entre las comunidades europeas y la Repùblica del Paraguay. Desarrollo duradero del Chaco (Protección del habitat de los indígenas y del medio ambiente)', *Plan Operativo Global*, vol. 3, Asunción: Unión Europea y Repùblica del Paraguay, Ministerio de Agricultura y Ganadería.

———— (1998b) 'Informe principal', *Plan Operativo Global*, vol. 2, Asunción: Unión Europea y Repùblica del Paraguay, Ministerio de Agricultura y Ganadería.

———— (1999) 'Responses to the points raised by Community Members delegations'. Copy of internal memorandum, in possession of the author.

Ramos, Alcida (1998) *Indigenism: Ethnic Politics in Brazil*, Madison: University of Wisconsin Press.

Renshaw, John (1989) 'Property, resources and equality among the Indians of the Paraguayan Chaco', *Man*, NS, vol. 23, pp. 334–52.

———— (1996) *Los indígenas del Chaco paraguayo. Economía y sociedad*, Asunción: Intercontinental Editora.

Rogers, Mark (1996) 'Beyond authenticity: conservation, tourism, and the politics of representation in the Ecuadorian Amazon', *Identities*, vol. 3, nos 1–2, pp. 73–125.

Rojas, Daniel E. (1996) 'Economía indígena y economía alternativa de desarrollo', *Suplemento Antropológico*, vol. 31, nos 1–2, pp. 251–73.

SETA (1992) *Paraguay. Desarrollo sostenible del Chaco Paraguayao. Informe provisional*, Comunidad Europea.

Stahl, Whilmar (1993) 'Antropología de acción entre indígenas chaqueños', *Suplemento Antropológico*, vol. 28, nos 1–2, pp. 25–42.

Stunnenberg, Petrus (1993) *Entitled to Land: The Incorporation of the Paraguayan and Argentinean Chaco and the Spatial Marginalization of the Indian People*, Saarbrucken: Verlag Breitenbach.

Susnik, Branka and Miguel Chase-Sardi (1995) *Los Indios del Paraguay*, Madrid: Editorial Mapfre.

Thorndahl, Marie (1997) 'Terrains de chasse et chasses gardées du développement: indigénisme et conflicts fonciers dans le Chaco paraguayan', Diplôme de Recherche, Institut Universitaire d'Études du Développement, Geneva.

Von Bremen, Volker (1987) *Fuentes de Caza y Recolección Modernas: Proyectos de Ayuda al Desarrollo Destinados a los Indígenas del Gran Chaco*, trans. Carlos Fernández-Molina, Stuttgart: Servicios de Desarrollo de las Iglesias (AG-KED).

———— (1994) 'La significación del derecho a la tenencia de tierra para los pueblos tradicionalmente no-sedentarios del Chaco Paraguayo', *Suplemento Antropológico*, vol. 29, nos 1–2, pp. 143–62.

Traditional Ecological Knowledge and Sustainable Development: Towards Coexistence

DEBORAH McGREGOR

Deborah McGregor is an Anishnabeg and member of the Whitefish River First Nation. She is Assistant Professor at the University of Toronto in the Aboriginal Studies Program and the Department of Geography. Her research focuses on First Nations and environmental issues.

Uncritical belief in Western science and technology as the only valid approach to resolving environmental problems has fallen by the wayside. In fact, science and technology are believed to be the cause of many of the problems that we now face (Mander 1991). Realizing the faults in its own system and recognizing the value of other knowledge in addressing global environmental concerns is a significant step for dominant Western society. Science and technology, at least on their own, cannot get us out of the situation that we are in now. Other approaches are required, especially ones with long, successful track records like Traditional Environmental Knowledge (TEK). TEK is increasingly viewed as a viable alternative to the status quo that caused the problems in the first place. Thus, TEK has received increased attention over the last couple of decades, particularly in the area of sustainable development (Williams and Baines 1993; WCED 1987).

Although there are protocols (the Convention on Biodiversity, for example) that promote and encourage the recognition and utilization of TEK as an integral part of moving towards sustainability, there has been little evaluation of the methods being implemented to achieve this sustainable future. Nor has there been much in the way of monitoring the level of achievement of its desired outcome: sustainability. In this chapter I will argue that the way in which TEK is understood and implemented within a Western perspective means that the insights into the nature of the environmental crisis and approaches to its resolution that TEK offers get lost.

What Does 'Sustainable Development' Mean?

From a Western perspective

Sustainable development is a concept derived from conventional Western ideology. It is the product of a particular world-view and its interpretation and implementation reflect Western culture and values. Though it is touted as a framework for addressing challenges faced the world over, these challenges and their solutions are defined through Western eyes.

The sustainable development concept emerged out of the recognition that there are 'strong links between economic development and environmental protection' (Courrier 1994: 508). *Our Common Future* (WCED 1987) popularized the term and brought it to the attention of the world. The WCED described the concept as 'development that meets the needs of the present without compromising the ability to future generations to meet their own needs' (WCED in Courrier 1994). Others have described it as 'economic development with due care for the environment' (Ramphal 1994: 680).

Whatever the specifics of its definition, sustainable development presents a major challenge to society. It requires us to 're-examine our current practices and procedures' (Dearden and Mitchell 1998: 22). It requires a shift in world-view. Despite initial enthusiasm for the concept and the stir created by the WCED Report (also known as the Brundtland Report, after the commission's chairperson), the debates around sustainable development remain (see Dearden and Mitchell 1998 for more on such debates). There has been no uncritical acceptance of the term and there is no consensus on what it means, although the definition provided in *Our Common Future* is the one most often cited.

The term 'sustainability' is often used interchangeably with 'sustainable development'. Sustainability is seen as less confusing. Sustainability 'refers to the capacity to persist and to be robust and resilient' (Dearden and Mitchell 1998: 26). Draper (1998: 13) describes sustainability as the 'ability of an ecosystem to maintain ecological processes and functions, biodiversity, and productivity over time'. The term 'sustainability' is fraught with many of the same shortcomings as 'sustainable development'. Proponents of both concepts, however, are faced with the challenge of encouraging a shift in societal world-views in order to achieve the goals they promote. People must 'learn how to sustain environmental resources so they continue to provide benefits to us, other living things, and the larger environment of which we are a part' (Draper 1998: 13). The dominant Western definitions of sustainability and sustainable development do not, despite some claims, actually propose to replace the status quo; it is simply the slowing down of the same old agenda. The purpose of sustainable development is to enable future generations to continue indefinitely with the same exploitive practices that have caused the problems we face in the first place. It is based on the notion of economic growth or development and a particular world order. In recent times, this growth has been threatened because environmental resources are running out.

Sustainable development does not challenge the power imbalances between Indigenous and Western nations in a meaningful way. It does not empower Indigenous nations. Although the Brundtland Report did recognize the value of Indigenous knowledge as a source of knowledge for moving towards sustainable development, such recognition was still framed within the dominant Western agenda. The conventional concept of sustainable development also tends to perpetuate tension between environmental and economic aspects. While recognizing that something is 'wrong', it concludes that changes must be made in order to survive as Western, economically 'developed' nations. Moreover, the so-called 'underdeveloped' nations are expected to 'catch up' with the rest of the world. Surviving the way Indigenous people have for thousands of years is not given serious consideration.

While interest in TEK as part of the solution to environmental crises is growing, using TEK to achieve the goals of Western society may not be what many Indigenous people have in mind. In fact, TEK research and implementation in support of sustainable development is arguably another form of colonialism. 'Development', in its various forms, has seldom benefited Indigenous people. Throughout the history of colonialism, Indigenous people have been dispossessed of their lands and subjected to policies aimed at 'developing' them, often with devastating effects. Sustaining this kind of development may indeed be counterproductive so far as Indigenous people are concerned. The way sustainable development is currently conceptualized, Indigenous knowledge is required to fit into the existing framework designed to fulfil the needs of Western ideals. We have been down that road before! What, then, might be an Indigenous view of sustainable development?

From an Indigenous perspective

There are superficial similarities between Indigenous views of sustainable development and those of Western society. Primary among these are the recognition that the path of progress upon which the current world order relies is not sustainable, and that fundamental changes are required. Despite such similarities, the two views remain fundamentally different. This should not be surprising as the two are products of very different world-views.

In the spring of 1997, I had the honour of working with Mahgee Binehns (Robin Greene) of Iskutewizaagegan No. 39 Independent First Nation[1] in northwestern Ontario. He is an Anishnabe (the name of the group of Indigenous people to which both he and I belong) speaker who was raised traditionally in his own culture, and for whom English is an acquired language. I worked with Mahgee Binehns on a 'Nationhood and Sustainability' submission for the Chiefs of Ontario Office (the 'Chiefs of Ontario', as it is generally referred to, is the primary political voice of the First Nations Chiefs in this province). This initiative was part of a larger undertaking initiated by the federal government to understand what sustainable development would mean at a practical level. The Chiefs of Ontario, in recognition of the fact that Aboriginal views would be very different from their Western counterparts, wanted to prepare a separate submission rather than integrate their views into a larger perspective. Before this time, I found myself always reacting and feeling uncomfortable with the dominant views of sustainability being imposed upon me. It was during my time with this group of First Nations people working in the environmental arena that an understanding of First Nations views of sustainability finally crystallized.

In the Nationhood and Sustainability working group, we began talking about the concept of sustainable development but did not really get anywhere. It was not until we started to discuss our world-view and the things that mattered to us that we realized that we have the Creation stories to tell us who we are and how we are supposed to live sustainably. Creation stories provide the fundamental understanding of our place in the world. They present us with teachings and lessons explaining how we are to relate to the rest of Creation. Once the discussion turned to our world-view, rather than trying to figure out how our understanding was supposed to fit into someone else's understanding (or agenda), we finally made some progress. Then came the 'insight'.

Before I convey the 'insight', I'll tell you about a rule of thumb I live by in my work with Indigenous knowledge. This is what I call the 'language rule', which I created for myself to enhance my own understanding. I apply it whenever I encounter a concept or construct (such as 'environment', or 'traditional ecological knowledge' or 'sustainable development') for which Aboriginal people are *assumed* to have an automatic affinity. In these cases I conduct the language test, which is simply this: I ask someone who was raised within a First Nations world-view and who learned their mother tongue before learning English or another colonizing language about the concept. These people are usually highly knowledgeable about their cultural traditions, values, and so on. I ask them to think about the concept I am interested in to see if there is a corresponding concept in their own language. Not surprisingly, often there is not. In many cases, expressing even a similar meaning takes a significant amount of time and involves constructing Indigenous knowledge in a variety of different ways. Coercive processes that force Native people to think and operate in non-Native terms frequently result in loss of meaning.

While talking with Mahgee Binehns, I asked whether there was any notion that corresponded with 'sustainable development' in his language. He had been listening intently to the other conversations and knew what the mainstream view was. He said there was no corresponding idea in the Ojibway language. The closest he could come was to explain that Aboriginal people concern themselves with (and have based their whole world-view on) the idea of learning how to give back to Creation, rather than taking away.

Using this as a starting point, it becomes apparent that Indigenous views of development are based not on taking but on giving. Indigenous people ask themselves what they can give to the environment and their relationship with it. The idea of sustaining, maintaining and enhancing relations with all of Creation is of utmost importance from an Indigenous point of view. Indigenous ways of life focus on this type of relationship with Creation. Indigenous people understand that with this special personal relationship with Creation comes tremendous responsibility; it is not something to be taken lightly.

Creation is regarded as a gift. To be sustainable means to take responsibility and be spiritually connected to all of Creation, all of the time. Everyone and everything carries this responsibility and has duties to perform. All things contribute to the sustainability of Creation. It is not a responsibility carried only by people. All of Creation contributes, and this includes everything from the tiniest animals to the powerful sun. It includes the land, the weather, the spirits – all of it. An important principle that emerges from the Creation stories is that we cannot interfere with the ability of these elements or beings of Creation to perform their duties. When we interfere, then the sustainability of Creation is threatened (as we now see).

Over many years Indigenous people developed ways of living that sustained this relationship with all of Creation. This relationship was based on giving. From an Indigenous point of view, all of Creation matters. Sustainable development therefore means the survival, not just of people, but of all Creation.

Since colonization, the ability of Indigenous people to live up to the responsibility of caring for all of Creation has been seriously inhibited. The sustainability of Indigenous peoples' lives has been compromised in every aspect of everyday life, resulting in destroyed lands, infant mortality, high suicide rates, and so on. Colonization and the accompanying oppression have been so pervasive that even Indigenous people themselves are sometimes disrespectful and harmful to Creation.

However, the strength and perseverance of Indigenous views of sustainability should not be underestimated; they remain in fact very powerful. Despite a concerted effort to eliminate Indigenous peoples as a recognizable group in Canada, First Nations have persisted and continue to pass on their knowledge. Many Elders remind us to be thankful to our ancestors, and that because of their courage we are still alive today. Every time you hear a prayer in the Indigenous language, it is a powerful reminder of how clever and strong our ancestors were.

Through our long history of oppression, our survival depended upon and still depends upon our traditions. This understanding permeates every aspect of our lives and efforts at nation-building (Mercredi and Turpel 1993). We have learned to resist and thus have survived. Understanding colonialism and its devastating impacts upon us, as well as learning how to resist various forms of colonialism (including internalized forms), constitute an important part of the our traditional teachings today (Fitznor 1998).

In summary, Indigenous views of sustainable development are concerned with giving rather than taking, and with what it is that we can contribute to creation. Indigenous views also include active resistance (sometimes to sustainable development itself) and the process of reclaiming our traditions. Resisting and reclaiming form an integral part of our concept of sustainable development.

What Does 'TEK' Mean?

The knowledge that Indigenous peoples have in relation to the environment has come to be referred to as 'Traditional Environmental Knowledge' (TEK). At national and international levels, TEK is currently a recognized term in the move towards increased environmental sustainability. However, its precise meaning, role and application remain elusive at both policy and operational levels. The last decade has seen quite an interest in TEK and it has now emerged as a field of study, complete with theory, research approaches, models and potential applications.

Despite the interest in TEK by environmental managers, policymakers, academics, consultants, environmentalists and Aboriginal communities themselves, the meaning of TEK remains both elusive and controversial. There is no commonly accepted view of the term. This matter is examined in more detail in recent texts (e.g. Battiste and Henderson 2000; McGregor 2000, 1994; Procter 1999). For the purposes of this chapter only some of the basic issues in defining TEK need be presented below.

Following are a few brief definitions. The most commonly heard views of TEK from a dominant or mainstream perspective tend to be variations of Martha Johnson's description, in which TEK is defined as:

a body of knowledge built up by a group of people through generations of living in close contact with nature. It includes a system of classification, a set of empirical observations about the local environment, and a system of self-management that governs resource use. The quantity and quality of traditional environmental knowledge varies among community members, depending upon gender, age, social status, intellectual capability, and profession (hunter, spiritual leader, healer, etc.). With its roots firmly in the past, traditional environmental knowledge is both cumulative and dynamic, building upon the experience of earlier generations and adapting to the new technological and socioeconomic changes of the present. (Johnson 1992: 4; see also Berkes 1999: 8; Doubleday 1993: 41; Nakashima 1993: 99)

In summary, while many of the non-Native definitions incorporate valid aspects of TEK, they tend to consider TEK as a 'body of knowledge', something that can be considered as being separate from the people who hold it. As we shall see, this constitutes a fundamental difference between the Native and non-Native views.

Aboriginal perspectives vary by nation and cultural group, though there are common themes that run throughout. In some cases the language used to describe TEK is similar to that of Western academics, as Aboriginal people have increasingly had to use the dominant language and terminology in order to communicate (AFN 1995). At the same time, this practice is being challenged by some parties with the result that alternative Aboriginal descriptions are emerging. Following is a sampling of Aboriginal views of TEK.

Elder Annie Catholique (in Raffan 1993: 49) states that, 'When the government people talk about land, I find it very funny, talking about all the things we use, all the things we survive on, like animals and caribou and those things. When I think about land, I think about the Great Spirit.'

Knowledge is regarded as inseparable from the land. According to Gleb Raygorodetsky (in Gwich'in Elders 1997: 14):

The term 'Land' … is not restricted to the physical environment only. It has a much broader meaning, used by indigenous people to refer to the physical, biological and spiritual environments fused together. The closest scientific equivalent of the 'Land', taken without its spiritual component, is 'ecosystem'.

Raygorodetsky also observes (in Gwich'in Elders 1997: 14) that 'Spiritual and ethical values have been woven into this knowledge, creating a system that has guided the people and helped them survive.'

Taiake Alfred (1999: 9) states: 'The Indigenous belief, reflecting a spiritual connection with the land established by the Creator, gives human beings special responsibilities within the area they occupy as Indigenous peoples, linking them in a "natural" way to their territories.'

Aboriginal participants in the 'Circumpolar Aboriginal People and Co-Management Practice' workshop (Roberts 1996) explain that

Traditional knowledge is an accumulated body of knowledge that is rooted in the spiritual health, culture, and language of the people and handed down from generation to generation. It is based on intimate knowledge of the land, water, snow and ice, weather and wildlife, and the relationships between all aspects of the environment. It is the way people travel and hunt. It is a way of life and survival.

Traditional knowledge is practical common sense, good reasoning, and logic built on experience. It is an authority system (a standard of conduct), setting out rules governing the use and respect of resources, and an obligation to share. For example, it tells people that they do not have the right to hunt all animals of a species, as in wolf kill programmes. The wisdom comes in using the knowledge and ensuring that it is used in a good way. It involves using the head and heart together. Traditional knowledge is dynamic, yet stable, and is usually shared in stories, songs, dance and myths. (Roberts 1996: 114)

In summary, Aboriginal people define TEK as much more than just a body of knowledge. While this is a part of it, TEK also encompasses such aspects as spiritual experience and relationships with the land. It is also noted that TEK is a 'way of life'; rather than being just the knowledge of *how* to live, it is the actual *living* of that life. One way of looking at the differences between Aboriginal and non-Aboriginal views of TEK is to state that Aboriginal views of TEK are 'verb-based' – that is, action-oriented. TEK is not limited, in the Aboriginal view, to a 'body of knowledge'. It is expressed as a 'way of life'; it is conceived as being something that you *do*. Non-Aboriginal views of TEK are 'noun-' or 'product-based'. That is, they tend to focus on physical characteristics. TEK is viewed as a *thing* rather than something that you do. Aboriginal views of TEK are inclusive of non-Aboriginal views, but tend to be broader in scope and holistic. The focus is not solely on the physical aspects, such as the natural environment. TEK is also viewed by Aboriginal people to be inherently sustainable and spiritual. Non-Aboriginal scholars and researchers see TEK as 'contributing' to sustainability, and that spirituality is merely an *aspect* of TEK.

One of the most significant differences between Native and non-Native views of TEK is the fact that Aboriginal people view the people, the knowledge and the land *as a single, integrated whole*. They are regarded as inseparable. As Roberts (1996: 115) points out:

Capturing a single aspect of traditional knowledge is difficult. *Traditional knowledge is holistic and cannot be separated from the people.* It cannot be compartmentalized like scientific knowledge, which often ignores aspects of life to make a point. However, traditional knowledge parallels scientific knowledge. (Stress added)

Aboriginal views of TEK are broad, and include spirituality, world-view and a way of life. Non-Native views tend to focus on 'ecological' aspects (similar to Lewis 1993; Nakashima 1993; and Richardson 1993). Such differences can be attributed to world-view. Aboriginal peoples' way of life is based on spirituality. A lifetime is spent enhancing and maintaining appropriate and sustainable relationships with the Creator and all of Creation. This is the essence of Indigenous science. Aboriginal people are reluctant to reduce TEK to simply 'ecological' aspects. Aboriginal views tend to move in the opposite direction to Western-trained researchers, scientists and scholars; that is, towards wholeness (pulling it together rather than taking it apart to understand it).

Barriers to the Use of TEK in Sustainable Development

In addition to the difficulty in defining TEK are the complications involved in applying it in various environmental and resource management applications. Barriers to the incorporation of TEK in environmental and resource management in Canada have been explored by a number of researchers and scholars. Many of the barriers are long-standing and have not been adequately addressed. Many are systemic and will require substantive restructuring of existing relations between Aboriginal and non-Aboriginal society in Canada in order to be resolved. Naskashima's research perhaps best summarizes the main barriers when he discusses the difficulties experienced in utilizing TEK in Environmental Impact Assessment, or EIA:

> Herein, however, lies the environmental scientist's dilemma. Traditional knowledge, in spite of its evident strengths, corresponds poorly with Western intellectual ideals of 'truth.' In our society, the acceptable norms of intellectual development have been rigidly institutionalized. University degrees, journal publications, conference presentations are the milestones which mark our narrow 'path to knowledge.' Guided by these inflexible norms, environmental scientists reject the traditional knowledge of Native hunters as anecdotal, non-quantitative and amethodical. Unable to overcome a deeply engrained and ethnocentric prejudice against other ways of 'knowing', they turn their backs on a source of data of exceptional utility to EIA. (Nakashima 1990: 23)

Environmental Impact Assessment is arguably the area where most of the TEK work in Canada is being applied. Nakashima's analysis holds true, however, for other resource management arenas, including forestry, as described in the literature and as found in my research. Nakashima's words were written a decade ago. Unfortunately, the attitudes that underlie the unsuccessful application of TEK in environmental and resource management still exist. In some cases there has even been a 'backlash' against attempts to use TEK (e.g. Howard and Widdowson 1997, 1996).

Barriers to TEK use include the cultural disruption that has occurred in Aboriginal communities as a result of colonization. Some TEK has been lost, at least for the time being, and there is a need to revitalize Native communities in order to maintain and develop what still exists and to begin to regain what has been lost. Kemp and Brooke (1995: 27) summarize this issue as follows:

> The most important lesson learned ... is that indigenous peoples must first and foremost control their own information. It has also become clear over the years that the knowledge base of indigenous peoples is vital, dynamic and evolving. Merely 'collecting' and 'documenting' indigenous environmental knowledge is in fact counter-productive. These knowledge systems have been under serious attack for centuries, and the social systems that support them have been seriously undermined. However, indigenous peoples must not just support 'salvage' operations of what now is often referred to as 'a rapidly disappearing knowledge base.' It is not just a question of recovery and recording indigenous knowledge; it is one of respect and revitalization. This information has to remain current and not be considered a relic of the past. Indigenous peoples must also insist that their knowledge not be reduced to an interesting research topic for western science to explore.

The literature reveals many similarities between Aboriginal and non-Aboriginal views of barriers to the incorporation of TEK in resource management. Some concerns are unique to Aboriginal people because they are the people from whom TEK is sought. This situation is complicated by the unequal distribution of power that characterizes Aboriginal/non-Aboriginal relations in Canada. Brubacher and McGregor (1998: 14) discuss this power imbalance in relation to forest management in Canada, noting that:

> Further compounding the distance between these understandings is the fact that dialogue around TEK takes place on the basis of a largely dis-empowered Aboriginal minority talking to the dominant culture, in the language of the dominant culture and within the existing institutional frameworks that govern forest management.

Healey (1993: 21) adds to this, suggesting that:

> It is difficult to separate political aspects of the relationship between the custodians of traditional ecological knowledge and those who wish to have access to that knowledge from legal, ethical and economic dimensions.... A consequence of this situation is that the relationship between traditional communities on the one hand and researchers, sponsors of research and development, and consumers of insights gained from traditional ecological knowledge on the other is generally a very unequal one. Power is concentrated on the side of researchers, sponsors and consumers, whether the power is political, economic or even military.... More often, at least in the contemporary world, the power relation is muted, masked, and benign; but not less unequal for all that.

This unequal power relationship and its impact on the utilization of TEK in environmental and resource management is also recognized by others such as Chapeskie (1995), Johnson (1992), Lukey (1995), and Stevenson (1997). The continued existence of such an imbalance means that the knowledge and the people who hold it remain vulnerable to exploitation.

The 'State of the Art' of TEK Application

The state of the art of TEK application in mainstream environmental and resource management framework remains weak. Most work in the field of TEK comprises collecting and documenting information. There is little in the way of meaningful application. This results from the fact that Aboriginal and non-Aboriginal people are coming from different world-views and their perceptions and experiences of the very same concepts, such as TEK and Sustainable Development, are quite different.

These differences are not fully appreciated. Non-Native scholars and resource managers may object and claim that indeed they understand and appreciate the differences. If this is the case, then one can justifiably ask, 'Why, then, do decision-makers continue to attempt to integrate TEK into environmental and resource management regimes created and designed by dominant society?' Most of the literature on TEK still suggests that 'integration' is desirable. Much of the effort expended in the field has been used in attempting to achieve this goal, but with relatively little success. This has given rise to severe criticism of TEK itself as well as of Aboriginal people (see Howard and Widdowson 1996), and has raised cynicism levels in many Aboriginal communities.

These disappointing results are in no way indicative of the importance of TEK and the potential contribution of Aboriginal people. 'Traditional Ecological knowledge is absolutely essential. Crafting a *relationship* between us is absolutely essential' (LaDuke 1997: 36). Cajete (1994: 192) adds that 'intellectual, social, and spiritual learning unfolds in a definite context of *relationships*' (stress added). From an Aboriginal perspective, positive relationships hold the key to a move toward sustainability and the fair use of TEK in environmental and resource management.

TEK and sustainable development are about relationships. Meaningful integration is difficult if not impossible to achieve in this larger social/cultural/political framework. Because of the existing power structure, integration has translated into 'assimilation' of Aboriginal TEK into dominant regimes. Chapeskie (1995: 27) observes that

> the discourse of resource management employed by the dominant non-aboriginal society which invariably forms the context of co-management discussions between

aboriginal groups and state agencies is plagued with ambiguity. The state largely controls the conceptual framework in which co-management negotiations take place.

This issue has been examined by a number of scholars and researchers (AFN 1995; Berneshawi 1997; Brubacher and McGregor 1998; Chapeski 1995; Feit 1998; Stevenson 1999; Wolfe et al. 1992). Assimilation has never been a desirable policy option for Aboriginal people in Canada, and the field of TEK is a microcosm of this larger social/political situation.

Significant changes to state environmental and resource management paradigms are called for. Merely wishing to include Aboriginal people and their knowledge is not enough. The dominant paradigms and the professionals (managers, planners, scientists, policymakers, decision-makers) who adhere to them are ill-equipped to deal with Aboriginal people and their concerns. Aboriginal people are expected to conform or acquiesce to the dominant paradigm in order to be 'involved' or 'consulted' (Stevenson 1999: 164). The knowledge of Aboriginal people is forced to fit into dominant frameworks that often render irrelevant the intellectual, social, cultural and spiritual contribution that Aboriginal people have made or can potentially make. Fully appreciating and utilizing Aboriginal knowledge must occur in the context of positive, equal and healthy relationships.

Aboriginal Interest in TEK

Despite the issues and challenges outlined above, Aboriginal people continue to find themselves in a position of sharing their knowledge and are frequently willing to do so to advance their goals and interests. In fact, Aboriginal people have been doing this for some time in Canada in an effort to protect their land and traditional life. Although not formally recognized as TEK, Indigenous environmental/ecological information was being collected and documented for various reasons in Canada prior to the explosion of the field in 1980s. The main reason for Aboriginal people sharing their knowledge was to protect their interests, including their land and the assertion of their rights via land claims (AFN 1995; Poole 1998; Roberts 1996). To a large extent, the reasons for sharing this knowledge with external interests remain the same.

TEK is being expressed in various environmental assessment and resource management areas, including issues relating to wildlife, forestry, fisheries and endangered species. Despite this, the meaning, theory and practice of TEK advanced little in its first two decades. It has only been in roughly the last five years that significant challenges to the mainstream concept of TEK have come forth, influenced by the increasing dissatisfaction among Aboriginal people of the misuse of their knowledge by external interests (see AFN 1995; McGregor 1999; Roberts 1996; Stevenson 1999). There has also been a backlash against TEK, particularly since in some mainstream processes, such as environmental assessment in the North, it has gained a secure foothold (see, for example, the position offered by Howard and Widdowson 1997 and 1996; and responses by Berkes and Henly 1997, and Stevenson 1997). The debate on the utilization of TEK continues (see Abele 1997; Wenzel 1999; Usher 2000).

In theory, the recognition of Aboriginal contributions to sustainability is generally well-intentioned. It is the practice and application (or lack thereof in some cases) that have come under scrutiny. Despite the interest in TEK, there is little to show for it on the ground. Aboriginal people throughout Canada are becoming increasingly dissatisfied with this state of affairs.

Further Thoughts on What TEK is About

So, what is TEK really about? Because of the past and continued colonial onslaught on Aboriginal people, the expression of TEK can be boiled down to our continued survival, which in turn is inherently intertwined with the survival of Creation. Before the term 'TEK' was ever coined, Frank T'Seleie, Dene from Fort Good Hope, stated during the Mackenzie Valley Pipeline Inquiry (arguably the first major TEK study in Canada) that:

> It seems to me that the whole point in living is to become as human as possible; to learn to understand the world and to live in it; to be part of it; to learn to understand the animals, for they are our brothers and they have much to teach us. We are part of this world.
>
> We are like the river that flows and changes, yet is always the same.... It is a river and it will always be a river, for that is what it was meant to be. We are like the river, but we are not the river. We are human. That is what we were meant to be.... We were meant to be ourselves, to be what it is our nature to be. (T'Seleie 1977: 16)

Water, in the form of a river, provides some of the greatest understandings of what TEK means to the people. T'Seleie (1977: 16–17) continues:

> Our Dene Nation is like this great river. It has been flowing before any of us can remember. We take our strength and our wisdom and our ways from the flow and direction that has been established for us by our ancestors we never knew, ancestors of a thousand years ago. Their wisdom flows through us to our children and our grandchildren to generations we will never know. We will live out our lives as we must and we will die in peace because we will know that our people and this river will flow on after us.

The river inspires connections, continuity and the feeling that the generations yet to come can 'rest and look over the river and feel that [they] too
[have] a place in the universe' (T'Seleie 1977: 17).

The river itself is a source of the knowledge that people require in order
to survive. This survival has a physical basis (we need water for our bodies),
but it also has spiritual (defining the role of humans in the world), emotional
(providing strength and vision), and intellectual (developing the minds of the
knowledge holders) aspects. The river provides a holistic metaphor for the
relationship between people and the rest of Creation, the essential core of
what TEK is, in my view.

According to Elders of the Grand Council, Treaty Number Three (in
Ross 1996: 254–5):

> Respect for each other and a universal appreciation for the power of the creator
> kept everyone walking down a path that encompassed honesty, truths, respect for
> everything in their immediate life or ecosystem, whether it was your fellow man
> or beast or plant life. It was a holistic respect for everything that the Anishinaabeg
> could see, smell, hear, taste and feel.

The relationship between people and Creation from an Aboriginal perspective can be aptly described as sustainable. The people *made sure* that relationships were sustained through duty, responsibility and reciprocity. It was not
and is not automatic. The people *care* for each other and their surroundings.
TEK, then, is practised by someone who takes care of his or her relations
(including Creation and the life it supports, and all the associated spiritual
aspects).

Coexistence: Re-creating an Old Relationship

TEK is about relationships: not just about *understanding* the relationships in
Creation, but about *participating* in those relationships. TEK is about sustaining a creative reciprocal relationship with all of Creation, and about fulfilling our lives as human beings in relation to Creation, as T'Seleie (1977) so
eloquently points out. This includes the spiritual core of Creation, not just
the physical environment that is noted by the five senses.

From a Western perspective, TEK and sustainable development (and sustainability) are discrete concepts. From an Aboriginal point of view, they are
intimately related and are in fact part of the same continuum (or circle).
They are both about relationships. They are both about relating to Creation
in a certain way. If people do not take care of their relations, then they are
not fulfilling their duties and responsibilities; they are denying their relationship with Creation, and dysfunction will result. In a reciprocal fashion,

non-human elements are expected to fulfil their responsibilities to Creation. Traditional teachings offer profound guidance about how to work with Creation and not to interfere with the other beings' ability to fulfil their duties and responsibilities.

Since the time of contact, a consistent message from Aboriginal people has been that they regard their relationship with the newcomers as one of nations interacting. The call for a nation-to-nation relationship between Aboriginal peoples and Canadians is thus not new or unknown among federal and provincial governments. In fact, this type of relationship has existed in the past and for a period of time was a key characteristic of the relationship between Aboriginal and non-Aboriginal peoples in North America. The knowledge and technology that Aboriginal people possessed enabled the newcomers to survive in these lands when the newcomers themselves lacked the capacity to do so.

The broader picture in terms of global sustainability is changing, internationally and nationally, and specifically includes calls for the meaningful participation of Aboriginal people. Can this be interpreted to mean that Aboriginal people and their knowledge and resources are now needed again? Many people seem to think so (LaDuke 1997; Low 1992). On what terms will Aboriginal people flourish in a climate of renewal and renegotiation? New relationships based on mutual reconciliation and peaceful coexistence are required. According to the Royal Commission on Aboriginal Peoples (RCAP, a Canadian federal government-funded five-year study completed in 1996), this renewed relationship must recognize that 'land is not a just a commodity; it is an inextricable part of Aboriginal identity, deeply rooted in moral and spiritual values' (RCAP 1996: 430). The new relationship must also recognize Aboriginal and treaty rights in a meaningful fashion – to embrace them as an expression of Aboriginal relationships to the land.

This new or renewed relationship RCAP calls for is based on the ancient Indigenous philosophical view that sought 'coexistence' among nations. It is founded on the belief that having separate world-views is not necessarily an undesirable thing, and that developing a framework that would respect different world-views would be an appropriate approach to take. This approach is based on the idea behind the Two-Row Wampum. A beaded belt describing part of a treaty of friendship between the Dutch and the Haudenosaunee (often referred to as 'Iroquois') peoples, the Two-Row Wampum consists of two rows of purple beads separated by rows of white beads. The purple rows represent the different vessels of the Dutch (a ship) and the Haudenosaunee (a canoe) travelling side-by-side down the 'river' of existence (the white beads). While the two vessels remain separate (i.e. the cultures remain distinct), the people from each vessel are meant to interact and assist each other as need be (see Ransom 1999 for a fuller description).

The Two-Row Wampum serves as a model for renewing and reconciling a damaged relationship between two peoples. It is a model that can apply to any interaction between two nations. In the current situation involving sustainable use of resources in Canada (and throughout the world), in which the participation of Aboriginal people and their knowledge is sought, the Two-Row Wampum and the principles it symbolizes can be appropriately applied. The principles of sharing and respect can apply to the intellectual tradition in the form of sharing knowledge. In the times when treaties were made based on the Two-Row Wampum, it involved the sharing of knowledge. Indigenous knowledge was used almost exclusively in the early years in order for the Europeans to survive. Aboriginal people shared their knowledge readily and it was also readily accepted. An important element to consider as well was the principle that both nations would come to the mutual aid of one another; again this applies to sharing knowledge.

At this point in the history of humanity, Aboriginal knowledge is needed to offer insights into sustainability and the contexts in which it finds meaning (e.g. spirituality). What has not been achieved in recent years are the conditions that make the principles of coexistence meaningful: equitable power relationships. Nation-to-nation relationships have as much relevance today as they did centuries ago. Only through a shift in power relationships can Aboriginal people and their knowledge be effectively involved in moving toward sustainability.

The model of coexistence is viewed as holding promise for environmental and resource management (Brubacher and McGregor 1998; Chapeskie 1995; McGregor 2000; Ransom 1999). Coexistence may serve as a potentially promising bridge between two world-views. Brubacher and McGregor (1998: 18–19) anticipate that the coexistence approach can function as a starting point for renegotiating an old relationship in a contemporary context:

> a co-existence approach would promote a focus on formally acknowledging Aboriginal people as legitimate partners in resource management. It would ensure their rightful place in the development and implementation of management policies and decision-making.... By drawing upon principles which express the values and perspectives of both Aboriginal and non-Aboriginal cultures, there is potential for developing an effective co-existence model, one that bridges distinctions by building upon shared values.

The coexistence approach does not devalue Western or Indigenous resource management practices and the knowledge that informs them. Coexistence does not allow for the domination of one over the other. Both systems are valued, and, most importantly for Aboriginal people, their cultural survival is assured. The Aboriginal world-view and all it has to offer will no longer be threatened, dominated or distorted. Relationships based on coexistence, if established on a broad scale, would greatly facilitate a global move towards sustainability.

Note

1. 'First Nation' is defined by the Canadian government (DIAND 1997: 406) as: 'A term that came into common usage in the 1970s to replace the word "Indian", which many people found offensive. Although the term First Nation is widely used, no legal definition of it exists. Among its uses, the term "First Nations peoples" refers to the Indian people in Canada.... Many Indian people have also adopted the term "First Nation" to replace the word "band" in the name of their community.' As an example of this latter usage, the 'Whitefish River Indian Band' is now the 'Whitefish River First Nation'.

References

Abele, F. (1997) 'Traditional knowledge in practice', *Arctic*, vol. 50, no. 4, pp. iii–iv.

Alfred, T. (1999) 'The people', in *Words That Come Before All Else: Environmental Philosophies of the Haudenosaunee*, Cornwall Island, ON: Haudenosaunee Environmental Task Force, Native North American Travelling College, pp. 8–14.

AFN (Assembly of First Nations) (1995) 'The feasibility of representing traditional Indigenous knowledge in cartographic, pictorial or textual forms', Ottawa, ON: National Aboriginal Forestry Association and National Atlas Information Service.

Battiste, M. and J. Henderson (2000) *Protecting Indigenous Knowledge and Heritage: A Global Challenge*, Saskatoon, SK: Purich.

Berkes, F. (1999) *Sacred Ecology: Traditional Ecological Knowledge and Resource Management*, Philadelphia, PA: Taylor & Francis.

———— and T. Henley (1997) 'Co-management and traditional knowledge: threat or opportunity', *Options Politiques (Policy Options)*, March, pp. 29–31.

Berneshawi, S. (1997) 'Resource management and the Mi'kmaq Nation', *Canadian Journal of Native Studies* 1, pp. 115–48.

Brubacher, D. and D. McGregor (1998) 'Aboriginal forest-related traditional ecological knowledge in Canada', contribution to the 19th Session of the North American Forest Commission, Villahermosa, Mexico, 16–20 November 1998. Ottawa, ON: National Aboriginal Forestry Association for the Canadian Forest Service.

Cajete, G. (1994) *Look to the Mountain: An Ecology of Indigenous Education*, Durango, CO: Kivaki Press.

Chapeskie, A. (1995) 'Land, landscape, culturescape: Aboriginal relationships to land and the co-management of natural resources', report for the Royal Commission on Aboriginal Peoples. Land, Resource and Environmental Regimes Project, Ottawa.

Courrier, K. (1994) 'Our common future', in R. and W. Eblen (eds), *The Encyclopedia of the Environment*, New York: Houghton Mifflin, pp. 508–9.

Dearden, P. and B. Mitchell (1998) *Environmental Change and Challenge: A Canadian Perspective*, Toronto, ON: Oxford University Press.

DIAND (Department of Indian Affairs and Northern Development) (1997) 'Information: Definitions', in D. McGregor and E. Doolittle (compilers) (2000) *Introduction to Native*

Studies, ABS 201, course readings manual, Toronto, ON: Canadian Scholars' Press, pp. 405–8.

Doubleday, N. (1993) 'Finding common ground: natural law and collective wisdom', in J. Inglis (ed.), *Traditional Ecological Knowledge: Concepts and Cases,* Ottawa, ON: International Program on Traditional Ecological Knowledge and International Development Research Centre, pp. 41–53.

Draper, D. (1998) *Our Environment: A Canadian Perspective,* Scarborough, ON: International Thomson.

Feit, H. (1998) 'Self-management and government management of wildlife: prospects for coordination in James Bay and Canada', in R. Hoage and K. Moran (eds), *Culture: The Missing Element in Conservation and Development,* Dubuque, IA: Kendall/Hunt, pp. 95–111.

Fitznor, L. (1998) 'The circle of life: affirming Aboriginal philosophies in everyday living', in D. McCance (ed.), *Life Ethics in World Religions,* Atlanta, GA: Scholars Press, pp. 22–40.

Gwich'in Elders (1997) *Nanh'Kak Geenjit Gwich'in Ginjik: Gwich'in Words about the Land,* Inuvik, NT: Gwich'in Renewable Resource Board.

Healey, C. (1993) 'The significance and application of TEK', in N. Williams and G. Baines (eds), *Traditional Ecological Knowledge: Wisdom for Sustainable Development,* Canberra, ACT: Centre for Resource and Environmental Studies, Australian National University, pp. 21–6.

Howard, A. and F. Widdowson (1996) 'Traditional ecological knowledge threatens environmental assessment', *Options Politiques,* November, pp. 34–6.

——— (1997) 'Traditional knowledge advocates weave a tangled web', *Options Politiques,* April, pp. 46–8.

Johnson, M. (ed.) (1992) *Lore: Capturing Traditional Environmental Knowledge,* Ottawa, ON: Dene Cultural Institute and the International Development Research Centre.

Kemp, W. and L. Brooke (1995) 'Towards information self-sufficiency: Nunavik Inuit gather information on ecology and land use', *Cultural Survival Quarterly,* vol. 18, no. 4, pp. 25–8.

LaDuke, W. (1997) 'Voices from White Earth: Gaa-waabaabiganikaag', in H. Hannum (ed.), *People, Land and Community: Collected E.F. Schumacher Society Lectures,* New Haven, CT: Yale University Press, pp. 22–37.

Lewis, H. (1993) 'Traditional ecological knowledge: some definitions', in N. Williams and G. Baines (eds), *Traditional Ecological Knowledge: Wisdom for Sustainable Development,* Canberra, ACT: Australian National University, pp. 8–12.

Low, P. (1992) 'Indigenous knowledge systems: the key to worldwide sustainable development', unpublished draft, Plenty Canada and Indigenous Network of Indigenous NGOs and Practitioners Involved in Development.

Lukey, J. (1995) 'Native and non-Native perspectives on Aboriginal traditional environmental knowledge', unpublished major paper, Faculty of Environmental Studies, York University, Toronto.

McGregor, D. (1994) 'Evaluating the use of traditional environmental knowledge in current resource management systems', Ph.D. thesis, Faculty of Forestry, University of Toronto.

——— (1999) 'Indigenous knowledge in Canada: shifting paradigms and the influence of First Nations advocates', in T. Veeman, D. Smith, B. Purdy, F. Salkie and G. Larkin (eds), *Science and Practice: Sustaining the Boreal Forest. Proceedings of the 1999 Sustainable Forest Management Network Conference,* Edmonton, AB: Sustainable Forest Management Network, pp. 192–7.

———— (2000) 'The state of traditional ecological knowledge research in Canada: a critique of current theory and practice', in R. Laliberte, P. Settee, J. Waldram, R. Innes, B. Macdougall, L. McBain, and F. Barron (eds), *Expressions in Canadian Native Studies*, Saskatoon, SK: University of Saskatchewan Extension Press, pp. 436–58.

Mander, J. (1991) *In the Absence of the Sacred: The Failure of Technology and the Survival of the Indian Nations*, San Francisco, CA: Sierra Club Books.

Mercredi, O. and M. Turpel (1993) *In the Rapids: Navigating the Future of First Nations*, Toronto, ON: Penguin Books.

Nakashima, D. (1990) 'Application of Native knowledge in EIA: Inuit, Eiders and Hudson's Bay Oil', Hull, PQ: Canadian Environmental Assessment Research Council.

———— (1993) 'Astute observers on the sea ice edge: Inuit knowledge as a basis for Arctic co-management', in J. Inglis (ed.), *Traditional Ecological Knowledge: Concepts and Cases*, Ottawa, ON: International Program on Traditional Ecological Knowledge and International Development Research Centre, pp. 99–110.

Poole, P. (1998) 'Indigenous lands and power mapping in the Americas: merging technologies', *Native Americas, Akwe:kon's Journal of Indigenous Issues*, vol. 15, no. 6, pp. 34–43.

Procter, A. (1999) 'Definitions and the defining process: "Traditional ecological knowledge" in the Keewatin Region, Nunavut', M.A. thesis, Natural Resources Institute, University of Manitoba, Winnipeg.

Raffan, J. (1993) 'Where God began', *Equinox* 71, September/October 1993, pp. 44–57.

Ramphal, S. (1994) 'Sustainable development', in R. and W. Eblen (eds), *The Encyclopedia of the Environment*, New York: Houghton Mifflin, pp. 680–83.

Ransom, J. (1999) 'The waters', in Haudenosaunee Environmental Task Force, *Words that Come Before All Else: Environmental Philosophies of the Haudenosaunee*, Cornwall Island, ON: Native North American Travelling College, pp. 25–43.

Richardson, B. (1993) *People of Terra Nullius: Betrayal and Rebirth in Aboriginal Canada*, Vancouver, BC: Douglas & McIntyre.

Roberts, K. (1996) 'Circumpolar Aboriginal people and co-management practice: current issues in co-management and environmental assessment', conference proceedings, Arctic Institute of North America and Joint Secretariat – Inuvialuit Renewable Resources Committees. Arctic Institute of North America, University of Calgary.

Ross, R. (1996) *Returning to the Teachings: Exploring Aboriginal Justice*, Toronto, ON: Penguin Books.

Royal Commission on Aboriginal Peoples (RCAP) (1996) *People to People, Nation to Nation: Highlights from the Report of the Royal Commission on Aboriginal Peoples*, Ottawa: Ministry of Supply and Services.

Stevenson, M. (1997) 'Inuit and co-management: principles, practices and challenges for the new millennium', prepared for Inuit Circumpolar Conference, President's Office, Nuuk, Greenland. NAMMCO International Conference, 'Sealing the Future', St John's, Newfoundland, 25–27 November.

———— (1999) 'What are we managing? Traditional systems of management and knowledge in cooperative and joint management', in T. Veeman, D. Smith, B. Purdy, F. Salkie and G. Larkin (eds), *Science and Practice: Sustaining the Boreal Forest. Proceedings of the 1999 Sustainable Forest Management Network Conference*, Edmonton, AB: Sustainable Forest Management Network, pp. 161–9.

T'Seleie, F. (1977) 'Statement to the Mackenzie Valley pipeline inquiry', in M. Watkins (ed.), *Dene Nation – The Colony Within*, Toronto: University of Toronto Press, pp. 12–17.

Usher, P. (2000) 'Traditional ecological knowledge in environmental assessment and management', *Arctic*, vol. 53, no. 2, pp. 183–93.

Wenzel, G. (1999) 'Traditional ecological knowledge and Inuit: reflections on TEK research and ethics', *Arctic*, vol. 52, no. 2, pp. 113–24.

Williams, N. and G. Baines (eds) (1993) *Traditional Ecological Knowledge: Wisdom for Sustainable Development*, Canberra, ACT: Centre for Resource and Environmental Studies, Australian National University.

Wolfe, J., C. Bechard, P. Cizek, and D. Cole (1992) 'Indigenous and western knowledge and resource management systems', University School of Rural Planning and Development, University of Guelph, Ontario.

WCED (World Commission on Environment and Development) (1987) *Our Common Future*, Oxford: Oxford University Press.

6

James Bay Crees' Life Projects and Politics: Histories of Place, Animal Partners and Enduring Relationships

HARVEY A. FEIT

Contradictions?

In 1994, Matthew Coon Come, who was then Grand Chief of the Grand Council of the Crees in Quebec, appeared before a committee of the Massachusetts Legislature to ask them to support the Cree struggle against the proposed Great Whale hydroelectric project by not buying Hydro-Quebec power. The Grand Council of the Crees had just signed a complementary agreement with Hydro-Quebec, the public electricity utility of the province, giving C\$50 million to the Crees and allowing new construction at the site of a hydroelectric dam that was part of the LaGrande project, which had been constructed over the previous two decades. A committee member asked:

> Why would you be so agreeable and so willing to modify an agreement, in light of the fact that we have heard that you folks signed the original agreement in 1975 under duress? In other words, if I were you, and Hydro-Quebec came to me and said, 'by the way ... we want to [install] four more sub-stations', I would be telling Hydro-Quebec to take a hike. (in Isacsson 1996)

The Grand Chief explained that 'we live in a society in which we have to see how we can coexist, how we can live together [with Quebec].' His questioner persisted, asking the Cree if it was true Hydro-Quebec needed Cree approval to undertake the construction. Grand Chief Coon Come confirmed that and explained that the Cree agreed to more construction in part because of the already compromised quality of these areas – the 'river ... is already dead'. But there was no escaping the implication that had been painted by the questioner: the Crees were not really interested in saving the rivers, animals and a hunting way of life, but in money.

This was a trap the Cree political leaders had clearly foreseen, and there were strong disagreements among them about whether to sign another in a series of agreements that made concessions to Hydro-Quebec, while fighting new project plans (in Isacsson 1996). The Cree participants in that debate had several reasons for signing, but they did not think that their actions were inconsistent, or opportunist. What they all were concerned about was that non-Crees would not understand the choices they were making, and thus they would be vulnerable to having the new agreement used against them. The differences among Cree leaders were over whether to take the risks.[1] The Crees have been accused of similar contradictions repeatedly by the media and non-Crees, by governments and developers, and by their allies and social analysts (see LaRusic et al. 1979; Feit 1985, 2004; Tanner 1999).

It is assumed by most analysts that the Cree organizations would, if they could, simply oppose large-scale development projects on their lands. This appears to make sense because these are projects which many Crees insist have detrimental effects on their lives and the lands they occupy, and the great majority of Cree leaders and people are unwilling to accept deals that give them cash for accepting destruction. Yet they have signed a series of agreements with Hydro-Quebec and Quebec that provide funds to improve Cree lives and communities and permit development projects, albeit mostly of modest scale. That most Crees do not see contradictions in the political actions the leaders pursue, even where their opponents, their supporters and social analysts do, suggests that Crees' agency does not arise solely as a response to development projects or from agreements that offer cash, but from a different setting. I will explore their actions as rooted not in opposition or opportunism, but in the practice of everyday life in communities and on the land.

Life Projects: Places, Histories and Animals

In James Bay Cree struggles against transnational hydroelectric and forestry developments Cree leaders address state institutions; forge access to transnational forums; build alliances with other Indigenous, environmental and human rights movements; and build relationships with international media and access to world financial centres (see Coon Come and Craik, chapters 9 and 10 in this volume; Rousseau 2001).

Yet James Bay Cree leaders also draw on powerful paradigms for collective agency provided by Cree hunters and hunting leaders.[2] The hunters embody practices and envision desired ways of living in the context of hunting on a land they know intimately. These hunting leaders typically live for half or more of the year on the particular tracts of land that they have inherited, used and stewarded over their lifetimes, and these tracts are places they have nurtured and made into their homes.

The processes of place-making (Gupta and Ferguson 1999) are accomplished not only through the actions of those on the land but also through their long histories of connections to markets and governments. As a result, their landscapes and their agency are not isolated or separate from the contexts that inform the struggles that Cree political leaders undertake; indeed, they are closely connected, as I will show. While many outside observers see Cree hunters as tied to the land in ways that isolate them from national politics and transnational markets, the experiences and lessons of hunting leaders are easily related and relevant to the decisions of Cree political leaders. This chapter develops an account of Cree agency in which I stress Cree statements, and my own understandings, of Cree hunters' life project politics. It is a case study for the analysis of Indigenous practices that are rooted in life projects closely linked to local places but that have wide connections to other places and broad political relevance.[3]

Cree hunters' lives and problems are place-based not universalist because they are concerned with communities and lands that are the intimate settings of their everyday lives. In a sense, they live in a world in which their communities and lands are centres, not the margins of some other cosmopolitanized place.[4] Yet they are connected widely. Cree hunters' communities and hunting lands are places where they encounter people from transnational corporations, trading empires, government agencies, diverse political ideologies, and international legal forums. Their lands and communities are also places to which they invite representatives from other communities to build understanding and connections (see, for example, Craik and McRae, chapters 10 and 7 in this volume).

Histories are part of both hunting and the processes of landscape making. Indeed, the land is layered with histories both personal and far-reaching. Place names known to and used by hunters who live on a particular hunting territory over many years cover nearly every feature of the landscape, and many are tied to stories of how the name came to be given – stories that recall past persons, events and associations. They also record past ties to Europe through the fur trade, as at 'Dress-up Creek', where hunters prepared to descend the last stretch of the Rupert river to enter the fur-trade post and meet the European traders. The presence of other Indigenous peoples is recorded, for example, by the Cree places named for Iroquois, or Haudenosaunee, who raided the area in the late seventeenth century by travelling along particular rivers that now carry their Cree names. Connections to Canada and the United States occur through the names of the first places where an early American sport hunter, known in Cree as a 'long-knife', did something memorable. They record corporate connections and histories of commercial fisheries, mines, sawmills and trading posts, now closed.

These localized histories are manifested as interrelated places, stories that are associated with particular Cree predecessors, personal memories and ongoing practices of occupying the land and of hunting. These intersections of places, histories, persons and activities tie the hunters to distant parts of the world and to the people who have come from those parts and entered into relationships here. They record the encounters that give hunters knowledge, experience and relationships to those other places, times and people that are rooted in their hunting places and in their own sense of identity. And they can draw on long and rich encounters with some of these others. Hunters are connected far and they have often been connected for long. But they are not connected universally. Their places, histories and relationships are always personal and specific, even as they are generalizable.

These hunters' relationships extend beyond the human world to the worlds of animals and other non-human beings that are part of the multi-person process of the hunt. Animals are hunted and are encountered as partners in the hunt, as I will indicate below. Animals are partners not only in the chase, but in the histories they produce, and they too are recorded and present in the place names that recall memorable encounters. They are also parts of the relationships that tie these places through time to other places far away, for they too are part of the fur trade, and they too are partners in the suffering that results from development projects.

When people come from other places they enter, whether they know it or not, Cree places in which their presence sets them into arenas of Cree life projects. To encounter these places, histories and relationships is to enter into new/old relationships not solely determined by the conditions and needs of the arrivees, even if they are unaware of the specificities of these places.

For example, the Crees as a nation have signed a treaty that governments consider to have significantly constrained Cree sovereignty over lands, although the legal reality is somewhat more complex because specific provisions of the agreement recognize Cree systems of territoriality and governance (the James Bay and Northern Quebec Agreement (JBNQA), 1975, between the Crees, Inuit of northern Quebec, Canada, Hydro-Quebec and the James Bay Development and Energy Corporations). The inequalities between Cree and governments profoundly shape how Crees and governments act on the land, and the very unequal consequences their actions have for the other. Therefore recognition of Cree tenure is clearly thought to be quite minimal by governments, both because they refuse to take them into full consideration, and because they consider the Cree hunting territories as isolated and exclusively involved with the Crees, not as places with far-reaching connections, recognitions and histories.[5] Whether governments ever recognize these dimensions of their obligations as such, or not, they constantly are engaged with them for there is no general Cree acquiescence to the unique sovereignty claimed by the governments of Canada and Quebec. Autonomy that does not recognize exclusive sovereignty is exercised every day by Cree hunters on the land they care for and nurture (see below). The contests over the imposition of more and more constraints by governments go on day by day, intrusion by intrusion, hunting territory by hunting territory, without Cree consent. Cree people's agency has its fullest expression in these very personal and yet shared practices of exercising an inherent ownership and governance of land, in the broadest sense. This exercise is embedded in Cree life projects.

Hunters' Life Projects in the Face of Development

The recent affidavits given by hunting leaders as part of their testimony for a court case against forestry companies articulate clearly the everyday problems the hunters face, the relationships out of which their actions emerge, and their assumption and exercise of inherent responsibility for the whole land. The series of court cases against the governments of Quebec and Canada and over twenty logging companies sought to get the courts to regulate forestry cutting because of the failure of governments to fulfil their obligations under the JBNQA to regulate forestry activities on Cree territories and to provide an effective voice for Crees in forestry management. Many Crees also emphasized that the companies, with government authorization, were accelerating forestry cutting and their destructive effects on forests, lands, wildlife and the Crees.

Allen Saganash, Sr. of Waswanipi, whose hunting lands had not yet been cut, described his inherent responsibilities of governance, as well as what he wanted to protect as a hunting territory leader, and on what he did and did not want to compromise.[6]

> I am the Ndoho Ouchimau [hunting leader] of trapline Wo5A [a government-initiated designation for hunting territories, see below]. I am 80 years old this year....
>
> As I said our land is uncut now but I know Donahue [a forestry corporation] plans to build a road into it.... This will seriously affect my hunting grounds.
>
> We had a consultation session with Donahue.... The idea was to try to protect some wildlife habitat....
>
> I am opposed to this road. Ours is good hunting and fishing land. The food is very good quality. The road will change all that; it will damage the habitat and open it up to hunters and fishermen....
>
> I want all of this considered in a full environmental assessment but they won't do it. I know the government well. I have seen how they work throughout my life. They refuse to consider all development together. I have no chance to get all these issues looked at. I worry all the time about what will happen when the

road comes. The road is not to come to the heart of my land. I don't want it. The government is not trustworthy....

We are pushed out of our land again and again. We are told to move our hunting grounds. I have seen this happen many times in Waswanipi.

They concentrate the cutting too heavily in one place. Too much is cut. There are too many roads.

Others support me on this....

The companies and the government don't listen to us. They take what is ours and push us aside. This must stop. (Affidavit of Allen Saganash, Sr, 22 July 1999)

Allen Saganash eloquently expresses his rights as Ndoho Ouchimau to a decisive say in what happens on his lands, his sense of loss and fear of destruction, and his experiences of government and corporate betrayals, domination, and failures both to protect the land and to respect the Crees. He implies that the Crees have shared the land enough.

Joseph Neeposh, an elderly hunting leader, indicated that he has shared because he recognized the needs of others, that he expected them to consider his needs in turn, but that continued sharing might not be appropriate under all circumstances.

I am the Ndoho Ouchimau or tallyman of the Ndoho Istchee or trapline now known as W-10....

Everyone in our community understands my authority and respects it. They know that I am the one that decides who can have access to the land and where they can hunt, fish or trap. They know that I must guide people to productive areas while I protect the land and the animals from overuse. Non-Natives and the logging companies do not understand or respect my role. They come to the land without my permission and take what they want.

All these roads, camps and activities lead me to believe that my Ndoho Istchee will soon be even more affected by forestry. I do not want this to happen. I want the game to stay....

I honestly think it is time for the cutting to stop in my hunting territory.

I understand that the forestry workers presently working in my hunting territory need their work for their families. If they wish to continue with forestry operations, they may do so. But they must consider my livelihood. The land is where I work and support myself. The forestry companies and those responsible for the cutting must do something to help me continue to live on my trapline. I do not want my Ndoho Istchee to be like some of the other Waswanipi traplines. I know they could eventually destroy it. I do not want to move ... to another hunting territory. It would be an expropriation of my hunting territory where I have hunted all my life. (Affidavit, Joseph Neeposh, 22 July 1999)

These testimonies echo the common themes of rights, destruction, betrayal, the need for restrictions on forest cutting, and a common call for respectful sharing. Throughout these affidavits Cree hunters eloquently reveal the sovereignty the Cree hunters still exercise, and their continuing determination to bring changes to the present relationships with governments and companies. These views have been repeatedly misunderstood by supporters of Cree struggles. The hunters assert basic and unchallengeable rights to their lands, yet they also express a willingness to respect the needs of others and an expectation that this will be reciprocated. As their assertions of ongoing governance of their lands indicate, this is not a compromise that arises out of subordination or a politics of the oppressed. It is a vision that arises out of the tie to the land and to all that has occurred on the land. It is embedded in the changing historical relationships of this place, as well as in their intimate relationships with the land and animals.

Histories of Relationships

The fur trade: commerce, relationships and reciprocities

The recent Cree histories of the abuse of lands and of ignoring the Cree that these affidavits express also allude to older histories of relationships, relationships that endured for decades and even centuries.

Cree stories of the fur trade have been reported in the recent literature (see Scott 1989; Feit 1994), but here I want to note the recent work by ethno-historians on the fur trade that echoes many of the Cree stories. The trade had begun in the James Bay area by the 1670s, and both Cree stories and recent research reveal rich and complex histories of alliances, partnerships and reciprocities in a trade in which the fur traders' practices were often adapted to Cree social values. There is not one fur trade but many (Francis and Morantz 1983). Here I will pick out some threads relevant to the newly realized aspects of much, but not all, of this trade.

The fur trade in the James Bay region was without doubt a very profitable and capital-making enterprise par excellence throughout almost all of its three centuries. Capital was accumulated as a result of substantial profits, mainly by the London-based Hudson's Bay Company (HBC), but also during several periods by Montreal traders. The trade produced exceptional profits in part because it exchanged generally easy-to-produce European goods with hunters, who welcomed them but had access to them only through traders. In exchange, furs and, until the mid-nineteenth century, especially beaver pelts were in high demand as valuable goods in Europe. From a Cree perspective, furs were labour intensive to produce, but many fur-bearers were also food staples, and trading their skins was not an inappropriately high labour cost over and above a subsistence hunting effort. A key feature of the profitability of the trade to Europeans was that it depended on Cree production on the land using Cree social and economic organization. It was to the advantage of HBC profitability to encourage Crees to produce furs because they provided most of their own subsistence needs, something European trappers would not do were the HBC to change its strategies and employ such production methods (Tanner 1979). In the twentieth century, with an increasing government presence, it was also in the interests of the HBC to promote exclusive Cree occupation and tenure of land as a barrier against itinerant trappers financed by competing non-resident traders.

From the Cree perspective the trade was beneficial for the increased security and labour-saving devices it brought, and although the Crees became dependent on the trade for these goods, their needs were specific and limited within a Cree economy of reciprocity (Scott 1983). The traders' records are replete with the difficulties of getting Crees to trap more than was required to secure their equipment and supply necessities and specific 'luxuries' (Salisbury 1976). Crees also demanded and generally got useful and quality trade goods, although their ability to affect the rates of exchange was limited primarily to pressure for stable prices and comparative pricing, when that was possible, among competing trading companies all setting prices for their traders in order to maximize profits.

The Crees also were able to shape the form and practice of the trade process itself, often not accepting a simple indebtedness created by traders' advances, and reshaping the relationships with traders into forms of partnership. To secure Cree efforts to trap more furs, and to try to tie Crees to their trading company, traders repeatedly adapted trade processes to Cree notions of reciprocity and enduring responsibilities. Traders often gave extensive gifts before trading began, sometimes up to half the value of the expected furs, and they gave special gifts and emblems of recognition to hunting leaders known as 'trading captains' (see Francis and Morantz 1983). Traders living in isolated trading posts were often not maximizing profits but rather trying to please their bosses by doing a bit better than last year's returns (Salisbury 1976). The traders themselves were sometimes dependent on Crees for food supplies, and more often for love and companionship. When not effectively prohibited by the HBC, 'country wives' and families were common while traders were in the region. In these ways Cree forms of kinship, leadership and partnership structured much of the trade process, and resulted in forms of relationships, reciprocity and mutual aid that were clear and enduring, if not universal.

The relationships were not egalitarian, but amidst their continual changes there were some periods of enduring relationships of respect and mutual reciprocity. Cree recollections of the fur trade sometimes speak of it as a satisfying exchange, sometimes as excessively profitable for and insufficiently reciprocated by the companies. But it is almost always talked about in terms of mutual responsibilities and their abrogation or fulfilment. That is, the fur trade is not, whether it was a good or a bad thing at the period being discussed, a simple market relationship between producer and commercial enterprise or between a buyer and merchant.

From these stories of decades and centuries of fur trading Cree hunters know that commerce and coexistence on the land with 'Whitemen' (a Cree term) can be conducted on a different basis than that employed by Hydro-Quebec and forestry companies today. Their approaches demand respect and reciprocity whether they are dealing with logging foremen in the field discussing how close to cut the forest along a stream, or with corporate lawyers or professional foresters discussing policy and best-practice guidelines.

Conserving beaver and co-governing territory

Cree hunters' stories of relationships with representatives of governments are equally complex and ambiguous, but also embedded in mutual dependency and recognition. The first on-the-ground intervention of governments in the James Bay region occurred when beaver reserves were established by Quebec in the early 1930s in response to the initiative of a concerned fur trader and his wife, working in dialogue with Cree hunters. Quebec was soon joined by Canada and the HBC, with the initial goal of restoring beaver populations depleted in the post-World War I boom years. The reserves excluded non-local trappers, who had been the main impetus for the depletion, as well as limiting Cree harvests until beaver populations recovered (Morantz 2002; Feit, in press). These initiatives had multiple origins, having been suggested in one form or another by fur traders, missionaries, anthropologists and Cree hunters from various communities.

When the time came actually to harvest beaver in the 1940s, the government claimed that its employees were exercising managerial authority over the beaver and the Crees. But the employees were confronted by their lack of knowledge of beaver dynamics and the distributions of beaver in the region. This made setting the quotas they envisioned difficult, as well as their decisions on how to allocate beaver harvest quotas to some Crees and not to others. To solve these problems government agents adopted and copied the Cree customary tenure system. Each hunting leader was paid to tally the number of active beaver lodges on his hunting territory, and to report them to government. The government then set the harvest quota and the hunting leaders were often left to allocate beaver taken on their territory to hunters whom they allowed to use their land. One government official described what was happening thus:

> When it is borne in mind that the Tallyman is the head of the family; that each
> district is a family trapping ground; that ... all boundaries are laid out by the

Indians themselves, it is apparent that we have not only adhered strictly to Indian custom but have actually improved on it since, through our Supervisor, we have maps of the districts and written records, which we can use to settle future disputes over trapping grounds. (Quoted in Morantz 2002: 167)

The claim that the beaver trapline system was an improvement obscured the fact that in practice it not only depended on the Cree hunting territory system; it left the Crees in charge of information and often allocation issues, and thereby left them to do what the hunting leader thought necessary on his land. The check the government had was when pelts were sold, but quota numbers were a function of Cree reports, and who killed beaver and where they were taken could be adjusted by Cree hunters, arranging among themselves who would do the selling or where they should report that the beaver had been caught.

The government beaver-reserve agents were more systematically dependent on the Crees than the reverse, although they claimed credit for the success of the scheme. Government officials and Cree hunters benefited from the plurality of practices and from the numerous ways they were interlinked. The Crees had exclusive use of their lands again as the government closed beaver reserves to other trappers; the appointment of hunting leaders as tallymen was taken by Crees as an acknowledgement by the government of the hunting tenure system, and it enhanced their legitimacy both within Cree society and by non-Cree. The government presented itself as having taken control of the governance of the lands and wildlife resources of the region, a claim that followed from the exercise of legislative authority, from the establishment of a new bureaucracy and from its control of public communications.

Under the beaver-reserve system, which lasted from the 1930s up to the 1970s, the Cree shared decisions about the use of the land for the first time, but on terms that were generally advantageous to themselves both in terms of decision-making and on-the-ground control of the land. Christine Saganash, the wife of Allen Saganash quoted above, said as part of her affidavit for the forestry case:

> I remember so many years ago when Indian Affairs [agents] came to draw boundary lines [of the hunting territories for the Beaver Reserves]. Allen was already the tallyman. They gave him a badge to show he was a game warden. I still have that badge and carry it with me....
>
> They must listen to us and respect us. We are the owners of the land. We are part of it. To cut our land is to destroy us and our way of life. (Affidavit of Christine (Jolly) Saganash, 22 July 1999)

Here government recognition not only acknowledges Cree governance; it affirms an expectation that lands would be used to protect a Cree way of life. The ambiguities over who was in control under the beaver-reserve system were heightened early in the 1960s as government-promoted mining, commercial forestry and sport hunting and fishing increased dramatically. These problems created by new resource uses came to a head in 1971 when work began on the James Bay hydroelectric project.

Choosing How to Fight Development Projects

When a youthful Cree leadership emerged to lead a regional Cree opposition to the hydroelectric development in the early 1970s, the hunting elders were turned to for advice on what position to adopt vis-à-vis the governments. They set the crisis in history but also suggested perspectives that drew on their own authority over the land that was threatened by these development projects. Philip Awashish, one of the emerging Cree political leaders of the time, wrote that the elders were saying that the present pattern was

> started by the arrival of the first white man into the area and still continues to this very day. Development is solely in the hands of people outside the region.... The region has been utilized almost exclusively by the Cree people who have no voice in the decision-making body which [is now] planning the development of resources in the area. (Awashish 1972b, discussed in Feit 1985)

When asked what they saw as the goal of their opposition, Awashish reported that 'most of the chiefs felt they would accept some form of hydro development under conditions that would be acceptable to the native people of the area. A negotiable development project would be the goal' (Awashish 1972a; see Feit 1985). The elders sought as a goal the experience of the sometimes respectful relationships of the past, but they now insisted that shared use of the land be explicitly negotiated and recognized.

The events put in motion by the ensuing court case and the negotiation of the JBNQA are described elsewhere in this book (see chapters 9 and 10 by Coon Come and Craik). Cree hunters' visions of recent agreements are reflected in the 1999 affidavits where hunters express their mistrust and frustration at the failures and betrayals of negotiations and agreements, and with the sham consultative relationships governments and corporations established during this period of industrial resource developments (see, for example, Feit and Beaulieu 2001).

Yet Cree hunters and Cree leaders seek to find means of sharing the land, and continue to offer and insist on reciprocity with governments and developers. To comprehend this dual insistence on recognizing their Cree rights and also again establishing respectful relationships, we need to examine how the life projects of Crees are envisaged in the light of long local histories of relationships that extend transnationally to institutions of commerce and governance. We must also consider how their life projects are embedded in relations to their lands and the non-human beings on the land.

Their Words Cannot Be Trusted: Asserting Land as Agency

As forestry expanded following the 1975 JBNQA, hunters like the late Noah Eagle tried throughout the 1980s and 1990s to communicate with forestry companies. When I talked to Noah two years after a first interview in which he reported to me that he had had talks with the companies about how to cut his land, he himself returned to the subject of forestry company practices because he wanted to report the results and wanted to make an invitation:

> Another thing I want talk about is the log cutting.... When they first started that business, they said they'd get the logs just in the bush not close to the river or creeks. But that is not true.... They don't do what they said, just to cut down the trees from far in the bush. That's how everyone's ground is....
>
> If anyone doesn't believe what we say, we could take them there to see or we'd take pictures of what we're talking about....

Then he described what was happening on the land:

> Some Indians that hunt up north say they have a lot of moose there, where their ground is not yet damaged. I guess the moose just takes off and goes to where the land is good and plenty of their food there. It can't stay where the ground is damaged, it's the same way with all the other animals.
>
> I don't know what will happen to us in the future, but right now we're okay, the way we're living. In the olden days I remember we didn't have any tea or sugar, all we had to drink was [the broth] from what we cooked, fish, rabbit and other game, we never had anything to make soup. And I think it's going to turn out that way pretty soon, by the way things look, in the past two years. (Noah Eagle, 8 May 1984; quoted in Feit and Beaulieu 2001)

Like those who gave affidavits more than a decade later, Noah is clear that he is dealing with people whose words cannot be trusted and who do not do what they say they will do. Yet he reaches out to seek recognition by forestry companies and his generalized listeners, and calls on them to recognize the dangers and act responsibly. His proposal is to invite his listeners to come and see what he has learned and seen on the land.[7] Here Noah actively seeks the re-creation of mutual understanding. He has experienced that this cannot be achieved by yet another conversation with forestry company representatives. Rather, they need to come onto the land. I think that for Noah there is no use in a discursive contest over truth, or even a discursive effort to convince others through argument about whose truth should prevail. He avoids words and in their place issues invitations to enter a place more fully. But why? I think that he is inviting the forestry operators to come onto the land and learn from what the land has to teach. This suggestion requires a brief discussion of Cree ontology.

In the Cree hunters' view there is no fundamental separation in kind between the social world and the natural world, or between humans and nature, and the land is not a thing. The social world of the Crees extends beyond Cree society not just to other humans: the whole of the cosmos is understood as being a social world. That is, the whole of the Cree world is conceived of by most Cree hunters as comprising beings that are like persons. The world of Cree hunters is a society of non-human persons with wills, idiosyncrasies, intelligence and capacities of communication. Hunters emphasize that they know the non-human persons of the lands they hunt as individuals, not only as generalized categories of persons. They know the world through the relationships they know intimately.

Animals as persons are not soulless machines; animals are active agents. Animals are full of subjectivity, awareness and social relations, and they re-spond to and convey meaning through their actions. This is true of many 'natural' phenomena as well. Thus in the early 1970s when I would ask about Chuetenshu, the powerful 'North Wind' person, I would get much more extended answers on cold and clear days associated with weather that arrived from the northwest. To talk extensively on warm days of the power-ful and potentially dangerous wind person who brought cold and winter was potentially disrespectful and made many hunters uncomfortable. They did not like to talk in the absence, or 'behind the back', of so powerful a person. It could know what was said and might think it was not being re-ferred to respectfully and could take offence.[8] That did not prevent joking, or complaints, but in appropriate contexts as in all social relationships. The same was true of animals. They knew what was said of them, and they knew of the needs of hunters and their families. Because of these needs animals were often willing to give themselves to hunters so that humans could feed themselves, but in return they expected respect and reciprocity, a mutual caring for the well-being of each others' societies. Thus the hunt was both an exercise in the skill of the hunter and a result of the willing participation of the hunted animals. Animals left signs and indications of their presence and possible willingness to be killed for the hunter to find, signs that made the hunt possible and more reliable. Nevertheless, animals would also often unexpectedly escape when they were not ready to give themselves. This world of non-human persons has been described by numerous non-Crees who have encountered Cree hunters, from missionaries to fur traders to anthropologists (Hallowell 1955; Preston 2002; Tanner 1979; Feit 1994; and Scott 1996). This cosmology has repeatedly been shown to underlie an ex-tensive system of traditional knowledge, hunting practice and effective game conservation (Feit 1994; Scott 1996; Berkes 1999).

Thus, Noah does not invite his listeners into the bush to see an essen-tialized nature, or an objective fact, but to come on to the land in order to learn about relationships from those who live there. When moose numbers have declined it is because, as he indicates, many moose are choosing to move away from cutting areas both because their food is scarce and because they judge the land is not 'good' where there is forestry cutting. Inviting foresters to the bush would allow a subject-laden land to pass its own messages to viewers willing to learn about what is good or bad in this place after forestry operations have transformed it.

When Noah proposes to take people onto the land, we cannot dismiss this as either metaphorical or naive. As the work by Tim Ingold (2000) and Bruno Latour (1993) emphasizes, listeners need to avoid imposing the culture–nature separation on ontologies and epistemologies not founded on the assumptions that underlie the modern world-view that has developed since the sixteenth century. When we do that we treat them as just interpretations, whereas they are statements about what both is known and what is (see McGregor, Chapter 5 in this volume), made not by a knower separated from a nature that is passively known but from a human engaged in relations with other active persons. They are, we can say, statements from within non-modern life projects.

But what is the purpose of such an invitation, especially if one suspects the invitee is blind to the possibilities of learning from the animals on the land? An answer emerges from other Cree statements and responses to the forestry crisis.

Life Projects and Relationships

The views that I have suggested are implicit in Noah's invitation became clearer to me in exchanges among Crees over how to deal with governments and forestry companies. In a telephone conversation in the late 1990s with a middle-aged Cree hunter about forestry cutting and the court action the Crees had initiated, I supported breaking off discussions with the forestry companies and accelerating legal action. He did not oppose court action, but he did oppose not talking at the same time to the companies. He said those Cree leaders who wanted to fight only in court were 'stupid', a strong word in his vocabulary, but one he thought I indirectly deserved. He asked rhetorically, 'Don't they' – those Cree leaders and myself – 'know that we cannot protect the land if we go around only blaming and accusing them?' He gave the example of declining moose numbers and the non-Cree sport hunt, saying we cannot simply blame the sport hunters. If we did that we could not respond effectively to the crisis because caring for the moose depends on working with the sport hunters and the government.

He claimed it was necessary to continue to seek relationships, even when they are not working, because only with such relationships can the animals and the land be effectively cared for and respected. To cut off relationships on an enduring basis in frustration would affect not only what can be in the future; it would affect the expression of relationships now. Cutting off communication denies the relationships one already has, and expresses a thoughtlessness and disrespect. His vision is not, however, modern in the sense that there is not any clear path to a defined objective or state: he does not offer a plan for establishing better or new relationships. He is committed to keeping relationships here and now, and by doing so to express here and now what is needed in the present and in visions of the future. Moreover, these relationships to animals and to others have implications for strategies of living.

Animal Agency and Surviving

These issues were expressed in the summer of 1998, when Waswanipi Cree hunters met to discuss possible responses to continuing forestry cutting on their lands. The leaders of the Cree communities had just accelerated their court case on forestry, and there was talk of blocking the provincial highway in protest against continued unregulated logging. The hunters heard from Cree negotiators about the modest changes that the forestry companies and the government of Quebec were proposing as their solutions. It was a meeting fraught with a sense of anxiety and frustration, although periodically relieved by humour. A middle-aged hunter and administrator said to Cree negotiators:

> Go to the government and tell them about forestry. This is what is pushing wildlife out.... How can we participate if they're not willing to participate with us? ... [logging companies] they're just going crazy and taking all the wood out and they're destroying the moose yards which are used in the winter time. They're destroying the mating grounds and they're destroying the playgrounds [of moose]. (Transcript, Waswanipi Cree Trappers Association Meeting, 26 August 1998)

It was a passionate speech, with a controlled but frustrated tone. The father of the speaker, himself an elder hunter, spoke next, and he said that what had been said was true. But he went on to say:

> The animals of this world love us, they can't leave us. I was told by my grandfather, who was a mean old man, ... if someone else kills your moose, it can happen that there will be more than what was killed. You showed love when you didn't say anything to the person who hunted on your territory, and that's how much love will be returned to you. (Transcript, Waswanipi Cree Trappers Association Meeting, 26 August 1998)

Although this sounds like a familiar story advising listeners to turn the other cheek, and the teller is an active Christian, the story is also embedded in

Cree storytelling traditions and hunting practices. Crees do hunt and kill moose, and moose are persons who consent. Thus this is a story about complex relationships. It asserts that respectful and life-supporting relationships do continue, and indeed can continue, even in the midst of disrespectful and destructive practices, even by Cree.

Even so, it is not a metaphor; it is descriptive. The speaker is reminding his listeners that animals remain generous in the context of denials of respect and destruction of habitats by other humans. These moose are material persons. They are hunted, forestry reduces their food yards, mating success and play, and many moose chose to move away as a result. But moose do not cease to be, they are still being hunted, and they are still giving themselves to hunters both on lands affected by forestry, and in larger numbers on lands not yet affected. Moose that move away respond to the destructiveness of forestry, and those that stay show that some may survive in its midst.

The Cree ability to continue to receive animal gifts in the midst of extensive destruction caused by forestry is experientially undeniable, even if game numbers are reduced by the destruction. This both results from and confirms the continuing respectful relationships sustained by Cree hunters through this crisis. Animals here are social as well as very embodied teachers. They are active agents who help and are at the same time models of how to seek to continue to survive. The moose both move and stay amidst forestry, reflecting the dilemmas and suffering Cree face as the choices expressed in Cree hunting leaders' affidavits. The continuing survival and the continuing generosity of animals reassure Cree hunters of their own future in the midst of great destruction and uncertainty for both Cree and animals. To have to give up the land completely is unthinkable, and the moose confirm that it need not come to be. This story bespeaks a capacity both to survive abuse and suffering, and to continue to seek to change abusive relationships.

Conclusions

For Cree hunters and Cree political leaders, their opposition to development and at the same time their invitations to relationships are both essential to living here and now.[9] The pursuit of relationships is not a request (waiting for others to act), a compliance (willing acceptance of failures of others to reciprocate), or an acquiescence to the control by others. It is an ongoing pursuit essential to maintaining the everyday lives and life projects of the Crees. It is in this knowledge that I think Noah Eagle offered his invitation.

Some readers will note with concern that seeking relationships with developers is a response that can be beneficial to state institutions and corporations. It is intended to be. This is not naive in the view of Cree hunting leaders. Recall the older hunter who defends the lessons of moose against too ready a dismissal by noting that his grandfather was 'a mean old man'. In doing so he highlights for his listeners that his grandfather did not act out of kindness when he did not confront those who killed moose on his hunting territory. He implies that this is the way things have to be done to benefit yourself as well as the moose. It is not just a morality but an ontology that motivates action here.

In seeking effective relationships within Cree life projects, the hunters reassert the power of their relationships to histories, lands, animals, to other places and peoples, and to the diversity of Crees and Cree communities. Contrary to what several analysts have suggested, this practice of inviting respectful relationships is not a sign of the need to compromise because the Crees have limited resources and power, although they do have limited means. It is not a turning to the moral because they cannot succeed in the political – they have had some significant successes (see Craik in this volume). It is not a sign of inconsistency in their commitment to their lands or a singular desire for monetary benefit. It is the means of re-creation of life projects and relationships for everyday living and survival in the midst of continuing destruction.

Notes

This chapter draws on the work of many Cree people and other scholars from whom I have drawn insights, including: Philip Awashish, Mario Blaser, Matthew Coon Come, Brian Craik, Paul Dixon, Sam Gull, Sr, Peter Harries-Jones, Peter Hutchins, Ted Moses, Matthew Ottereyes, Alan Penn and Colin Scott. Many others go unnamed. I also want to acknowledge financial support from the Social Sciences and Humanities Research Council of Canada, and the Arts Research Board of McMaster University.

1. The film-makers who caught part of this debate on video (some scenes look like they may have been re-enacted) themselves felt the contradiction enough to have to explain it to viewers, by stressing that offering an agreement at this time was part of a divide-and-rule tactic by Hydro-Quebec, which it was.

2. I use the term 'hunting leaders' for the generally elder Cree hunters who are the 'bosses' or 'tallymen' (see below) of family hunting territories. There are approximately 300 hunting territories in the region, and they range from about 200 to over 1,000 square miles. The territories are a key part of the Cree social and customary legal structures. Several elder and respected hunters or community leaders would also be included among this group of leaders as elders, although they do not have their own hunting territories. The designation is also intended to include spouses and women elders of the community.

3. I take the concept of life projects from Bruno Barras's chapter (3) and Mario Blaser's Introduction (Chapter 2) in this volume, but see also Escobar 1995: 212.

4. I am indebted to Wendy Russell for making this clear to me (see Russell, Chapter 8 in this volume).

5. Similarly, in the very nature of the treaty-making process itself the government also acknowledges and acquiesces to some Cree sovereignty by acknowledging the relationship as one that requires treaty-making and agreements, and not just decrees and contracts.

6. The affidavits were prepared by legal counsel for the Cree in preparation for this court case. All were given verbally in Cree and were translated and transcribed into English.

7. He offers them photos if they cannot come because he recently worked with staff of the Grand Council of the Crees to photograph sites that exemplified the changes he was taking about.

8. For similar experiences, see Black 1977.

9. In 2002 the Cree signed a new agreement with Quebec which gave them a new role in forestry management, as well as consenting to new hydroelectric installations (see Craik in this volume).

References

Awashish, Philip (1972a) 'Report of Philip Awashish. Communications Worker Indians of Quebec Association on the James Bay Development Project. April 10–May 5, 1972', Huron Village, 11 May 1972.

——— (1972b) 'Report of Philip Awashish Communications Worker. James Bay Development Project', Huron Village, 23 June 1972.

Berkes, Fikret (1999) *Sacred Ecology: Traditional Ecological Knowledge and Resource Management*, Philadelphia: Taylor & Francis.

Black, Mary B. (1977) 'Ojibwe power belief systems', in R.D. Fogelson and R.M. Adams (eds), *The Anthropology of Power*, New York: Academic Press, pp. 141–51.

Escobar, Arturo (1995) *Encountering Development: The Making and Unmaking of the Third World*, Princeton: Princeton University Press.

Feit, Harvey A. (1985) 'Legitimation and autonomy in James Bay Cree responses to hydro-electric development', in Noel Dyck (ed.), *Indigenous Peoples and the Nation State: Fourth World Politics in Canada, Australia, and Norway*, St John's: Memorial University, Institute for Social and Economic Research, pp. 27–66.

——— (1994) 'Hunting and the quest for power, the James Bay Cree and Whitemen in the twentieth century', in R.B. Morrison and C.R. Wilson (eds), *Native Peoples: The Canadian Experience*, 2nd edn, Toronto: McClelland & Stewart, pp. 181–223.

——— (2004) 'Contested identities of "Indians" and "Whitemen" at James Bay, or the power of reason, hybridity and agency', in T. Irimoto and T. Yamada (eds), *Ethnicity and Identity in the North*, Osaka: National Museum of Ethnology.

——— (in press) 'Co-governance and the uses of co-management', *Anthropologica*.

——— and Robert Beaulieu (2001) 'Voices from a disappearing forest: government, corporate, and Cree participatory forestry management practices', in C.H. Scott (ed.), *Aboriginal Autonomy and Development in Northern Quebec and Labrador*, Vancouver: University of British Columbia Press, pp. 119–48.

Francis, Daniel and Toby Morantz (1983) *Partners in Furs: A History of the Fur Trade in Eastern James Bay, 1600–1870*, Montreal: McGill-Queen's University Press.

Gupta, Akhil and James Ferguson (eds) (1999) *Culture, Power, Place: Explorations in Critical Anthropology*, Durham, NC: Duke University Press.

Hallowell, A.I. (1955) *Culture and Experience*, Philadelphia: University of Pennsylvania Press.

Ingold, Tim (2000) 'Culture, nature, environment: steps to an ecology of life', in *Perception of the Environment: Essays in Livelihood, Dwelling and Skill*, London: Routledge, pp. 13–26.

Isacsson, Magnus (dir.) (1996) *Power – One River, Two Nations*, film, Montreal: Cineflix and the National Film Board of Canada.

LaRusic, Ignatius et al. (1979) *Negotiating a Way of Life*, Montreal: Indian Affairs and Northern Development Canada.

Latour, Bruno (1993) *We Have Never Been Modern*, Cambridge, MA: Harvard University Press.

Morantz, Toby (2002) *The White Man's Gonna Getcha: The Colonial Challenge to the Crees in Quebec*, Montreal: McGill-Queen's Press.

Preston, Richard (2002 [1975]) *Cree Narrative*, Montreal: McGill-Queen's Press.

Rousseau, Jean (2001) 'Les nouveaux défis des Cris de la Baie James à l'heure de la globalisation', *Recherches amérindiennes au Québec*, vol. 31, no. 3, pp. 73–82.

Salisbury, Richard F. (1976) 'Transactions or transactors: an economic anthropologist's view', in B. Kapferer (ed.) *Transaction and Meaning*, Philadelphia: Ishi, pp. 41–59.

Scott, Colin H. (1983) 'The semiotics of material life among the Wemindji Cree hunters', Ph.D. thesis, Department of Anthropology, McGill University.

——— (1989) 'Ideology of reciprocity between James Bay Cree and the Whiteman state', in Peter Skalnik (ed.), *Outwitting the State*, New Brunswick, NJ: Transaction Press, pp. 81–108.

——— (1996) 'Science for the west, myth for the rest?', in Laura Nader (ed.), *Naked Science: Anthropological Inquiry into Boundaries, Power, and Knowledge*, New York: Routledge, pp. 69–86.

Tanner, A. (1979) *Bringing Home Animals. Religious Ideology and Mode of Production of the Mistassini Cree Hunters*, St John's: Memorial University, Institute of Social and Economic Research.

——— (1999) 'Culture, social change, and Cree opposition to the James Bay Hydroelectric Project', in James F. Hornig (ed.), *Social and Environmental Impacts of the James Bay Hydroelectric Project*, Montreal: McGill-Queen's University Press, pp. 121–40.

7

Grassroots Transnationalism and Life Projects of Vermonters in the Great Whale Campaign

GLENN McRAE

Connections

Jim Higgins was not certain what the result would be when he forwarded a message to the Grand Council of the Crees[1] in the spring of 1989 through the Mohawk nation bordering his home state of Vermont. Jim, an ardent wilderness canoe enthusiast had been running the rivers that flowed east to James Bay or north to Ungava Bay in northern Quebec for a decade. He had watched with concern as survey markers started appearing in wilderness areas, and reports of a great herd of Caribou[2] being drowned from a surge in dam releases filtered south. What brought him to the point of trying to contact the James Bay Crees was his discovery that Vermont utilities had entered into negotiations to increase their purchase of power from Hydro-Quebec, the provincially owned utility, and that Hydro-Quebec was aggressively marketing power to the northeastern United States in order to guarantee funding for the Great Whale Project, a new massive hydroelectric development on lands claimed by the Crees.

The first journey of Crees coming to Vermont, stimulated by Jim's message, was the first ripple of a great many circles that would connect James Bay Cree and Vermont communities in a series of exchanges, both personal and political, that continue to the present (McRae 2001). In this examination of grassroots transnationalism, I look at the Great Whale Campaign from viewpoints in Vermont. Numerous accounts of this and other campaigns have been written from the perspective of the Crees, and by the Crees themselves (as in Coon Come's contribution to this volume, Chapter 9). What I believe to be missing, and what I hope to contribute, is an understanding of these movements that goes beyond the portrayal of them as forging 'common cause' between the First World activists and the empowered activist bodies of the Third and Fourth Worlds (to use an outdated paradigm). I believe that within the framework of a grassroots transnationalism we can observe a range of interests and identities expressed and, in the process of interaction, changed. I contend that interests and identities are not changed in a manner that creates more homogeneity or even shared and common interests or identity. Rather I will advance the idea that what is newly forged is a set of linkages that create a dynamic stream of communication and understanding of the relative socio-political positions.

The Great Whale Campaign as it unfolded in Vermont in the early 1990s is a case study in the initiation of a local Indigenous resistance that grows it-self into a translocal movement. I will examine how the homogenous message that initiates the campaign becomes a heterogeneous but connected set of messages based in actions grounded in local landscapes. I will also discuss the expanding critique of globalization, centred on the simple epigram, 'there is no away', that is inspiring the growth of a critical localism at the root of both new indigenist, environmental and democratic movements, but that is also reshaping some localism in the form of corporate environmentalism.

Taking Life Projects across the Border

The development of a movement contesting the Hydro-Quebec contracts to sell electricity to the northeastern United States created a ripple effect that confronted thousands of Vermonters with questions about their daily lives and practices and about the democratic principles they valued and how they were applied in their institutions. The expression by the Crees of their special relationship to the land had particular resonance for Vermonters, who see their history as one guided by a tradition of land stewardship and see themselves as particularly successful at managing a variety of forces that might degrade the land in Vermont. This point of connection provided Vermonters with a story and connection to share through their existing affinities and self-identities. The small groups of Vermonters who had direct contact with the Crees took the stories of those contacts, and the resulting new convic-tions, to others through their personal and organizational networks, whether an association, neighbourhood church, or family. There were many levels at which participants found they could interact with the campaign. This might have included the act of voting against the contracts in a local referendum, or hosting a Cree family when they came to Vermont, or, as in the case of many students, reading a book and acting out a simulated debate as a way of better understanding the various perspectives involved. Each act built on previous actions and stimulated new ones.

The Crees came to Vermont to articulate a message that their way of life was at risk, and that the cause was directly linked to decisions that people in Vermont were making about their lives. Where they were successful they connected to Vermonters' common themes and questions about their own resistance to or acceptance of development in the last fifty years — years that have evidenced tremendous change in the Vermont way of life (Bryan and McClaughry 1989; Sherman 2000). Yet these actions did not homogenize the Cree or the Vermont experience. They instead forged deft and strong links between two distinctive localities in struggle. The struggles that ensued intersected at numerous points, but also took on independent manifestations. Indeed, despite the mobilization inspired by the Cree intervention, some Vermont activists remained strongly tied to earlier forms of environmental action aimed at working within market institutions and values.

The grassroots surge of support for the Crees, the flow of Vermonters travelling to James Bay and Crees travelling to Vermont, and active questioning of public policy in Vermont over the next five years were the framework for a transnational support network that extended beyond Vermont and were at least partially responsible for the eventual cancellation of the Great Whale Project. This successful conclusion for the Crees was preceded by a marginally successful campaign in Vermont that led to the utilities in the state not increasing the amount of power they purchased from Quebec. While not successful in their aim of cancelling new contracts, activists in Vermont noted that the new contracts, for the same amount of energy that Vermont had previously purchased, could not be used to help leverage financing for new hydro development.

The activism embodied in this effort led some Vermonters to question Vermont's own development. But it was also compatible with community activism rooted in corporate environmentalism. At least three distinct threads of resistance and protest can be found in these interactions. There was the direct connection of Crees and Vermonters, with Vermonters working to give voice and re-enact the Cree message directly in Vermont. There was also the ongoing corporate environmentalism that argued against contracts with Hydro-Quebec and Vermont having a part in further efforts to import large blocks of power, based on standard economic models and projections that sought to promote energy efficiency and local sources of power as alternatives. Finally, there were the restimulated efforts at addressing some of the incongruities between Vermont's image of itself as a model of local democracy and government accessibility and the increasingly visible bureaucratic system that guided decision-making in the state. As these three threads make up the larger strand of action during and since the campaign, they provide a fertile ground for analysis of the interactions between Indigenous and other activists.

The literature surrounding the relationships between social justice and environmental activists from the United States, Europe and Canada working to save the environment, and the Indigenous peoples who rely on it, usually presents the relationships as flowing one way. Help is provided to Indigenous peoples to support their struggle and preserve the rainforest (or whatever environment is under threat from development).[3] Although, increasingly, the relationships between Indigenous communities and their far-distant supporters are being presented in a more complex manner (Rabben 1998; Gedicks 1993), what has been missing is an analysis of the effects that these interactions have on the First World activists and their communities that step forward to help in Indigenous struggles. The activists, and the organizations they work for or are members of, are often portrayed as coming to the battle fully developed, and leaving wholly unchanged after the outcome.[4]

There were three sectors of transformative action in Vermont affected by these interactions. The first sector encompassed those people in communities where the Crees visited, spoke and interacted with residents. The Crees' expression of their own disenfranchisement from decisions that affected their lives created room for discussion in Vermont communities concerning just how much control Vermonters still had over decisions affecting how they wanted to live their lives and express themselves.

The second sector involved the hundreds of individuals who actually went to visit the James Bay communities, and returned with that experience. For the most part these individuals came back having experienced both a political and a personal transformation.

This personal and political transformation of individuals in turn impacted on the final sector of transformative action: institutions. Institutional change took place primarily within the environmental and economic justice organizations in the state that had previously worked on energy issues. These institutions sought change within the traditional market-based system; as one environmentalist put it:

> We made a conscious campaign choice not to appeal to the emotional arguments about the impact this project would have on the Crees, a kind of 'save the Indian' campaign. Instead, we focused on the economic argument that the PSB [Public Service Board] and the utilities were making a bad financial decision for themselves and for Vermont ratepayers. (Cited in McRae 2001)

While the institutional environmental work remained anchored in the existing systems of marketplace economics, the individuals involved often went beyond this thinking in their direct interactions in the community and personal experience with the state's corporate and political infrastructure.

It is my contention that the conditions for bringing increased attention to a new sense of the local, as a focus for social action, requires a corresponding level of study of specific local campaigns as they have developed in spaces like Vermont. The strength of Indigenous resistance movements in places such as James Bay and corresponding movements in places like Vermont are interrelated. Resistance to the Hydro-Quebec contracts in Vermont was not simply a matter of 'saving Great Whale', but some of it was also part of what Dirlik (1997) proposes as shifting resistance to counter the coercive elements of modernization. The Cree resistance stimulated and strengthened local life projects in Vermont.

Great Whale Campaign through the Local Lens of Vermont

Vermont is situated in a unique geopolitical and historical position for consideration of its role in the Great Whale Campaign. Vermont has a long history of social justice advocacy (from banning slavery in its state constitution upon adoption in 1791, to passing legislation in 2000 creating 'civil unions' – i.e. same-sex legal unions). Since the 1960s it gained national prominence for its environmental quality (at least in part based on twenty years of tourism promotion of its green mountains, clean air and water, fall foliage, and bucolic rural settings) and environmental activism, particularly the anti-nuclear-power organizing of the 1970s.

When the Crees started their contacts and campaign to stop the Great Whale Project, they employed moral approaches to elicit response and action from people and organizations they encountered in Vermont and other states. From 1989 to 1992, the state of Vermont was the scene of an extensive debate over energy policy and development choices, in the background of which were moral questions. The moral opposition staged by the Crees and interpreted by supporters in Vermont pushed the debate in a direction totally unexpected by the utilities or the regulators. The debate was framed in questions that did not fit into the legislative or regulatory structure, but were clearly associated with strongly held values in Vermont. Vermonters listening to the debate were forced to ask (and were presented with these questions continuously by the media) why there was a separation between their values and the social power structure that they assumed grew out of those values.

Should Vermonters only be concerned with environmental degradation in our own backyard? If so, encouraging the trashing of northern Quebec's environment would be a good idea because we will get our electricity without ever seeing the direct effects.[5] Could Vermonters assume that decisions would be made fairly and justly in Canada?[6] Or should they go beyond these assumptions, as the Crees and Inuit urged, and ensure that these decisions corresponded with their values of fairness and justice? Could

Vermonters justifiably complain about fossil fuel emissions from Midwest power plants that degrade Vermont's environment, then turn around, get their power from James Bay, and ignore their impact on that environment?[7] In Vermont, where state government has long prided itself on improving conditions for children, Mayor Sappa Fleming of the Inuit community of Kuujjuaraapik at the mouth of the Great Whale River, asked Governor Kunin of Vermont, what about the future of the children? 'The lives of everyone's children up there are at stake.' To which Kunin is reported to have replied, 'I have to think about *my* children's future.'[8] The question remained as to why any children anywhere needed to be at risk as a result of decisions made in Vermont.

These questions and the debates that surrounded them were framed by the participation of a variety of interest groups. Some groups were formed in direct response to Cree interventions, but few of these outlived the campaign. Other groups brought their previously informed ethos of environmental and social justice to the campaign activities, and were informed and in many cases strengthened by their interactions with the Crees and the issues that emerged during the campaign. Still other groups working within the environmental and progressive economic development framework they developed in Vermont kept a distance from the Crees and groups working more directly with them. These groups saw benefit in the Cree-inspired actions, but also viewed them as a possible diversion from other agendas. The Crees asked directly that the contracts not be consummated, and that Vermont look to other options. This new effort helped initiate and, in part, direct the tone of how Vermonters debated their future in terms of energy choices and the future shape of its economy, communities and institutions of democracy.

Vermont: The Global in the Local

In setting the stage for this drama to play out, the economic connections have to be considered alongside those of values. Vermont's geographic location has also placed it in a unique position for relations with Quebec and as a conduit for the export from Quebec of electric power. Vermont's major population centre is in the north, thirty miles from the Canadian border, and situated on a historical north–south trade route. Upon the untimely death of Governor Snelling in 1991, Lt-Governor Howard Dean came into the governorship. In a letter to the new governor, who had not had much time to evaluate all his responsibilities, former governor Salmon wrote to provide support and strong advice on the need to preserve Vermont's 'unique relationship with Quebec', and to honour the contracts for purchase of electric power from Hydro-Quebec as a continuation of that unique relationship.

> As you know, we have no greater friend in the world than Canada, in general, and the Province of Quebec, in particular. No stone should be left unturned to continue to exploit this sound relationship for the greater good of our mutual societies.

This echoed Governor Snelling's vision of establishing a long-term foreign trade relationship with Quebec as a strategy for growing the Vermont economy. Salmon also noted in his letter to Dean that the contract with Hydro-Quebec had 'so much to say about Vermont's economic future' (McRae 2001).

In addition to direct trade relations, Vermont is also situated as a conduit for Quebec electricity exports to the United States, a conduit that has great value in the long-range plans of Hydro-Quebec and Quebec economic planners. Although there are other possible routes, the already established Vermont linkages provide an existing infrastructure to be exploited.

The Crees offered the opportunity to link their campaign to a Vermont campaign that changed from being James Bay-centric to a Vermont-centric activity focused on Vermont issues. This was a critical point of connection, strengthened by the continual flow of people-to-people contacts in trips of Crees to Vermont and Vermonters to James Bay. Six years after the conclusion of the campaign, a Cree activist, Matthew Mukash, who had become chief of the Great Whale community, reflected that the 'neighbour-to-neighbour' connection was a critical step, but what was just as important was for the Crees to know that Vermonters had and would articulate their own efforts to address conditions in Vermont, so that Vermont would not be a contributor to future problems in Cree territory (McRae 2001).

> We also need to get white people to look at themselves, not at us. They need to focus on healing themselves. People should not think to study us except where we can hold a mirror up to them to show them what they need to look at.

During the Great Whale Campaign, the actions by both the Crees and the Vermonters who supported them amounted to more than the visible direct acts that occurred around the courtrooms, corporate boardrooms, government policy meetings, and voting booths. The responses of Vermonters who supported the Crees created an opportunity for personal and social critique. In the end, some Vermonters did more than simply demand a change or restitution from a corporate structure to the Crees; they opened the possibility for social experimentation and reinvention in Vermont.

In responding to the requests and challenges presented by the Crees, Vermonters turned back to institutions they assumed were the embodiment of values considered to be at the core of their identity as Vermonters. Yet Vermonters found that their institution's actualization of those values fell short of the rhetoric.

In the Vermont economic sector, rather than emphasizing self-reliance, private-sector initiatives and governmental policy favoured the purchase of large blocks of energy from out-of-state, requiring the export of significant economic resources to obtain guaranteed sources of energy. Activists in Vermont, as well as the Crees, vigorously argued that such a policy diminished Vermont's self-reliance, by tying it to sources of power that it had little control over, and by exporting significant resources rather than investing those resources locally. These fragile economic relations were indicators of how much Vermont was becoming tied in to global economic systems.

Vermont's system of government and state administration are regarded by most in Vermont as being more direct and accessible than they are in other states. Unlike other states, a number of local utilities in Vermont were bound by charter to bring the contract decision before town voters. In the campaign, there were some significant successes in direct intervention through grassroots organizing and voting; but, for the most part, direct participation in decision-making was restricted for Vermonters. Activists, environmentalists, and even some significant business interests in Vermont considered the signing of the contracts with Hydro-Quebec a monumental decision, made with little citizen input.[9] Three successive governors said that there was nothing they could do. Three successive legislative sessions failed to produce legislation requiring a broader overview of such projects. The regulatory bodies responsible for review of the contracts stated clearly that they must abide by the law that restricted what they could consider and how.

Throughout the process, activists and citizens remarked that they felt shut out. They had no viable recourse that made a difference. Bryan and McClaughry (1989) argue that, even at the town-meeting forum, much vaunted in Vermont for its 'direct democracy', the survival of local direct democracy as a tradition in Vermont is tied, at least in part, to the fact that the vast majority of its 250 towns have fewer than 2,000 people each. Face-to-face relationships dominate social networks, and over short periods of time it is not uncommon for the majority of citizens in a town to have served in one or more leadership positions. This builds an expectation for all levels of government to work in a similarly responsive and direct manner (Bryan and McClaughry 1989). More often than not, citizens advocating against the contracts were rebuffed. The rise of bureaucratic governmental structures and elite power brokers, and the influence of money, were blamed for the failure of their efforts.[10]

The green of Vermont's hills has often been described in a manner that makes it a reflector for the 'green' values of its inhabitants. When George P.

Marsh published his classic tome on environmental stewardship in the 1860s he did not look at green hills, but rather at a denuded landscape threatening an ecological disaster due to overgrazing and deforestation. In the next hundred years, through stewardship, an economic shift that drove sheep farming from the state, and population loss, Vermont's landscape came to resemble the more pastoral setting people value today. Bryan and McClaughry (1989) call it an environmentalism of use that is maintained by a strong sense of localism. They disparage other environmentalisms as representative of central, undemocratic, elitist controls. Yet Vermont's green reputation develops from these other environmentalisms: its land-use regulation, its bottle bill, its ban on billboards, and its distinction as being the last state to have a Wal-Mart store and the only state still without a McDonald's in its capital city. All of these are centralized initiatives.

On the issue of Great Whale, neither the local working environmentalism nor the legislated environmentalisms availed activists, who saw the project as anti-environmental on all levels. The tension between the need for power and the lack of will to meet that need locally is still unresolved. One of the reasons is that environmentalism in Vermont, as elsewhere, has become closely tied to centralized and corporate decision-making and market interests. Nevertheless, the Cree Great Whale Campaign became a process that moved many activists to a clearer awareness of this contradiction.

Joe Sherman (2000), in his commentary on themes in contemporary Vermont history, looks on the 1990s as a 'decade of concern'. Sherman hypothesizes that there was too much concern, and it left the state fractious and unfocused. It did, however, in his words, identify what he called an 'undercurrent of morality, fairness'. Vermonters expected that their actions reflected this: 'This sense of morality ... nourished much of the public debate, from education spending to affordable housing to condom giveaways to what to do about the garbage. The burning question was, "Are we doing it right?"' (Sherman 2000: 179). The lack of justice in the decisions to sign the contracts seemed to bother Vermonters most. It was a theme that the Crees hammered on continually. Could Vermonters, by either action or inaction, actually contribute to the destruction of an environment and a culture just to have cheap electricity? This question was underscored by what the Vermont activist Jim Higgins saw as clear-cut support for the Crees from Vermonters who could identify with either being on the socio-economic margins or who had their identity threatened, like those who still hunted and trapped in Vermont and lived a more subsistence lifestyle.

> Poor people in Vermont really understood this. The poorer towns voted in solidarity with the Crees, even with all the hype about higher electric rates. There was some real solidarity built. I would often talk to people about this, and it surprised

me how many knew about it; even the janitor at city hall in Burlington told me he was against the contract. (McRae 2001)

Organizing for this campaign drew on each of these core values in the Vermont identity. In confronting those values, activists felt the strength of having a common and recognized ideal to rally around, but as the campaign continued the clear weaknesses in the 'reality' behind the rhetoric appeared to some. Sherman (2000) speaks of Vermont as the 'late great fairy-tale state' that came into the twentieth century some sixty years late. Vermont maintained a self-image that translated into a public image yearned after in other regions of the country, but was not able to maintain the structure to support those values as it grew into its modern state role. Vermonters organizing to support the Crees failed to create a collective state action on this issue that matched the values Vermont projected. Perhaps for this reason the desire and need to take personal control and action became such a prominent activity of some of those in the campaign, as exemplified in the journeys going north and the hosting of Crees when they came to Vermont.

Disturbing Dialogues

Grassroots transnationalism creates unexpected changes

These traditions of protest in Vermont intersected with new forms of protest exhibited by an Indigenous activism that is consciously seeking out interfaces with environmental and social activists who are not solely or even primarily focused on Indigenous issues. Activism is starting to share an increasingly similar set of variables across these geographic and cultural borders without creating homogeneity. There is an increase in the study and exchange of techniques and strategies between Indigenous activists and non-Native allies they have affected,[11] as well as among themselves. Solidarity visits from representatives of different Indigenous movements to James Bay during the Great Whale Campaign from Guatemala (Rigoberta Menchú) and Brazil (Kayapo leaders) gave substance to the environmental metaphoric connections 'Arctic to Amazon'. The multiplying and interconnected networks of Indigenous nations and movements make it highly likely that unique attributes that might be found in campaigns like Great Whale will increasingly be reconstructed and reinvented within numerous localities throughout the world, just as they have often been shared through networks of environmental and social justice groups that have operated globally.

Without consciously planning it, the Crees, in the development of their networks, established a framework of transnational activism that has connected them to struggles throughout the world. But these networks changed them, just as they changed others. Many of the Crees' connections are based on their ability to identify, isolate, re-create and use, in the context of the Cree discourse, such values as environmentalism and human rights. Neither of these values was intrinsic to the Cree discourse prior to their active opposition to the mega-hydroelectric developments in their territory in the 1970s. In the twenty years prior to the Great Whale Campaign the Crees incorporated these discourses into their own to enable others to better identify and relate to their struggle.

In appropriating and incorporating these values, the Crees effectively separate values such as environmentalism from having an intrinsic attachment to particular persons, kinds of groups or places. The redeployment of local environmental and social values is perhaps best illustrated by the way the Crees used these very values to identify and make visible the externalization of Vermont's environmental costs.

Learning that there is no 'away'

> I was asked to speak at a community gathering in Brattleboro. I had to drive down in a raging snowstorm. It was a really crazy trip. The meeting ended up in a church basement with ten people. One of them, a young person, was not hostile but quite challenging, indicating that hydro was the best choice for energy because of air quality issues from other sources. I talked to the group about the fact that the Crees do not have any separate word for 'air' and therefore could not address this argument. It might seem crazy to the Crees – as it should to others – to destroy their environment and way of life to improve local 'air' conditions elsewhere. (Brian Craik, Cree Embassy, quoted in McRae 2001)

Vermont's pristine environment, or at least the ascription of pristine environmental conditions to Vermont, plays a key role in the identity of the state and its people both internally and externally. The park-like ambiance of Vermont's landscape was achieved over the last hundred years via the proactive stewardship of farmers and local communities and the neglect of vast areas that natural forces restored to forest. Beginning in the 1970s, at the same time that the Crees were facing the intrusion of a world-view that segmented the environment into resources and waste, Vermont was establishing a structure of environmental management that segregated and categorized the environment. Air, waste, water, land management, forests, parks, fish and wildlife (game and non-game), and agriculture all became departmentalized approaches to achieving a unified goal of preserving the environment and placing it in the service of Vermonters. Vermont government and citizens focused greater attention on the environment and its 'quality' in a new context that clearly designated the environment as a foundation for the economic well-being of the state.[12] The environment became an attribute of the marketplace. State environmental policy in the last thirty years had followed a path of 'sending problems away' if they could not be easily dealt with.[13]

In the last thirty years Vermont's population, industry and, as a result, impacts on its environment have all grown. Paralleling this growth has been a systematic dismantling of the old infrastructure for self-reliance in producing what it needs, and managing what it produces (e.g. wastes). Currently, almost all energy resources (electricity, oil, gas) consumed in the state are produced elsewhere and transported into the state. Vermont also imports most of its food and other basic necessities. On the output end Vermont has next to no capacity for managing the wastes (ranging from domestic to nuclear) it produces in-state.

Vermont also enacted legislation to restrict any objection to this approach of sending problems 'away'. At the beginning of its hearings on the Hydro-Quebec contracts, the Public Service Board (PSB) was quite clear that its mandate to consider the environmental or social impacts of importing power ended at Vermont's border. The Board did have the clout to require evidence that the power was being imported from an area that had a comparable review process. It did not, however, evaluate the implementation of that review process.

In 1991, Larry House, the representative from Chisasibi to the Grand Council of the Crees, provided testimony[14] to the Vermont Senate Committee on the Environment, specifically concerning what the Crees were not allowed to present to the PSB. It was also an appeal to look 'beyond the borders of Vermont and to establish laws that will address the impacts of the decisions made in Vermont on the environment and on the way of life of those who live outside of your borders' (cited in McRae 2001).

For the Crees, the idea that Vermont and other localities should own their problems was the core message that they presented in Vermont and throughout their efforts in the United States. The appeal was not to 'help' the Crees in Quebec, but to stop those behaviours in Vermont that threatened the Crees directly and indirectly. They desired Vermonters to tend their gardens in a manner that did not harm their neighbours. No Vermonter tolerated a neighbour who constantly sprayed pesticides on their own garden that then drifted over to the next. Currently, Vermonters do not tolerate Midwestern coal plant emissions that create serious air quality problems in Vermont. The Crees were simply requesting that Vermonters apply that standard to themselves in governing their impacts on others.

When House was confronted with challenges that the Crees had already changed and that development was inevitable, he chose not to dispute it, but said:

Our way of life is ancient. It is built upon a respect for the land and for other people. We have ceremonies and traditions that are sacred. We have our own language that is different from that of the people around us. We seek to protect these things and also we seek to develop and adapt our way of life to the changing world. We are not against development. We encourage it. The mega-hydroelectric projects proposed by Hydro-Quebec are not development, they are degradation of the environment and of our way of life. (Cited in McRae 2001)

House puts forth the contradictions inherent in what has been shown to him as being Vermont's representation of itself: a culture that at its core claims a 'respect for the land and for other people' (cited in McRae 2001). In this statement he creates a link between the Crees and Vermonters, and exposes the contradiction. Vermont's caring for its land is managed by the destruction of other lands, and its responsibility for the effects of its actions is legislated to end at its borders. House, and the Cree narrative in general, invited Vermont to join in the practice of what Dirlik (1997) identifies as a 'contemporary localism'. In this Dirlik seeks to distinguish a 'critical localism' from localism that acts as an ideological articulation of capitalism.

The critique that House provides of Vermont is another lens with which to examine the predicament of the local. If anything, Vermont's self-representation, and the external representations that have developed around it, define it as 'local' in all traditional senses. In his regional analysis of New England, Pierce (1976) coins the phrase (which could have been taken directly from a tourism brochure): 'Vermont is perhaps the only place in America a stranger can feel homesick for – before he has even left it.' He also speaks directly to Vermont's 'natural inclination for localism and citizen control'. Although it is not comparable to the genocidal 'localisms' embodied in the conflicts in Indonesia, the Marshall Islands, or Kosovo, what the Crees are insinuating in their critique of Vermont's localism is that it was being expropriated by and used as a tool of capitalism and modernity, rather than existing as the narrative articulated by Pierce which invokes a resistance to and repudiation of the meta-narratives of modernization.

Localism, Markets and Decolonization

Critical localism or local criticism?

The attributes of Vermont's localism, as expressed in the Great Whale Campaign, often aligned themselves against, not with, the ecological consciousness that Dirlik assigns to the emergence of a contemporary localism of liberation. Despite the changes emerging from the joint campaigns of the Crees and Vermont activists, Vermont's decisions on the Hydro-Quebec contracts were made on the basis of a scientific and economic rationality that supersedes local knowledge. Most Vermont towns voted in favour of their local utilities signing contracts with Hydro-Quebec. Thus despite a growing self-reflectiveness among a sector of the Vermont activists that encompassed a critical sense of their earlier assumptions about self-sufficiency, environmental responsibilities to others and local democracy, these changes were not pervasive enough within the time frame of the electric supply contract decisions to alter their outcome decisively. Many sectors of the Vermont movement, as well as the Vermont public, remained entrapped in a localism bound to market environmentalism.

Tanner (1999) contends that the environmental and other supporters of the Crees in the United States, although they opened opportunities for Crees to speak, paid little attention to Cree knowledge. These opportunities for the Crees to express themselves were largely staged as events for the media. 'As a result the main opposition to the project has been couched in Western "environmentalist" terms without the benefits of Cree concepts and perspectives' (Tanner 1999: 127). While Tanner's observation may be accurate in a broad survey of Cree interactions in the United States, I believe that the deeper analysis of these interactions in a locale such as Vermont suggests that the reality is more complex. In some ways the Crees contributed to this effect through their incorporation of the human rights and environmental discourses in what became a powerful strategy of forcing the reflection back on both the proponents of these discourses and the social structures that have been established to contain them. In using these tools the Crees may not have been as critical of them as they needed to deepen their support beyond what Tanner points out are superficial levels. However, at least in Vermont the Crees expanded their critique beyond this, pointing out some of the more visible contradictions in Vermont institutions and image. I do, however, agree with Tanner that the Vermont institutional opposition largely sidestepped the 'Cree voice', and allowed the Crees to express themselves, but then addressed their arguments within the social, economic and political structures at hand. Few were self-critical in this context.

In correlating localism with a localism at the service of modernization, Dirlik's thesis[15] also identifies the process of establishing rigid political forms (especially national borders), as opposed to the creation of 'more porous borderlands'. The Public Service Board's ruling that they remained bound by Vermont law not to consider any impacts of the contracts that could not be demonstrated within the borders of Vermont is an effective example of this. Less clear, but equally rigid, were other barriers established by many of the Vermont opponents of the contracts. For example, Ben, a Vermont businessperson and an ardent opponent of the Hydro-Quebec contracts, thought that the environmental and human rights arguments did not work as well as an economic argument.

> The issues were always couched as the cultural hippie environmentalists versus the industrial, profit-minded, chamber-of-commerce types. The environmental- ists were always marginalized. They were not speaking to the issues most people could listen to, understand and take action on. I wanted to make an economic argument – one that other businesses and most people could respond to because it affected their profits or costs. I took pains to divorce myself from the groups and work that were pursuing this issue based on the human rights side. (Cited in McRae 2001)

Ben spoke from what he articulated as a new discourse of business and capitalism – one that was based on and reinforced a sense of 'social re- sponsibility'. It also promoted and sustained a construction of localism that excluded the Cree narratives, as well as the 'local' discourses of environ- mentalism and human rights. In Dirlik's representation of the predicament of localism, he alludes to the evolution of capitalism towards what he terms 'Global Capitalism'. This is a process of the transnationalization of capitalism in production that is increasingly grounded in localities without concern for past distinctions (First/Third World), and management that by necessity emerges as supranational, leaving the nation-state in a position 'betwixt and between'. The disassociation embodied in the narrative that Ben proposed guided a significant portion of the Vermont opposition to the Hydro-Quebec contracts. It dismissed a connection to a local voice, and positioned his narrative alongside other competing but relatively homogeneous narratives of a global capitalism.

Localisms and connections, a yet-to-be-fulfilled potential

Gupta and Ferguson (1997), following Foucault, note that any discourse is simply a tactical component that operates in a field of relationships, and that multiple discourses can be hosted under a single strategy.

> Practices that are resistant to a particular strategy of power are thus never innocent of or outside power, for they are always capable of being tactically appropriated and redeployed within another strategy of power, always at risk of slipping from resistance against one strategy of power into complicity with another.

This slippage from resistance to complicity is illustrated by Dirlik (1997) in the expropriation of the radical ecological slogan 'Think Globally, Act Locally' by transnational corporations in a manner that makes them much better practitioners of it than any radical social force. The global thinking of transnational corporations requires them to think locally in a manner so as to incorporate localities into the service of global capitalism as specific but interconnected sites of production and consumption.

This, then, is the dilemma of linking resistance and protest movements of Indigenous and previously colonized peoples with groups of activists and social movements that have developed in the dominant Western cultures. Apffel-Marglin takes up this dilemma in what she lays out as the 'operative features of the path for decolonization' (Apffel-Marglin 1998: 236–7; see also Esteva and Prakash 1998). She indicates that most of the present social movements in the West are not presenting real alternatives to the current mainstream imperialistic social order there. The analysis of most environmental and social action groups does not run deep enough to denounce the 'aggressive nature of imperialism', or to move past simple verification of the symptoms of environmental degradation. For the most part, neither individuals nor groups in the West are willing to relinquish their privileged status and the material wealth associated with that in order to advance more harmonious relations with other peoples.

Apffel-Marglin does, however, indicate that there is an undercurrent of new social resistance movements in the privileged West that may be difficult at this time to identify clearly. It is being born of what she identifies as an increasing dissatisfaction – expressed as a failure of the trust of citizens in reason, a disenchantment with progress, a revulsion for continuing environmental degradation, and a rejection of the increasing pace of change for the sake of change (Apffel-Marglin 1998: 237).

The experience of the Crees in Vermont indicates that one way these new social movements emerge is through the links that develop between Indigenous resistance movements and groups and individuals who support them from their location in the dominant social orders. As part of the resulting actions, in seeking to change those dominant social orders their changing processes of control can become clearer. Where the actions of that resistance results in a focus on the local – not just the Indigenous local, but also the local of the supporters – new social forms are being created, people-to-people, organization-to-organization, and locality-to-locality. The Crees nurtured (and continue to nurture) those connections. The evolution of their requests in Vermont indicated a clear learning of how to develop and sustain those connections. Initial appeals focused on the broad and distant values of environmentalism and human rights. As the Crees interacted directly with Vermonters, they shifted into more direct connections and asked Vermonters to be more like Crees, reflecting on what should be shared values and concern for neighbours. Finally, as the Crees came to understand more about Vermont, and as Vermonters began to articulate their own values, history and vision, the message became one of Vermonters really needing just to build on the values and essence of what they believed they were.

The focus on the local, whether by Indigenous resistance movements or the mirrored reflection of a local support community, can, in Dirlik's (1997) words, sow the seeds of resistance. It is difficult to quantify the level of transformation that might have occurred on the local level as a result of this interaction and the continuing interactions between the Crees and other northern Indigenous communities throughout the rest of the decade. Have Vermont communities and citizens become more closely aligned with the values and identity that are associated with Vermont? Many of the citizen activists who participated in the campaign in Vermont have gone on to work on other local campaigns and to build links with other communities in shared struggle. While many individuals still speak of and point to the transformations that the campaign had in their individual lives, the question remains as to whether these changes extended themselves to change in communities and institutions that would influence future debates similar to Great Whale.

Three indicators might substantiate some institutional change. In the late 1990s Vermont passed a landmark campaign-finance reform bill to reduce the power of special interests and increase government's connectedness and accountability. In addition, the state created the nation's first energy-efficiency utility, putting responsibility for conservation in the hands of an entity that had no conflict of interest, with the sole purpose of decreasing the need for finding ever-increasing sources of outside power. Also of note have been the emergence and replication of various community visioning groups, and of networks of 'healthy community' initiatives, around the state that have brought citizens together to discuss the values that they hold in common, and to devise strategies to actualize them on a local level. While none of these developments grew directly out of the Great Whale Campaign in Vermont, the community level interactions certainly contributed to them.

The rapt attention of global capitalism to localities, as it consumes their cultures, can make the local aware of itself in relation to global capitalism, and presents the local as a site of possible resistance. These localities can be in James Bay or in Vermont. How those localities become aware of their potential as sites of resistance relates back to the activities embodied in the core of the Great Whale Campaign in Vermont – a campaign that has become a continuing story of journeys and exchanges. The strength and significance of future local resistance movements will be bound up with the nature and strength of future journeys and exchanges among as yet emerging networks of local movements.

Notes

1. The Grand Council of the Crees now maintains a website (www.gcc.ca) that includes current activities and some history of previous actions. They are much easier to reach than they were in the 1980s.
2. Chronicled in Williams 1985.
3. As in Schmink and Woods' (1992) extensive account based in Amazonia, or as is found in the documented work of organizations such as Cultural Survival (www.cs.org).
4. Coutin's study of the US sanctuary movement that provided support for Central American refugees fleeing political terror is a notable exception.
5. Jan Beyea, senior staff scientist of the National Audubon Society, *Burlington Free Press*, 29 January 1989. Also see Gedicks and Grossman in this volume.
6. George Sterzinger, Commissioner of the Public Service Department, in 'Cree Strike Out with Kunin', *Vanguard Press*, 5 April 1990, pp. 7, 22.
7. Burlington Mayor Peter Clavelle quoted in Burke 1990.
8. Quoted from Posluns 1993: 135.
9. Lew Milford, former director of the Conservation Law Foundation's Vermont office, opposed the contracts and outlined the magnitude of the deal in a conversation with me: 'We got a US$4 billion deal. That is staggering given the size of Vermont. Vermont is not as big as many cities in the US, and yet it was playing with terms and commitments that were way beyond its means. Vermont's debt to a foreign country, because we are obligated to the Quebec government that owns Hydro-Quebec, has us in a similar position to what many Third World countries face.' Personal interview, February 2000.
10. Some campaigners became directly involved in the push for campaign finance reform as a direct result of their experiences on this issue. A reform bill was passed in 1997.
11. See, for example, the activities and work of the Indigenous Environmental Network, Honour the Earth Foundation, Indigenous Women's Network, and the Seventh Generation Fund. For a review of North American Indigenous resistance and protest efforts in this vein, see also: Gedicks 1993; LaDuke 1999; Lewis 1995; Wadden 1996; Whaley and Bresette 1994.
12. Governor Richard Snelling, in his farewell address after four terms as governor in 1985, laid out the narrative of the fragmented but inseparable nature of Vermont's environment and economy that presents an ongoing predicament for Vermont policy-makers and citizens.

    > Indeed, we know that part of our economic strength has come from the recognition by others throughout the United States that the quality of life in Vermont will continue to be attractive and enjoyable for the foreseeable future.
    >   The record clearly shows that the economy of the State of Vermont and the economic circumstances of our people have been strengthened by our determination to develop our resources thoughtfully while maintaining vigilance in the protection of our environment. (10 January 1985; recorded in the *Journal of the Senate of the State of Vermont Biennial Session*)

13. Interview with former Vermont Environmental Agency head (McRae 2001).
14. Extracted from written testimony, 21 February 1991 (House 1991).
15. Dirlik (1997) identifies elements of what he sees as a post-modern consciousness that serve as enabling and producing conditions for a contemporary localism. In addition to the attributes cited above, also included would be 'the adjustment to nature against the urge to conquer it; heterogeneity over homogeneity; over determination against categorically defined subjectivities; ideology as culture, and culture as daily negotiation;

enlightenment as hegemony; Native sensibilities and spiritualities as a supplement to, if not a substitute for, reason; oral against written culture; and political movements as "politics of differences" and "politics of location"' (1997: 89).

References

Apffel-Marglin, Frédérique (ed.) (1998) *The Spirit of Regeneration: Andean Culture Confronting Western Notions of Development* (compiled with PRATEC), London: Zed Books.

Bryan, Frank, and John McClaughry (1989) *The Vermont Papers: Recreating Democracy on a Human Scale*, Post Mills, VT: Chelsea Green.

Burke, Don (1990) 'The southern campaign', *Macleans Magazine*, 21 May.

Burlington Press, 29 January 1989.

Coutin, Susan Bibler (1993) *The Culture of Protest: Religious Activism and the US Sanctuary Movement*, Boulder, CO: Westview Press.

Dirlik, Arif (1997) *The Post-colonial Aura: Third World Criticism in the Age of Global Capitalism*, Boulder, CO: Westview Press.

Esteva, Gustavo, and Madu Suri Prakash (1998) *Grassroots Post-modernism: Remaking the Soil of Cultures*, London: Zed Books.

Gedicks, Al (1993) *The New Resource Wars: Native and Environmental Struggles against Multinational Corporations*, Boston, MA: South End Press.

Gupta, Akhil, and James Ferguson (1997) 'Culture, power, place: ethnography at the end of an era', in Gupta and Ferguson (eds), *Culture, Power, Place: Explorations in Critical Anthropology*, Durham, NC: Duke University Press, pp. 1–32.

House, Larry (1991) 'Written testimony to Vermont Senate Committee on the Environment', copy provided by Cree Embassy, Ottawa, Ontario.

LaDuke, Winona (1999) *All Our Relations*, Boston: South End Press.

Lewis, David Rich (1995) 'Native Americans and the environment: a survey of twentieth-century issues', *American Indian Quarterly* 19, pp. 423–51.

McRae, Glenn (2001) 'Protest journeys: Vermont encounters in a campaign of translocal solidarity with the James Bay Crees', Ph.D. thesis, Anthropology Dept, Union Institute and University, Cincinnati.

Peirce, Neal R. (1976) *The New England States: People, Politics, and Power in the Six New England States*, New York: W.W. Norton.

Posluns, Michael (1993) *Voices from the Odeyak*, Toronto: NC Press.

Rabben, Linda (1998) *Unnatural Selection: The Yanomami, the Kayapo and the Onslaught of Civilization*, Seattle: Pluto Press.

Schmink, Marianne, and Charles H. Wood (1992) *Contested Frontiers in Amazonia*, New York: Columbia University Press.

Sherman, Joe (2000) *Fast Land on a Dirt Road*, South Royalton, VT: Chelsea Green.

Tanner, Adrian (1999) 'Culture, social change, and Cree opposition to the James Bay hydro-electric development', in James F. Hornig (ed.), *Social and Environmental Impacts of the James Bay Hydroelectric Project*, Montreal: McGill-Queen's University Press, pp. 121–40.

Vanguard Press (1990) 'Cree strike out with Kunin', 5 April, pp. 7, 22.

Wadden, Marie (1996) *Nitassinan: The Innu Struggle to Reclaim Their Homeland*, Vancouver: Douglas & McIntyre.

Whaley, Rick and Walt Bresette (1994) *Walleye Warriors: The Chippewa Treaty Rights Story*, Warner, NH: Writer's Publishing Cooperative.

Williams, Ted (1985) 'What Killed 10,000 Caribou?', *Audubon*, March, pp. 12–17.

8

'The People Had Discovered Their Own Approach to Life': Politicizing Development Discourse

WENDY RUSSELL

Wendy Russell is Assistant Professor at the Centre for International Studies at Huron University College in London, Ontario. Her current research is into the impact of neo-liberal economic policy on local economic practice in the Mushkegowuk community of Fort Albany.

In this chapter, I address what can be called the political economy of economic development in a northern Canadian Indigenous community. I have chosen the term 'political economy' to underscore the central place that economic, cultural and political interconnection has in local development analysis in the Fort Albany First Nation settlement, an Indigenous community on the west coast of James Bay in northern Ontario, Canada. Fort Albany's discourse on the problem of development is parallel to the critiques of development that are being made in a number of other national contexts, discussed below. These critiques have amply demonstrated the need for understanding Indigenous and local responses to economic development through local agency. Local initiatives are continuous with past forms of negotiation with colonial and national opponents, and are not merely momentary, reactionary developments to an immediate threat. These are, instead, acts of building consciousness that are thoroughly tied to the economic conditions through which people reproduce themselves and their society. Most important to my argument here is how the critique of development as global capitalist expansion can also be used to emphasize economic diversity as a condition of life for the economically marginalized, as I show below. I thus begin with a discussion of the necessity of a fully fledged political economy of economic development in Indigenous communities in northern Canada, and then present some of the development discourse from the 'development frontier' of Fort Albany, and how it deals with the problems of local agency, relationships with the nation-state, and the prospect of renewing local autonomy through economic development.

The Persistence of Small-scale Economies and Development Critique

Analysis of the political economy of economic development in the Canadian north consistently details the north's identity as a resource base for industrial economies in the south (Coates 1985; Coates and Powell 1989). Various studies of economic development and Indigenous communities in Canada document the effects of these boom-and-bust or resource extraction economies on the highly localized small-scale and subsistence economies of Native communities (Gagné 1994; Paine 1977; Rees 1988; Salisbury 1986). While these analyses show the political economy of Canada in international relations, and the subsequent marginalization of Indigenous peoples within the state, there are few reviews of local Indigenous responses to such economic development (Asch 1979; Brody 1988; Niezen 1998). This is especially remarkable given a diverse literature on community responses to development in those regions drawn into development as 'the undeveloped Third World'. This literature locates the failure of modernization projects in their biases to Western social forms (Boserup 1970) and the consequent invisibility of economic diversity (Escobar 1995; Ferguson 1990). Exploring the hegemony of growth-obsessed and market-oriented forms of capitalism, the literature critical of the hold modernization has over development thinking assumed that the livelihoods of much of the world have been left outside of development. Highly localized, small-scale and subsistence economies, despite successful articulations with capitalism (Lee 1992), are situated in opposition to capitalist development.

It is understandable, then, that 'struggle' is now a point of departure for analysing and understanding the situation of 'undeveloped' communities during the current era. Small-scale, subsistence or land based economies continue to be linked with capital, but in shifting contexts of wider trends to further capital mobility and pressures to dismantle national services and remove subsidies for the subsistence pursuits of the poor, economically marginal or geographically remote. The continuing crisis of development is not just capitalist advance into new territories, but the creation and re-creation of struggles of those at the new and shifting frontiers of capital to maintain their capacity to reproduce a normal social, economic and ecological context. Maria Mies and Veronika Bennholdt-Thomsen (1999) suggest the 'subsistence perspective' to express the specifics of the crisis facing these economies as they are conquered and dismantled by capitalist appropriation of labour and land, as well as a name for the struggles to maintain the priorities of the social/environmental webs that are the primary 'wealth' of these economies. June Nash similarly argues that the reproduction of small-scale economies is a struggle for survival under the ever-changing, expanding and contracting reach of capital (Nash 2001). Like Mies and Bennholdt-Thomsen, Nash conflates informal, domestic and non-market economic activity as 'subsistence', arguing that these economic forms are drawn together by the common threat capitalism poses to their security, but most especially by their common struggle 'to assert the right to live in a world with a diminishing subsistence base' (1994: 10). As portrayed in these works the struggles for self-determination and self-sufficiency are significantly linked, and it is this tie that I want to emphasize as a means to keep available the possibility of economic diversity.

This 'diversity' is discursively relegated to the margins of hegemonic capitalism when we identify it as 'non-capitalist', 'traditional' or 'pre-capitalist' (Gibson-Graham 1996: 6–7). Self-consciously to deny this marginality created by a particular construction of 'capitalism' moves subsistence and informal economies from the fringes and portrays them instead as belonging to the plural, unruly and ungovernable set of economic practices that make up 'capitalism'. Myriad economic forms, especially those that combine subsistence with market-oriented production, are thus not 'unconquered' or 'remnant' because they contain a traditional component. Thus we are not required to account for the unity of, for example, land-based pursuits and the cash sector in the overall economy, or mistakenly to portray subsistence pursuits as anachronistic fragments at the margins of an otherwise total capitalist economy. Gagné makes this error in an analysis of the economic engagement between the James Bay Crees and their Euro-Canadian partners, and interprets the land-based portion of their mixed economy as fulfilling basic needs resulting from their dependency on mainstream capitalism. She writes: 'The James Bay Cree are more fortunate than First Nations Citizens residing in urban areas, because they can supplement their employment income by hunting and trapping' (1994: 62). The primacy attributed to the cash sector here, and in effect one version of economic relations called 'capitalism', erases the persistence of Cree localizing economic, social and cultural practices. This local agency is seen to have dissipated under 'outside' threat, and local practices remain only as desperate attempts to survive the onslaught of forced economic change, and not as central to engagement in that conflict. These are, after all, conflicts that are regularly renewed as capital's interest in regions and territories and even neighbourhoods diminishes just as surely as it will again intensify.

Capital's new frontiers continue to be sites of engagement and negotiation. Newly (re)identified resource and development frontiers are thus always potentially sites of new visions of local autonomy in a globalized world.

J. Peter Brosius (1997) and Dan Jorgensen (1999) argue for Malaysia and New Guinea that the responses of the dispossessed to nationalist development projects are heterogeneous within regions, and are certain to include the manipulation of such projects to meet locally articulated goals. William H. Fisher (1994) argues that these goals need to be understood in part as gaining authority in national and international discourses through devices as diverse as nongovernmental organizations, international, regional and local structures. William F. Fisher, analysing the links between local, national and international action around the Sardar Sarovar dam in India, argues that heeding this flourishing 'civil society' shows 'the extent to which human beings can alter otherwise determinant structures [and] encourages us to consider unexpected possibilities' (1995: 40). Economic development in the global context is thus best understood as a context for specifically local action (Kean 2000), and one route through which local populations seek meaningful footing in the political and economic relations that connect a locality simultaneously to a region, to the nation-state, and to the international sphere.

The process of demanding authority within these interconnections often posits a local, territorially and historically grounded collective identity that explicitly contrasts with national identity and both the political and the economic practices of the state (Tsing 1993; Nash 1997; Watts 1999). Within such regional historical politics, assertions of collectivity can serve as the foundation of appeals for social change, as Gustavo Esteva (1999) argues for the post-democracy discourse of the Zapatistas. The growing global phenomenon of Indigenous and local resistance to poverty happens through movements for gaining real autonomy, and signals the necessity of a fully realized political economy of development. How does economic development pose not just a threat but a potential for gaining real authority in economic relations without necessarily resorting to the same economic forms pursued in national and industrial schemes?

The struggle that has been brought to life and reproduced through capitalist development for Indigenous communities in the Canadian north is common to the global Fourth World, especially in the recurring loss of land and livelihood to national progress. Indigenous communities in the north have seen their economies and territories decimated by national resource extraction economies, such as hydroelectric development and mining (RCAP 1996a: 467–91). National projects directed to Canada's 'remote' regions and underserviced Indigenous communities have served the same kinds of national 'development' goals as they have in the Third World, while the north has been a resource-rich or strategically important hinterland, much like the global Fourth World (LaDuke 1994: xiii). Militarization has had significant impacts in northern regions, as military bases near or in

Indigenous communities left behind varying levels of contamination; while these bases have been closed for decades they are only recently being investigated (Environmental Sciences Group 1999; Katapatuc and Associates 1999). And even in this context of national significance, social development for Indigenous northerners has been very similar in practical ways to that provided to the majority of the population in the Third World. In the Canadian case, as elsewhere in the world working within restricted development budgets, these very services have been chronically underfunded parallel to the earliest United Nations-sponsored development in the Third World (Kaufert et al. 1993; Milloy 1999; Sargent 1982). Indigenous communities in Canada have had their autonomy sacrificed to national projects such as modernizing health care and providing education.

In the Canadian north, national projects have supplanted *local* development processes. As the mainstream economy has prospered, the economies of Indigenous communities have been brought 'to the point of impoverishment' (RCAP 1996b: 777) by the interference of government through programmes and policies directed specifically to assimilating Indigenous people, while only superficial action was ever taken to strengthen their local economies. Development thus enters communities in the Canadian north as an institutionalized and apolitical response to problems that are disguised by its seemingly natural and mutual goals. The global localization of economies, or the liberation movements that are seeking local forms of economic stability and autonomy, all disclose the uneven benefits and unwanted consequences of development. It is one local analysis of the problems and promise of economic development that is the focus of this chapter.

The overriding interpretation in Fort Albany of Indigenous peoples' place in the Canadian north's economic history is that strategic government interference has combined with government neglect, thus eroding local social and economic autonomy. In this discourse, investment in infrastructure and public services was reserved for mid-northern Ontario urban centres while Fort Albany received economic development solely through the interventions of a state-sponsored religious mission. This differential access to economic improvements was a direct result of the village's identity as an Aboriginal community under federal policy. The federal government regularly fulfilled its obligations in treaty territories through various surrogates, most famously religious missions but also in federal hospitals, schools and police outposts, always at the expense of local autonomy. In local discourse, the practices of neglect and interference have steadily diminished the strength of the village's economy relative to its non-Native and urban neighbours. The net economic result of this history is that today the cash incomes of Fort Albany households form a stable income base whose spending benefits enterprises centred in the mid-north or elsewhere in the industrial south, even while the community is now tasked with performing economic development. The process of formulating economic development for the community under these conditions has required politicizing the very practice of development itself and of reflecting on the history of the conditions under which it occurs in Fort Albany. But beyond this political economy of economic development in the Canadian north, development planning in Fort Albany is a site of social action through imagining a different future in which the economic values and practices, social and cultural norms indigenous to the region can be renewed by gaining some power in regional economic relationships. As I describe below, economic development is both an inadequate model for pursuing community needs and a process that continues to generate models for analysis of the ongoing conflict over 'development'.

Fort Albany First Nation and Underdevelopment

Fort Albany First Nation is an Inninowuk[1] community located on the Albany River near its confluence with James Bay in northern Ontario. The settlement has a band-list population of over 1,200, and the settlement is home to around 800 people, the majority Cree speakers. Even a fairly straightforward history demonstrates some of the complexity of the settlement's place in history and within the wider region formed by that history. This passage marks how the settlement was carved out of a wider territory by federal administration more than two hundred years after the fur trade first brought Crees into relationships with Europeans:

> Families of the Fort Albany First Nation have lived on lands along the Albany River, its tributaries, and along the adjoining James Bay Coast for hundreds of years. The Fort Albany reserve was established in 1905, when some area families signed Treaty Number 9.
>
> The community is located about 120 kilometres north of Moosonee (or 580 km north of Timmins), 10 kilometres upstream from James Bay on the Albany River, in northeastern Ontario. Fort Albany is situated about 52 degrees latitude, and 81 degrees longitude. (Fort Albany Band Economic Development Office 1993)

Treaty 9 assigned a negligible segment of Cree territory to the official category 'Reserve', adding a layer of definition within a region that had been mapped and remapped in Cree use since before colonization, which began in this region in the 1680s with the fur trade.

The territory around the contemporary settlement of Fort Albany was part of a regional economy before the fur trade where Crees camped together, harvested and preserved food. In the immediate area of the present settlement people came to the lake on the mainland to harvest fish and berries, and spent some of the spring and fall in goose camps near the flats where the Albany River meets James Bay. The existing regional economy proved especially important to the Hudson's Bay Company, which depended on Cree people's skills to bring the region's resources into their trading post, while Crees adapted European goods to their own purposes. Crees integrated trapping, trading and labour at the post into the existing land-based economy. This mixed economy remained a regional economy because the trading post was only one point in Cree maps that included pathways for travel between harvesting areas and to other trading posts. The settlement was the location through which this region became part of an international (and later national) economy.

Roman Catholic missionaries to the Crees in the region around Fort Albany ended forty years of itinerant missions in 1892 when they set up permanent residence alongside the Hudson's Bay Company trading post. Like the traders, the missionaries participated in the mixed economy by hiring Cree families as seasonal labourers and harvesters, activities crucial to sustaining the practices of the mission. The difference between the trading post and the mission's settlement, however, was scale: the missionaries envisioned a town, and in 1903 created a 'new' settlement for Catholic Crees. The mission's settlement was the locus of Euro-Canadian attempts to control the economic, cultural and spiritual life of Cree people through its own economy, residential education and religious evangelism. But the mixed economy, Cree language and culture persisted. The Fort Albany settlement has developed through its role as one point on a larger map of cultural, economic, social and political links within the region, and between the region and international and national interests.

Local linkages continue to serve as a meaningful context for settlements throughout the north, as described in the *Final Report of the Royal Commission on Aboriginal Peoples*:

> The northern Aboriginal community is not just a collection of buildings. It extends beyond dwelling places to include land for fishing, gathering, visiting, trapping and hunting, and memorable places where important events occurred. Northern Aboriginal peoples' tenure in the settled communities of today is relatively recent; they have lived in more mobile, family-centred communities for centuries. In modern times, the attachment to the land and the strong sense of collectivity remains. (RCAP 1996c: 400)

Settlement does not imply a complete isolation from the region or loss of its specific values in Indigenous practice and imagination. Contemporary patterns of harvesting[2] in Fort Albany reflect this continuous relationship.

For participants in the mixed economy today, like their ancestors, the settlement is one part of a larger territory. Interconnection throughout the region today remains much as it has throughout the past three centuries for Crees, in that their own territorial uses are accomplished by the blend of technological innovations with detailed knowledge of the territory, both processes part of the heritage of Cree people here. But residents of the village also find interconnection the source of local subordination to mainstream, Euro-Canadian ideas, interests and economic practices.

The regional position of Fort Albany is both materially and socio-politically the role of an isolated outpost, an identity made real in various ways for residents pursuing a livelihood today: people frequently travel to mid-northern urban centres to shop, attend secondary and post-secondary school, or visit children attending high school. Every encounter village residents have with the mainstream economy is inflected by their isolation as well. The extremely high prices of basic goods in the village's Northern Store are attributed to costs added by shipping into a fly-in community. Getting cash, cashing cheques or depositing cheques into personal bank accounts are all complicated by the village's isolation from the nearest bank in Moosonee, and all of the solutions to the problem have costs attached, whether it is service charges for using point-of-purchase debit or (for people with bank accounts) the automatic teller machine. Cashing pay, personal and income-subsidy cheques at the Northern Store remains the only option for the large number of people who do not have bank accounts, to the store's benefit. An entire industry of expediters (enterprises which organize shipment of goods) and charter air services thrives in mid-northern towns and cities, facilitated by the spatial relations of this region. In official inside/outside relations members of the village are incorporated into federal and provincial policy through received social welfare, employment and education programmes at the same time that villagers' cash incomes derived from those programmes are leaked out of the local economy by the Northern Store providing basic food and goods.

In quantitative terms, roughly 75 per cent of household incomes are in cash; 25 per cent in land-based resources. Given existing economic forces throughout the region, these figures show that about 75 per cent of the value of Cree incomes ends up generating sustainability for businesses from outside of the community: the telephone company, the Northern Store and other suppliers of goods and services. The local economy fails to capture and build profit from cash exchanges. In comparison with the mainstream economy, Fort Albany's economy is simply 'underdeveloped', a condition that could just as easily be resolved through the provision of federal development aid. This aid brings with it the bundle of social, political and economic patterns that are embodied in the process of 'development', while it also constantly disguises the traditions of economic marginalization that make today's exploitation possible.

Arturo Escobar's post-development critique argues that engaging in development transforms the consciousness of those parties to be developed, inculcating a self-consciousness of underdevelopment simultaneous with the highly specific socio-economic practices that promise progress (Escobar 1995). Esteva argues that this process appropriates the agency of those to be developed, as this moment of engaging development 'converts participation into a manipulative trick to involve people in struggles for getting what the powerful want to impose on them' (1996: 8). These appropriations of consciousness and agency are precisely the dynamics that are contested in the local discourse about development that has emerged in Fort Albany, along with a vital commentary on the causes of Fort Albany's poverty today. Despite the substantiation of 'development' in the band's Economic Development Office, an institutional 'body' that enacts the typical development work of proposal writing and planning, the actual practice of these formalities generates a critique of development's goals and its ahistorical, apolitical assumptions, while pressing forward the vision of distinctive local forms of development made possible by everyday life in Fort Albany.

The Problem with Development

Formal discourse on development in Fort Albany emphasizes the community's position within social, political and economic relationships throughout the region and discloses their historical foundations. This link between current and historical dynamics evokes a comparison between colonial and 'development' strategies for interfering in Cree life, and posits local economic practice as distinct from both. Fort Albany's community development plan for 1995–96 opens with a clear articulation of a long-standing conflict between Indigenous and imposed economic forms:

> Families of the Fort Albany First Nation have pursued their ways and their livelihood on lands along the Albany River, its tributaries, and along the adjoining James Bay Coast for thousands and thousands of years. *The people had discovered their own approach to life* that was entirely different from and thus strange compared to the practices of the business-oriented Europeans. (Fort Albany Band Economic Development Office 1995: 4, emphasis added)

By equating the fur trade economy with 'business', this passage roots today's economic problems in colonial relations, indicating that both the economic exploitation of Fort Albany's cash incomes and the pressure to 'develop' are signs of deep conflict. 'Economic development' itself presents a crisis parallel to the crisis of economic underdevelopment, in that both are generated by an alien and inappropriate model of social and economic relations. The passage continues to argue that underdevelopment today has in fact been caused by economic development:

> In the 1600s, the area was reconditioned as a major trading post by the strangers from overseas and it was such a success, being in a strategic location, that even today the Northern Store still exists and still retains a profit. However at the end of the fur trade, nothing was left – animal life was depleted, people were lost, nothing had been gained for the people. No profits were received or shared, no infrastructure built or inherited, hence no progress for the people. (Fort Albany Band Economic Development Office 1995: 4)

As a commentary on development generally, this passage shows that the seemingly natural solutions presented by development serve to mask the causes of the condition of underdevelopment, here the very specific relations between inside and outside that still characterize the village's place in the mainstream economy. As an expression of community goals, the formal plan identifies the reality of the economic crisis facing Fort Albany (economic exploitation and marginalization) without acquiescing to the socio-economic norms of development, as 'the people had discovered their own approach to life'.

Within the fuller historical context provided in the planning document, the following account of the village's economic situation is explicitly a consequence, and not a neutral condition of 'underdevelopment':

> We are hindered in our quest for economic development in that the First Nation has no revenue/funds of its own and is totally dependent on government grants. They say we have no land except the reserve land, they say it is incumbent for the office to create wealth. Wealth is looked at in the sense that the community has more – more healthy people, more resources, more tools, more infrastructure, and in the end, more funds and revenue. As it is now, the First Nation has none of these and if they are available, then the machines, the tools, the buildings are outdated or substandard. (Fort Albany Band Economic Development Office 1995: 4)

The situation of the village today is thus an accumulation of past actions even while the village's capacity to gain some power in the mainstream economy steadily diminishes. Economic development in Fort Albany can only be achieved if the habits of exploitation and marginalization, past and present, are addressed. These passages from formal development discourse echo commonly articulated understandings of both the crisis facing Fort Albany today and its roots. I turn now to a discussion of the distinctions made between appropriate and inappropriate economic relations in everyday discourse.

Missionary Development

The distinction made between business-oriented and Cree socio-economic relations that is apparent in the document cited above is revealed even more sharply in daily life in Fort Albany. In common narratives of community history, people comment on the conflict between appropriate and inappropriate economic relations and how they have shaped the village. In this process of narration, a local knowledge of events at this place and the groups brought together here is reproduced across generations.

This local knowledge is often inscribed in the landscape, so that the territory and features of the settlement can act as reminders of specific patterns of relationships between identified groups of people, usually missionaries, and local people. In this way, the land and its features act as cues capable of evoking entire interpretive frameworks. And as Cruikshank (1998) and Santos-Granero (1998) demonstrate in comparable Indigenous territories, it is not only a primordial landscape, but also the changing, colonized landscape that is recorded by colonized peoples in such local narratives. In Fort Albany, most people know the sites that are relics of mission enterprise in the village, such as the barn, and the heap of broken concrete partially blocking a stream that flows through the village, which was the mission's hydroelectric dam. People know where the various buildings in the village have come from, and distinguish between those built with local materials, those scavenged from the derelict radar base, and prefabs supplied by the federal government through Indian Affairs. Commonplace narratives communicate a wide variety of themes central to community life, including disruptions in the use of the land base caused by building, patterns of exploitation of labour necessary to the mission's enterprise and social institutions (such as the radar base) which caused social disruption. Alongside this everyday knowledge, the location of the Old Post, where both Anglican and Roman Catholic missions functioned beside the Hudson's Bay Company, is the home of an annual Cree cultural gathering, during which the site is reanimated as a regional centre and not as a fur-trade or mission post. At this gathering, Cree people are made central to the history of the region, their presence predating and outlasting any other interest in the region.

These commonly known and understood sites all mark process and interconnection, each site used to represent the practical shape of the links among Indigenous people and between Cree people and the various visitors who have shared interest in this region. Though the mission's agricultural developments at the present village site have disappeared (most of the buildings have been torn down and the farm itself was converted to an airstrip), detailed stories about the functioning of the farm and local people's tenure as workers are commonplace, told in reference to or in the presence of specific sites.

The landscape of the village itself is used as corroboration in these narratives, as during interviews and conversations people would point out specific sites (such as the hydroelectric dam), or would use the large treeless area of the village as evidence of the enormity of the mission's economy, and as a symbol of the extent of Cree participation in that enterprise.

The last examples show that remembering the mission's enterprises is an interpretive act, often an act of highlighting specific qualities of the mission's relationship to local people, and most often a means of characterizing the mission's economy as inappropriate, as in the following circumstance. On a summer day in 1995 I noticed the boys' team of high-school students employed for the summer through the band economic development office working at the missionary residence under the direction of the two elderly Jesuit Brothers. Shortly after I met with one of my community advisers, and because our conversations had frequently turned to the mission's working arrangements in Fort Albany I asked about the project.

My adviser began his response by reminding me, as many had before, that between 1950 and 1952 Cree people had constructed the building in which we were sitting, the mission-run St Anne's Residential School, made from cement blocks manufactured on site. He then told me that the formula for cement devised by the mission from local materials was never shared with the workers, and thus was held back from the community as a whole. Since building materials for housing, town services and private household needs are rendered extremely expensive by shipping costs, this formula for cement represents a valuable innovation for the community as it pursues development today. My adviser's insistence that the formula for cement was held back echoes the report I quoted above that there was 'no progress for the people' in the economic relations dominated by outside interests at the settlement. This lack of 'progress' is further underscored in another commonly known account that when the mission finally gave up its control over village life in 1974, it sold the school and contents to the federal government for C$400,000. The school itself is used as a symbolic reminder of the hierarchical material and social relationship between local people and missionaries, through which the mission habitually appropriates Cree agency to its own purposes. On that day, the boys' work was being taken 'dishonestly', replicating old exploitations. The added element of the formula for cement, however, makes this exploitation symbolize the even more brutal sacrifice of the village's future for the simple economic benefit of a powerful, detached institution.

A related feature of narratives about the school is that the mission's workers on this and other projects were paid with rations and what is called 'mission money', an innovation through which Cree workers further subsidized the mission's prosperity. After its largest economic and territorial expansion in the 1930s, the Roman Catholic mission to Fort Albany began to mint this currency in order to hire Cree labourers to build and rebuild the mission's hospital, residential school and staff residences. The mission required labour to clear land, work on their farms[3] and provide food for the missionaries. For the mission, its initiative of hiring Cree workers converted subsistence hunter–gatherers into honest workers, leading them 'unconsciously' to 'civilization' through the discipline of labour. The transformation the mission sought on the economic front was comprehensive of gender and kin relations as well, and so their practices focused on wage-earning heads of nuclear families who would provide for their dependants. The mission sought to normalize this nuclear family by re-creating the capitalist division of labour among its workers, streaming men and women, boys and girls, into jobs considered gender-appropriate.[4] At the core of their enterprises, mission money was central to the project of repatterning Cree lives, and serves as a special symbol of the mission's project in local discourse. In particular, it is described as a way of isolating local people from the 'real' economy, as the money was only redeemable at the mission store.

Mission money is best known, however, for the lengths to which the mission went to have it destroyed when it was replaced in about 1965 by pensions and baby-bonus payments made in cash to individuals. Practically, this change spelled the end of the mission's settlement economy. Mission staff collected the money and had it dropped into the water at a northern river where it would be washed away in the spring break-up. This event is recounted as a clear attempt to conceal the existence of mission money because it was used to exploit workers for the benefit of the mission, and not the community. The secrecy attributed to the attempt to destroy the money has also elicited questions about the pact between the federal government and the mission through which the mission was partially funded, especially whether or not the mission channelled money intended for residents of the village to its own use through the mission money system. The refusal to comply with the concealment of the money represents a questioning of the appropriateness of the entire mission project among Cree people.

Symbols such as the residential school and mission money serve as interpretive frameworks for novel events, as expressed in the conversation cited above, and act as reminders of how economic exploitation remains rooted in the colonial relations of the past. Such narratives are acts of disclosing the social, cultural and political specificity of inappropriate economic relations, but they also reproduce and communicate the possibility that appropriate economic relations can be renewed. Rejecting the forms of exploitation that seem so particular to the cash economy does not imply an outright rejection of economic development, however, but instead emphasizes the need for a revolution in the inside/outside relationships that take place here every day.

To illustrate how locally appropriate forms of development anticipate this revolution, I now turn to a discussion of the appropriate forms of economic relations that are alive in the village every day, and how these are applied to the work of economic development.

Politicizing Development

In 1994 Fort Albany was included in the regional government's Entrepreneurship Training Program (ETP), a typical training programme designed, staffed and monitored by the regional development coordinator. The region's Band Economic Development Officers were responsible for coordinating the programme delivery within each community, finding participants and assisting the hired trainers with local logistics. Trainers provided classes five days a week and individual consulting on business plans in the afternoons and evenings. The course content covered a description of entrepreneurship, the demands on the entrepreneur, and training in the skills required to create a business proposal that would satisfy a granting agency or a bank manager reviewing a loan application.

The ETP was popular in Fort Albany, and attracted a fairly wide variety of male and female students with an equally varied set of proposals, from a bakery to a small, home-based retail business. In my interviews with part of this group in the wake of the formal programme, it was clear that the popularity of the programme was owed almost exclusively to a long tradition of entrepreneurship within the community. Entrepreneurship is a feature of community life in Fort Albany, and new entrepreneurship was made consistent with this tradition in this passage I recorded in 1994:

> It's something that I've always wanted to do, I've always wanted to run a business of my own. I used to admire my uncle, he used to run a business, I used to look at him and say, maybe that's what I want to do.... That's what gave me the idea. From him that's where I get to know that's what I want to do. More or less determined to do it, not to fall from grace, I don't want my business to go down, I always keep it going. (Anonymous 1994a)

The tradition of entrepreneurship in Fort Albany predates the formal development promise of small enterprise and owes its existence to the settlement's mixed economy. Blending subsistence pursuits with limited market-oriented production (of fur, fuel and food), the mixed economy is sustained today by the combination of harvesting, wage labour and formal income subsidies, much as it has been for three hundred years. Entrepreneurship represents another innovation consistent with the requirements of the mixed economy: it is small in scale, flexible, requires small investments and has always been combined with other pursuits in providing for the household. But the mixed economy continues to generate much more than 'incomes',[5] as it is a framework that reproduces crucial aspects of social and cultural life.

The mixed economy is a route through which individuals demonstrate their competence in necessary, highly valued skills, skills which individuals combine in the process of providing for their families. Traditional skills, those learned in family networks and which tie people to the resources of the land, are especially valued, and commonly remarked upon. And entrepreneurs demonstrate this pattern: the most established entrepreneurs in the village are also among those who have demonstrated their competence in traditional skills, as tanners, sewers and harvesters. One entrepreneur commented that 'keeping' these skills was among his accomplishments, as in another case during my research period a woman combined a cottage industry (based on exceptional sewing skills) with running a small business outside of the home to provide income for her extended family. Cottage industry based on producing and selling goods using traditional materials, methods and skills is well established in Fort Albany.

Individual competence is proven only in relation to collective interests, as it is in providing for household self-sufficiency that competence is achieved. Each household participates in the mutual obligation and support networks of an extended family, a collective that is made secure through sharing work, resources and tools. At the heart of these redistributive and reciprocal exchanges in Fort Albany is an ethic of 'sharing' that is recognizable in this speaker's opposition to accumulation in a manner that would deprive others of a similar status:

> If I was really into money, I guess I'd be open all day. But I try not to make big money. If I made a lot of money, I'd be living in a big mansion, in a new building, but I don't do that. I try to stay the way people are in Fort Albany. I'm not trying to be, like I'm better, whatever. I try to be the same, like other community members, the way they're living, so I don't have any high standards, no limos and all of that. That's what I believe in, I'm not really into that at all, being a big guy, I just opened it because the community, maybe they're bored with TV, that's the only reason why I opened this kind of business I guess. (Anonymous 1994a)

The practice of entrepreneurship as it has developed in Fort Albany is consistent with the fundamental values of the mixed economy. It was in fact this form of entrepreneurship that was the template for students who joined the ETP.

The gaps between the local and the ETP form of entrepreneurship are fairly obvious: collective versus individual orientations in economic relations, individual competence versus individual economic power, redistribution versus individual accumulation. However, it was not this dissonance between two systems that led to what I consider the failure of the ETP. The programme was, in fact, hijacked by community values, as participants proposed to develop businesses to support their families and that involved their available kin. Participants made proposals to provide improved and necessary community services (e.g. a translation service), and to undermine the power of the Northern Store in the village economy (by opening a hardware store that would compete with Northern's hardware department). In local interpretation, the ETP was made consistent with the traditional form of entrepreneurship in the community, and was thus grasped as an opportunity to address common grievances about economic exploitation, material poverty and the experience of underdevelopment.

The failure of the ETP can instead be attributed to the ahistorical analysis of the problems in the village economy. The ETP was justified by the most straightforward understanding of this economy as 'underdeveloped', defined conventionally through measures of income and employment levels, both figures demonstrating the failure of the local economy to provide for and integrate the entire local population. Income subsidies and unemployment levels are consequently high when evaluated against the assumed 'norm' of the mainstream capitalist urban economy. The remedy to this problem just as typically implies both a particular constellation of exchange relations and a specific set of social roles that must be fulfilled, most obviously in the ETP in the role of 'employed worker'. But the programme never took into account the decades of federal neglect of village infrastructure, which in 1994 meant that very few homes had running water, that there were too few buildings to accommodate even official services, and that there were too few houses for the village as a whole. The ETP's version of economic development, therefore, did not acknowledge either these realities or their historical basis. This failing was not lost on participants either, who were left with business plans but little hope that they could overcome the pre-existing constraints on their plans. The ETP provided small investments in individual villagers, but was not contained within a comprehensive plan for redressing the marginalization of the entire community. Such individual investments, like the missionary economy and income subsidies before them, signal the inadequacy of governmental response to the real needs of developing northern economies.

Even more generally, the ahistorical underpinnings of economic development schemes such as the ETP serve to perform a kind of violence to local knowledge by precluding a radically different kind of future. The assumption that Fort Albany's economy is simply an incomplete version of the mainstream economy, and not a unique economy in itself, assumes that the histories of places as different as Fort Albany and Timmins are similar enough to project a similar destiny. And it is the assumption that these communities have developed and *will* develop along similar courses that is most contested by local people, and that most obscures the 'causes' of Fort Albany's poverty today: Fort Albany, like Indigenous communities throughout the north, has not received the same supports and basic infrastructure development found in the larger urban and mainstream communities, the same places which draw on Fort Albany as a market. And so while 'economic development' is accepted as necessary to improve the future of the village, the current constellation of common sense, the hegemonic discourses of poverty and dependency, perpetuate thinking and practice at odds with Fort Albany's needs, and may even further undermine its interests. Each development or training project which receives mixed reviews within the community is potentially seen as a failure; without a context in which such failures can be interpreted as the result of inappropriate and misdirected development planning, the presupposition of local deficiency is confirmed and the proposed remedy is normalized. The validation of a local, historically grounded political economy of development is ruled out and the future that might be imagined in this thinking is unrecognizable.

Conclusion

The ETP served as an opportunity for community members to politicize the development process, just as the 'trainees' consistently demonstrated an acute awareness of the history of the weaknesses in the settlement economy today. Common understanding of the history of the settlement was pressed into service as an interpretive framework for the ETP, just as economic development is interpreted locally in terms of the appropriate economic relations that are alive in daily life in the village. The reality of a collective as the basic unit of economic exchanges in village life was reproduced through trainees' plans to assist their own extended families and to reorient the entire settlement's relationship to the mainstream economy. The ETP promoted investment in individuals, rather than in this collective, bound by social and kin networks, and by their shared history in this region. The collective goals of development expressed by entrepreneurs are echoed in this passage from the formal development plan for 1995–96:

> The underlying philosophy of including everyone in our actions and activities was developed and refined by our elders thousands and thousands of years ago. We call the system the 'wholistic[6] approach'.... The wholistic approach preaches inclusion of all people in all actions and in all activities. No one is to be left behind. This is the aim of the Band Development Office – to provide equal and fair opportunities for everyone to help him/herself. (Fort Albany Band Economic Development Office 1995)

Reimagined within the daily life of the village, development can be faithful to the values of the mixed economy in which individuals are given the opportunity to demonstrate their competence. This is not a concession to individualism, but an expression of the core of collectivity that is ideally generated in the practices of the mixed economy.

As a 'development frontier', Fort Albany is a rich social, political and historical context in which economic development has been reinvented as the process of investing economic relations with the collective goals of renewing local autonomy on the community's own terms. As a locally specific political economy of development, Fort Albany's discourse provides new critiques of development's apolitical and ahistorical foundations. This local analysis thus finds that the real limitations to economic development are rooted in the old habits of exploitation and marginalization. Fort Albany's discourse on development is an appeal for change in the inside–outside relations that normalize these habits, and thus seeks change through participation in civil society. Local elements of this civil society are emerging in the social agencies, such as the Band Economic Development Office, within which local priorities are consolidated and communicated to other agencies, regional and national. It is such formal elements of social life, along with informal structures of community, kin group and family, through which change will be made. Such community-based development proposes a new era of cooperation among Indigenous communities in the region and between Fort Albany and those partners in the local economy that have grown accustomed to having access to the village's incomes. For people from Fort Albany, negotiating this cooperation will be continuous with three centuries of engagement with 'outside' interests, an engagement that has only relatively recently seen a drastic decline in their local economic authority.

Notes

1. Also known in anthropological literature as Swampy Cree, and in some local and regional usage as Omushkego. The term 'Cree' was in common usage in the region during my field research, and I use it here in that manner to refer to the descendants of the earliest inhabitants of the region.
2. I use the term 'harvesting' throughout to refer to all activities that make land-based resources available for consumption by individuals, family groups and communities. 'Harvesting' thus includes subsistence hunting, trapping, fishing and gathering.
3. Children worked as farm labour as well in the residential school, which was partially funded by the federal government from 1905 to 1974.
4. Neither extended families nor the Cree division of labour submitted to the European division of labour, however, as both patterns are maintained in village life today.
5. The mixed economy is vital to the reproduction of people's relationships to one another and to the region, as harvesting is made possible by access to cash incomes with which necessary equipment is purchased.

6. This is a neologism that the author of this document, Alex Metatawabin, uses to emphasize the role of completeness in community action, associating this word with the English word 'whole'.

References

Anonymous (1994a) Personal communication.

———— (1994b) Personal communication.

Asch, Michael I. (1979) 'The economics of Dene self-determination', in David H. Turner and Gavin Smith (eds), *Challenging Anthropology: A Critical Introduction to Social and Cultural Anthropology*, Toronto: McGraw-Hill Ryerson, pp. 339–51.

Brody, Hugh (1988) *Maps and Dreams: Indians and the British Columbia Frontier*, Vancouver: Douglas & McIntyre.

Brosius, J. Peter (1997) 'Prior transcripts, divergent paths: Resistance and acquiescence to logging in Sarawak, East Malaysia', *Society for Comparative Study of Society and History*, vol. 39, no. 1, pp. 468–509.

Boserup, Ester (1970) *Women's Role in Economic Development*, New York: St Martin's Press.

Coates, Kenneth (1985) *Canada's Colonies: A History of the Yukon and Northwest Territories*, Toronto: Lorimer.

———— and Judith Powell (1989) *The Modern North: People, Politics and the Rejection of Colonialism*, Toronto: Lorimer.

Cruikshank, Julie (1998) *The Social Life of Stories: Narrative and Knowledge in the Yukon Territory*, Lincoln, NE: University of Nebraska Press.

Dove, Michael (1986) 'Peasant versus government perception and use of the environment: a case-study of Banjarese ecology and river basin development in South Kalimantan', *Journal of Southeast Asian Studies*, vol. 17, no. 1, pp. 113–36.

Environmental Sciences Group (1999) 'Environmental assessment plan for 15 mid-Canada radar sites in Ontario', Kingston Ontario: Royal Military College Environmental Sciences Group.

Escobar, Arturo (1995) *Encountering Development: The Making and Unmaking of the Third World*, Princeton, NJ: Princeton University Press.

Esteva, Gustavo (1996) 'Development', in Wolfgang Sachs (ed.), *The Development Dictionary*, London: Zed Books, pp. 6–25.

———— (1999) 'The Zapatistas and people's power', *Capital and Class* 68, Summer, pp. 153–82.

Ferguson, James (1990) *The Anti-Politics Machine: Development, Depoliticization, and Bureaucratic Power in Lesotho*, Cambridge: Cambridge University Press.

Fisher, William F. (1995) *Toward Sustainable Development: Struggling over India's Narmada River*, New York: M.E. Sharpe.

Fisher, William H. (1994) 'Megadevelopment, environmentalism, and resistance: the institutional context of Kayapó Indigenous politics in Central Brazil', *Human Organization*, vol. 53, no. 3, pp. 220–32.

Fort Albany Band Economic Development Office (1993) 'Community Economic Development Operational Plan 1993–94', Chris Metatawabin, Band Economic Development Officer, unpublished report, Fort Albany, Ontario (in possession of the author).

———— (1995) 'Community Economic Development Operational Plan 1995–1996', unpublished report, Fort Albany Ontario (in possession of the author).

Gagné, Marie-Anik (1994) *A Nation within a Nation: Dependency and the Cree*, Montreal: Black Rose Books.

Gibson-Graham, J.K. (1996) *The End of Capitalism as We Knew It: A Feminist Critique of Political Economy*, Cambridge, MA: Blackwell.

Isbister, John (1998) *Promises Not Kept: The Betrayal of Social Change in the Third World, Fourth Edition*. West Hartford, CT: Kumarian Press.

Jorgensen, Dan (1999) 'The conquest of Nena: property, identity and the politics of mining in Papua New Guinea', paper read at the Annual Meeting of the American Ethnological Society, March 1999, Portland, Oregon.

Katapatuc and Associates (1999) 'Remediation of site 050 of the Mid-Canada Radar Line: identifying potential sites of concern utilizing T.E.K.', Moose Factory, Ontario: Katapatuc and Associates.

Kaufert, Patricia A. and John O'Neil (1993) 'Analysis of a dialogue on risks in childbirth: clinicians, epidemiologists, and Inuit women', in Shirley Lindenbaum and Margaret Locke (eds), *Knowledge, Power and Practice: The Anthropology of Medicine and Everyday Life*, Berkeley: University of California Press, pp. 32–54.

Kean, Peter (2000) 'Economic development in the Siki settlement scheme, West New Britain', *Critique of Anthropology*, vol. 20, no. 2, pp. 153–72.

Kelm, Mary Ellen (1998) *Colonizing Bodies: Aboriginal Health and Healing in British Colombia, 1900–50*, Vancouver: University of British Columbia Press.

LaDuke, Winona (1994) 'Foreword', in Al Gedicks, *The New Resource Wars: Native and Environmental Struggles against Multinational Corporations*, Montreal: Black Rose Books.

Lee, Richard B. (1992) 'Art, science or politics? The crisis in hunter–gatherer studies', *American Anthropologist*, vol. 94, no. 1, pp. 31–54.

Milloy, John (1999) *A National Crime: The Canadian Government and the Residential School System 1879–1986*, Winnipeg: University of Manitoba Press.

Mies, Maria and Veronika Bennholdt-Thomsen (1999) *The Subsistence Perspective: Beyond the Globalized Economy*, London: Zed Books.

Nash, June C. (1994) 'Global integration and subsistence insecurity', *American Anthropologist*, vol. 96, no. 2, pp. 1–31.

—— (1997) 'The fiesta of the word: The Zapatista uprising and radical democracy in Mexico', *American Anthropologist*, vol. 99, no. 2, pp. 261–74.

—— (2001) *Mayan Visions: The Quest for Autonomy in an Age of Globalization*, New York: Routledge.

Niezen, Ronald (1998) *Defending the Land: Sovereignty and Forest Life in James Bay Cree Society*, Boston: Allyn & Bacon.

Paine, Robert (ed.) (1977) *The White Arctic: Anthropological Essays on Tutelage and Ethnicity*, St John's, Newfoundland: Institute of Social and Economic Research, Memorial University.

Rees, William E. (1988) 'Stable community development in the north: properties and requirements (an econo-ecological approach), in Gurston Dacks and Ken Coates (eds), *Northern Communities: The Prospects for Empowerment*, Occasional Publication Number 25, publication of the Boreal Institute for Northern Studies, pp. 59–75.

RCAP (Royal Commission on Aboriginal Peoples) (1996a) 'Looking forward, looking back', *Final Report of the Royal Commission on Aboriginal Peoples*, vol. 1, Ottawa: Canada Communication Group.

—— (1996b) 'Restructuring the relationship', *Final Report of the Royal Commission on Aboriginal Peoples*, vol. 2, Ottawa: Canada Communication Group.

—— (1996c) 'Perspectives and realities', *Final Report of the Royal Commission on Aboriginal Peoples*, vol. 4, Ottawa: Canada Communication Group.

Salisbury, Richard (1986) *A Homeland for the Cree: Regional Development in James Bay 1971–1981*, Kingston, ON: McGill-Queens University Press.

Santos-Granero, Fernando (1998) 'Writing history in the landscape: space, myth and ritual in contemporary Amazonia', *American Ethnologist*, vol. 25, no. 2, pp. 128–48.

Sargent, Carolyn (1982) *The Cultural Context for Therapeutic Choice: Obstetrical Care Decisions among the Bariba of Benin*, Boston, MA: Kluwer.

Tsing, Anna Lowenhaupt (1993) *In the Realm of the Diamond Queen: Marginality in an Out-of-the-Way Place*, Princeton, NJ: Princeton University Press.

Watts, Michael John (1999) 'Collective wish images: geographical imaginaries and crisis of national development', in Doreen Massey, John Allen and Philip Sarre (eds), *Human Geography Today*, Cambridge: Polity Press.

PART II

Strategies:
States, Markets and Civil Society

9

Survival in the Context of Mega-Resource Development: Experiences of the James Bay Crees and the First Nations of Canada

MATTHEW COON COME

Matthew Coon Come was the National Chief of the Assembly of First Nations of Canada, the organization that represents 'Indian' peoples of Canada, from 2000 to 2003. Matthew entered politics, becoming the Chief of Mistissini from 1981 to 1986. From 1987 to 1999 he was the Grand Chief of the Grand Council of the Crees.

I want to begin with a story. I remember my mother taking me in 1995 to a place where my grandmother had stood (my grandmother was 94 years old then):

> This is where Gookam [Grandma] stood, and I'll remind you of what she said. As she looked to the lake she said: 'One of these days they will come and they will block our rivers. They will make them flow backwards.' Then she looked to the mountains, and she said, 'I see something eating the trees.' And then she said, 'Even the very water that you drink, someday you will have to pay for it.'

I have seen that vision come to pass. I have stood where the big dams have been built. I have seen where the rivers have been made to flow backwards. And every spring I am told in Mistissini that I cannot drink that water because it is contaminated, and I have to pay so that I can drink water. So what my grandmother and her generation have prophesied is true, because they are one with the land.

My people identify themselves with the land as hunters, as fishermen and as trappers. I am talking about my father, who never went to school. I am talking about my grandfather, who is 103 years old and is still out on that land. It's not in a museum, it's not in a textbook. Our people and their way of life are still thriving; they are flourishing. We have learned to live with the animals. We have maintained some of our traditions and customs, but we have survived because we have adapted. A fancy word used by anthropologists is that we have 'acculturated'. I am very familiar with some of their work, because I am one of the Crees who really read some of the meticulous research that they have done.

We have survived because we have adapted. When I went with my dad there were no snowmobiles, there were no airplanes. We walked on the land with snowshoes. We paddled up there. Now when I go, I use a snowmobile to go out on the land. It is easier, it is faster, we adapt. That is how we have survived, and we call our land 'Eeyou Istchee' (the people's land). We have governed and occupied this land and have managed the resources so as to allow us to continue that Cree way of life.

When the Europeans came to our land, we saw that they arrived in boats. These boats were made of curiously carved and shaped wood and so, to this day, we call them 'Wemistigoosheeyiw' (the shaped-wood people). You have heard of a wooden Indian? Well, we called them something like that first.

We had no idea that they had come because a king across the sea had scratched on a piece of paper saying that he 'gave' our lands to his cousin Prince Rupert. Similarly, in 1873 when the same lands, our lands, were ceded to Canada by the Hudson's Bay Company, this was not of significance to us. We were not asked or told, and we continued to live as usual. Once again in 1898 and 1912, when our lands were transferred by Canada to the Province of Quebec, we did not know about this. We continued to pursue our way of life, and also we fed and clothed the small number of Wemistigoosheeyiwits who were living among us.

In a way, we developed along with the Europeans in a symbiotic if not always mutually beneficial relationship, which continued until the middle of the last century. When the Europeans first contacted our society it was primarily for trade purposes. For more than three hundred years of our relationship, the Crees continued to occupy the land as we had always done. This is how it was through centuries of colonial dealings with our lands.

In the 1950s certain government services began to be available to the Crees, including some limited health services, some educational opportunities, and monthly old-age pensions, which led to increasing settlement of the Crees around the former trading posts. Until that time our society had been organized around the extended family unit and the *ouchimau*, or family head. It was also at this time that this leadership was supplemented, and somewhat replaced, by a system of government based on chiefs and band councils that the Canadian government encouraged us to adopt. I can tell you stories about how we used to mock that, because it was foreign to us.

By the late 1960s and early 1970s our lands were increasingly targeted by forestry and mining companies and Hydro-Quebec, the provincial electricity utility. At first forestry and mining provided supplementary income to some Crees who combined subsistence hunting with part-time employment in forestry or sometimes in mining and mining exploration. However, these activities also led to increased social tensions on the territory as the people who were the original inhabitants were increasingly treated as squatters in their own lands.

Our communities of Nemaska, Waswanipi and Ouje-Bougoumou are prime examples of this. All these communities were closed as a result of so-called development activities. Those Crees seeking to participate in the wage economy built shack towns on the outskirts of the company communities that grew up around these development activities. The community of Ouje-Bougoumou, for example, while it tried to stay together, was relocated many times to accommodate the wishes of the developers. Gradually it disintegrated into approximately five settlements, mostly groupings of shacks along the sides of the roads.

In 1972 I was a young student in Hull, and I read in the newspaper one day about Quebec's 'hydroelectric project of the century'. I looked at a map and saw that my community's lands at Mistissini were to be submerged because they were going to use Lake Mistissini as a reservoir. It was then that our people realized that the plans of Hydro-Quebec to dam and divert more than a dozen rivers in our territory would spell an end to our way of life. For the Cree people, the land is part of us. My people still live off the land. We are sustained by what it provides; I guess we can say that we are the land.

Eeyou Istchee, although it is vast, is a familiar place to us. Every bend in the river is known and named. A Cree map of our vast lands is crowded with place names. The footsteps of my people are everywhere. When I go with my dad to the hunting ground, he tells me, 'That's where grandpa killed his first moose. That's where we buried someone. That's where there was a lot of game. That's where the fish spawning grounds are.' We do not have to move a hundred yards and he has a story to tell.

A Cree person is not an adult until he or she is familiar with life on the land. From infancy we are taught to respect the land and to take only what we need. We have a traditional system of family territories where we manage the resources, rotating our use from one year to the next, to allow the resources to replenish. This has been our practice for several millennia.

Then a 400-mile road was built, and next, at Matahonansheesh (the spring gathering place), they began construction of the LG-2 dam, a massive twenty-storey dam to block the La Grande River. We reacted by going to court. After six months of testimony, we won an injunction. This was a historic ruling: the court affirmed that my people had certain 'undefined' rights to our lands. But when a city wants to build a new airport or highway, does it declare that the rights of those who live there are 'undefined'? It appears that only Aboriginal peoples who have lived in a place since time immemorial get this dubious honour.

The court's injunction did not last. Three judges of the Quebec Court of Appeals disposed of our rights in less than six hours of deliberations: first suspending the ruling recognizing some rights, and then later ruling that we were squatters in our own lands. The judges said our rights in and to our lands had all been extinguished, because in 1670 King Charles II had 'given' the Hudson's Bay watershed to his cousin Prince Rupert and the Hudson's Bay Company.

Now, as the Quebec government proceeded with its plans to dam and divert the La Grande, Eastmain, Caniapiscau, Little Whale, Boutin, Great Whale, Coates, Nottaway, Broadback, and Rupert rivers, we were finally aware of the significance of what had been going on all those years after 1670 when King Charles had signed that piece of parchment far away in England. How on earth could this be, we wondered. We have always been here. We were put here as a people by the Creator, to live in and take care of this land.

This is the law of the country, our leaders were told. Your territory was *terra nullius*, or land belonging to no one, when King Charles made his grant in 1670. Your society has no concept of ownership or jurisdiction over land. And so, according to our laws, your rights were extinguished, and Rupert's land became Crown land (government land).

We knew that the La Grande Project, which was already under way, would be complete before our case could be heard at the Supreme Court, and that it was also possible that we would not get a favourable ruling. So we decided to negotiate an agreement. Canada refused to intervene on our behalf, and Hydro-Quebec held a gun to our heads – the destruction of our lands and rivers continued daily while we negotiated. Thus it was that on 11 November 1975 we signed the James Bay and Northern Quebec Agreement (JBNQA).

Cree hunters on their hunting territories could see the power of the 'Whitemen', as we call non-Aboriginal people in English. They were moving whole mountains and turning a whole river around so it would flow away from the sea and down another river. This we knew we could not stop. So my people put their hopes in the new relationship we were promised: in return for permitting one project, we were promised health care, education and other benefits, and protection for our hunting, fishing and trapping way of life.

Over the last nearly thirty years since signing the JBNQA we have learned the many ways that this was not a good agreement. We have been in and out of courts since 1975 to get the governments to implement it. They still refuse and delay, and many of the benefits we were promised have failed to materialize. These benefits are things that all who live in Canada enjoy as a right. My people had to bargain for clean water supplies and sanitation, for clinics and schools, for our rights and our way of life.

There is something fundamentally wrong that needs to be identified here. At the same time that these negotiations concerning the JBNQA were taking place, Canada had signed and was participating in the development of the International Covenant on Civil and Political Rights and the International Covenant on Social, Economic and Cultural Rights at the United Nations. Article 1 of both of these covenants provides that: 'Under no circumstances shall a people be deprived of its own means of subsistence.' Yet this is precisely what had just been done to us, as the waters of the La Grande hydroelectric mega-project rose around us and flooded our ancestors' graves. I believe that the governments knew then what they were doing: depriving the Cree people of our own means of subsistence in violation of our fundamental human rights.

The evidence is in the JBNQA itself, and in its implementation. In the agreement the simple promise was made: in response to this damage to your lands, your economy, and your way of life, we will ensure that we assist your people. We will assist you in the transformation you will undergo. We will ensure that the opportunities for your hunters are maintained and enhanced. We will ensure that your people get trained to be involved in new activities and economic development and that, when they are trained, they will gain employment. We will ensure that your communities are serviced, have infrastructure, and are viable. Sadly, while we have received some benefits, many of these promises in the agreement have never materialized. It is an ongoing battle, in the courts, in the court of public opinion, and around the table with the governments, to try to get them to live up to their obligations.

Hydro development has not provided long-term opportunity for Cree employment. The La Grande Project currently has approximately 750 permanent employees. For the most part these employees are flown in from southern Quebec on shifts that last a couple of weeks at a time. The number of Cree employees hired by Hydro-Quebec has never been more than five people, or less than 1 per cent of those employed at any one time. While the Crees managed to get some employment during the construction phase of these projects, during the operations phase there has been very little access to employment. Can you imagine a company from Ontario building a large hydro project in front of Quebec City, flooding the Old City and the Plains of Abraham, and then not even hiring any of the local people? Can you imagine such an employer not even putting in place programmes to bring local workers into full-time employment? This is our situation.

The La Grande experience, a nightmare for us, has taught us a great deal. The project flooded natural habitats over an area more than half the size of the state of Vermont. The water in the reservoirs is managed on an unnatural cycle, which builds up the reservoir's water levels from spring until winter, only to release it through the dams in the coldest months, when the electrical heating demand in southern Quebec is the greatest.

We have realized that programmes to build hunters' campsites beside the reservoirs are not worthwhile, because the animals do not live there. One hunter discovered a beaver lodge twenty feet high on the edge of a reservoir. The beavers had kept building higher to keep ahead of the rising water all summer. When the winter came, the water was drawn down and the beavers froze. We have discovered that the boat access ramps are useless in areas where the trees are left standing underwater, because the trees block boat access to the shore. Furthermore, the fish are highly contaminated by mercury leaching out of the rotting vegetation; if we eat the fish, one of our staples, we get methylmercury poisoning. We have discovered that beaver and lynx relocated by helicopter from the areas to be flooded very often die from the shock of the move. We have discovered that the engineers' promises that they could manage the flows appropriately were untrue, when 10,000 caribou drowned trying to follow their traditional migration paths.

We have discovered that people who have lost their family lands are at great risk of losing their traditions and values. The activities and knowledge that bind a family become a painful memory when the land is gone. We have discovered that our way of life, our economy, our relationship to the land, our system of knowledge, and our manner of governance are an interlinked whole. Remove us from the land, and you destroy it all. We are then left with social disruption, suicide, epidemics of disease and violence, and loss of hope.

So, reluctantly, we have also learned to fight, peacefully. In 1989, Hydro-Quebec announced that it would proceed with C$62 billion worth of further hydro mega-projects, including James Bay Phase II on the Great Whale River. We decided, at a general assembly of my people, to oppose these new projects. We could see, after fifteen years of experience with the first phase of the James Bay Project, that it would not benefit our people.

We are only 13,000 people, so we decided to take our story of the impacts of these projects upon us to the Canadian and American peoples. We took two messages. First, in spite of a provision in the JBNQA that says we may not oppose future hydro projects on sociological grounds in official hearings, we helped the people who had already lost their lands to tell the media and the wider public of the social and environmental impacts.

Second, we were also sure that there were other ways to make energy that did not entail destruction of the land. So we also talked about the alternatives in energy conservation, wind energy and co-generation projects. We undertook studies about the effect of electricity subsidies for the aluminum and magnesium industries in Quebec on the rates ordinary consumers pay for their electricity. We researched the impacts on future electricity rates of building these projects and of the impacts in US states buying the energy. We studied and publicized co-generation and conservation potentials. We participated in formal hearings on the export contracts in Canada and in Vermont, New York and Massachusetts and intervened before international tribunals in Europe.

We Crees became the environmental and economic conscience that the Quebec government did not have. Hydro-Quebec and the government of Quebec led a media campaign against us. When we said that cheaper alternatives were available, that the impacts on the land were catastrophic, they accused us of spreading lies, of leading a smear campaign. When in 1990 the president of Hydro-Quebec stated that Quebeckers could run short of electricity if there were delays for environmental review, nobody questioned the accuracy of his statements except the Crees. The Quebec minister of energy actually warned Quebeckers they would freeze by candlelight if the Great Whale Project was delayed. Just one or two years later, all jurisdictions in the northeastern part of North America had huge energy surpluses.

As a result of our campaign in the United States and Europe, through our legal efforts in the courts, and through our participation in the first phases of the environmental assessment of the Great Whale Project, it became clear that the project was not viable, and it was abandoned by Quebec premier, Jacques Parizeau, in November 1994. So the threat of the Great Whale Project was removed from over my people's heads. The rivers of the Great Whale watershed still flow free and towards the sea.

Now a few years have passed since the project was cancelled, our people can now see that little or nothing has changed. Our rate of unemployment continues to rise, and our housing shortage remains acute. The land and wildlife continue to be degraded around us, as multinational forestry corporations clear-cut the boreal forests around our communities. The permits for this destruction were issued by the government of Quebec in the late 1980s and early 1990s in contravention of many of the provisions of the JBNQA. And yet the cutting continues, and the federal government stands by and is silent or conspires with Quebec to permit the destruction. Many of the laws and the provisions of the agreement relating to environmental protection continue to be ignored.

Our treaty is often referred to as the first modern land-claims agreement in Canada. It is very long and very detailed, but we are learning that it is actually not very new. It is true that since we entered into our agreement with Canada and Quebec, things have improved socially for the James Bay

Crees. We have obtained schools, clinics, local administrations, and certain programmes and services. But these are things that all other peoples in Canada take for granted. The reality is that our treaty is built on the same structure as all the treaties that went before it. Its foundation is the extinguishing of our Aboriginal rights. Consider this: on the one hand, Aboriginal rights are now guaranteed and affirmed in the Constitution of Canada. At the same time, the federal government still insists, as a condition of reaching agreements with Aboriginal peoples, that these rights be extinguished or given up. This is not consistent with any civilized view of fundamental rights. Our experience with the implementation of our treaty is that, while the governments now insist that we deliver to them all our obligations with respect to the land and to the extinguishing of our Aboriginal rights, at the same time they twist the meaning of their obligations and minimize or deny the promises they made to us.

It is thirty years since the hydroelectric mega-projects came to our lands. At the beginning, and for the fifty previous years, it was very much the case that we Crees were 'in the way' of development. Various means were used to get us out of the way, such as forced relocation, treating us as squatters, and flooding and clear-cutting. The legal techniques that have been applied against us when we have been 'in the way' of development are actually more diabolical than the flooding and relocation. These are the doctrines of extinguishment and *terra nullius*. One does not have to be an Aboriginal person to understand that any dispossession of our legal status and fundamental rights is a root cause of our ongoing social disadvantage and underdevelopment.

The link between the denial of our fundamental rights and our political and economic exclusion is not abstract. Taking our lands and resources has resulted in mass dislocation and the involuntary resettlement of hundreds of thousands of First Nations people ('First Nations' is a general term that many 'Indian' Aboriginal peoples of Canada use to refer to themselves). It has resulted in great damage to the social and economic fabric of our communities and societies. It has also resulted, as in the case of the Crees, in the removal of billions of dollars of resources from our lands each year, while we are forced to seek annual handouts to govern and administer our communities.

Thankfully, the news is not all bad. Our people and our societies have been patient and resilient in the face of these policies and practices of dispossession and discrimination. Our people's identities, economies and ways of life have survived, and our societies are developing in important ways. All the credit is due to the courage and spirit of our elders and our women and our youth.

However, as pointed out by the Royal Commission on Aboriginal Peoples (RCAP), Aboriginal peoples remain at the top of the scale on all indexes of social distress in Canada. In our Cree communities in James Bay, for example, our people face a critical shortage of housing. We live in seriously overcrowded conditions, with the result that there are outbreaks of infectious disease. The ability of our young people to form new families is being hindered. Many of our communities still lack adequate sanitation, safe water and other essential infrastructure.

We Crees are aware that many other Aboriginal peoples in Canada are in worse shape than we are. Both levels of government frequently point this out to us when we attempt to get them to implement their treaty and other obligations to us. But we are not willing to permit comparisons to the lowest denominator. Rather, we believe that the correct approach is to compare our socioeconomic and other conditions with those of *non-Aboriginal* communities. When these objective comparisons are made, there is considerable socio-economic work to be done.

For the first time in Canadian history, a concerted exercise was recently undertaken by the Royal Commission on Aboriginal Peoples to examine relations with Aboriginal peoples within Canada. The Royal Commission's work was conducted over a period of five years. In hearings across the country it heard thousands of witnesses and received thousands of briefs. It consulted hundreds of experts, corporations, governments and individuals, both Aboriginal and non-Aboriginal. The Commission process was really an exercise of the wisdom in the counsel of many.

It has been argued by some that the Royal Commission was too costly, that it took too long, and that its recommendations were too numerous and too far-reaching in terms of political or legal change. Some of these criticisms have even been echoed by prominent First Nations leaders, who have apparently said that some of the Commission's recommendations are too broad and not supportable. But not dealing with these recommendations and not addressing the plight of the First Nations is a social time bomb.

Of course the work and approach of the Commission was broad. I believe firmly that nothing less will do in the face of the challenges to address meaningfully the effects of centuries of discrimination, oppression and dispossession carried out against more than a million Aboriginal people in Canada. I believe that the burden is still on governments to show, with respect to each recommendation, why it should *not* be implemented.

This status quo of social and economical exclusion is the root cause of our dependence on governments. For example, the terms of the Cree nation's agreement with Canada and Quebec were, for all intents and purposes, imposed on us in 1975. It is clear, from the way governments are now interpreting the agreement, that it does not provide any substantial foundation for a sustainable Cree economy or Cree self-sufficiency.

On the contrary, governments, Crown corporations and multinationals are now removing resources to the value of over C$5 billion from our traditional lands *each year*. The federal and Quebec governments spend a small fraction of this sum on the Crees. These expenditures, per capita, now amount to little more than average per capita expenditures on all other Canadians, and much less than is spent per capita in the Northwest Territories, a similarly remote and costly region of the country.

Thousands of jobs have been created for non-Aboriginal Quebeckers as a result of the extraction of resources from our traditional lands. In contrast, as I have indicated, few jobs have gone directly to Crees, in spite of treaty promises that we would have priority for these positions and for contracts in Eeyou Istchee.

Possibly the single most important finding of the Royal Commission is that Aboriginal peoples are confined on a fraction of the lands that would be required for even a small measure of economic self-sufficiency. The Commission recommended that there must be a meaningful redistribution of lands and resources in favour of Aboriginal peoples in this country.

This is a simple choice for the rest of the country: do we want Aboriginal peoples to be dependent wards of the state forever, or do we want them to be socio-economically viable? If the latter option is preferred, plain economics dictates that the present formula of distribution of lands and resources *away* from Aboriginal peoples must be reversed. It must be accepted, in the words of the commissioners, that 'Federal, provincial and territorial governments, through negotiation, provide Aboriginal nations with lands that are sufficient in size and quality to foster Aboriginal economic self-reliance and cultural and political autonomy' (RCAP 1996: Recommendation 2.4.2). It is also necessary to 'ensure that Aboriginal Nations ... have ... exclusive or preferential access to certain renewable and non-renewable resources, ... [and a] guaranteed share of the revenues flowing from resources development' (Recommendation 2.4.3). In addition, the commissioners recommended that Aboriginal nations should receive substantial financial transfers for the benefit of their people, as do the provinces under present federal arrangements.

By any measure, whether it is justice, fairness or economics, the present formulas and arrangements *do not work*. With respect to the necessary conditions for socio-economic success, a key factor identified by the Royal Commission is the requirement for full recognition of our status and rights as peoples, including our right to self-determination and self-government. At present, in my opinion, First Nations do not exercise self-government. We exercise a form of self-management, because as long as we are receiving government handouts we are administrating the policies of the government. In other words, we are forced to become administrators of our own poverty.

Numerous studies in the United States have demonstrated that the only North American Indian tribes that have thrived and developed are those that, in addition to adequate land and resource bases, have the highest levels of sovereignty, jurisdiction and control over their lands, resources and various institutions. The universal Aboriginal experience in Canada is that federal and provincial governments are permanent opponents of full recognition and development of the inherent rights we have as Aboriginal peoples.

The Royal Commissioners recommended that 'All governments in Canada recognize that Aboriginal peoples are nations vested with the right of self-determination' (Recommendation 2.3.2), and that

> Self-determination entitles Aboriginal peoples to negotiate the terms of their relationship with Canada and to establish governmental structures that they consider appropriate for their needs ... in practice there is a need for the federal and provincial governments actively to ... implement [Aboriginal nations'] right of self-determination. (RCAP 1996: 'Self-Determination and Self-Government: Overview')

The Royal Commission stressed that this recognition would pose no threat to Canada or its political and territorial integrity. We have always sought coexistence, cooperation and harmony in our relations with other peoples. We want to find our rightful place as partners in the Canadian federation. There was a 97 per cent 'no' vote in our own Cree Special Referendum of October 1995 concerning Quebec secession. There can be no clearer proof that we are seeking full and meaningful *inclusion* in Canada and Quebec, and all that such an involvement has to offer.

The Royal Commission also said, and I agree, that if what Aboriginal peoples thought we had won had been delivered – a reasonable share of lands and resources for our exclusive use, protection for our traditional eco-nomic activities, resource revenues from shared lands, and support for our participation in the new economy being shaped by the settlers – then the position of Aboriginal peoples in Canada today would be very different to what it is. Many would be major landowners. Many Aboriginal communi-ties would be economically self-reliant. Many would be prosperous. Instead, every Aboriginal people in Canada can testify to the efforts of countless governments, through countless policies, to deny us these benefits and our fundamental human rights.

This approach cannot last forever. I know that my people, the James Bay Crees, do not intend merely to survive in the face of mega-development. We intend to ensure that it takes place only under conditions that are environmentally sustainable, consistent with our human rights, and equitable in a way that benefits our people.

We are no longer going to tolerate our exclusion. We will insist, at last, that we are still here, that we will be here for generations to come, and that we intend to share equitably in the benefits of this land.

References

Anonymous (1975) *The James Bay and Northern Quebec Agreement*, Quebec: Editeur officiel du Québec (JBNQA).

International Covenant on Civil and Political Rights, Article 1. 1966.

International Covenant on Economic, Social and Cultural Rights, Article 1, 1966.

RCAP (Royal Commission on Aboriginal Peoples) (1996) *Report of the Royal Commission on Aboriginal Peoples*, 5 vols, Ottawa: Royal Commission on Aboriginal Peoples. Also on CD-ROM: *For Seven Generations*, Ottawa: Libraxus, 1997.

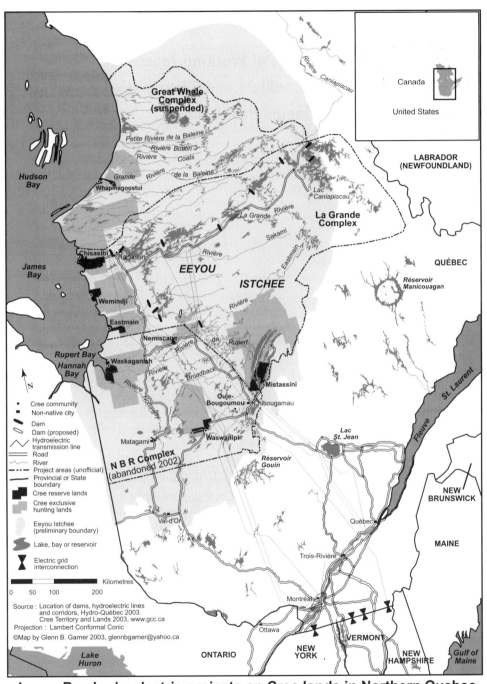

Canada

United States

LABRADOR (NEWFOUNDLAND)

Hudson Bay

Great Whale Complex (suspended)

Petite Rivière de la Baleine

Rivière Boutin

Rivière Coats

Grande Rivière de la Baleine

Whapmagoostui

Rivière Caniapiscau

Lac Caniapiscau

La Grande Complex

La Grande Rivière

Chisasibi
Radisson

Sakami

EEYOU

ISTCHEE

QUÉBEC

Réservoir Manicouagan

James Bay

Wemindji

Rivière Eastmain

Rivière

Eastmain

Nemiscau

Rivière de Rupert

Rupert Bay
Hannah Bay

Waskaganish

Rivière

Broadback

Rivière Nottaway

Mistassini

Ouje-Bougoumou

Chibougamau

Lac St. Jean

Fleuve St. Laurent

N

Matagami

Waswanipi

N B R Complex
(abandoned 2002)

Réservoir Gouin

NEW BRUNSWICK

• Cree community
■ Non-native city
◊ Dam
◊ Dam (proposed)
⌇ Hydroelectric transmission line
═ Road
〜 River
–·– Project areas (unofficial)
— Provincial or State boundary
■ Cree reserve lands
▓ Cree exclusive hunting lands
░ Eeyou Istchee (preliminary boundary)
▰ Lake, bay or reservoir
⧓ Electric grid interconnection

MAINE

Val-d'Or

Québec

Trois-Rivière

Kilometres
0 50 100 200

Source : Location of dams, hydroelectric lines
 and corridors, Hydro-Québec 2003.
 Cree Territory and Lands 2003, www.gcc.ca
Projection : Lambert Conformal Conic

©Map by Glenn B. Garner 2003, glennbgarner@yahoo.ca

Montréal

Ottawa

VERMONT

NEW YORK

NEW HAMPSHIRE

ONTARIO

Lake Huron

Gulf of Maine

James Bay hydroelectric projects on Cree lands in Northern Quebec

10

The Importance of Working Together: Exclusions, Conflicts and Participation in James Bay, Quebec

BRIAN CRAIK

Brian Craik is Director of Federal Relations for the Grand Council of the Crees. He has been an applied anthropologist and political strategist for thirty years. He played a central role in both the 1989–94 campaign that stopped the Great Whale River hydroelectric project and the implementation of the 2002 agreement with Quebec.

In 1971, when the La Grande River Complex, first phase of the James Bay hydroelectric development, was announced, the James Bay Crees organized to resist the development. While they lost in the courts, they managed to negotiate the James Bay and Northern Quebec Agreement (JBNQA) in 1975. The first phase of the project was built, but the agreement kept the Crees in the middle of debates on Aboriginal policy and development in northern Quebec, Canada and internationally. In 1989, when the government of the province of Quebec announced that it would finish the final two phases of the project, the Crees resisted this once again and in the face of daunting challenges managed a campaign that led to the cancellation of the next phase of the project in 1995. In 2001, the government of Quebec proposed a smaller hydroelectric project, which would divert new rivers into the existing installations. But when the project was rejected by the Crees, and another conflict loomed, the government offered to negotiate on a new basis. Early in 2002, the Cree leadership and community members approved an agreement that permitted this project to proceed in the conviction that they had negotiated a new relationship with the government of Quebec and that the Crees were assured the substantially increased resources from Quebec needed for their own social and economic development. Many who have supported the Crees and followed their struggles were surprised by this apparent reversal of events.

It is my contention that the diverse Cree practices and the varied outcomes can only be understood by considering the most intransigent problems the Crees have had to face throughout the last three decades and the diverse but critical sources of power they have developed to affect political and economic decision-making within and beyond Quebec and Canada. I show that the need for social and economic development of the Cree communities has been a key problem of growing proportions. It is a problem that the La Grande hydroelectric development and the JBNQA provisions failed to ameliorate, although they had promised to address it. Most Crees supported the recent negotiations because they offered what many Crees think may be a way out of this dilemma. I also show that among the several forms of political and economic power that the Crees have mobilized, standing in the way of development designed to serve others has been the most critical. The story of their diverse struggles provides lessons from which others may draw insights, both for planning protest strategy and for anticipating long-term opportunities and risks.

The First Phases of Development Conflicts

The Grand Council of the Crees was born of the conflict over hydroelectric development in northern Quebec in the early 1970s. Before that time the Crees, or Eeyouch, as they call themselves, occupied Eeyou/Eenou Istchee (the people's land), an area drained by the rivers flowing into eastern James Bay and southern Hudson's Bay. They were united by a common language, Eeyouayiminanoch, and culture; by pursuit of *ntohonanoch*, a hunting, fishing, gathering and trapping way of life on a common area of land; and by history and mythology.

During the mid-twentieth century the opening of community clinics and schools increased year-round Cree presence at the trading posts where they had traded their furs for three hundred years. In spite of this increased sedentarization into the 1970s, for a Cree person to work in Eeyou Istchee meant to hunt. It was in the early 1970s that the government of Quebec, through its wholly owned corporation Hydro-Quebec and its newly created development companies – the James Bay Energy Corporation and the James Bay Development Corporation – began large-scale exploitation of the water, forest and mining resources on Eeyou Istchee.

It was in response to this threat to their way of life that the Crees decided to create a Cree governing body, Winnebegoweeyouch Notchimeeweeyouch Enadimadoch, roughly translated as 'Coaster and Inlander Cree Working for One Another's Interests' and known in English as the Grand Council of the Crees.

The Canadian west and north had been opened in the nineteenth century by means of treaties that promised Aboriginal peoples the right to hunt on their traditional lands but that, in fact, soon confined them to reserves set out of the way of development. Because the treaty commissions that opened the west to Europeans never came to eastern James Bay, there was no treaty in the region in 1970.

The Crees challenged the right of governments and corporations to build hydroelectric projects based on Cree rights in the land and won an injunction in the lower courts against the construction. Although the appeals court quickly reversed the decision, the first court ruling had shown that the outstanding question of Cree fundamental rights could disrupt tightly planned construction schedules and force a negotiation process that defined some of those rights and provided a place for the Crees in the development of the territory. Unable to stop the ongoing project, the Crees negotiated the James Bay and Northern Quebec Agreement (JBNQA), which promised both protection to the traditional Cree hunting life and participation in the employment and contract benefits of development.

The Failure of the Treaty

The agreement was an out-of-court settlement in 1975 that involved the Inuit of northern Quebec, the Crees, Hydro-Quebec, the James Bay Energy and Development Corporations, and the governments of Canada and Quebec. It approved the La Grande Hydroelectric Complex, then already well under construction on the La Grande River, and provided for certain possible future developments. Most of the document sets out Cree and Inuit rights to programmes and the institutions to govern themselves. Education, health care, income security for trappers, environmental and social protection, police and justice services, wildlife management, local and regional government and community membership, community and economic development, as well as a regime for land rights, are all included. Compensation was fixed and divided between the Crees and Inuit according to population. In 1982 Cree and Inuit rights in the agreement were confirmed as protected by the Constitution of Canada.

The Crees' portion of the compensation funding was C$130 million, which was paid out to them over twenty years and invested by professional investment companies under the direction of an elected board of Cree directors. In addition, the Crees negotiated, on the basis of the 1975 agreement, a new local government act and funding for the communities that gave them an increased level of local autonomy and more adequate funding to maintain local services and some regional government services. Earnings on compensation funds have been spent on economic development and on the protection and advancement of Cree rights.

Between the signature of the agreement in 1975 and 1989, when Quebec decided to proceed with Phases 2 (the Great Whale Project) and 3 (the Nottaway, Broadback, Rupert Rivers Project) of the James Bay hydroelectric developments, the agreement was the cause of much controversy. First there was an ongoing fight with Quebec and Canada for adequate funding of the school and health boards and for adequate housing. Then in 1980 an epidemic of gastroenteritis caused the deaths of several people in the communities. This was caused by growing community populations and the lack of sewer and water systems, another unfulfilled treaty promise. Similarly, government obligations to economic development were not implemented effectively. Provisions in the agreement for economic and social development were to have gone ahead hand in hand. In this way, as sectors of the Cree population grew rapidly, employment both in and outside the communities would have expanded so that Crees would have had opportunities apart from hunting. This would have helped Cree families to afford to bear more of the costs of housing and freed up Cree and public funding to expand the housing stock and improve community infrastructures for the growing population. Instead, the Crees, who represent between 30 and 75 per cent of the population in different parts of the region, had less than 5 per cent of the jobs in development and had a 40 per cent unemployment rate.

The 1975 agreement promised the crafting of development policies to the particular circumstances in the territory. In addition to the Crees benefiting from jobs and revenues from resource development, the land and traditional way of life based on it were to be accommodated by special development policies. However, throughout the 1980s forestry companies were clear-cutting at an ever-accelerating rate, without regard to the hunting rights or presence of the Crees. At the same time, mining activities were accelerating on the territory. Cree involvement was almost non-existent.

By the late 1980s special protections for land had still not been implemented, and government commitments to all types of services were weak. There was a growing housing shortfall, clinics and schools were understaffed and inadequate, and Crees were still almost absent from the regional workforce in resource development. This reflected a long-standing policy of not providing adequate resources for social and economic development to Indigenous communities across the country. The Crees continued to be marginalized and were excluded from the development of their lands and resources, despite the provisions of the 1975 agreement. It was in this context that Phases 2 and 3 of the hydroelectric project were proposed.

United in Exclusion

In 1989 the Cree communities sent over a hundred leaders and delegates to meet in Montreal to discuss the proposals for new hydroelectric projects. They reviewed their experience to date with the treaty and with the La Grande Complex. There were many in the room who had benefited from the 1975 treaty: those who administered the Cree corporations and organizations and those who had found work in the construction of the first project.

The hunters were there also, and they were highly critical of the impact of the La Grande Project. They pointed out that there were very few animals near the La Grande Project and that the promised compatibility of the project with Cree hunting had proved false. The contamination of fish in the reservoirs by mercury and the danger that this represented to people's health were large issues.

Others spoke about the fact that the Crees still had not been hired in any numbers by Hydro-Quebec, or by forestry, or by mining companies; the lack of community development, adequate housing, fire protection, police services and promised funding for the Cree Trappers Association; and other major problems in the implementation of the treaty.

The treaty called for special programmes and commitments for the Crees while Quebec and, to a greater degree, Canada continued to pursue uniform policies for all Indigenous peoples. Moreover the Crees themselves had problems in the execution of treaty mandates due to insufficient training, lack of qualified people, and the absence of internal policies and structures to support the new institutions created by the agreement. As a result of these various problems, there was also a lack of growth in the Cree private sector. The physical isolation of the Cree communities from the development project sites was another problem that would have required special initiatives to deal with. These issues escalated into a growing problem of Cree exclusion from both development and the wider national societies.

While the individual treaty issues and the impact of development were important, they were also evidence of a larger problem: serious faults in overall treaty implementation. The political commitment evident when the treaty was signed was no longer present once the governments got the dams and resources they wanted, when the Crees were no longer in the way.

At the meeting in Montreal the new proposals for more flooding were described and discussed. There were a few Crees in the room with commercial interests in mind who argued that the Crees should negotiate an agreement, as this would create employment and be good for their businesses. The obvious problems with the preceding agreements; ongoing problems with community development, environmental damage and unemployment;

and the absence of any detailed discussions with governments about these issues made the proposals for negotiation seem ridiculous. The intractable problems of the treaty and subsequent agreements made signing a new agreement an unreasonable move.

The decision was not made with bravado, but with a measure of desperation. It was the combination of the desire to protect the land, and the unfulfilled promises to meet the growing need for development, that jointly united the Crees. In the end the assembly of over a hundred leaders and representatives decided to oppose the new projects. At first there were some who wanted to announce that the proposed projects would be subject to Cree rights. Others in the assembly complained that the Crees had stated this before in the face of modifications to the La Grande Complex and that each time since (in the Fort George Relocation Agreement 1978, the Sakami Agreement 1979, the La Grande Agreement 1986) they had eventually accepted a monetary settlement. To make the statement now was the same as putting out a For Sale sign. They said that if the people were truly against the projects, they should just state that they opposed them. And this is what they did.

The mandate was given to the Grand Council to use the means that were required to stop the proposed projects. The next day the chiefs met to decide how this could be done. They pointed out that the proposed projects were designed to supply electricity to the United States and decided that this should be the major target of a public campaign.

A Public Campaign to Stop Development

In part the focus was on a public campaign because the younger Cree leaders thought that the old formula of leaving the main thrust of Cree opposition to a legal battle essentially removed the Crees from day-to-day involvement in the efforts to accomplish the goals set by the people. Moreover, they thought that the Quebec, Canadian and American publics should know about the reasons for their opposition, and that without public support and interest the courts would tend to favour the political and business elites in Quebec and Canada.

In spite of this preference for a public campaign, it was necessary to file Cree interventions in legal, political and administrative forums. A general legal action was initiated, based on the treaty rights of the Crees; work on this was allowed to proceed slowly, however. Using the courts at strategic points in the campaign on points that were clearly winnable reinforced the effectiveness of the campaign and the seriousness with which it was taken.

Allies without Marriage

The first and most obvious place to begin the campaign was the state of Maine. Maine was debating whether to buy a large amount of energy from Hydro-Quebec or to support the local forest-products industry, which since the Carter administration had been re-equipping itself with profits made by producing electricity in combined-cycle generators (the use of excess energy from industrial processes augmented by natural gas to produce electricity for internal use and public sale). The Maine group 'No Thank Q Hydro-Quebec', headed by Pamela Prodan, had already informed the Maine population about the issues. It was good for both their cause and that of the Crees when the Grand Chief at that time, Matthew Coon Come, flew to Augusta at the invitation of a Maine legislator, Conrad Heeshin, and held a press conference in the legislature.

Cooperation with the Maine group raised important issues for the Cree campaign. While there was not any formal decision, over time it became evident that it would be best not to be drawn into other organizations by accepting funding from them or by joining larger coalitions in a manner that would allow others to make the decisions. Rather, with a few small exceptions, the Crees kept at arm's length but maintained very cooperative and friendly relationships with other groups. They encouraged these groups to raise funding and to use it for their own efforts against the projects. In most cases, the groups that were working with the Crees on the campaign were starved for funds and needed to use whatever money they raised to support their own efforts. In this way, the Crees were able to maintain control over what they did and left others in charge of their own campaigns.

Because of this arm's length but friendly relationship, conflicts between Cree goals and those of other groups usually did not become obstacles to cooperation. The most obvious one was the contradiction between the Greenpeace campaign against fur trapping and Cree efforts to protect their traditional fur-trapping and hunting economy. Perhaps because the Crees were not dependent on Greenpeace for funding, Greenpeace made no attempt to force the Crees to support their issues. In fact, the first priority was to save the 8,000 to 11,000 square kilometres of land to be flooded. Other issues could be left aside, as the habitat was the primary focus. Without the habitat, the fur-trapping debate would be moot, at least in the affected area.

Cooperation with other groups was an essential part of the campaign. Without it the efforts of the Crees would have been much more difficult and less effective. Local groups knew their political landscape better than anyone else. They knew who was trustworthy, powerful and effective, and they knew the current political and policy debates and how the Cree issue fitted into this. Moreover, many groups had credibility in their milieu that benefited the Crees. This was the case with the Audubon Society, the Natural Resources Defence Council, Greenpeace Quebec and Les Amis de la Terre (Friends of the Earth) from Montreal, to name only a few. While one may think that the Cree elders know more about the birds or other wildlife, there are always people who will listen first to the Audubon Society or to a well-known environmental group. It is sometimes important to use one's own expertise to choose allies rather than trying to be the expert to everyone on everything.

Local People Must Be Very Involved

The Crees of Whapmagoostui and the Inuit of Kuujjuaraapik (the twin Cree and Inuit communities at Great Whale) decided early in the campaign to build a large canoe (8 metres or 24 foot long) that was made to look like a kayak in the stern and a canoe in the bow, called the *odeyak* (from *owut*, 'canoe' in Cree, and *kayak* from the Inuit language). This was a symbol of the cooperation of the two communities in their opposition to the project.

In 1991, they paddled the *odeyak* to New York City and arrived on Manhattan Island at the end of April. Because the trip was organized in a hurry the arrangements were very dependent on the cooperation of local community groups and organizations along the route, which included Quebec, Vermont and New York State. Local press along the way recorded stories, and the Canadian press followed their progress. Most nights there were events organized in local churches and town halls. All of this, culminating with carrying the *odeyak* onto the Earth Day stage in Times Square, provided a powerful energy to the Cree campaign in the United States. The idea for the trip came from Deny Alsop, who had made a similar trip by himself to bring attention to the state of the rivers in Massachusetts. The people of Whapmagoostui, with the help of an American river-raft expert, also organized rubber-raft expeditions on the Great Whale river and invited important political figures to come and see the river for themselves. The personal involvement of many people created friendships and demonstrated to people in the Cree communities that they were not powerless but had enormous capability to fight for their issues (see also McRae in this volume).

The people of Whapmagoostui were crucial in the Cree campaign. They held a referendum early in 1990 that revealed that community support for stopping the project was almost unanimous; only one person voted in favour of the project. Moreover, they called on the other Cree communities to support them, which they did. Each year between 1989 and 1994, when the Great Whale Project was shelved, resolutions were passed at the Cree Annual General Assemblies to affirm Cree solidarity in opposition to the projects.

A Strong Mandate and Trust in Leadership Are Strategic Advantages

The Cree media campaign was carried out without an overall plan. Cree leaders sometimes commented that it was carried out the same way that they hunted, planning the next move in relation to the last and taking advantage of opportunities as they arose. One advantage that the Grand Council had was that it was given a strong mandate by the Crees. Cree leadership could thus support council staff internally when they made decisions quickly to respond to breaking news, sometimes without much consultation with the local communities. If there had not been good judgement expressed in the exercise of this liberty, if the internal support of the Cree local and national leadership had not been present, then the Crees would not have been able to be nearly as effective as they were. Where it took governments and corporations days and sometimes weeks to respond, the Crees could respond in a matter of hours on most issues.

Internal Dissent Can Be Costly

Internal support was crucial to the campaign. But it was not always automatic. Those interested in exploiting the commercial prospects of the proposed hydro development never ceased trying to force their agenda on the leadership. In one instance a Cree corporation launched a food-produce distribution business on the basis of a business plan that was made public and premised that the Great Whale Project would be approved. When the project was dropped in 1994 much of the future market for this company disappeared, and the business lost millions of dollars because of this and other factors and was eventually closed. The Cree leadership did not allow contradictions of this sort to dissuade them from their political mandate to stop the project. This was one of the reasons that the mandate had to be reaffirmed each year.

There were times during the campaign when local agendas led the leadership to raise the issue of local versus national Cree priorities. Political actions could interfere with attempts to attract investment or to raise funding for local projects. These were almost always dealt with internally, but they raised the spectre of the campaign losing its local support. In every case the local community members supported the defence of Cree rights.

Your Back Yard Must Be Their Back Yard

If you want people to put your concern for the land and your way of life ahead of their perceived economic benefits from cheap electricity or some other commodity, those people must see and be familiar with your land and way of life. Some of the main issues in mounting a campaign are isolation, lack of knowledge and exclusion. People tend to care about what they know and value. As a result the Crees decided that they had to take images of the area to the larger public audience. Initially this was done through a slide show put together with the help of the Sierra Club. It brought pictures of Cree culture and communities and the rivers to a very wide audience.

In addition the Grand Council commissioned a film, *The Land of Our Children*, that highlighted problems in forestry and hydroelectric development in northern Quebec. Although the Quebec media deemed it too pro-Cree, it was shown on Ontario television and on local channels throughout the American northeast in subsequent years. These local showings of the film helped make the Cree issue a local issue, as did posters, T-shirts and presentations brought to those in the south.

Formal interventions were made in important international institutional, quasi-judicial and legislative forums. The Crees intervened successfully with international institutional investors in Hydro-Quebec bonds, beginning with the 'Ivy League' US universities, a number of which (including Dartmouth, Tufts and Harvard) were persuaded by their student bodies to divest their holdings (as they had their South African investments). The Crees also presented their case to the International Water Tribunal sitting in the Netherlands, where the Great Whale case was paired with Three Gorges in China. The tribunal did not rule against the project but did rule that the JBNQA was not a full manifestation of the Crees' right of self-determination. In addition, the Crees cooperated with US state legislators in Massachusetts and other New England states in efforts to enact laws requiring that Great Whale electricity imports be subjected to state environmental assessment. While these interventions were not always strictly 'successful', they always added to the moral status of the campaign and enhanced sympathy for the Crees as the underdog vying with the big machine.

There Is Nothing More Compelling than a Good Story

Crucial to effectiveness in such a public campaign is a clear message and a thorough understanding of the issues. Most of the Cree campaign was directed by a small group of people that included the Cree leadership and Cree and non-Cree staff. These people, because of their daily involvement, became immersed in the facts of the projects and the politics. When they did not have the technical expertise, they relied on advisors. When the forum called for a more personal approach, they would bring in local Crees.

The Cree leadership took a one-day course of media training to gain some of the skills that everyone speaking to the media should know. It reinforced the importance of deciding what you want to say before the interview and not being led by the interviewer to say something that you did not want to say. Coherence in what is said by the various spokespersons is important also, as is keeping the story in the mind of the public from day to day. The public starts to listen for the next turn in the story. Through keeping a list of press contacts and speaking with them almost every day, the campaign becomes shaped around a consistent and truthful story. This requires detailed work to bring out the facts of the case. Good technical advisors are essential, as they will bring facts to bear that have not been considered before. Dealing with facts brought out by opponents to the campaign is also essential to maintaining the trust of the wider audience. You must always be thinking of what the public wants to hear and how this could help your campaign. Most of the media have to put together a story every day. As a result, it is essential to maintain constant contact with the press and build a relationship based on reliable information.

Because the team was small, when an issue arose it was easy for them to discuss the matter over the telephone or in person and to decide on a position consistent with what had already been decided. In this way the story line of the campaign was often conducted by the Crees and not by proponents of the project. The public often understood the issues from a Cree perspective. This is not easy for governments or corporations to subvert, as the Cree view on these matters was often also the most compelling.

People Are the Best Asset

There is an old maxim that you are no more than six contacts away from anyone else in the world. This has worked time and time again for the Crees. Being part of a society based on everyday personal contact, many Crees have an exceptional ability in dealing with others on a one-to-one basis. This has given others confidence that the Cree leadership can carry off a meeting with anyone, and carry it off well. Personal contact has brought the Cree leadership into meetings with the Pope, even though they are not Roman Catholics, and with political leaders in the United States, Europe, Canada and elsewhere. Moreover, contacts during the Great Whale Campaign brought the Crees into contact with music stars, making possible the support of the Indigo Girls, Sting, Bruce Cockburn and others, and brought the campaign free publicity in *Sports Illustrated*, *Time Magazine*, and *Newsweek* and other publications. Individuals interested in supporting a campaign often bring contacts with others that can be very important to getting the message out.

Criticism Requires the Presentation of Better Alternatives

The message has to deal with the issue of alternatives. If you want others not to do what they planned, then you must demonstrate what they can do instead to solve the problem.

Behind every large project there is an analysis of why it makes economic sense to build it. There are also environmental, social and political reasons of importance. However, all the effects of the project will have economic implications, so the economics of the project in relation to its alternatives must be examined in detail. Moreover, the weight given to the social and environmental factors tends to be emphasized by those most affected, whereas economic factors are emphasized most by those the furthest away from the project area.

In the case of Great Whale, a large percentage of the Cree effort went into hiring experts who had credibility within the hydroelectric and energy economics sectors to study the project and alternatives to it in order to see where the proponent had exaggerated its claims. They succeeded in showing that programmes to save energy or to make Quebec industry more energy efficient were underdeveloped. Some economic parties in Quebec and the United States were interested in having more emphasis on these areas.

Arguments and Experts Must Be Professional and Convincing

In New York State the government study of the profitability of the proposed long-term contract with Hydro-Quebec concluded that it would be too expensive in light of alternatives (mostly electricity generated by natural gas). The Crees' technical advisors helped to focus the attention of the review on important elements of the contract that otherwise could have been undervalued. Vermont reached a similar conclusion, again with Cree input at a hearing process. New York decided to cancel its proposed long-term contract with Hydro-Quebec, and Vermont decided to reduce its contract proposal but did go ahead with 90 per cent of it.

Experts, public-relations companies, lawyers and advisors hired by governments, utilities and corporations were always numerous, well prepared and had access to overwhelming resources. It was impossible to meet them head-on in quantity, but it was possible to meet or better the quality. It was often an advantage to appear to be totally outgunned. But whether in court, before international forums, in environmental-assessment processes, or testifying before legislators, one cannot be imprecise or ill-equipped or have an inadequate strategy. The Crees had learned this lesson well before the struggle over Great Whale. Being well prepared can be expensive but is worth the cost, and fortunately the Crees had the means to do much of what was needed.

Successful Opposition May Create Conditions for Other Successes

While a group may be willing to risk everything on a particular issue, it must weigh the possible outcomes. If one examines the times when the Crees were in serious conflict with governments and compares them with times when they settled problems in the implementation of the treaty, one finds that it was during the greatest conflicts that major issues were resolved. During the Great Whale Campaign (1989 to 1995) construction of the access roads to the Cree communities was settled (except for Waskaganish, which refused the road at the time), the Cree school-board funding dispute was resolved, and a five-year agreement was reached on the funding subsidies for the Cree community and regional governments. The roads issue had been outstanding since 1975, the school-board issue since 1978, and the government subsidies since 1984. However, in other political and social contexts a government might resort to force and opt to endure the public-relations and international problems created by such a campaign.

In the Cree–Quebec context the main negative impact was from the fact that the Crees' own funds had to be used for political problems rather than for immediate local needs. The investment in solving the political problems paid off in the long term, however, whereas compensation funds never could have resolved the larger problems.

Good Strategic Analysis Is Important to Clarify Key Questions

The dilemma of the Crees is that the large-scale development projects that have gone ahead in their region have provided some financial resources to support Cree commercial ventures and community development, but not enough. Long-term benefits of development seem to aid people from the south, whereas Crees have not gained access to long-term employment in development or to long-term revenue sources from development with which to finance the growth of their communities and government. For many Crees development projects have done nothing but reduce their access to the land and their source of traditional food. In addition, as I noted above, government programmes to support community development and employment have not materialized or have not been adequate to the task. The traditional economy based on fur trapping and hunting provides subsistence only with the aid of the Income Security Programme for trappers and hunters. The question of where long-term Cree employment and growth will come from has not been answered. Hence ongoing attempts by some Cree leaders to find large-scale resource-development proposals that could work is met by scepticism by many Crees because of their experience with short-term supply and construction contracts on such development projects. Many Crees still ask, where does a long-term solution come from?

Opposition Takes New Forms

The Great Whale Project was shelved early in 1994 as the separatist government under Premier Jacques Parizeau decided that it was a higher priority to promote Quebec independence; in their view, Cree campaigns in the United States and Europe put the province in a negative light.

The project of Quebec's political independence from Canada became the most important issue for the new Quebec government. The Crees had temporarily won their fight against dams, but if Quebec separated from Canada, what would happen to the rights that the Crees had fought so hard to achieve and that were protected by the Canadian Constitution? As inadequate as they were, Cree rights in Canada were protected by the amendment process that required consent from a majority of the provinces and probably Cree consent as well. Moreover, Quebec claimed the right to separate from Canada but denied the right of its constituent Aboriginal nations to decide for themselves. What rights would an independent Quebec deny to the Crees?

In this new context, the Crees had to promote their right to self-determination and to stay in Canada should the efforts of the Quebec separatists succeed. In doing so, they provided a constant critique of the Quebec positions on territorial integrity; on the principle of territorial integrity not applying to administrative units within states, such as provinces; on the right of self-determination applying to Quebec; and on other details in terms of Canadian and international law. The Crees published a legal analysis of these issues entitled *Sovereign Injustice* (Grand Council of the Crees 1995), and later a popularized version entitled *Never without Consent* (Grand Council of the Crees 1998). They also intervened in the federal reference of these matters to the Supreme Court.

Moreover, they commissioned a poll, which showed that if Quebeckers thought that separation would mean losing northern Quebec, a substantial number would vote against separating from Canada. This finding influenced the federal government to adopt a tougher position in the public debate on these issues. The Crees also held their own referendum on whether to leave Canada and go with Quebec if it voted to separate; 97 per cent voted not to get into that boat.

New Projects, Old Problems, Exploring Relationships

After the Quebec referendum narrowly decided against separation in October 1995, the Crees had to return to business as usual. This was not easy, as the Quebec government and the Crees had to set out a new agenda for themselves, and relations between them were somewhat bruised. The first Cree peacemaker was former grand chief Billy Diamond. He was appointed by the Grand Council as their negotiator for discussions with the province.

Billy Diamond brought the community problems to the provincial government. He took Quebec's negotiator on trips to see the need for infrastructure and housing and to view Cree economic initiatives such as the joint-venture sawmill and forestry companies. The communities had waited a long time, since 1989, with little in the way of positive development and with growing housing and employment needs. It is to their credit that they weathered the storms of the fight over the hydro dams and then the separation fight and held to their principles in the face of growing local problems.

At the time, some wanted to hold high-level discussions with Quebec to resolve differences on the implementation of the treaty and on development. The Quebec government chose a route to reconciliation that refused to deal with the Grand Council, preferring to establish relations directly with the Cree communities. What was called in the Cree camp a Memorandum of Understanding (MOU) process, after the legal form the agreements were given, saw high-level Quebec officials in discussion with the communities. But the communities would only discuss projects that at the time were described by the Crees as the 'non-James Bay Agreement project'. They were still in court on the significant treaty issues and refused to negotiate them community by community.

The MOU process was a rolling development plan for the communities, amended year by year. It brought some funding for community projects, including a community-access road for Waskaganish and funding for the sawmill expansion at Waswanipi, as well as some infrastructure expansion and youth centres in the other communities. However, the MOU process was fraught with complications resulting from the number of individual projects, the detailed quarterly financial reporting required for each, and the irregular means of payment, and it became somewhat mired down by administrative complexity.

Hydro-Quebec, for its part, adopted a policy of not going ahead with projects if local communities did not approve. It sounded rather enlightened. But the key word was 'communities'. The policy was another attempt to undermine the unity of the Cree Nation. Hydro began a series of initiatives aimed at convincing the so-called impacted communities to accept the new Eastmain–Rupert Diversion Project. They undertook fieldwork with

Eastmain and Mistissini, two of the Cree communities that would be affected by flooding on their traplines. Nemaska and Waskaganish, the other two communities that would be affected, refused to participate. Hydro-Quebec proposed a partnership in which the Crees would take out loans guaranteed by Hydro and would invest in the new project in return for a fifty-year annual payment from the profits.

Their approach was slow and diplomatic. Crees were hired in Mistissini to help with surveys and water measurements, and they began to ask Hydro-Quebec about issues concerning the past agreements and things that remained outstanding. Hydro-Quebec's approach was unusually soft in comparison with the past, although there was always the question of whether they would try to force the issues if there was no unanimity among the communities. However, there was always the fact that the Grand Council, as the protector of all Cree rights and signatory of the James Bay Agreement, would have to consent to any amendment to the agreement, which such a project would require.

In July 2001 the issue came to a head at a special assembly of the Grand Council held in Waskaganish. At the meeting Waskaganish told Hydro-Quebec that the community did not want the project. It asked for and received support from the other communities. The Hydro-Quebec initiative was dead. In the face of this stalemate the new premier of Quebec, Bernard Landry, asked Cree grand chief Dr Ted Moses if it would be possible for the two parties to make peace. The stakes were high for both. If the attempt to resolve their differences came to nothing, the Crees would have to continue to cope with a worsening social situation in the communities caused by the lack of employment opportunities and housing and other problems. Premier Landry would face the prospect of again fighting the Crees over development. This would mean more court actions on hydro and forestry and would put him and his party into the same pot from which Jacques Parizeau had extricated them by freezing the Great Whale Project.

The discussions would be difficult because each outstanding issue had its separate audience, and each of these would use public and perhaps legal pressure to get their way. Forestry and mining companies, Hydro-Quebec, the environmental lobby, consumers groups, and others would all want a direct say in the discussions. Because the situation was delicate, it was agreed that the initial talks would be held with small teams of two negotiators per side. On 23 October 2001, after three weeks of negotiations, the parties came to a proposal. The Agreement in Principle (AIP) dealt primarily with the outstanding obligations of Quebec under the JBNQA in the areas of community and economic development.

The Cree aim in the discussions was simple: instead of repeating the James Bay Agreement model of setting up committees to set policy and to access government resources, implementation either would follow new policies established during the negotiations or would flow from making the required cash available. This procedure also met the Cree government's need for its sources of revenue to be guaranteed over a long period. The other principle that structured the negotiations was that the rights in the JBNQA could not be diminished by any new arrangements.

The AIP contained the following:

1. A Quebec and Cree commitment to deal with one another on a nation-to-nation basis.
2. The Crees' assumption for fifty years of certain JBNQA obligations of Quebec for Cree community and economic development.
3. Settlement of outstanding Cree lawsuits against Quebec.
4. Quebec's payment to the Crees of C$24 million the first year, C$46 million the next year and C$70 million each year for the next 48 years.
5. Indexation of payments with possible increases, according to increases in the volume and value of mining production, forestry and hydroelectric production from the full extent of the Cree traditional lands in the James Bay Territory.
6. A new regime to regulate forestry, and new logging practices to be implemented in cooperation with the Crees, using mosaic cutting and management of the cutting area on the basis of Cree trapline territories.
7. Quebec's support of Cree involvement in future development.
8. Crees' consent to the Eastmain–Rupert Diversion Project.

Several of the provisions that benefited the Crees had been refused repeatedly by Quebec since 1974–75, particularly recognition of the Crees as a nation and Cree participation in revenues collected by Quebec from natural-resource developments. After the signature of the AIP the Grand Council made a consultation tour of the Cree communities. Each of the nine communities was visited and the AIP explained. The process upset many people, but after explanation many were surprised by the extent of Quebec's commitment and liked the deal. The Grand Council gave the Cree negotiators a mandate to complete the negotiation and to propose a final agreement. The chiefs of all nine Cree communities consented to finalize the AIP.

The final agreement, called 'A New Relationship', was completed by the end of December 2001, and a new round of community consultations was carried out in January and early February 2002. The main item added to the list in the final agreement was the renunciation by Hydro-Quebec and Quebec of any rights they had in the James Bay Agreement in respect to the Nottaway, Broadback, Rupert River Hydroelectric Project, which would have flooded 8,000 square kilometres of territory, compared to 640 square kilometres for the Eastmain–Rupert River Diversion Project.

The process for making the decision in each community was left to the communities to decide. All the communities opted for a local referendum, and each set its own rules. The result was a 70 per cent approval of the agreement by those who voted. About 55 per cent of the eligible voters cast their ballots. In the communities most directly affected, 80 per cent of the voters were in favour of the agreement. Chisasibi, the community that experienced the most extensive effects of the La Grande Project, was almost evenly split in the referendum and was the only community narrowly to reject the new agreement.

Opposition to the new agreement among the Crees was the most vocal and active that had developed to date. It was the second time that the issue of development was debated by Cree people, who felt empowered to decide whether a project would go ahead. The first was in the 1989 Great Whale decision, and in that case the decision was to oppose. In the present case the possibility of the Crees becoming involved in the development of the territory, rather than being compensated to step aside, was on the table for the first time. Those who opposed the agreement articulated a view of the Crees as stewards of the land and stated that the people should not accept the diversion of the river and more flooding. They spoke of the fish and wildlife and how in Cree tradition the people stood in a relationship with the animals. They also claimed that the proposed project would ruin the Cree way of life and that the land should be preserved for future generations.

Those who promoted the agreement pointed out that the Crees were the traditional occupants and owners of the land and could decide whether to develop the territory's resources. They eschewed the vision of the Crees as stewards and spoke of this view as portraying them as janitors, taking care of the territory so others could develop it. They claimed that the Cree way of life would continue, as the harmful affects of the project would be relatively small in comparison to the La Grande, Great Whale or Nottaway, Broadback, Rupert River projects, and they pointed to the growing population of unemployed young Crees who needed opportunities.

The debates about the agreement and its significance and content will go on for years as it is implemented. What the new agreement is and who the Crees think that they are, are questions that will be answered over the coming fifty years.

Conclusions: Understanding a Complex Relationship

I believe that Canada has a huge problem with its present land-claims policy and with the future of Aboriginal communities. While they are often surrounded by resource-rich land, the Aboriginal communities are too often islands of unemployment and poverty. The Canadian policy is one of maintaining this status quo. Rather than bringing Aboriginal communities into the revenue streams created by the development that surrounds them, and rather than recognizing the interests of Aboriginal peoples in development, the Aboriginal-claims policy promotes one-time payments and asks Aboriginal peoples to accept exclusion. If they do benefit from development over the full extent of their lands, this policy permits them to do so only as individuals. It does not address problems of community and of economic, social and cultural linkages between the Aboriginal and non-Aboriginal societies.

John Bodley stated in his collection of essays, *Tribal Peoples and Development Issues*:

> A major problem with development policies promoting integration is that their aim is usually to benefit individuals, often at the expense of the community. When development undermines a community's ability to defend and manage its own resources, or when imposed by outsiders, genuine benefits can hardly be expected. (Bodley 1988: 3)

The Crees signed an agreement in 1975 that promised participation, community development and protection of their the traditional way of life. The Great Whale fight was in large part a reaction to the lack of the promised participation and the problems in community development. Its success posed the question for the Crees of where they would go as a society, and this raised the question of who they wanted to be. For the answer they look as a society to both their past and their future. Is development imposed? For the Crees, they can say that they have had the ability to stop development that they do not want, and they have already done it. They may not always succeed, but their skills and resources are such that their capacity to stop some developments cannot again be ignored by developers.

This time, however, they chose development. In doing so, they questioned the stereotypes that they have seen in themselves and that others see in them. They have also tried to step across the boundary between standing in the way of development and gaining the means needed to initiate some developments that they can control, not just oppose, stop or suffer.

In addition, the Crees have to come to a first understanding with Quebec as to the nature of their relationship. The agreement describes it as a nation-to-nation relationship. Quebec is, of course, a province in a nation-state. However, within Canada and across the world one of the outstanding conundrums is how the relationship between nation-states and peoples, including Aboriginal peoples and the Quebeckers, will be maintained.

In the case of the Crees there are potential lessons to be learned in this regard. Sectors of Cree society that would directly benefit from large-scale developments have applied constant but not decisive pressures for Cree agreement to such developments. Cree leadership and administrators who need steady sources of funds for programmes have shown a continuing interest in such agreements. But widespread community visions have supported opposition to projects seen as degrading Cree lands and serving the development needs of others and not of the Crees.

In 2001 and 2002 one of the things that made a difference was the growing community recognition of the need of many Crees for new resources, on a scale not available under Indigenous policies and programmes in Canada, to facilitate meaningful and productive lives, on Cree terms, for a growing population. In this sense, government-inflicted poverty and exclusion were key to creating the conditions for widespread Cree acceptance of some large-scale resource developments. The other key difference was the negotiation of a new form of agreement with significant changes on the part of the government, changes such as removing planned projects and providing access to ongoing resource-generated revenues that had been declared non-negotiable for three decades. These afforded recognition and the means for Cree-controlled, locally based community and economic development. It was also clear that Crees would reject negotiated agreements that were heavily dependent on government promises to fulfil complex undertakings rather than establishing direct relations and resource transfers.

These changes were possible because Cree opposition to earlier development projects had convinced governments of their capacity to oppose government-sponsored development projects effectively. In this sense, being in the way of development has made possible more effective negotiations and relations.

Participation as a community, as a nation, in development and governance, is now part of the Cree relationship with Quebec. They are shaped in the continual process of working out this relationship, which involves conducting business with respect for each other, without the arrogance of power. Ultimately I also believe that this new relationship involves accepting a measure of change, uncertainty, risk and more than a little ambiguity, for this is the stuff out of which new potentials are created.

References

Bodley, John H. (1988) *Tribal Peoples and Development Issues: A Global Overview*, Mountain View, CA: Mayfield.

Grand Council of the Crees (1995) *Sovereign Injustice: Forcible Inclusion of the James Bay Crees and Cree Territory into a Sovereign Québec*, Nemeska, Quebec: Grand Council of the Crees.

Grand Council of the Crees (Eeyou Astchee) (1998) *Never without Consent: James Bay Crees' Stand against Forcible Inclusion into an Independent Québec*, Toronto: ECW Press.

Indian reservations and mining sites on Chippewa ceded lands in Northern Wisconsin

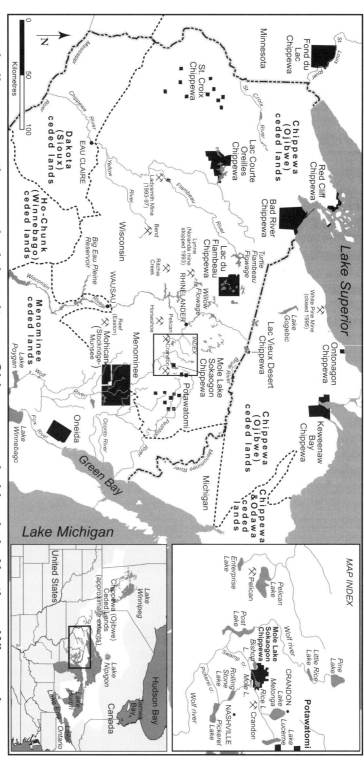

Legend:

- ⛏ Metalic ore deposits
- ● City or Town
- ∿ River
- Lake or bay
- - - - Treaty boundary
- ──── State boundary
- ▨ Indian reservation
- ☐ Map extent
- ☐ Chippewa (Ojibwe) ceded lands
- State or provincial boundary

Inset (Bottom)
Chippewa (Ojibwe) ceded lands

MAP INDEX

Source: http://www.treatyland.com
©Map by Glenn B. Garner 2003, glennbgarner@yahoo.ca

11

Defending a Common Home:
Native/non-Native Alliances against
Mining Corporations in Wisconsin

AL GEDICKS AND ZOLTÁN GROSSMAN

Al Gedicks is an environmental and Indigenous rights activist and scholar. In 1977 he founded the Center for Alternative Mining Development Policy to assist Indian tribes and rural communities in the upper midwestern US in resisting ecologically destructive mining projects. He teaches at the Department of Sociology in the University of Wisconsin – La Crosse.

Zoltán Grossman is Assistant Professor of Geography and American Indian Studies, University of Wisconsin – Eau Claire. He has been a long-term organizer for Native American rights and environmental protection. His Ph.D. dissertation (2002) focuses on treaty conflicts and environmental cooperation between Native American and rural White communities.

Native resistance to multinational mining corporations in northern Wisconsin has been growing for over two decades. It started in 1975 when Exxon discovered the large Crandon zinc/copper sulphite deposit in Forest County, one mile upstream of the wild rice beds of the Mole Lake Chippewa Reservation, five miles downwind of the Forest County Potawatomi Reservation, and 40 miles (via the Wolf River) upstream of the Menominee Nation. A quarter-century later, after a series of five mining companies were involved in the project, the proposed mine has been defeated and the mine site is owned by two neighbouring tribes.

The site lies on territory sold by the Chippewa (Ojibwe) Nation to the United States in 1842, and directly on a 12-square-mile tract of land promised to the Mole Lake Sokaogon Chippewa in 1855 (Danziger 1978: 153). Treaties guaranteed Chippewa access to wild rice, fish and some wild game on ceded lands. But the economic, cultural and spiritual centre of the Mole Lake Chippewa is their wild rice lake. The rice, called *manomin*, or 'gift from the Creator', is an essential part of the Chippewa diet, an important cash crop, and a sacred part of the band's religious rituals.

The Crandon/Mole Lake mine would have extracted approximately 55 million tons of sulphite ore during the thirty-year life of the project. Over its lifetime, the mine would generate 44 million tons of wastes – the equivalent of eight Great Pyramids of Egypt (WDNR 1986: ii; *World Book* 1987: 810a). When metallic sulphite wastes have contact with water and air, the potential result is sulphuric acid, plus high levels of poisonous heavy metals such as mercury, lead, zinc, arsenic, copper and cadmium. The mine would also use toxic chemicals in ore processing (including up to 20 tons of cyanide a month) and reduce groundwater tables in the area because of the constant dewatering of the proposed underground mine. The Chippewa were not reassured when Exxon's biologist mistook their wild rice for a 'bunch of lake weeds'. Frances Van Zile, a tribal elder and leader of the opposition to mining, says 'these people [from the mining company] don't care about us. They don't care if we live or die. All they want is that copper and zinc' (personal interview 1994).

The construction of the largest toxic mine waste dump in state history at the headwaters of the pristine Wolf River poses an unacceptable economic and environmental risk to the downstream tourist industry on this Class I trout stream. As local opposition increased, Exxon withdrew from the project in 1986, citing low metal prices. But in 1993, Exxon returned, this time with a new partner, the Canadian-based Rio Algom.

Much had changed since Exxon had first proposed the mine. The Mole Lake Chippewa, Menominee, Potawatomi and Mohican (Stockbridge–Munsee) had opened casinos, generating income that enabled them to fight mining companies more effectively in the courts and in the arena of public opinion. The four tribes formed the NiiWin Intertribal Council (*NiiWin* is Chippewa for 'four'). NiiWin immediately began hiring lawyers and technical experts to challenge Exxon/Rio Algom's mine permit application. They also purchased a NiiWin house on a seven-acre parcel across the road from the proposed mine site, to monitor all activities at the site. The Oneida Nation, which is downstream from the mine near Green Bay, also joined the opposition.

To protect tribal resources and assert tribal sovereignty, the Mole Lake Chippewa developed a multifaceted strategy that includes: (1) building national and international support by networking with Native rights groups, and challenging Exxon through shareholder resolutions; (2) developing a state-wide alliance to educate the non-Indian public about mining, and pass a mining moratorium law; (3) joining in local alliances with their non-Indian neighbours in the town of Nashville to oppose the mine and develop economic alternatives to mining jobs; and (4) developing tribal regulatory authority under the provisions of the federal Clean Water Act.

The attitudes of neighbouring non-Indian communities had also changed since the Chippewa treaty rights controversy of the late 1980s. After a federal court decision recognized Chippewa treaty-rights in 1983, White sportsmen had held sometimes violent protests against Chippewa off-reservation spearfishing. Anti-treaty groups had accused the Chippewa of destroying the fish and local tourism economy, even though the tribes never took more than 3 per cent of the fish (Strickland 1990: 24). Although tribal members themselves tended to frame their identities around their tribal ethnicity, the protesters grouped all Indians together as a single 'race' that was afforded 'special treatment'. Riot police from around the state were deployed at northern lakes during the spring spearfishing seasons, while anti-treaty mobs attacked Chippewa spearers and their families with rocks, bottles, boat and vehicle assaults, sniper fire and pipe bombs. The anti-treaty groups were practising 'geographies of exclusion', which portrayed the Chippewa as 'out of place' outside the boundaries of their reservations. This attitude was summed up in the ironic White protesters' chant of 'Indians Go Home'.

The Chippewa received support from Witnesses for Nonviolence, who monitored the anti-Indian harassment and violence with cameras and recorders. By 1992, increased cultural education, a federal court injunction against anti-Indian harassment, and the deterrent effect of the Witnesses' presence lessened the violence at the boat landings. The spearfishing conflict had ironically overcome the 'invisibility' of Native Americans in Wisconsin, and educated the non-Indian majority about the legal powers of Native sovereignty on the reservations, treaty rights outside the reservation, and the continuing vitality of Indigenous cultures. Prejudice against Native Americans continued, but the organized anti-Indian groups went into a decline.

The spearfishing and mining conflicts in Wisconsin tell a story of racial/ethnic confrontation turning into environmental cooperation, of distinct boundaries between reservations and non-Indian towns blurring with common watersheds, and of places of fear turning into places of opportunity. These changes took place in the 1990s in areas of the state where they were least expected – where tension between Native Americans and non-Natives had been the most intense. In the process, two communities that had viewed each other as 'outsiders' began to redefine each other as 'insiders' in a common place, under siege by new and more threatening 'outsiders': multinational mining corporations.

Treaties as Obstacles to Mining

When Exxon, Noranda, Rio Tinto and other companies renewed their interest in metallic minerals in Chippewa-ceded territory around 1992, the same treaties became a factor in the mining controversy. The treaties do not cover mineral rights, but Native nations interpret their guarantees to mean that any degradation of off-reservation resources would be an 'environmental violation' of the treaties, giving them legal standing in federal court to challenge harmful projects. Mining proponents took a position against treaty rights as a potential legal obstacle to development of a mining district in the lands ceded by Chippewa treaties. State administration secretary (and former Exxon lobbyist) James Klauser had in 1990 unsuccessfully pressured the Mole Lake and Lac du Flambeau Chippewa to 'lease' their treaty rights in exchange for money. The Wisconsin Counties Association, viewing the treaties as a potential legal obstacle both to county timber income and to mining, took the lead in organizing county governments around the USA to oppose treaty rights. Yet on the question of mining, the perspective of most environmentally minded sportfishers was closer to the tribes. When the tribes asked anti-treaty groups to take a stand against mining's potential environmental threat to the fishery, the groups either refused to take a stand or sided with the mining companies.

Because anti-treaty groups refused to oppose the mining companies, they began to lose their 'environmentalist' image in the eyes of many of their followers, and the tribes saw new opportunities to build bridges to certain sportfishing groups. Even at the height of the spearing clashes, the late Red Cliff Chippewa activist Walter Bresette had predicted that non-Indian northerners would realize that environmental and economic problems are 'more of a threat to their lifestyle than Indians who go out and spearfish … we have more in common with the anti-Indian people than we do with the state of Wisconsin' (Midwest Treaty Network 1991: 1).

The irony of the treaty rights conflict in northern Wisconsin had been that Chippewa spearfishers and anti-treaty protesters shared certain basic values. Fishing has long been a central cultural icon for both groups, and the northwoods region was a strong source of territorial identity. The difference between the groups involved how the fishing would be exercised, and especially where it would take place (Silvern 1995: 269–73). The two groups constructed 'place' identities in different ways, with the Chippewa expanding the view of their territory into the treaty-ceded lands where they had been excluded for decades, and the sportfishing protesters (with backing from state regulatory authorities) seeing the Chippewa 'in their place' only within the boundaries of the reservation. Both groups, however, portrayed their fishing method or ethic as best suiting the long-term conservation of the fishery.

The most pejorative term used throughout both the spearing and mining conflicts was the label 'outsider'. Anti-treaty protesters used the label against both the Chippewa and the non-Native treaty supporters. Mining companies deployed the label, often successfully, against urban-based environmental groups such as the Sierra Club. Local environmentalists and tribal members, however, quickly labelled the multinational companies 'outsiders', and in so doing increasingly won the support of their former local White adversaries. In so doing, they began to use 'geographies of inclusion' to redefine parts of northern Wisconsin as a common home for both Native and non-Native residents. Instead of continuing the conflict over allocation of the fishery, both groups began to cooperate to protect the fishery against a common outside threat.

In 1993, Rio Tinto's Kennecott company opened the Ladysmith mine, 100 miles to the west of the Crandon deposit in northwestern Wisconsin, and 30 miles south of the Lac Courte Oreilles Chippewa reservation. The mine opened despite a successful court challenge by the tribe and the Sierra Club, charging that the Wisconsin Department of Natural Resources (WDNR) had failed to conduct endangered resource surveys in the Flambeau River as required by law. The court issued an injunction against mine construction until a supplemental environmental assessment of endangered species was completed. The tribe and the Sierra Club accused the WDNR of conducting a whitewash study but were unable to pursue the case because of a lack of funds (Gedicks 1993: 159). The mine closed after four years.

Native and non-Native opponents, however, stopped Noranda's plans to open the Lynne mine in Oneida County, 30 miles south of the Lac du Flambeau Chippewa reservation. The area was one of the hotbeds of militancy against spearfishing, but local environmentalists nevertheless built a working relationship with Lac du Flambeau after Noranda announced its plans in 1990. Sportsmen also joined the opposition, to protect the rich fishing and hunting grounds around the Willow Flowage. The unexpectedly strong opposition, combined with questions about the mine's potential damage to wetlands, convinced Noranda to withdraw by 1993.

This multiracial alliance of tribes, environmentalists and sportfishers was strengthened by renewed opposition to the Crandon mine along the Wolf River. In a series of meetings and gatherings in 1992–95, different grassroots groups met to coordinate opposition to the mine. As tribes won their treaty rights and opened new casinos in the early 1990s, their legal and financial ability to protect the off-reservation environment was improved, to the advantage of Native and non-Native communities alike.

Building National and International Support

The mining battle in northern Wisconsin received increased attention in 1994, when the Indigenous Environmental Network and Midwest Treaty Network co-sponsored a gathering at Mole Lake that drew a thousand participants from around North America. As part of the gathering, a citizen-initiated Wisconsin Review Commission on the Track Records of Exxon and Rio Algom heard testimony by native people from Colombia, Alaska, New Mexico and Ontario about the environmental, cultural and economic practices of the two companies then planning the Crandon mine. Although the commission had no official standing, its findings were reported in statewide media. The International Indian Treaty Council also helped bring Mole Lake's concerns about the Crandon mine to the Working Group on Indigenous Peoples, held at the United Nations in Geneva.

The Mole Lake Chippewa have also developed ties with various church groups that held stock in several mining companies and who were willing to raise issues of social and corporate responsibility through shareholder resolutions. Shortly after Exxon announced its intention to seek mining permits at Crandon/Mole Lake, the Sinsinawa Dominican Sisters of Wisconsin, along with six other religious congregations, filed a shareholder resolution on behalf of the Mole Lake Chippewa and the other Native communities affected by Exxon's proposed mining operations. The resolution specifically asked Exxon to provide a report to shareholders on the impact of the proposed mine on Indigenous peoples and on any sacred sites within Indigenous communities. The resolution also called on Exxon to disclose 'the nature of and reason(s) for any public opposition to our Company's mining operations wherever they may occur' (Exxon 1994: 16).

After an unsuccessful attempt to omit the Sinsinawa resolution from their 1994 proxy statement, Exxon's board of directors had to face the Chippewa on the company's home turf. Tribal judge Fred Ackley and Frances Van Zile spoke to the resolution and explained to shareholders that the very existence of their culture was at stake in the proposed mine. The resolution received 6 per cent of the vote, representing 49 million shares. Most shareholder resolutions of this type receive less than 3 per cent of the vote. While the resolution was defeated, the Chippewa won enough votes to reintroduce it at the 1995 shareholders' meeting and remain a thorn in Exxon's side.

Building Statewide Coalitions

By 1996, the Wolf Watershed Educational Project (a campaign of the Midwest Treaty Network) began to coordinate a series of anti-mine speaking tours around the state, bringing tribal representatives to communities that had never heard a Native American speak publicly. A spring 1996 speaking tour along the Wolf and Wisconsin rivers educated twenty-two communities about the Crandon mine, and the company's proposed 38-mile liquid waste pipeline from the mine to the Wisconsin River. The tour culminated with a rally of a thousand people in Rhinelander, at the company headquarters and the pipeline's proposed outlet.

Fishing organizations and sportsmen's clubs began strongly and publicly to oppose the Crandon mine and the metallic mining district proposed by pro-mine interests. The tourism industry – the Wolf River watershed's economic lifeblood – also began to realize that urban tourists may not be drawn to the area's clean lakes and rivers if mines were allowed to open. Mining companies had perhaps felt that sportfishing groups would never join hands with the tribes, yet some slowly realized that if metallic sulphite mines were allowed to contaminate rivers with sulphuric acid, there might not be edible fish left to argue about. The American Rivers group had already identified the Wolf River as the fifth most endangered river in the USA, and the Federation of Fly Fishers would later warn that the river is the most threatened in the country.

Sentiment against metallic sulphite mining spread throughout the state in 1996. A blockade by Bad River Chippewa prevented trains from supplying sulphuric acid to a mine in Michigan's Upper Peninsula. The Chippewa were concerned that a spill from tankers would poison their reservation water. But they were equally concerned about the mining company's proposal to inject sulphuric acid into old mine shafts and pump the solution out of the mine and recover the minerals that the acid dissolved. The blockade received so much non-Indian public support that the mine operation was closed. A spokesman for the Crandon Mining Co. told a reporter they were viewing the conflict 'with a little more heightened tension' (Imrie 1996). The blockade convinced mining opponents and proponents alike that the tribes and their allies will never back down even if a Crandon permit is ever granted.

Sinking Roots in Local Alliances

In the same year of 1996, the Mole Lake Chippewa joined with their non-Indian neighbours in Nashville (which covers half the mine site and includes the reservation), not only to fight the mine proposal, but to chart economic alternatives to mining development. In December 1996, the Nashville town board signed a local mining agreement with Exxon/Rio Algom, after a number of illegally closed meetings and despite the objections of a majority of township residents. The former town board was replaced in the April 1997 election by an anti-mining board that included a Mole Lake tribal member. In September 1998 the new town board rescinded the local agreement. Without this agreement from the town, the state cannot grant a mining permit. The mining company has sued the town for violation of contract. The township countersued the company, charging that the local agreement 'resulted from a conspiracy by the mining company and the town's former attorneys to defraud the town of its zoning authority over the proposed mining operations' (Seely 1999). To raise funds to defend itself, the town set up its own website to explain how people can donate money for a legal defence fund in what the town calls a 'David and Goliath' showdown. In January 2002 a state appeals court upheld the 1996 local agreement.

Cooperative relations between the town and the Mole Lake tribe were further strengthened when they received a US$2.5 million grant from the federal government to promote long-term sustainable jobs in this impoverished community. Together with surrounding townships, the Menominee Nation, the Lac du Flambeau Tribe, and Mole Lake formed the Northwoods NiiJii Enterprise Community (*NiiJii* being the Chippewa word for 'friends'). Now Indians and non-Indians are working together to provide a clear alternative to the unstable 'boom and bust' cycle that mining would bring to their communities. If successful, the unique project could bring in an additional US$7 to 10 million to these communities over the next decade. This effort, combined with casinos that have made the tribes the largest employers in Forest County, has dampened the appeal of mining jobs for many local residents. Indian gaming, while not providing an economic panacea for many tribes, has enabled some tribes to finance legal and public relations fights against the mining companies. One of these fights used federally recognized tribal sovereignty to enhance environmental protection of reservation lands.

Tribal Water and Air Regulatory Authority

Tribal lands were ignored in the original versions of many federal environmental laws of the 1970s, including the Clean Air Act and the Clean Water Act. To remedy this exclusion, amendments to these laws have been enacted to give tribes the same standing as states to enforce environmental standards. In 1995 the Mole Lake Chippewa became the first Wisconsin tribe granted independent authority by the US Environmental Protection Agency (EPA) to regulate water quality on their reservation. The tribe's wild rice beds are just a mile downstream from the proposed Crandon mine. Tribal regulatory authority would affect all upstream industrial and municipal facilities, including the proposed mine. Because Swamp Creek flows into the tribe's rice lake, the tribe has to give approval for any upstream discharges that might degrade their wild rice beds.

Within a week of EPA approval of Mole Lake's water quality authority, Wisconsin Attorney General James Doyle sued the EPA and the tribe in federal court, demanding that the federal government reverse its decision to let Indian tribes make their own water pollution laws. A petition urging Doyle to drop the lawsuit was signed by twenty-six environmental groups, two neighbouring townships, and 454 people in 121 communities around the state. In April 1999, the US District Court in Milwaukee dismissed the Wisconsin lawsuit and upheld the tribe's right to establish water-quality standards to protect its wild rice beds. The state appealed this decision. Four townships downstream from the proposed mine signed on as 'friends of the court' on the side of the EPA and the tribe. In June 2002, the US Supreme Court let stand the lower court decision.

Meanwhile, after five years of opposition from the state of Wisconsin and the state's largest business lobby, the Forest County Potawatomi won approval of their Class I air quality designation from the EPA. This allows the tribe to designate their 11,000 acres as Class I, the highest air designation possible. No new facilities that release more than 250 tons of particulate per year would be permitted. The mine is expected to emit about 247 tons of particulates into the air each year. If either tribal air or water quality standards should be violated by the proposed mine, the tribes can deny air or water quality permits necessary for mine approval.

The Mining Moratorium Campaign

Besides building local alliances between the tribes, environmental and sport-fishing groups, the Wolf Watershed Educational Project's speaking tours in 1996–97 built public support for legislative passage of a sulphite mining moratorium bill that would prohibit the opening of a new mine in a sulphite ore body until a similar mine had been operated for ten years elsewhere and closed for ten years without pollution from acid mine drainage. The movement for a sulphite mine ban originally developed out of the Rusk County Citizens Action Group in Ladysmith (site of Rio Tinto's Flambeau mine) and was developed into a piece of legislation at the initiative of the Menominee Nation's Mining Impacts and Treaty Rights office and with the assistance of State Representative Spencer Black (D–Madison). The legislation became a rallying point for the Native American, environmental and sportfishing group coalition as well as for the powerful pro-mine lobby in the state.

The mining companies and pro-mining Wisconsin Association of Manufacturers & Commerce (WMC) responded to the speaking tours and the moratorium campaign with newspaper ads, radio ads, a US$1 million blitz of television ads, and a US$1 million lobbying effort. Nevertheless, in March 1998, the legislature passed the moratorium bill after initially successful attempts to weaken it, and pro-mining Republican Governor Tommy Thompson was forced to sign the bill to ensure his re-election. The Crandon project appeared doomed to many when the 'mining moratorium' law was signed;

yet the new law did not stop the mine permit process, but rather provided another hurdle at the projected end of the permit process in about 2004.

The upsurge in environmental activism around the state, however, convinced Exxon to turn the Crandon project over to its partner Rio Algom. The Canadian company put the pipeline plan on the back burner, instead proposing on-site waste treatment in perpetuity. It submitted three 'example mines' to meet the criteria of the moratorium law (even though two of the mines had not been both open and closed for periods of ten years). In May 2002, the WDNR rejected the only example mine that had been both open and closed for periods of ten years because it failed to demonstrate that it had operated without harm to the environment. Finally, in August 2002, the WDNR concluded that potentially polluted groundwater from the mine may travel twenty-two times faster and reach pollution levels five times higher than the company's predictions, thus threatening local drinking water (Imrie, 2002).

A New Type of Environmental Movement

The moratorium and subsequent mining battles in Wisconsin have seen small grassroots groups using old-fashioned education and organizing to slow down the multinational mining corporations. They drew on Wisconsin's history of environmental ethics, as the home of John Muir, Aldo Leopold and the Menominee Chief Oshkosh. They also drew on Wisconsin's tradition of populist and progressive politics, with a dose of mistrust of corporations and their collaborators in government. The groups identified with a regional resentment by people (regardless of race) in northern Wisconsin, which has been historically poorer than the south, and neglected by the state government, while at the same time respecting Native nations' perseverance in defending their tribal sovereignty and treaty rights.

Resource corporations are used to dealing with stereotypical environmental groups, made up largely of White, urban, upper-middle-class twenty-somethings. The companies and Wise Use groups have been able to portray such groups as hippies and yuppies who do not care about rural joblessness. Wise Use groups arose in the western United States as an environmental backlash to grassroots rural environmental victories in the 1970s and 1980s. Much of the funding for this movement comes from mining, oil and timber interests in favour of opening up more federal lands for extractive resource development (Deal 1993). What the companies faced in northern Wisconsin was a rural-based multiracial, middle-class and working-class environmental movement, made up of many older people and youth. The companies slowly learned that they could not successfully use the same divide-and-conquer tactics that had worked so well elsewhere in the country.

First, they tried to split northerners by race. The treaty conflict did not, however, prevent sportfishers from joining the anti-mine alliance, or Nashville voters from electing a Mole Lake Chippewa to their new anti-mining town board in 1997. When Governor Thompson threatened the same year to close the casinos if the tribes did not back off on their treaty rights or federally backed environmental regulations, many non-Indian communities supported the tribes.

Second, the companies tried to split rural from urban people, by portraying anti-mining forces in their ads as 'well-funded' and based in urban groups. Yet the moratorium concept had emerged from rural groups, and rural legislators quickly learned that their constituents strongly supported it. Hundreds of signs sprouted on northern roads, and the theme of regional pride was claimed by anti-mining groups before Wise Use groups could use it, creating a lack of support for emerging pro-mine groups.

Third, the companies tried to split people by class. In one of its television ads, the mining company displayed a Milwaukee Steelworkers Union local president, who backed mining because many Wisconsin plants manufactured mining equipment. Yet Rio Algom's uranium mines in Ontario had killed dozens of Steelworker members in the 1970s, and Wisconsin union members formed the Committee of Labor Against Sulfide Pollution (CLASP) to expose the company's health and safety track record. Union locals and labour councils (many of whose members enjoy fishing in the north) passed resolutions against the Crandon mine.

The mining corporations have not been able to divide Wisconsin residents by race, region or class; the longer the Crandon project was delayed the more the global mining industry expressed frustration. The industry journal *North American Mining* in 1998 discussed Wisconsin as one of the industry's four main global battlegrounds, where 'increasingly sophisticated political manoeuvring by environmental special interest groups have made permitting a mine … an impossibility' (1998: 3). The journal of the National Mining Association earlier complained that Wisconsin 'barbarians in cyberspace' were spreading anti-corporate tactics around the world through the Internet (Webster 1998). The *Mining Environmental Management Journal* in 2000 portrayed the Wolf Watershed Educational Project as an 'example of what is becoming a very real threat to the global mining industry' (Khanna 2000: 19).

A Broader Anti-Corporate Movement

The movement against the Crandon mine has linked up with other environmental issues in northern Wisconsin, partly due to other vulnerabilities of the project. The Crandon mine would need enormous amounts of electrical power to process the ores, but it does not have adequate access to electricity. Proposed transmission lines from Duluth, Minnesota, would take power from hydroelectric dams that flood Manitoba Cree lands, transmit it on high-voltage lines that threaten northwestern Wisconsin farmers and the Lac Courte Oreilles Chippewa Reservation, and use it to power the Crandon mine at Mole Lake (LaDuke 2000). The transmission lines are under heavy criticism from a new rural alliance called Save Our Unique Lands (SOUL), in the process casting a shadow over the Crandon mine's future electrical needs. In recent public hearings on the lines project conducted by Wisconsin's Public Service Commission (PSC), virtually all the testimony has been critical of the project, prompting one official to comment that in his sixteen years at the PSC, 'no other project has met such strong and organized opposition from protesters' (Kamp 2000).

The alliance against the transmission lines closely resembles the grassroots Native/non-Native alliance against the Crandon mine, and successful concurrent opposition by central Wisconsin farmers and the Ho-Chunk (formerly Winnebago) Nation to a groundwater pumping plant proposed by the Perrier corporation. The three rural anti-corporate alliances have co-operated closely, holding a large rally in April 2000 at the state capitol, and organizing high-school and college students to join the growing state-wide movement, in the spirit of anti-corporate protests that emerged in Seattle and globally in 1999–2000.

In 2000, Rio Algom was purchased by the London-based South African company Billiton, which merged the following year with Australian mining giant BHP to form the world's largest mining company, BHP Billiton. Company spokesman Marc Gonsalves soon reported that the company had received an 'endless stream of emails' from Crandon mine opponents around the world (Kallio 2000). Mine opponents proposed a ban on cyanide use in Wisconsin mines to prevent the kind of mine-spill disaster that struck in Romania in 2000. They also proposed a bill to end 'special treatment' for the mining industry in state environmental laws. Meanwhile, anti-corporate organizers convened a 'Citizens' Assembly' in spring 2001 to bring together rural and urban grassroots groups with common concerns of protecting local governments and economies from corporate control and promoting environmental and cultural sustainability.

Beginning in December 2000, the Wolf Watershed Educational Project had demanded that BHP Billiton withdraw applications for mining permits and open a dialogue to negotiate the sale of the site. An alliance of environmental, conservation, local and tribal governments released a detailed proposal calling for the purchase of the Crandon mine site (more than 5,000 acres of land and mineral rights) as a conservation area devoted to sustainable land-management practices, tribal cultural values and tourism suitable to this environmentally sensitive area. The main goal of the purchase would be to end permanently the controversy over permitting the Crandon mine by taking the land out of the hands of mining companies.

'Our proposal will support low-impact sustainable development instead of destructive mining at the headwaters of the Wolf River', said Chuck Sleeter, board chairman of the town of Nashville. 'We want to protect natural and cultural resources and grow our economy wisely, instead of endangering it with risky, short-term mining' (Sleeter 2002). Less than a year after the mine opponents' proposal, BHP Billiton sold the Nicolet Minerals Company to the former site owners, a local logging company. The company unsuccessfully attempted to search worldwide for a multinational mining firm that would serve as a partner.

On 28 October 2003, Mole Lake and Potawatomi leaders announced that the two neighbouring tribes had jointly purchased and divided the 2,939-acre Crandon mine property for US$16.5 million. Mole Lake acquired the Nicolet Minerals Company, and quickly dropped mine permit applications. The bombshell announcement not only brought the 28-year battle to a dramatic end. It demonstrated that tribal gaming revenue could be used for the benefit of northern Wisconsin's environment and economy. It also showed the power of the tribes' cultural renaissance, and their work in alliance with non-Indian neighbours. The alliance had driven down the site price by tens of millions of dollars, by driving away potential mining company partners.

As he tacked up a giant 'SOLD' sign on the company, Potawatomi mine opponent Dennis Shepherd exclaimed, 'We rocked the boat. Now we own the boat.' The tribes held a large celebration powwow, where they honoured Natives and non-Natives who had opposed the mine. The less wealthy of the two tribes, Mole Lake, inherited a 'mortgage' from the company, and set up a Wolf River Protection Fund to help pay for its half of the purchase.

By 2003 the political landscape of northern Wisconsin had become very different, compared to the tensions before 1993. The relationship between Native and non-Native communities before 1993 had been framed in terms of 'exclusion'. Native Americans who left the reservations to spearfish were viewed as 'outsiders' by White residents, who tried to exclude the Chippewa (and later the Menominee) from treaty-ceded territories. Conversely, the Native nations enhanced their sense of non-Indians as 'outsiders' who did not understand their cultural ways or the environment of northern Wisconsin.

Also by 2003, the intense conflict over natural resources had been replaced by cooperation to protect natural resources. The relationship between Native and non-Native communities was increasingly framed in terms of 'geographies of inclusion'. The tribes and their White neighbours had begun to include each other as 'insiders' within a common place, such as the Willow Flowage or Wolf River watershed. This was not simply because the spearing conflict had been put behind them, but because their sense of 'exclusion' had been largely redirected away from each other and towards 'outsider' mining companies and state agencies. Furthermore, this shift to a 'place identity' was not limited to environmental cooperation, but had signs of being expanded to increase local economic cooperation and greater cultural understanding. Large gaps remained between the communities, and individuals' racial prejudice obviously continued, but the tribes and white 'border towns' were clearly moving away from mass confrontation and towards substantial cooperation.

These shifts in thinking not only happened despite the treaty rights tensions of the late 1980s and early 1990s, but occurred at least partly because of the tensions. The area between Mole Lake and Lac du Flambeau that had seen the greatest conflict during the fishing 'war' developed levels of environmental cooperation higher than those of other northern areas that had been spared conflict. The conflict had educated the non-Native community and strengthened the territorial identity of both groups and their commitment to protect the fishery and the relatively clean environment of northern Wisconsin.

The environmental cooperation began to redefine the Native and non-Native concepts of 'home'. Before 1993, most Natives and non-Natives possessed a meaning of 'home' that stopped at reservation boundaries. But by 2003, the Native American 'home' and the white majority's 'home' had begun to encompass both tribal and non-tribal lands in a common home. Mole Lake tribal member Frances Van Zile describes this shift in consciousness when she says that many local white residents now 'accept Mole Lake as part of home. It's not just my community. It's everybody's home.' She concludes:

> This is my home; when it's your home you try to take as good care of it as you can, including all the people in it.... We have to take care of this place, including everybody in it. I mean everybody that shares these resources should take care of it. It's not just my responsibility ... everyone in the community takes care of home. (Personal interview, 1994)

What mining companies are confronting in northern Wisconsin is an environmental movement that they have not yet experienced, at least in North America – a broad multiracial, rural-based grassroots alliance. This kind of movement, where livelihoods rather than environmental consciousness are at the forefront of environmental movements, is not new in the Third World (Taylor 1995). The alliance has brought together not only Native American nations and sportfishing groups, but environmentalists with unionists and retired local residents with urban students. The movement does not just address endangered species, but also endangered Native cultures and endangered rural economies. The tribal purchase of the Crandon mine site has brought the intercultural relationship full circle from conflict to cooperation and marks a small roll-back in the history of Native land dispossession.

The growing movement also recognizes that treaties and sovereign status offer Native nations unique legal powers to protect the local environment and economy for Indians and non-Indians alike, strengthening intercultural cooperation based on a territorial attachment to a common place. By connecting its seemingly local issues to a state-wide and global anti-corporate movement, the alliance is helping to create a broader vision of a democratic and sustainable society.[1]

Note

1. For more information, visit the Midwest Treaty Network, www.treatyland.com; Wisconsin Resources Protection Council, www.wrpc.net; and Wolf River Protection Fund, www.wolfriverprotectionfund.org.

References

Danziger, Edmund Jefferson (1978) *The Chippewas of Lake Superior*, Norman: University of Oklahoma Press.

Deal, Carl (1993) *The Greenpeace Guide to Anti-Environmental Organizations*, Berkeley, CA: Odonian Press.

Exxon (1994) Exxon Coal and Minerals Co., Proxy Statement, Houston: Exxon.

Gedicks, Al (1993) *The New Resource Wars: Native and Environmental Struggles against Multinational Corporations*, Boston: South End Press.

Grossman, Zoltán (2002) 'Unlikely alliances: treaty conflicts and environmental cooperation between Native American and rural white communities', Ph.D. thesis, Geography Dept, University of Wisconsin, Madison.

Imrie, Robert (1996) 'Rail blockade not solely about acid shipment', *St. Paul Pioneer Press*, 5 August.

———— (2002) 'New concern raised on pollution', *Wisconsin State Journal*, 31 August, p. B1.

Kallio, Nikki (2000) 'New mine owners face opposition', *Wausau Daily Herald*, 18 October.

Kamp, Jon (2000) 'Minnesota aquarium feud fuels power line dispute', *Dow Jones Energy Service*, 8 December.

Khanna, Tracey (2000) Editorial comment, *Mining Environmental Management*, vol. 8, no. 3, May, p. 19.

LaDuke, Winona (2000) 'Dams, transmission lines, and mines', *Potawatomi Traveling Times*, 1 December.

Midwest Treaty Network (1991) *Wisconsin Treaties: What's the Problem?*, Madison, WI.

North American Mining (1998) 'Troubled times; brighter future', vol. 2, no. 4, August/September, p. 3.

Seely, Ron (1999) 'Firm, town trade barbs', *Wisconsin State Journal*, 18 June.

Silvern, Steven E. (1995) 'Nature, territory and identity in the Wisconsin treaty rights controversy', *Ecumene*, vol. 2, no. 3, pp. 267–92.

Sleeter, Chuck (2002) 'Wolf river headwaters protection purchase proposed as final end to Crandon mine controversy', press release, 20 June.

Strickland, Rennard et al. (1990) 'Keeping our word: treaty rights and public responsibilities', Madison, WI: Report to the US Senate Committee on Indian Affairs.

Taylor, Bron Raymond (1995) *Ecological Resistance Movements: The Global Emergence of Radical and Popular Environmentalism*, Albany: State University of New York.

Van Zile, Frances (1994) Personal interview, 18 June.

Webster, Bob (1998) 'Barbarians at the gates of cyberspace', *Mining Voice*, vol. 4, no. 1, January/February, pp. 38–43.

WDNR (1986) *Final Environmental Impact Statement, Exxon Coal and Minerals Co. Zinc–Copper Mine, Crandon, Wisconsin*, Madison, WI: Department of Natural Resources.

World Book (1987) Vol. 15, Chicago: World Book.

Pehuenche communities and locations
of hydroelectric dams on the Bío-Bío river

Pehuenche Communities

Callaqui	Ralco-Lepoy	Rivers	
Malla-Malla	Trapa-Trapa	Lakes	
Quepuca		Administrative boundary	
		Dam	

Source : Pehuenche Communities and location of dams
http://www.mogensgallardo.com/ecobiobio/english/ralcoeng.html#pehuen

©Map by Glenn B. Garner 2003, glennbgarner@yahoo.ca

Projection : WGS 84

12

Chilean Economic Expansion
and Mega-development Projects
in Mapuche Territories

ALDISSON ANGUITA MARIQUEO

Aldisson Anguita Mariqueo is the former general coordinator of the Consejo Inter-regional Mapuche, an organization created in 1993 to provide a common platform for a variety of associations and initiatives of the Mapuche people.

In the deepest part of the sea lived a big snake whose name was Kai Kai.
It ruled over all the waters.
Once, it ordered the sea to cover the earth.
There was another snake, Xen Xen, who was as powerful as the first and who
   lived on top of the hills.
Xen Xen advised the Mapuche to climb over the mountains when the waters
   were starting to rise.
Many Mapuche could not climb and drowned, becoming fish. The waters rose
   and rose.
The hills floated and rose as well.
The Mapuche put small pots on their heads to protect themselves from the rain
And repeated this song to encourage the snakes in their fight:
'Kai Kai.'
And they answered:
'Xen Xen, Xen Xen.'
They prayed and the waters calmed down.
Those who survived came down from the hills and populated the land.
That is how the Mapuche were born.[1]

We, the Mapuche people, are one of the first peoples in the southern part of the Americas. We live in the middle and southern regions of what today are Chile and Argentina. When the Spaniards invaded our territory in 1541, our people numbered nearly a million. Then, one of the cruellest wars started; it lasted for over three hundred years. During the war our braves gave their lives to defend our independence and freedom. At the beginning, the Spaniards were unable to subjugate our people by military means, so they proposed and signed a peace treaty on 6 January 1641 at Quillin Tolten. By that treaty the Mapuche–Huiliche (Mapuche of the South), Mapuche–Lafquenche (Mapuche of the Coast), Mapuche–Picunche (Mapuche of the North) and Mapuche–Pehuenche (Mapuche of the Pewen[2]) were recognized by the Spaniards as independent nations occupying the southern part of contemporary Chile. However, the conflicts continued as the Spaniards regularly raided Mapuche territory searching for slaves to work in the northern regions, where disease had decimated the Aboriginal populations.

Once the *criollos* (people of European descent who were born and lived in the Americas) obtained independence from Spain and established the Chilean republic, new pressures were exerted in order to occupy the Independent Territories of the Mapuche nation. There were long debates among the *criollos*, but all concurred with the objective: the occupation of our lands. In 1868, using the Chilean army, they started an extermination war against the Mapuche. Many lives were taken in these wars. Terror spread through our territories as the army came burning houses, taking the women, killing the children and making prisoners of the men. Their intention was to force the men to work, or execute them as a 'pedagogical' measure. This massacre was called 'the Pacification of the Araucanía'. At the same time, with the same purposes and methods, the Argentinian army carried on with their 'Campaigns to the Desert' to take over the Mapuche territories in the Argentinian Patagonia.

The 'pacification campaigns' resulted in a military defeat for the Mapuche people. Thus began a long and different fight for survival. Our communities were forcefully relocated to reserves, where the lands were unfit and insufficient to sustain life. In 1880, the Mapuche territory comprised approximately 5 million hectares. After our military defeat all this territory was decreed state land. In 1890 a commission for Indigenous peoples' resettlement (Comisión Radicadora de Indígenas) concluded; it awarded only 475,000 hectares of land to 78,000 Mapuche.

Even then reserve lands were permanently under encroachment by big landowners. In fact, through the years, Chilean governments passed laws about land and property that were meant to open the way for big landowners to take over Mapuche lands in the shortest possible time. For example, during Augusto Pinochet's dictatorship a decree was passed segmenting communal lands into individually owned holdings, thereby intensifying the vulnerability of the communities and promoting the disintegration of our collective land rights. Nevertheless, we have managed to survive.

During the nineteenth and the first half of the twentieth century, we saw our territories drastically reduced and our people driven to poverty and marginality. Repeated visits by our *lonko* (leaders of the Mapuche communities) to the national authorities obtained nothing. On the contrary, the ensuing years were marked by laws that were negative for the communities as they promoted and forced the massive migration of our people to the urban centres, where they ended up working as servants and living in the poor peripheries. According to the national census of 1992, there are 1.5 million Mapuche living in the rural and urban areas of Chile. They constitute approximately 11 per cent of the total population of Chile. Of the total Mapuche population, at least half a million live in the capital city, Santiago.

In 1993, under the democratic government that followed the long military dictatorship, Law 19253, known as the 'Indigenous peoples' special law', was passed. Under this law the state is committed to protect and promote the development of the Indigenous peoples. A series of articles in the law addresses issues pertaining to Indigenous education, culture and land rights. The law also creates an organization, Corporación Nacional de Desarrollo Indígena (National Corporation for Indigenous Peoples' Development, known as CONADI), which is in charge of mediating relations between the government and the Indigenous peoples. We have experienced how the Chilean government respects this law.

Chilean Economic Expansion and the Mapuche People

Chilean commercial expansion and dominant free-market policies result in an unrestricted drive to gain access to natural resources, still abundant in Mapuche territories. These policies, therefore, constantly threaten the survival of Mapuche communities. This is the case with activities such as forestry, hydroelectric power plants and expansion of the highway system.

Forestry is an activity to which the Chilean state has given important support since 1973, when it provided subsidies to promote pine tree plantations. This activity has been carried out mainly by big corporations, in lands that are being claimed by Mapuche communities in many regions. In all these cases, Mapuche communities have been claiming what is rightfully theirs, since these lands were among the lands that the state 'gave' to the Mapuche in 1890. The documents proving this have been systematically ignored, and the lands have been usurped through deceitful laws and arbitrary measures taken during the military dictatorship and since.

The forestry industry in Chile has also received the support of several multilateral organizations, such as the World Bank and the Inter-American Development Bank. But multilateral support lent to the industry is channelled through many routes. For example, the United Nations Development

Programme, the Food and Agriculture Organization, and the Chilean National Commission of Forestry (CONAF) have joined in a programme that promotes a forestry action plan for Chile in which forestry experts are taken as consultants, thereby co-opting them for the transnational forestry industry. Thus, few experts in the industry recognize that successive massive replanting of pine trees has degraded the lands and resulted in serious environmental damage, further intensifying problems of poverty in the area. Indeed, in some places the use of pesticides has affected not only wild animals but also animals raised by the Mapuche who live in the area.

For the forestry companies, Indigenous communities are an annoyance since they refuse to sell their lands and put permanent obstacles in the way of the companies' plans for expansion. These big transnational corporations, claiming proprietary rights over the lands, use all their economic might to influence the state to thwart the legitimate owners' claims. For example, in December 1997 the police fought Mapuche protestors from the communities Pichi–Lincoyan and Pilil–Mapu. The communities were claiming their lands, and this generated a conflict because the government ignored Mapuche demands. The response of the 'democratic' government of Chile was to arrest twelve Mapuche under the legal umbrella of the Internal Security Law. This law, inherited from the military dictatorship, allows the security forces to search private residences and to arrest and interrogate any 'suspicious' individual without judicial intervention. Once Mapuche protestors were taken away under this law, no information was given to their families as to their whereabouts, intensifying the confusion, fear and hopelessness among their families and communities.[3]

Since the Chilean republic was created, legislation on Indigenous peoples' affairs has been tied to a certain concept of land as property. Acting on this concept, the Chilean state has caused poverty and marginality among the Mapuche. The first stage of these policies was the relocation of the Mapuche into non-contiguous reserves of little or no agricultural value. The second stage was encroachment on those communities' lands, since the private sector wanted them for different purposes. This generated poverty and marginality. However, until recently, the Mapuche–Pehuenche lands were spared from intense encroachment because they were relatively poor for agriculture and difficult to reach. Nevertheless, once the market found value in the water courses that pass through these lands and feed the Bío-Bío river, the government began to argue that it was necessary to undertake the challenge of developing the area. In order to do this, it plans to relocate Mapuche–Pehuenche families to even more marginal areas.

The Bío-Bío, one of Chile's main rivers, is located in the central part of the country. From its source in the area of the Lonquimay volcano to its mouth at the Pacific Ocean, the Bío-Bío gives life to hundreds of animal and plant species, making it a place of incalculable value that is recognized by both the national and the international scientific communities. Given that the river has a constant flow and that the geography it traverses is mountainous, it has become an appetizing target for hydroelectric companies that want to build dams in the valleys to produce electricity. The Empresa Nacional de Electricidad (National Electricity Company, ENDESA), created by the Chilean state and privatized during the military dictatorship, plans to build a series of six dams at different points on the Bío-Bío. One of these dams has already been built at Pangue.

ENDESA's project has produced alarm at the national and international levels. However, the company denies that its plan is to build that many dams.[4] In fact, Pangue, whose operations started in 1997, was built with the authorization of the military government, when neither Indigenous peoples' laws nor environmental laws were in place. The arguments used to legitimize the construction were the country's need for economic growth and the negligible environmental and social impact of the project. When democratic rule began, the new government gave all its support to the project, and the president of the Republic, Eduardo Frei Ruiz-Tagle, even inaugurated the dam. Fifty Mapuche–Pehuenche were relocated, and 500 hectares of land were flooded.

As soon as the Pangue hydroelectric facility was working, ENDESA publicized its intention to build a second dam upstream from Pangue. The dam they intend to build in Ralco will flood 3,500 hectares of land, almost all of which belongs to approximately a hundred Mapuche–Pehuenche families, who will be forcefully relocated. The big difference in this case is that, in contrast to what happened with the construction of Pangue, under a democratic government there are laws that protect Indigenous peoples and the environment. Thus, ENDESA had to produce several environmental and social-impact assessments to comply with these laws. In 1996, all the regulatory institutions, plus the affected communities, rejected the plans for mitigation of the social and environmental impacts presented by ENDESA. Nevertheless, after making cosmetic changes to the documents and putting pressure on the government, ENDESA obtained approval from the Comisión Nacional de Medioambiente (National Commission for the Environment, CONAMA) to go ahead with the project. This very murky approval resulted in the resignation of CONAMA's director. Nevertheless, ENDESA still had to obtain approval from CONADI for the relocation plans. Here is where the conflict began to show who has leverage over the government's decisions, for the government openly asked for the resignations of those directors of CONADI who publicly opposed the Ralco project.

ENDESA's Social and Cultural Effects on the Mapuche

ENDESA has invested enormous resources in a double tactic: public campaigns to press for relocation and enticements to individual Pehuenche families to approve the project and accept the proposed relocation. Through these actions families have been divided, causing a break in the way of life and in community ties that were intact until the arrival of ENDESA in the area.

In general, the concepts, language and values within which experts and politicians frame this project are rather alien to the communities and hard for them to understand. In addition to evident and regular misinformation, the use of highly technical language by experts and politicians has made any potentially meaningful communication ineffective. Severe problems of miscommunication affect relations both within the communities and between the communities and non-Indigenous people from outside. The experience of repeatedly receiving contradictory information from ENDESA's employees, government officials and NGOs, who had become involved because of the environmental consequences of the project, has been traumatic for the communities. In fact the situation has created a climate of confusion and mistrust within the communities.

For example, ENDESA promises employment. But people in the communities say that when Pangue was built employment was only temporary; once the dam was built ENDESA brought in its own personnel and did not train or hire any member of the communities. CONADI is supposed to protect Indigenous peoples' rights, but ENDESA keeps working even without its authorization. CONAMA, the environmental agency, is very strict with the Pehuenche who cut trees, but it does nothing to stop ENDESA, which is going to flood thousands of hectares of forest and is clear-cutting wide areas to open up roads.

This is another aspect of 'development' that is affecting Mapuche communities. In effect, growing economic activity in this area, which includes what is referred to as the Eighth and Ninth Regions of Chile, has meant an increase in the number of roads being opened up. The expansion of a road network serves to connect urban centres and ports with places where natural resources are being exploited. The plans have already affected several communities of the Mapuche–Lafquenche, who have seen their lands suddenly expropriated, in some cases divided and in others simply 'vanished'. For example, in the city of Temuco, which has become an important node in this network, the construction of a highway has been started. The project provoked conflicts with Mapuche communities who opposed the project. However, the government, unwilling to accept any other alternative, exerted pressure and offered monetary enticements that finally broke down the resistance.

The Chilean state's conception of development is one without any trace of equity. For example, the public services that are supposed to bring welfare and assistance to all Chilean citizens are almost non-existent where Mapuche communities are located. This is especially the case in the Pehuenche area. Here, programmes for improving health care, housing, education, local infrastructure and roads, social assistance, and employment conditions are insufficient when they are not totally absent. Representatives of the government have recently shown up in the area because of the conflict that has been generated, not because of any honest interest in the well-being of the Pehuenche.

In all these conflicts, the government has argued that the country's development must take precedence over other concerns. Using this as justification, the government has been free not to question its own assumptions about a given project. Each time that dialogue has been called for, this justification is made by the government, and proposals for alternatives are ignored. For us, it is clear that in the plans for development, promoted by the government and the markets, Mapuche territory is doomed to disappear. Development, as it is pursued today, pronounces a death sentence over the land and over Mapuche culture, for it attacks the communities, atomizing them and rendering them vulnerable to the markets and their projects. We are not going to accept this.

Notes

1. 'Mapuche' means People of the Land (*mapu* = land; *che* = people).
2. Pewen is a tree that grows in the Southern Andes; its fruit is the staple food of Mapuche from the Pewen.
3. For details about this conflict, see http://members.aol.com/MAPULINK/.
4. See the reports on the International Rivers Network (IRN) website at www.irn.org, as well as the American Anthropological Association Committee for Human Rights website at www.aaanet.org/committees/cfhr.

13

Hydroelectric Development on the Bío-Bío River, Chile: Anthropology and Human Rights Advocacy

BARBARA ROSE JOHNSTON AND
CARMEN GARCIA-DOWNING

Barbara Rose Johnston is Senior Research Fellow at the Center for Political Ecology, Santa Cruz, CA, and emeritus chair of the American Anthropological Association's Committee for Human Rights. She has edited numerous volumes on human rights and environmental conflicts and activism.

Carmen Garcia-Downing is a faculty member in the College of Public Health at the University of Arizona. She collaborated as the cultural consultant with Ted Downing, her husband, in the evaluation of the Pehuen Foundation that was mandated to address the needs of the Pehuenche people of Chile.

Until recently, the Bío-Bío river cascaded through the heart of Pehuenche territory. Today the river is harnessed by the Pangue dam and the soon to be completed Ralco dam. The hillsides have been stripped of their timber and the river valleys flooded. Many of the Pehuenche – a cultural group often described as the last Chilean Indigenous group to live by traditional means on traditional lands – have lost their homes and are being forced to accept resettlement in the distant and difficult mountains. The Pehuenche had no opportunity to participate in the decisions to dam their river, deforest their hills or flood their valleys. And the Pehuenche had no opportunity to help shape the varied remedies offered by project developers as meagre compensation for the loss of ancestral lands, resources, community cohesion and way of life. Inept planning and inadequate local involvement in decision-making resulted in hydroelectric dam development without adequate assessment of the real human and environmental costs. The end effect is that a small, poverty-stricken band of Pehuenche Indians have been forced to subsidize Chilean hydroelectric power development at the cost of their economy, resources and culture.

As illustrated in the previous chapter by Mapuche activist Aldisson Anguita, the Pehuenche and their neighbours have not accepted their fate quietly or with ease. The struggle to secure Pehuenche rights to participate in development decisions has been a lengthy, tumultuous process involving local, national and international actors whose efforts to draw public attention to inequities and abuses have been successful, yet meaningful remedy remains elusive. In this chapter we outline the events and actions that structure this dam development controversy; describe efforts to document and remedy institutional failures in World Bank-funded development planning, impact assessment, resettlement planning, and implementation of mitigation programmes; describe efforts to encourage institutional action by filing human rights complaints within the World Bank, and when these failed to produce meaningful remedy, to file human rights complaints in an independent forum of a scientific organization (the Committee for Human Rights of the American Anthropological Association); summarize the political outcome of these efforts; and, finally, we briefly discuss some of the lessons emerging from this decade and more of struggle to halt dam development on the Bío-Bío river.

Dam Development Decisions and Controversy

In 1989 hydroelectric dam development on the Bío-Bío river was first proposed by Empresa Nacional de Electricidad SA (ENDESA) – a private energy and resource development corporation in Chile. In 1990, the newly elected Chilean government approved plans for hydroelectric development of the Bío-Bío river. Implementing this project would require invoking the Electrical Services Law (decreed during Augusto Pinochet's regime in 1982) to privatize Pehuenche reservation land. ENDESA applied for a loan to the private-sector arm of the World Bank Group – the International Finance Corporation (IFC) – to finance the construction of the state-sanctioned, privately owned Pangue Dam. ENDESA did not request, nor did the IFC make any reference to, involvement in another five hydroelectric dams on the Alto Bío-Bío river. In 1990 the IFC began appraising the Pangue Dam proposal.[1]

In December 1992, the IFC board approved the decision to invest US$150 million in the Pangue dam project. On 22 October 1993, the IFC and ENDESA signed an investment agreement providing a US$170 million loan to ENDESA to build the Pangue dam, and US$4.7 million in equity for the Pangue project. Both parties accepted the state of New York as the legal jurisdiction. Since the agreement was secret, the Pehuenche had no way to know that arrangements were being made about them.[2] The loan agreement, in addition to containing plans that would determine the fate and livelihood of an Indigenous nation, granted the IFC a 2.5 per cent equity interest in Pangue SA, a subsidiary wholly owned by ENDESA (then a Chilean company). Pangue SA would build and operate the hydroelectric facility. At the same time that the IFC finalized its Pangue funding agreement with ENDESA, work began to develop the initial plans for the second dam, the Ralco dam, immediately upstream from the Pangue.

Development plans and financing decisions occurred despite the many and vocal protests by various Pehuenche, Chilean citizens, and nongovernmental organizations who expressed deep concern over the environmental and social impacts of building the first and then second of a proposed series of six dams on the Bío-Bío. Beginning in 1991, the Pehuenche community and their advocates participated in public protests and letter-writing campaigns, and provided testimony to the Chilean public, Chilean government and international forums. They expressed opposition to the dam project and their desire to retain their ancestral lands. As the years went by and development decisions fuelled the early stages of dam construction (clearing of hillsides, building of roads), local protests continued and were further strengthened with increased references to Chilean laws protecting Indigenous land rights. These laws include the Chilean Constitution adopted in 1990, the October 1993 Indigenous Peoples Law, and the March 1994 Environment Law. Under the 1993 Ley Indigena (Indigenous Peoples Law), the Pehuenche control their lands. The national Indigenous development corporation, Corporación Nacional de Desarrollo Indígena (CONADI), a government agency formed by this law, has the fiduciary right to accept or refuse transfers, exchanges, privatizations or expansions (*permutas*) of Indigenous lands.[3] And, under the 1994 Environment Law, a similar commission – Comisión Nacional del Medio Ambiente (CONAMA) – was established to review and approve all development-related decisions affecting the natural environment. The Chilean environmental organization GABB – Grupo de Alto Bío-Bío – emerged as a major force in Chilean politics, educating citizens about the environmental impacts of dams on the Bío-Bío and the importance of enforcing the newly created laws. GABB developed close collaborative ties with a number of international NGOs, most notably the International Rivers Network (IRN), whose educational efforts brought the issue to the awareness of tens of thousands of environmental activists around the world.[4]

Dam development protests citing violations of Chilean national law were dismissed by ENDESA as irrelevant, since the project was approved prior to the formation of these laws. Furthermore, ENDESA argued that under the 1982 Energy Law, the nation's need for energy superseded Indigenous rights. In response, dam opponents argued that Pangue was designed to work in conjunction with a large reservoir dam upstream (Ralco), that the government should consider environmental and social effects of building two dams before giving approval to build Pangue, that new development proposals should be assessed for their individual and cumulative impact, and that development decisions should reflect full compliance with current Chilean law.

Public protests against the World Bank funding of the Pangue dam were widely covered in the Chilean and international media, and this coverage raised considerable concern among private investors who were brought in following the initial IFC/ENDESA financing agreement. Pangue project supporters, including IFC staff, produced rebuttal arguments describing Pangue as a single, stand-alone dam unrelated to ENDESA's other dams, and a hydroelectric development project that was located adjacent to but not on Pehuenche lands. Thus, the project reportedly would not involve any involuntary resettlement of Pehuenche.[5] The IFC's assurance that Pangue was a stand-alone dam, and ENDESA's assurance that it would only use IFC funds for this single dam, calmed investor fears, and the project proceeded. In 1996, despite long and intense protest in Chile and abroad, the Pangue dam was completed and its reservoir filled.

Efforts to Halt Further Dam Development and Seek Redress for Problems Resulting from Pangue Dam Construction

The intense period of national and international protest in the early and mid-1990s provoked a wide array of responses. The Pehuenche and Mapuche communities became increasingly politicized by their conditions and experiences, and their place-based issues involving land and resource rights increasingly came to be seen as national issues. National and international nongovernmental organizations developed close collaborative ties to communicate and encourage political action. The Chilean government was continually challenged by the contradictions between rights-protective legislation and the lack of political will or power to enforce the law (challenges that produced significant political fallout). And the World Bank saw its image and actions placed under increasingly critical international scrutiny.

In 1995, in response to Chilean and international advocacy criticizing Bío-Bío dam development and human rights abuses, the IFC hired Dr Theodore Downing (President Emeritus of the Society for Applied Anthropology) to conduct an external audit of the social impacts of the Pangue dam. Specifically, Downing was asked to evaluate the efficacy of the Pehuen Foundation, an organization created by IFC and ENDESA to offset the socio-economic impacts of hydroelectric development. In October 1995 Downing travelled to Chile and met with some sixty stakeholders representing different sides of the dam development conflict. Downing presented the evaluation plan to the IFC, which accepted it, completed his fieldwork in November and December 1995, and submitted his report to the IFC in May 1996 (Downing 1996).

The Downing audit findings supported conclusions that the Pehuen Foundation implemented a programme of resettlement that failed to incorporate the rights of Indigenous peoples, and failed to compensate all affected peoples adequately – in direct violation of the World Bank Group's involuntary resettlement and indigenous policies. In addition to these and other critical findings, Downing documented those instances where Foundation objectives were being met, and also offered a number of specific recommendations to address past failures and improve the ability of the Pehuen Foundation to address the socio-economic needs of the Pehuenche community.

On 17 November 1995, while Downing was in the field conducting his Pehuen Foundation evaluation, a group of nearly four hundred Chilean citizens, including Pehuenche Indians, environmentalists and other concerned individuals, filed a complaint with the World Bank's Inspection Panel.[6] This complaint was unrelated to Downing's investigation. The Chilean NGOs, led by GABB, alleged that the IFC had violated Bank rules on environmental assessment and its own environmental and social policies on dam and reservoir projects, Indigenous peoples, involuntary resettlement, management of cultural property, wildlands protection and management, and project supervision, as set forth in 'IFC: Environmental Analysis and Review of International Finance Corporation Projects'. They were unaware that Downing had discovered and was reporting the same conclusion from within the IFC. Both the Downing report and the Chilean complaint charged that IFC funds allocated to Pangue SA were appropriated and applied to the Ralco project, in clear violation of the loan agreement and the IFC's assurances that its loan funds would be used only for Pangue, not Ralco.

The World Bank Inspection Panel, in reviewing the November 1995 petition filed by GABB, rejected the complaint on the grounds that the IFC, while a member of the World Bank Group, sponsored private/public partnerships whose actions fell outside the Panel's jurisdiction. The Inspection Panel refused to investigate. Responding to the concerns of the Bank's executive directors, however, World Bank President James D. Wolfensohn promised an 'impartial, internal review' of the Pangue loan, and reiterated that 'the IFC has no plans to provide financial support for Ralco' (cited in Cockburn 1997).

In May 1996 the IFC received Downing's report. According to Downing's statements, on the day he submitted his report, IFC and ENDESA announced their new agreement to use the Foundation to mitigate the social impacts of Ralco dam construction – especially resettlement. Two weeks later IFC staff submitted a summary of Downing's report to ENDESA for their approval before releasing it to the Pehuenche in completion of the participatory evaluation. ENDESA rejected the summary and threatened to sue the IFC and Downing if they released the report to the Indians or the public (Downing, personal communication). The IFC agreed to suppress the Downing report and terminated the final phase of his investigation – a reporting requirement included in Downing's consultant contract that involved disseminating findings and recommendations to Pehuenche and the broader Chilean community.

At the same time that the IFC accepted and then censored the Downing report, in the spring of 1996, GABB commissioned a critique of the Ralco environmental impact statement (EIS). The resulting report prompted the Chilean environmental agency CONAMA to declare the Ralco environmental impact statement unsatisfactory. The GABB critique found that not only did the EIA omit an analysis of environmental impacts, it lacked details on resettlement plans for the more than five hundred Pehuenche who would be moved for the Ralco dam. Subsequent pressure from ENDESA and government officials prompted CONAMA to retract its finding.

Also in the spring of 1996, World Bank President James Wolfensohn contracted Jay Hair, President Emeritus of the National Wildlife Federation, to evaluate ENDESA's compliance with the IFC/ENDESA agreement (including environmental and social-impact mitigation plans) and review the findings of the still censored Downing report. Commissioning another independent evaluation provided a legitimate excuse to delay the release of the Downing report (a tactic that ultimately kept the Downing findings secret until the Ralco comment period had passed and development plans were approved). Wohlfensohn's actions also served to deflect public criticisms over the failure of the World Bank Inspection Panel to investigate the environmental and social complaints associated with Pangue dam.

In February 1997, in response to the abundant evidence of project failures and political pressures emerging from all quarters, the IFC served notice to ENDESA that failure to meet the environmental conditions of their loan would result in a declaration of default. Rather than take action to comply with contracted obligations, ENDESA found a way to deflate the power of the World Bank in this affair by seeking financing elsewhere. In March 1997, the World Bank Group/IFC loan was repaid by ENDESA with funds secured from a German private development bank consortium (Dresdner Bank). This action reduced IFC participation to its 2.5 per cent equity in Pangue SA.

In March 1997, CONADI released a report stating that the Ralco project was illegal according to Chile's 1993 Indigenous Law. In response, Chilean President Frei fired CONADI's director, Mauricio Huenchulaf, a strong

Pehuenche supporter. ENDESA then announced that the Pehuen Foundation would be the vehicle for Ralco resettlement.

Jay Hair submitted his report in April 1997. On 15 April 1997 participants at a workshop in Gland, Switzerland, co-sponsored by the World Bank and the World Conservation Union (IUCN), discussed the findings of a review of fifty World Bank-funded dams, carried out by the Bank's semi-independent Operations Evaluation Department (OED). The need for a truly independent review of dams was identified, with workshop participants concluding that the primary operating assumption behind dam funding – the benefits of large dams 'far outweighed' their costs – was based on inadequate data and flawed methodology. The IUCN and World Bank agreed to fund an independent 'World Commission on Dams'.[7]

On 16 April 1997, Juan Pablo Orrego, director of GABB, was awarded the Goldman Environmental Prize, the equivalent of the Nobel Prize for environment protection. This award further increased international attention to the issues and concerns surrounding the hydroelectric development of the Bío-Bío.

On 25 April 1997, the IFC and ENDESA signed a private agreement to address outstanding environmental and social impacts resulting from IFC's investment in Pangue. Like the original agreement between IFC and ENDESA that established the Pehuen Foundation, agreement was negotiated without the awareness or involvement of the Pehuenche, and without disclosing the complete terms of the agreement to the affected people, the Chilean government or the public.

In June 1997, CONAMA approved the Ralco project environmental assessment with three conditions: increasing minimum river flows, increasing technical assistance to the Pehuenche from four to ten years through the Pehuen Foundation, and establishing a biological reserve to replace forest resources lost through dam construction and subsequent flooding.

Human Rights Complaints

In the months while Hair was producing his report, Downing continued to seek public dissemination of his findings. His efforts generated significant internal discussions but no satisfactory resolution. On 16 December 1996, after sending scores of memos to IFC management about the violations of IFC Indigenous and resettlement policy in the Pangue project and the need to ensure that the Pehuenche were opportunely informed, Downing filed the first human rights complaint ever made inside the World Bank Group (Downing 1996). He alleged that specific management and staff had intentionally and wilfully violated the human and civil rights of the Pehuenche.

Among the key elements of the Downing complaint is the concern that withholding key documents containing evidence of the failures of the Pehuen Foundation to meet the social, environmental and resettlement obligations of the Pangue Project violated the political and civil rights of the Pehuenche, especially given that this information was central to determining the validity of Ralco dam project plans, which relied on the Pehuen Foundation to implement social impact and resettlement programmes. Downing's complaint was assigned to the IFC senior vice-president and chief counsel for investigation. Two months latter, executive vice-president Lindbak informed Downing that the complaint had been thoroughly investigated by his chief legal counsel and was without merit. Downing responded with a second human rights complaint to the World Banks ethics officer, alleging an IFC cover-up, noting that he, as the complainant, had never been interviewed during the thorough investigation. This complaint was similarly dismissed.[8] One result of Downing's efforts to demand from the World Bank public disclosure of his findings was the Bank's threat of a lawsuit garnering Downing's assets, income and future salary if he disclosed the contents, findings and recommendations of his independent evaluation.

In July 1997, IFC staff released to its board and to the public a heavily redacted version of the Hair report, explaining: 'The remaining portions of the Report are not released based on the advice of external legal counsel' (Lee 1997: 3; Cockburn 1997). Portions totalling one-third of the document had been deleted, including much of the material describing social impact and possible human rights violations. And the report was edited in ways to distort Hair's findings. Large sections of still-censored Downing report on the social impacts had been copied, almost verbatim, into the Hair report and were redacted again. Enough did get through to indicate that, while Hair found that the IFC failed to comply with 80 per cent of its environmental and social directives, the IFC version of his report says: 'The IFC considers the Pangue Project complied with five out of eight policies and procedures applicable' (quoted in Crawford 1997).

In September 1997, CONADI publicly questioned the legitimacy of individual resettlement agreements between Pehuenche families and ENDESA, saying that ENDESA had omitted key information on the resettlement site's location and setting when gathering signatures. Nine Pehuenche lonkos reiterated their previous opposition to Ralco and their refusal to move. In fall 1997, the Chilean public had an opportunity to review and comment on the Ralco dam EIS, which proposed mitigating adverse social impacts through the Pehuen Foundation. In October 1997, six of the seven Pehuenche band leaders met to review the Ralco EIS and voted to reject resettlement.

In the fall of 1997, unable to get the IFC to release his findings, and concerned that the Ralco development decision would be finalized without key information, Downing formally filed his third human rights complaint, this time with the American Anthropological Association Committee for Human Rights (CfHR). In November 1997, the AAA invited Downing, Chilean sociologist Claudio Gonzalez Parra, and representatives from the IFC and World Bank to present their sides of this story to the AAA membership at an Open Forum, and to discuss the human rights complaints in greater detail at a meeting of the AAA Committee for Human Rights. In addition to the censorship complaint, the CfHR received testimony that in the building of the Pangue dam some Pehuenche families were forcibly evicted from their lands, receiving no resettlement assistance. Most notable was the experience of the Sotomayor Riquelme family: their home and property were flooded, resettlement assistance was not provided, and the Pehuenche family were struggling to survive while living in the animal shed on relatives' land.

The CfHR found the case to be within its area of concern, and voted to investigate the complaint. Over the next four months, through testimony, interviews and review of public reports, planning documents and various communications, the CfHR explored whether the IFC-sponsored development of the Pangue dam violated the rights of an Indigenous community; whether censorship of the Downing report violated the rights of an independent evaluator to disseminate scientific findings in ways that reflect ethical, human subject and contractual obligations to an affected community; and whether this censorship violated the rights of that community to information concerning the terms and performance of organizations operating on their behalf.

The CfHR review was partially enhanced by unanticipated access to the censored Downing report. On 24 December 1997, Downing finally received notice from the IFC that it would not seek legal remedy if he copied and distributed his report, providing that he added a qualifying statement that the report was not an official IFC document. The IFC granted this permission to release Downing's research findings after the public review period for the Ralco project had expired. Thus, while the CfHR had the opportunity to review the Downing evaluation as part of their inquiry into human rights abuse, the Chilean people did not have access to this critical information when they most needed it. During the eighteen months that the IFC kept Downing's report secret, ENDESA negotiated resettlement packages with individual Pehuenche families, with the assurance that the Pehuen Foundation would implement the resettlement programme. These assurances were made despite ENDESA having on file the evidence provided by Downing that the Pehuen Foundation failed to meet the economic, social, cultural and environmental needs of the Pehuenche already affected by the Pangue dam, and lacked the technical means to mitigate adequately the impoverishment that would result from resettlement associated with further dam development.

By withholding this crucial documentation on the functional viability of the Pehuen Foundation from the people that the foundation was supposed to serve, the IFC and ENDESA prevented the Pehuenche from making an informed decision about their future.

On 8 January 1998, despite lack of approval from CONADI, ENDESA announced that it would complete agreements with contractors in February 1998 and begin bidding in March 1998 for two civil construction projects: a tunnel and the dam itself. Construction of Ralco dam required the displacement of more than 1,000 people, including 600 Pehuenche from the communities of Ralco-Lepoy and Quepuca-Ralco. ENDESA relocated some Pehuenche on farms in the snow-covered Andean highlands above the dam and others onto downstream settlements. Construction in the area has continued, as have civil protests.

AAA Committee for Human Rights Findings

In March 1998 the AAA's CfHR released the results of its inquiry in the form of a briefing paper (Johnston and Turner 1998). This report included quotations from statements and press releases issued by Carol Lee, vice-president and general counsel of the IFC, acknowledging that some of the IFC's decisions and actions were flawed; noting that the IFC should have taken a more systematic approach to analysing environmental and social impacts in the Pangue project before funding; acknowledging that the IFC should have handled the Indigenous peoples' issues more thoroughly, especially the project's indirect impacts on Indigenous people; and admitting that the lack of informed participation by Indigenous people has been a weakness of the project (IFC 1997b: 2, cited in Johnston and Turner 1998). According to Lee, problems associated with the project should be understood as part of IFC's 'learning curve', and IFC shortcomings, while unfortunate, were 'consistent with the environmental procedures in place at the time' (Lee, statements to the CfHR and IFC 1997b: 4, cited in Johnston and Turner 1998). And, Lee argued, the project itself was improved as a result of IFC's involvement. IFC's contributions included requiring an environmental-impact statement, publicly disclosed in Chile; involvement of a wide variety of stakeholders in development planning and project implementation; establishment of an ecological station to monitor downstream effects; establishment of the Pehuen Foundation, an innovative mechanism for returning corporation profits to the community; and revision of the Foundation operating procedures to include some changes recommended by Downing (increasing Indigenous participation in the Foundation and including Pehuenche personnel in Foundation activities; development of a culturally appropriate information and participation programme; adopting the Pehuenche language as a working language of the Foundation). Finally, the IFC noted that the public controversies and experience have prompted a number of changes at IFC, including adding staff, creating an environmental review unit, and drafting proposed human and environmental policies and procedures.

However, while acknowledging that mistakes were made and people and their environment suffered as a result, the IFC did not acknowledge responsibility for providing meaningful remedy to the varied problems resulting from their past failures. The CfHR review concluded that the IFC refusal to release Downing's 1996 report not only violated professional ethics and contractual obligations of an individual scientist and his obligations to the 'human subjects' involved in his study, but violated the civil and political rights of an Indigenous nation.

The CfHR confirmed Downing's human rights allegations, noting that the IFC failure to release Downing's 1996 report to the Pehuenche in a culturally appropriate and timely manner meant that the Pehuenche were asked to sign resettlement agreements – exchanging ancestral land rights for land high in mountains, several hours distant from their homes – without an understanding of the effects of the Pangue dam development or the potential effects of the proposed Ralco dam. And, the Pehuenche were not informed about how the Pehuen Foundation is structured, what role it is supposed to play in funnelling income back into the Pehuenche community, or of their constitutionally protected right to participate in the decision to build a dam within their ancestral territory. The CfHR concluded that, in censoring Downing's evaluation findings, the IFC was able to protect the economic interests of its private partner, by knowingly withholding from the Pehuenche information that directly affected their constitutional rights, their social welfare, and their ability to recognize and address developing threats to their cultural survival.

Disseminating CfHR Findings to Encourage Meaningful Remedy

On 19 March 1998, AAA President Jane Hill submitted a copy of the CfHR report with a covering letter to World Bank President James Wolfensohn. In this letter Hill urged Wolfensohn to consider concrete actions that might provide remedy to those individuals, families and communities whose lives have been irreparably harmed by the IFC behaviour in this case; and actions that might minimize and prevent the incidence of similar abuses in other development projects. She requested an apology to Dr Downing and the reinstatement of his working relationship with the World Bank; the adoption of a uniform and uniformly binding commitment to guarantee the human rights of all groups impacted by World Bank development projects; the institution of organizational changes that will prevent project-level implementation from ignoring the Bank Group's directives on human rights, resettlement and participation by local populations; and improvement in project information flow and accountability for human rights within the Bank Group's structure, and beyond the Bank to public groups and peoples affected by those projects.[9]

In an effort to educate its professional membership and the international human rights community about the details of this case, the AAA posted the CfHR briefing paper on its website, together with related correspondence between the AAA and the World Bank. Within a few weeks, a number of non-profit organizations created weblinks to the AAA report. The report was translated into Spanish by GABB.[10] The AAA also worked to inform its membership and other professional organizations about the investigation findings and recommended actions. The CfHR report authors developed news articles for the *Anthropology Newsletter* and the American Academy for the Advancement of Science (Johnston and Turner 1998b) and published an abstracted version of the report in the journal *Identities* (Johnston and Turner 1999).

In April 1998, while attending the Summit of the Americas meeting in Chile, World Bank President James D. Wolfensohn apologized for the Bank's alleged participation in the Ralco hydroelectric project in southern Chile, noting that it will displace some 96 Indigenous Pehuenche families from their homes on the upper Bío-Bío river. Wolfensohn said to reporters covering the Summit that Ralco 'was not one of the high points in the bank's experience'.

On 30 September 1998, having received no response from the World Bank to the earlier letter and report, AAA President Hill sent a follow-up query. On 21 October 1998, World Bank President James D. Wolfensohn replied, noting that while 'there were serious shortcomings in the way that IFC handled the Pangue project' as a result of close scrutiny and review of Pangue and other projects, IFC has expanded its review staff and put into place 'new and more stringent environmental and social review procedure' and 'safeguard policies which follow closely those of the World Bank'.[11] Regarding the 'lack of progress made in responding to the March 1998 report' Wolfensohn suggested that it was 'important to recognize that IFC's capacity to influence outcomes of the projects it helps finance varies, depending on when in the project cycle intervention is needed', and that the responsibility for defining the issues addressed by client companies in private-sector projects 'must, by their scope and nature, be in the domain of the national government'. Thus, according to Wolfensohn, IFC in its current relationship to ENDESA has 'no leverage to address existing deficiencies in the social area'.[12]

In late 1999, recognizing the growing need for some mechanism to allow project-affected parties the opportunity to lodge complaints and resolve conflicts, the IFC and the Multilateral Investment Guarantee Agency (MIGA) established the Office of the Compliance Advisor/Ombudsman. This office receives and explores the environmental and social concerns voiced by people affected by projects financed or insured by IFC and MIGA.[13] In May 2000 the IFC held a public meeting introducing to the nongovernmental community their new ombudsman, Meg Taylor. CfHR member Linda Raben attended, and raised questions concerning the status of complaints associated with the Indigenous peoples involuntarily displaced by the IFC-financed Pangue dam, especially the status of the Sotomayor Riquelme family. IFC Ombudsman Meg Taylor indicated a lack of familiarity with the development project and its social complaints, and requested additional information, promising that her office would look into the matter.

In July 2000, with no evidence of action coming from IFC, the CfHR provided copies of its briefing paper and associated AAA–World Bank correspondence to Claudio Gonzalez Parra, the Chilean sociologist working with Pehuenche peoples displaced by the Pangue and Ralco dams on the Bío-Bío river in Chile. Gonzalez used these materials to support a formal request for intervention by the IFC ombudsman to examine, among other concerns, the case of involuntary displacement experienced by the Pehuenche Sotomayor Riquelme family. Also in July 2000 the CfHR provided a copy of its briefing paper 'The Pehuenche: Human Rights, the Environment, and Hydrodevelopment on the Bío-Bío river, Chile' to the World Commission on Dams (WCD) for consideration during its July 2000 meeting in South Africa. The WCD was considering using IFC-financed Pehuen Foundation as an example of an innovative model appropriate for public involvement in hydro-dam development. Review of the CfHR report allowed the WCD to consider some of the human and environmental problems emerging from the performance of the Pehuen Foundation, and this case study helped inform the WCD's recommendations on social impact mitigation and equity participation in future dam development.

On 7 February 2001, the AAA and its CfHR sent a letter of concern to Meg Taylor, noting the lack of action on the July 2000 complaint filed by Gonzalez Parra on behalf of the Sotomayor Riquelme family. The 7 February 2001 letter also cited findings from the World Commission on Dams review of hydroelectric dam development on Chile's Bío-Bío river, which noted a range of unresolved mitigation issues. With this letter, the AAA formally added its name to the 150 nongovernmental organizations from 39 countries who endorsed the WCD report and called for the World Bank and other public financial institutions and agencies involved in dam building to adopt WCD guidelines and provide reparations to affected communities.

The Impact of Human Rights Advocacy
on the Ground and within the World Bank

In July 2001, AAA member Ted Downing reported to the CfHR that ENDESA (Spain) had arranged for the Pehuenche Sotomayor Riquelme family to receive 30 hectares and a house. No arrangements had been made to compensate them for pain and suffering associated with five years of involuntary displacement.

In Chile, the Ralco dam development proceeded, as did public protests over construction and forced resettlement. In March 2002 a massive protest took place in the upper Bío-Bío, with Pehuenche families and their supporters blocking the road and inhibiting transport of a generator meant to power the hydroelectric plant at Ralco dam. Police response was violent, and fifty-five people – the majority of them Pehuenche – were arrested and charged in military courts for alleged attacks against the police.

On 1 July 2002, GABB filed a 'Petition to address outstanding issues of IFC financed and partly owned Pangue/Ralco projects' with the IFC office of the ombudsman. This petition requested the Ombudsman's assistance in shaping concrete remedies to resolve outstanding issues arising out of IFC involvement in the Pangue/Ralco hydroelectric project in the Upper Bío-Bío. The petition was filed by GABB with the signed support of Pehuenche and other residents in the immediate and downstream regions of the Pangue and Ralco dams. The complaint was filed against the IFC as it financed Pangue/Ralco projects and was partial owner of Pangue. Shortly after receiving the complaint, the IFC quietly sold its remaining 2.5 per cent ownership of Pangue.[14]

On 2 September 2002 the IFC office of the ombudsman announced its intent to mount an investigation into unresolved issues surrounding its financing of Pangue dam and the subsequent construction of Ralco. The field mission was scheduled to begin on 18 November 2002, with a report due by the end of that year. The ombudsman's office will present its findings to ENDESA, IFC and the complainants.

The previously isolated Bío-Bío region is now characterized by unchecked in-migration, land speculation and deforestation. The area has attracted a number of independent timber contractors who give Pehuenche landowners small sums of money, harvest their trees and leave, making the landowners unwittingly responsible for the violation of Chilean forestry laws, which require permits and reforestation. Fines have been levied, and a number of Pehuenche, unable to pay the steep fines, live in fear of losing their land rights or are currently threatened with eviction. As indicated in the previous chapter in this volume and evidenced in recent events, the Ralco dam development controversy continues as Pehuenche communities resist resettlement, protest dam development activities and related deforestation, and deal with the difficult outcomes of increasingly violent confrontations.

On 6 November 2002 the Chilean Anti-terrorist law 18.314 was invoked in relation to filing charges against Victor Ancalaf Lalaupe, a leader in the Mapuche activist community. Victor Ancalaf was charged with participating in a civil protest over Ralco construction that resulted in the explosion of an ENDESA subcontractor truck. The Pehuenche and the broader Mapuche community are increasingly concerned that their struggle to halt further development will be formally recast as a terrorist movement.[15]

In December 2002 the Organization of American States' (OEA) Inter-American Human Rights Court in San José, Costa Rica, accepted an amicus brief filed by Chilean and international advocates on behalf of people affected by the Pangue and Ralco dams. On 12 December 2002 the OEA court ordered the Chilean government not to allow any further negotiations between ENDESA and Bío-Bío area residents 'until the Inter-American Human Rights Court has adopted a definite position'. The Costa Rica-based court was to conduct an in-depth analysis and issue a final ruling in mid-February 2003. Also on 12 December 2002, ENDESA announced that Nicolasa Quintraman, an elderly Pehuenche woman and one of the leaders in Ralco protests, had signed a 'promise of exchange' with ENDESA representatives exchanging 3.1 hectares for a 77-hectare plot of land near Santa Barbara and compensation of some US$290,000. By mid-January 2003 other Pehuenche families had issued a statement indicating that they would not negotiate with ENDESA and would remain claimants in the OEC petition.

In May 2003, the Office of the Compliance Advisor/Ombudsman for the International Finance Corporation and Multilateral Investment Guarantee Agency released their report evaluating IFC involvement in the Pangue dam. It is a highly critical indictment of IFC actions with recommendations including: immediate publication of the Hair report; publication and translation of the Downing report to allow dissemination of his findings and communication of how the IFC has responded to his recommendations in a culturally appropriate manner; and acknowledgements that IFC obligations remain concerning the Pangue dam and the related Ralco dam projects. Most significantly, the report calls for a system-wide review of projects to determine whether similar existing obligations remain in other IFC partnership agreements, especially those involving equity investment (IFC 2003).

The Creation and Erosion of Human Rights Protection Mechanisms

This case illustrates the importance of local, national and international communication and advocacy in lodging human rights complaints and applying the sustained political pressure that may eventually produce some measure of remedy. It also illustrates the relative lack of power that World Bank con-sultants – let alone affected organizations and communities – have in com-municating flaws in the decision-making process and encouraging remedy for problems resulting from an imposed vision of 'development'.

The fact that the Sotomayor Riquelme family received compensation for their losses is a hugely significant fact, in that it represents an example of World Bank action that acknowledges some measure of responsibility and produces some measure of remedy. Their compensation was the result of negotiations between IFC and ENDESA, which in turn were a direct re-sponse to the many years of advocacy efforts by Downing, Claudio Gonzales Parra, and the support provided by national and international organizations (GABB, International Rivers Network, and many others) and professional groups (such as the AAA Committee for Human Rights). Whether this sin-gular measure of remedy is a reparations precedent that can be built upon remains to be seen.

This case reflects in many ways the social trajectory and experiences of large dam development projects around the world. The World Commission on Dams (WCD) thematic review, 'The Social Impact of Dam Development on Indigenous Peoples and Ethnic Minorities', found a number of commo-nalities. Dam development typically produced cultural alienation; resulted in the dispossession of land, resources and the means to sustain a self-sufficient way of life; involved a lack of consultation and meaningful participation in decision-making processes; involved a lack of, or inadequate, compensation; generated human rights abuses; failed to spread the benefits of development; and lowered living standards. The WCD found that problems are rarely the simple result of failures of a single actor such as the state, but more typi-cally involve failures of multiple actors including states, public and private financing institutions, and private organizations and entities engaged in plan-ning, designing, building and implementing mitigation measures (including compensation and resettlement programmes), and managing dam develop-ment projects. This is certainly the case in the development of Pangue and Ralco dams.

The WCD, in its final report, called for reparations for dam-affected communities, noting that such remedy is warranted under existing interna-tional law, and that moral and legal culpability includes those parties who planned and authorized projects, as well as those who benefited from dam development projects – including states, funding institutions, contracting and construction companies, and energy and water system management companies. The WCD also noted that meaningful reparations require efforts to repair, make amends and compensate for damages. Given the nature of damages resulting from loss of land and a way of life, reparations imply remedies that:

- acknowledge and attempt to repair, make amends and compensate for past failures;
- address human environmental needs and reflect a commitment to restore human and environmental integrity;
- involve equitable decision-making processes;
- create or strengthen rights-protective mechanisms where claims can be made, damages assessed, culpability assigned, and remediative activities devised and implemented (see also Johnston 2000).

The conclusion that those who funded, built and operate the enterprises associated with large-scale development have some obligation to people whose lives and livelihoods were adversely affected along the way is, as things stand, an illusive ideal. Under prevailing conditions, the control of power in development decision-making and implementation lies in corporations and political institutions, rather than with project-affected peoples.

For a brief period of time (much of the 1990s), the international political climate and the operating culture of institutions and corporations increasingly supported endeavours that enhanced human rights and protected the environment (as evidenced by global treaties, social and environmental rights-protective policies, ethical codes of corporate conduct). However, while the nations of the world passed human rights and environment legislation, and organizations like the World Bank became increasingly transparent (see Cernea 1997), a major shift occurred in development financing. The financing of public utilities – water supply, electrical generation, and telecommunications networks – increasingly occurred via privatized processes. By the late 1990s the mode of operation evidenced by the IFC/ENDESA relationship – where public financing was used in private partnerships to fund development projects that first and foremost meet the interests and needs of the private partner – became the norm. What this case suggests is that international development financing through private partnerships require that institutions and agencies negotiate in secret, retain control over 'sensitive' human and environmental information, and thus have the means to circumvent rights-protective laws, policies and procedures presently contained in national governments and multinational lending agencies. This case demonstrates a culpability gap – one that is likely to widen in the years to come.[16]

Notes

1. Sources for the events reported in this timeline include the 1996 Downing report; letters and documents published on the Mapuche Foundation worldwide website (the Consejo Inter-regional Mapuche, Mapuche Inter-regional Council, website

is www.bounce.to/cim). Also articles and supporting documents published on the International Rivers Network website (www.irn.org), including: *World Rivers Review*, August 1997; IRN Press Release of 30 July 1997; Letter from James Wolfensohn, World Bank President, to Andrea Durbin of Friends of the Earth, 2 June 1997; *World Rivers Review*, June 1997; *World Rivers Review*, April 1997; IRN/CIEL Press Release of 26 February 1997; *World Rivers Review*, June 1996; *World Rivers Review*, January 1996; *World Rivers Review*, Fourth Quarter 1994. Also, 'Bío-Bío Updates', nos 1–7, Grupo de Accion por el Bío-Bío of Chile (Action Group for the Bío-Bío – GABB), translated by the International Rivers Network and published on the IRN website. News on Ralco construction plans derived from translated press reports from *El Mercurio* and *El Diario*, provided by International Rivers Network, 22 January 1998; and subsequent updates posted on the Rehue Foundation website covering Mapuche and Pehuenche issues in the Alto Bío-Bío (www.xs4all.nl/~rehue).

2. The anthropologist Downing would later argue both within the IFC and in his complaint to the AAA that the formation of a secret agreement without the knowledge of the people, or their government, was a human rights violation.

3. CONADI is composed of representatives from the different governmental ministries and eight Indigenous representatives.

4. See the Bío-Bío campaign briefings, newsletters and reports on the IRN website, and broader analysis of the adverse impacts of large dam development in McCully 1996 (2002).

5. From the viewpoint of the IFC staff and ENDESA, this meant that there was no need to provide the assurances and planning that would have been necessary had the dam affected Indigenous peoples or involved involuntary resettlement (known as Operational Policies 4.20 and 4.30 at that time; see www.displacement.net for additional detail.)

6. The World Bank Inspection Panel is a fact-finding body that operates on behalf of the Board to investigate the performance of the Bank and not the borrower. The Inspection Panel was established by resolution of the Board in 1993; its stated purpose is to review available material and determine whether there is a serious Bank failure to observe its operational policies and procedures with respect to project design, appraisal and/or implementation. The Inspection Panel examines only those material adverse effects, alleged in the request, that have totally or partially resulted from serious Bank failure of compliance with its policies and procedures.

7. The World Commission on Dams was later established in May 1998. The WCD was an independent, international multi-stakeholder process involving twelve commissioners representing science, industry, government, funding agencies, NGO advocates, and project-affected peoples. The WCD commissioned intensive reviews of large dam projects from around the world; thematic reviews of funding, development, and operational issues; and held a series of hearings soliciting testimony from tens of thousands of dam-displaced peoples. The Commission's final report, 'Dams and Development: A New Framework for Decision Making', was released in November 2000. Reports, thematic reviews, briefing papers and related materials can be found on the WCD website at www.dams.org.

8. Downing reports that in a conversation regarding the status of this second complaint, the ethics officer asked, 'What do you expect me to do with a complaint filed against my boss?' As a result of his whistle-blowing efforts, Downing was blacklisted by the World Bank Group, ending his thirteen years of consulting on social development issues.

9. Letters on the Pehuenche matter are posted at www.aaanet.org/committees/cfhr/pt-pehuenc.htm.

10. See, for example, the Lawlink website, Aboriginal Justice Advisory Committee page on the Mapuche People, www.lawlink.nsw.gov.au/ajac.nsf/pages/mapuche. For the Spanish translation, see www.derechos.org/nizkor/espana/doc/endesa/aaa.html.

11. Within the World Bank Group, the Pangue case became known as the private-sector Narmada – meaning that it was a watershed event in which a cluster of issues changed how the organization did business. In this case, it was how they approached social issues. Before Pangue, the IFC had almost no staff social scientists. Following Downing's complaint, they brought over anthropologist and resettlement specialist Dan Aronson from the IBRD for temporary assignment to build a social science core staff which now is reported to be about fifteen professionals.

12. Letter posted at www.aaanet.org/committees/cfhr/rptpehuenc.htm.

13. The role of the ombudsman includes: advising and assisting IFC and MIGA in dealing with sensitive or controversial projects, either at the request of the president or IFC's or MIGA's management or on the suggestion of the ombudsman; assisting in efforts to respond to complaints from external parties affected by IFC or MIGA projects; investigating complaints, as appropriate, in consultation with affected parties, project sponsors and IFC's or MIGA's management, with the goal of correcting project failures and achieving better results on the ground; communicating directly with complainants and affected parties, while respecting the confidentiality of sensitive business information; reporting on his or her findings and recommendations to the president, who will determine what actions are required; and making recommendations to the president regarding to what extent and in what form the findings will be disclosed to the IFC or MIGA Board of Directors, affected parties and the public. Abstracted from the Office of the Compliance Advisor/Ombudsman for the International Finance Corporation (IFC) and the Multilateral Investment Guarantee Agency (MIGA) webpage, www.ifc.org/cao/ImpactCAO.pdf. See also the Compliance Advisor/Ombudsman (CAO) article, 'Building Accountability From the Ground Up', *IFC Impact Magazine*, vol. 3, no. 4, Fall 1999.

14. This sale was confirmed in a 7 November 2002 conversation between Barbara Rose Johnston and the executive assistant to the IFC Director of Corporate Power.

15. Source: www.mapuche.nl/news/list, 15 November 2002.

16. For a detailed analysis of the human rights culpability gap within the World Bank, see Clark 2002. In this essay Clark not only criticizes the lack of effective mechanisms for airing complaints and resolving conflicts; she assess the impact of recent changes in World Bank social and environmental policy that suggest significant erosion of basic human rights and rights protective mechanisms. In addition to the critique, Clark outlines creative suggestions for developing remedial mechanisms.

References

Cernea, Michael (1997) 'The risks and reconstruction model for resettling displaced populations', *World Development*, vol. 25, no. 10, October, pp. 1569–88.

Clark, Dana L. (2002) 'The World Bank and human rights: the need for greater accountability', *Harvard Human Rights Journal* 15, Spring, pp. 205–26.

Cockburn, Alexander (1997) 'Wolfensohn, Indian killer', *The Nation*, 30 June, p. 9.

Crawford, Leslie (1997) 'Chile dam row shows IFC's problems with Projects', *Financial Times*, 8 August.

Downing, Theodore (1996) 'A participatory interim evaluation of the Pehuen Foundation', prepared for the International Finance Corporation by T.E. Downing, AGRA Earth and Environment in collaboration with Downing and Associates. Submitted to the International Finance Corporation on 7 May. [NB: the IFC has asked that it be made clear that this report is not an official IFC document.]

Gonzalez Parra, Claudio (1997) 'Indigenous peoples and the mega-projects: the example of the Pehuenches in the Alto Bío Bío, Chile', paper submitted to the American Anthropological Association Committee for Human Rights. An earlier draft was presented to the international conference, 'Human Rights as an Instrument for the Eradication of Extreme Poverty', organized by Centro de Estudios Sociales y Educacion (Sur), Asociacion Latinoamericana de Organizaciones de Promocion (ALOP) and Comparative Research Programs on Poverty (CROP), Santiago, Chile, 22–28 September.

GABB (Grupo de Accion por el Bío-Bío of Chile – Action Group for the Bío-Bío) (1995) 'The Bío-Bío Update', no. 1, 18 December (updates are translated by the International Rivers Network and published on the IRN website).

——— (1996a) 'The Bío-Bío Update', no. 2, 6 January.

——— (1996b) 'The Bío-Bío Update', no. 3, 31 January.

——— (1996c) 'The Bío-Bío Update', no. 4, 28 February.

——— (1996d) 'The Bío-Bío Update', no. 5, 2 April.

——— (1996e) 'The Bío-Bío Update', no. 6, 10 May.

——— (1996f) 'The Bío-Bío Update', no. 7, 5 December.

——— (2002) 'Petition to address outstanding issues of IFC financed and partly owned Pangue/Ralco projects', filed with the IFC Office of the Ombudsman, 1 July.

Hair, Jay D., Benjamin Dysart, Luke J. Danielson and Avra O. Rubalcava (1997) 'Pangue Hydroelectric Project (Chile): an independent review of the International Finance Corporation's compliance with applicable World Bank group environmental and social requirements'.

IFC (International Finance Corporation) (1995) 'Terms of reference for an interim evaluation of the Pehuen Foundation' (consultancy contract with Theodore Downing). 26 July.

——— (1997a) 'Annual Report', Washington.

——— (1997b) 'Statement of the IFC about the report by Dr Jay Hair on the Pangue Hydroelectric Project', 15 July.

——— (2003) 'Assessment Report: Assessment by the Office of the Compliance Advisor/ Ombudsman in relation to a complaint filed against IFC's investment in ENDESA Pangue S.A.', May 2003, posted on the Compliance Advisor Ombudsman (CAO) webpage at www.cao-ombudsman.org/.

IRN (International Rivers Network) (1996) IRN Bío-Bío river, Chile Campaign Information Package.

——— (1997a) IRN/CIEL Press Release of February 26: 'World Bank threatens Chilean dam-builder with default'.

——— (1997b) 'Chilean dam builders slip through the noose: ENDESA pays off World Bank to avoid loan conditions', World Rivers Review, April.

——— (1997c) 'Background on the Bío-Bío dams', World Rivers Review, June.

——— (1997d) IRN Press Release of July 307: 'Independent review blasts World Bank over Chilean dam project'.

——— (1997e) 'Review panel blasts World Bank over Chilean dam', World Rivers Review, August.

——— (1997f) 'Review of IFC's policy on disclosure of information' (Draft 11/17), Draft Environmental, Social and Disclosure Policies and Review Procedure, posted on IFC website through 20 March 1998.

———— (1998) Translated articles from *El Mercurio* and *El Diario*, provided by International Rivers Network, 22 January.

Johnston, Barbara Rose (2000) 'Reparations and the right to remedy' (July 2000). World Commission on Dams Contributing Paper, Prepared for Thematic Review 1.3: Displacement, Rehabilitation, Resettlement, Reparations and Development. www. damsreport.org/docs/kbase/contrib/soc221.pdf.

———— and Terence Turner (1998a) 'The Pehuenche: human rights, the environment, and hydrodevelopment on the Bío-Bío river, Chile', American Anthropological Association Committee for Human Rights, published at www.aaa.net.org/committees/cfhr/ptpe-huenc.htm.

———— (1998b) 'Censorship, denial of informed participation, and human rights abuses associated with dam development in Chile', *Professional Ethics Report*, Publication of the AAAS Scientific Freedom, Responsibility and Law Program, in collaboration with the Committee on Scientific Freedom and Responsibility, vol. 11, no. 2, Spring.

———— (1999) 'The Pehuenche: human rights, the environment, and hydrodevelopment on the Bío-Bío river, Chile', *Identities*, vol. 6, nos 2–3, pp. 387–434.

Lee, Carol F. (1997) Carol F. Lee, Vice President and General Counsel for the International Finance Corporation, personal statements to CfHR Forum, American Anthropological Association Annual Meeting, November 20, Washington, DC, and to members of the CfHR in closed meetings.

McCully, Patrick (1996) *Silenced Rivers: The Ecology and Politics of Large Dams*, London: Zed Books; revised edition published 2002.

Pehuen Foundation (1997) 'Minutes No. 41 of the Special Meeting of the Board of Directors, May 28'.

Wolfensohn, James (1997) 'Letter from James Wolfensohn, World Bank President, to Andrea Durbin, of Friends of the Earth, June 2', published on the International Rivers Network webpage, www.irn.org.

World Bank (1991) 'Operational directive 4.20: Indigenous Peoples', 17 September.

———— (1994/1996) 'Resettlement and development – the Bankwide review of projects involving involuntary resettlement, 1886– 1993', Washington, DC: World Bank (internal policy review document).

———— (1998) 'Social and environmental policy guidelines for the International Finance Corporation', www.worldbank.org.

PART III

Invitations:
Connections and Coexistence

14

Revisiting Gandhi and Zapata:
Motion of Global Capital, Geographies of Difference
and the Formation of Ecological Ethnicities

PRAMOD PARAJULI

Pramod Parajuli is an interdisciplinary scholar, educator and anthropologist. Originally a native of Nepal, he has published on the topics of sustainability education, bio-cultural diversities, knowledge systems and environmentalism of the global South. Parajuli co-founded and is the executive director of the Portland International Initiative for Leadership in Ecology, Culture and Learning (PIIECL), an interdisciplinary graduate programme at Portland State University, Portland, Oregon (www.piiecl.pdx.edu).

Tortured Bodies and Altered Earth

Among the Indian ethnic groups of Latin America (there are about 200), this *tortured body* and another body, the *altered earth*, represent a beginning, a rebirth of the will to *construct a political association*. A unity born of hardship and resistance to hardship is the historical locus, the collective memory of the social body, where a will that neither confirms nor denies this writing of history originates. 'Today, at the hour of our awakening, we must be our own historians.'

(Michel de Certeau 1986: 225)

Those who loot water, forest and the earth
Government or the rich, will not be spared.
Only people have the rights over these.

(slogan in *Padayatra* (footmarches), Jharkhand, India)

Michel de Certeau's twin metaphor of 'tortured bodies' and 'altered earth' in the quotation above aptly characterizes the existential crises faced by groups of people whom I call 'ecological ethnicities' (Parajuli 2001a, 2001b, 1998). I call them ecological ethnicities because the conventional categories based solely on caste, tribe, language, or even religion, are not adequate to describe their agonies as well as struggles today. Not only do I include Indigenous populations (known as *adivasis* in India) within the rubric of 'ecological ethnicity'; I also include peasants and other cultures of habitat such as fisherfolk, seedkeepers, forest dwellers and nomadic shepherds. The notion of ecological ethnicity refers to any group of people who derive their livelihood through day-to-day negotiation with their immediate environment. What gives them a common identity today is that all these groups are marginalized by the extractive processes of the global motion of capital that is now accelerated by neoliberal policies such as those of the World Trade Organization (WTO). Thus, about 500 million Indigenous people constitute a crucial part – but by no means are they the only element – of ecological ethnicities. For example, in this chapter, I look at how peasants and farmers of India and Mexico are experiencing the loss of their land, seed and a rich tradition of knowledge, just as many Indigenous communities are.

Within the rubric of Gandhian and Zapatista legacies, I will also explore the commonalities shared by Indigenous peoples and peasants, fisherfolk and pastoralists. Both Mahatma Gandhi and Emiliano Zapata are ignored in mainstream environmental discourses. It is true that they were not championing singularly environmental causes. But, as I argued in a recent article, their strategies and visions are at the very core of what I call the 'environmentalism of the Global South' (Parajuli 2002). Although a wide range of groups I refer to in the global South do not affiliate officially with Mahatma Gandhi or Gandhism (a term that Gandhi did not approve himself), Emiliano Zapata or Zapatism, I find that both Gandhi and Zapata are reflected in many of the struggles to create a livable economy for the 'ecological ethnicities' of the world. These environmentalisms are also distinct from what could be considered environmentalism of the Sierra Club, the Nature Conservancy, and even some aspects of deep ecology. By elaborating a variety of interrelated issues and concepts common to Gandhi, Zapata and ecological ethnicities, I will illustrate that the gaps between environmentalism of the global North and global South are wide and profound.

Time is ripe to articulate what an environmentalism of the South might be. In an effort similar to mine, Laura Pulido articulates subaltern environmentalism in these words:

> Subaltern environmental struggles are not strictly environmental. Instead, they are about challenging the various lines of domination that produce the environmental conflict or problem experienced by the oppressed group in the first place. Since they must confront multiple sources of domination that include economic marginalization, patriarchy, nationalism and racism, it is difficult to discern where the environmental part of the struggle begins and where it ends. Indeed, trying to do so may misrepresent the very nature of struggle, as it suggests that environmental encounters are not coloured by political economic structures. This tendency to disaggregate environmental concerns is a reflection of mainstream environmentalism's propensity to deny that its own environmental interactions are couched within a context of political economic privilege. (Pulido 1997: 193)

In Mexico, anthropologist Victor Toledo characterizes various movements of Indigenous peoples and peasants as 'neo-Zapatista ecologism'. Like the resurgence of Mahatma Gandhi's notions of *gram swaraj* (village self-rule) in India, Emiliano Zapata's discourses resonate with most of the tribal–peasant struggles globally today. In this chapter, I will revisit what both Mahatma Gandhi and Zapata were proposing and what could be their legacy and relevance today.

I then explore emergent notions and institutions of watersheds, foodsheds or seedsheds that can be considered the contemporary versions of Gandhian local economy and Zapatismo ecologism. These new place-based identities have given people the true 'council of the place' where, as Gandhi had envisioned, individuals are at the centre of a community but are always ready to perish for the interest of larger community. On occasions, an individual inhabitant is willing to go against his or her own economic self-interest in order to give preference to the common interest of the community. This is the way watersheds, foodsheds or seedsheds transcend the logic of economic man and the simple articulation of interest groups.

The Interface of Ecology and Social Justice

Indeed, as de Certeau had used these metaphors to describe the predicament of Indigenous peoples of Latin America, and globally also, the immediate human toll of environmental destruction has usually been borne disproportionately by the people who are least able to cope with it. That is precisely the irony of this situation. While the metaphor of 'altered earth' signifies a crisis of nature and survival for them, the metaphor of 'tortured bodies' signifies the crisis of social justice. I use the imagery of 'altered earth' to show that there are visible biophysical limits to wanton extraction from nature and it cannot continue further as usual. As Herman Daly (1996) has pointed out, the accelerated trade in goods creates spatial separation between the places that suffer the cost of ecological extraction and those areas that reap the benefits. Be it forest products, minerals or food, the local economy erodes and gradually global supermarket goods flood in and replace the local market. Consequently, there is a widening chasm between those who produce the goods and those who consume them. It is only due to the naked logic of market that England imports as much butter and beef from economies as far away as Australia and New Zealand, as it exports to those countries and other countries. It is only due to the same bizarre logic that I had the option of buying New Zealand cheese in the supermarket of Oaxaca City in Mexico in the spring of 2001. Oaxaca is a city where Oaxacan cheese is available and is indeed very popular. Getting New Zealand cheese in

Oaxaca City might make economic sense, but it is a hopeless proposition for the local economy; it has eroded local Mexican economy, employment and livelihoods.

It is not only that their earth is altered to such an extent; ecological ethnicities are like 'tortured bodies' because of the uneven ways ecological costs are borne by those who are rich in natural economy (including biodiversity) but have been unduly exploited by the market economy. Increasingly, those who are least able to cope with environmental collapse are beginning to be aware and assertive of their interests. What I am referring to as ecological ethnicities corresponds closely with what Gustavo Esteva and Madhu Prakash have called the 'social majorities' of the world (Esteva and Prakash 1998). In their view, the 'social majorities' have no regular access to most of the goods and services defining the average 'standard of living' in the industrial countries. They have their own definitions of what a good life is, and share a common rejection of the 'global forces'. The 'social minorities', on the other hand, are those groups that, in both North and South, share homogeneous ways of modern (Western) life all over the world, and usually adopt as their own the basic paradigms of modernity. They are usually classified in the upper classes of every society and they are fully immersed in the institutions of the 'formal economy'.

Globally, ecological ethnicities are coming to be at odds with the logic of the market because they are used to depending largely on the maintenance and regeneration of ecosystems for their livelihoods. That is why they are causing tremendous barriers to the motion of global capital today. As ecological ethnicities carefully ensure continuity in the symbiotic connection between the human collectivities and the non-human collectivities, they stand in the way of wanton resource extraction demanded by the corporations with global reach. In order to maintain the rhythm of circularity in human and natural economy, they cultivate appropriate cosmovisions, observe related rituals, and practise prudence in harvesting from nature's bounty in everyday life. Moreover, they are reluctant producers as well as consumers in and for the global market.

The salience of the notion of ecological ethnicity is that although ecological ethnicities might be internally fragmented with respect to religion, caste or language, those internal distinctions cannot always be considered as antagonistic to each other. Despite their differences in human terms, they share an ecosystem and might already have or can inculcate a sense of ecological community based on, to borrow Gary Nabhan's apt notion, their 'cultures of habitat'. What seems common in all these 'geographies of difference' is a combination of a distinct geographical and ethnic make-up, cultural and linguistic assertions resulting in aspiration for varying degrees of political autonomy (Parajuli 2001a, 2001b). As I will show later in this chapter, their demand for autonomy is not merely about political representation; it is about altering the very relations of ruling – the question of what is power, what is governance and what are other possible roles of state, civil society and communities.

I have identified five crises that ecological ethnicities are experiencing and some responses in which they are engaged in a globalized economy. The five crises are those of nature, social justice, survival, knowledge and identity, and governance. Such crises are inevitable when global capital expands semiotically and tries to incorporate peasants and other ecosystem people within its own grid. By 'semiotic expansion of capital', I am referring to a phase in which whatever was previously considered as 'external', or off-limits to the market, is now internalized as a 'commodity'. For example, now both biophysical nature and cultural knowledge are released for capitalist exploitation and appropriation (Guha and Martinez-Alier 1997; Parajuli 1998). In other words, it puts a private property label on nature's bounty – soil, biomass, fish, water, forests, minerals and so on. So are the cultural fabric of ecological ethnicities – their dances, their rituals, seeds, medicinal plants, and their knowledge systems – opened up for egregious exploitation (Parajuli 2001b). The degree and extent of these crises fluctuate in relation to how the global motion of capital has to articulate unevenly other economies and cultures into its own orbit. As I have commented elsewhere, globalization is a phase in which 'capital' is naturalized, while simultaneously 'nature' is capitalized (Parajuli 1998). In this phase, whatever was previously considered as 'external', or off-limits, to the market is included as 'internal'. Put simply, if capital is nature, nature is capital, too. Saving nature becomes equivalent to ensuring the reproduction of capital.

As expressed in the post-Rio and post-Johannesburg environmental discourses, the planet as a whole is our capital that must be managed in a sustained way. What is alarming, and at the same time challenging, for ecological ethnicities today is the fact that the relationship of capital to nature and humans has acquired a qualitatively different dimension and depth than before. Today, the old logic of capital accumulation is turned upside down when the trade in software of knowledge, information and consumption surpasses the hardware of production of raw materials and material goods. Ecological ethnicities feel the crunch on both realms in the sense that while the extraction of raw materials continues unabated, they do not have any ownership over the software that is a product of their own knowledge, a product of their historical heritage.

The ethno-ecological movements suggest that economy should be only a subsystem of an ecosystem. Thus their search is for the optimal scale of the macro-economy relative to what is possible within the environment. The key reasons why ecological ethnicities are plundered by the globalizing economy are the speed of production and extraction that the regime of globalization heralds. Such an accelerated pace violates the very bio-geo-chemical cycles of nature necessary to allow regeneration and re-newal. In other words, 'economic time outdoes biological time' (Altvater 1994; Parajuli 1998). When I look at the global motion of capital and its spatial articulations, it becomes clear that the accumulation of capital itself produces development and underdevelopment as mutually determin-ing moments of the uneven and combined movement of capital. In that sense, regional and spatial inequalities are built in as a necessary means of survival of profit-seeking capitalism (Harvey 1996). Thus contradictions that arise between the requirements of an extractive global economy and the ethno-ecological characteristics of regions are irreconcilable. A regional unevenness is experienced in the arena of biological wealth such as land, water, forest and soil, and in human-made wealth such as labour, skills and technologies. Politically, the conflict arises between the necessity to regu-late the uneven extraction centrally, and the desperate need of ecological ethnicities to protect themselves by taking power at the community level. That is the drama this chapter seeks to unveil.

The Twin Crisis of Nature and Ecological Justice

The movements that ecological ethnicities are involved in today have two facets. First, they are expressions of resistance against the uneven appropri-ation of their natural economy by others. Overall, it seems that the history of the motion of capital is predicated upon the 'resource transfer' from ecological ethnicities to what Gadgil and Guha (1995) in India have called the 'omnivore' class. While ecological ethnicities have to maintain the fine balance between what is 'extracted from nature' and what is 'replenished back' into nature's processes in the immediate environment, the 'omnivore' class is primarily concerned with the flow of goods for consumption in the supermarkets, far away from the points of production. Unfortunately, Gadgil and Guha show that the flow of these modern goods and services starts from the rural hinterlands, where ecological ethnicities are, and moves to urban supermarkets (Parajuli 1998). It is not simply a geographical accident that most of the tribal belt in middle India is rich with hydro, forest and mineral resources. While their own natural economy is overused and over-drawn, ecological ethnicities do not have the access to the market economy; nor do they have command over human-made capital. On the other hand, the omnivores, who are the beneficiaries of these state-mediated projects, are given access to resources at highly subsidized rates and therefore do not care if the process is grossly inefficient and wasteful.

That is why whenever and wherever there are violations of human rights, environmental justice is violated, and where we see the violation of environmental justice, human rights are also neglected. Take the example of Chico Mendes, the leader of the rubber tappers' movement in the Brazilian Amazon who was killed by the bullet of a neighbouring rancher. Shanker Guha Niyogi, the leader of Chattisgarh Mukti Morcha in Chattisgarh, India, was killed by the industrial houses in India. Ken Saro-Wiwa, the leader of the Ogoni People's Movement against the Shell oil company in Nigeria, was hanged by the military junta of his own country. The murder of these three ecological activists demonstrates the seriousness of the deadly 'war over resources' worldwide.

The country of India as a whole offers one of the clearest examples where ecological ethnicities signify the double burden of 'tortured bodies' and 'altered earth'. Today, India is polarized to such an extent that while for the many the issue is no less than the 'right to life', for the few the issue is the 'right to property'. As a result, an increasing number of India's citizens are experiencing marginalization because their rights over resources have been violated. Their access to the means of production is diminishing, and consequently they have been pushed out of their land and into the vagaries of an unorganized labour market that is neither stable nor disciplined by the labour laws and trade-union organizations. While they have been pushed out of their own resource base, they do not have the entitlement over their own labour processes (Sharma 1996). Although this form of marginalization builds upon and perpetuates other relations of domination and discrimination based on gender, caste, ethnicity and class in Indian society, it has some distinct dimensions that require specific analysis. My own research over a decade has amply demonstrated that patterns of discrimination based on gender, caste, ethnicity and class are intertwined with the issues of ecology, survival and the deadly 'war over resources'. Moreover, the situation is compounded by the fact that these groups are searching for identity and an appropriate mode of governance in the form of autonomy at the level of the village and geographical region.

Similar trends within the crises of justice and nature are evident in the United States, where it is known as environmental racism, with clear evidence that racial minorities are disproportionately exposed to environmental hazards (see Bullard 1994; Gedicks and Grossman, this volume).

My claim is that the movements of ecological ethnicities are proposals about initiating alternative modes of production, consumption and distribution; in short, they imply alternative modes of environmental transformation. The most significant part of these struggles is that 'ecology', 'environment' or 'nature' gets politicized in the fullest sense of the term. While involved in political actions to restore these ecosystems, these struggles also produce competing discourses vis-à-vis the global discourse of environmental crisis and management. Political geographer David Harvey argues that environmental modernization is 'fundamentally a class project, whether it is exactly called that or not, precisely because it entails a direct challenge to the circulation and accumulation of capital which currently dictates what environmental transformations occur and why' (Harvey 1996: 401). I am not confining the plight of ecological ethnicities to rigid class analysis; nor have I ignored the crucial role it plays (see Parajuli 2001b for a critique of Harvey).

Owners of Soil, Land and Knowledge

For the last decade or so, Indian peasants have been enraged by the politics of patent. Let us take the patent on basmati (aromatic rice especially grown in North India and parts of Pakistan) as an example. The American company Ricetec had been granted a patent on the rice grown outside India. Ricetec, which has already staked a claim on the international basmati market with brands like 'Kasmati' and 'Texmati', which claim to be 'basmati-type' rice. One of the direct consequences of this new patenting regime will be that India will lose out on the 45,000-tonne US market, which forms 10 per cent of total basmati exports, but also its premium position in vital markets like the European Union. Stunned by the development, the commerce ministry, the Indian Agricultural Research Institute, the Indian Council of Agricultural Research, and the basmati industry have together decided immediately to challenge the patent given to Ricetec by the US government. The initial verdict has been in favour of India.

The issue here is not merely legal. For centuries ecological ethnicities have been the farmers, seedkeepers and seed breeders. Basmati, neem, jowar lentils and many kinds of millet are only a few of the diverse plants and crops that ecological ethnicities have nurtured in their fields and used as their food, in their medicine and as part of their spiritual repertoire. Throughout peasant culture, no agricultural activity is done without the corresponding ritual of thanksgiving and celebration. For example, as Vandana Shiva notes, in central India at the beginning of the agricultural season, farmers gather at the village deity, offer their rice varieties and then share the seeds. This annual festival of *Akti* rejuvenates the duty of saving and sharing seed among farming communities. But the new biotech and seed companies such as Monsanto and Cargill are involved in what is touted as 'termination of germination'. Through terminator technologies, companies ensure that this year's harvest does not make seed for next year. As a strategy of capital accumulation, farmers are compelled to buy seeds every year from these companies. Vandana Shiva aptly notes:

There can be no partnership between the terminator logic, which destroys nature's renewability and regeneration and the commitment to continuity of life held by women farmers of the Third World. The two world-views do not merely clash – they are mutually exclusive. There can be no partnership between a logic of death on which Monsanto bases its expanding empire and the logic of life on which women farmers in the Third World base their partnership with the earth to provide food security to their families and communities. (distributed over the Internet; for a description of the patent status of various plants, visit the Vandana Shiva website at: www.vshiva.net)

The second trend is even more troublesome. In 1998, more than 110 cotton farmers committed suicide in Andhra Pradesh state, India, due to heavy losses incurred in farming this capital-intensive crop, which in peasant semiotics is considered 'white gold'. Why did members of these farming families come to this tragic conclusion? The root cause lies in the familiar story of the 'corporate-chemical-and-cash-chain' that has engulfed smaller and subsistence farmers all over the globe. Enticed by the promise of quick cash, many marginal and small farmers had switched to cotton from their subsistence production in Andhra Pradesh. This shift required a major investment in order to purchase seeds, fertilizers and, above all, costly pesticides. Many farming families ended up putting their entire wealth – including the golden ornaments of their womenfolk – into the crop. On top of that, they were coerced into borrowing substantial amounts from private moneylenders. Regrettably, institutional credit from banks and development agencies was not forthcoming, and many of the loans were taken from private lenders at usurious interest rates; often these were the very same pesticide dealers to whom they needed to pay that money. While hopes of achieving a healthy return were high, no reliable services were offered by the agricultural extension agencies or by the irrigation department – that is, a steady supply of water. Lured by quick profit, pesticide dealers advised the farmers to use more and more pesticide, so much that the pesticides, instead of killing the pests that infested the crop, ended up killing predators like field rats, which were feeding on those pests and therefore helping to control the damage.

While the crop yields decreased, farmers were desperate to sell their crop in order to repay the loans. Under the pretext of oversupply, the price of cotton fell from an average of Rs 2,500 per quintal to as low as Rs 1,700 per quintal. Despite several appeals from the farmers, agencies of the state and of central governments, like Markfed and Cotton Corporation of India, did not intervene in time to stabilize prices to a remunerative level, until tragedy ensued. Distressed by the critical situation and helpless to find sources of support, farmers, and in some cases the whole family, ended their lives by swallowing the same pesticide that was supposed to help them grow their 'white gold'.

Ironically, the same 'resource-rich' but 'cash-poor' people are blamed for the environmental crisis. A classic argument has been the idea that 'poverty is the largest pollutant' (see Kothari and Parajuli 1993 for a critique). The logic here is that ecosystem people are desperate and will forsake their future for mere survival in the present because of hunger, famine and destitution. This is the epistemology behind the somewhat infamous 'tragedy of the commons' syndrome Garrett Hardin discussed. My data clearly show instead that ecological ethnicities exemplify 'commoners' tragedy'. The issue I consider is how the commoners may have access to commons so that they can use it by applying the practices of prudence, reciprocity and sharing among members. Rather than blaming the destitute ecological ethnicities for cutting forests to sell in the market or overfishing the river beds, I observe how the encroachment on resources gets worse when the industrial economy also banks upon the rural resource for its use. This is well illustrated by the fisherfolk struggle against large trawlers in India (Kurien 1993).

This aggressive form of capitalist incorporation has also given rise to new awareness and action among peasants in India. For example, a farmers' charter was announced on 7 March 1996 in which peasants pledged to protect their land, water, animals, seeds, intellectual capacities, and livelihoods. The charter states:

> We consider the purchase of land by non-agriculturists such as foreigners, multinational corporations, the export industry, and corrupt politicians as illegal. We will reclaim these lands for farmers and cultivators and ensure that illegally acquired village public land is returned to local bodies.

And, further, on the right to breed seed:

> We are original breeders of seed and our resource and intellectual rights are prior to, and set the limits for, corporate monopolies from any intellectual property rights regimes. This further includes our fundamental rights to exclude patents on plants and life forms because they violate our ethical values and cultural traditions. (Lokayan Bulletin 1996: 67–70)

Indigenous people join in this chorus and thereby challenge the entire scientific and technological enterprise, including biotechnology and patent rights, and its right to tinker with their culture, artefacts and knowledge systems. Clause 2:8 of the Mataatua Declaration seeks 'a moratorium on any further commercialization of indigenous medicinal plants and human genetic material until Indigenous communities have developed appropriate protection mechanisms' (see Posey 1999: 564–6 for the full text). Such declarations have influenced subsequent discussions on biodiversity and patent rights, and now it is accepted that *in situ* biodiversity conservation in the hands of peasants and Indigenous communities is perhaps the best way to enhance biodiversity.

By demanding patent rights for the community rather than accepting them as the right of an individual farmer, peasants are challenging the very idea of knowledge as private property. For example, an organization called Navadanya (Nine Seeds) is engaged in promoting species diversity, genetic diversity, and output diversity in farming and rural ecosystems as a whole. Navadanya does not promote diversity in close-knit laboratories, but *in situ*, in the ordinary farms of peasants (Navadanya 1995; see also www.vshiva.net). What is being articulated is a regime of 'common property rights' as opposed to 'intellectual property rights'. The cases of neem, basmati rice, and other medicinal plants for pharmaceutical research and production will continue to be the main issues of contestation in the future.

The Urge for Political Autonomy

It is a common saying that while Chiapas is the richest region in Mexico for natural resources, the Mayans of Chiapas are perhaps the poorest. The continued uprising in the Chiapas region in Mexico is an attempt to correct this anomaly. Geographically, the Chiapas region is a high-elevation plateau, composed of rugged terrain known as the Chiapas Highlands. Annexed to Mexico from Guatemala after its independence in 1910, the Chiapas region has remained crucial to the resource economy of Mexico, but is neglected in terms of respect and security for its Indigenous inhabitants.

Before the reform of 1991, Article 27 of the Mexican Constitution of 1917 obliged the state to redistribute land to those petitioners who fulfilled necessary legal requirements. The *ejido* land system consisted of individual plots and communal property, none of which could be legally sold, rented or used as collateral until the 1991 reforms which removed these specific provisions and opened up the land for privatization. The impact of this reform has been devastating. First, the sale of *ejido* plots is causing a reconcentration of land in the hands of large landowners. Second, permission for the collateral use of land arguably risks farm foreclosure and loss of land rights. Third, there was a risk that unresolved land petitions would be rejected. This amendment ended the progress of agrarian reform that has been carried out sporadically since the Mexican Revolution of 1917 (Collier and Quarantiello 1994).

George Collier and Quaratiello's book, *Basta! Land and the Zapatista Rebellion in Chiapas*, accurately shows how the so-called insular Mayan communities were in fact forced into the global motion of capital through the oil boom of the 1970s, followed by structural adjustment in the early 1980s and the resultant Mexican debt crisis. The Zapatista uprising thus can be attributed to a series of factors. Among them, the book identifies the most immediate trigger as the foreclosure of land reform and putting the *ejido* lands up for grabs by private business and multinational companies in the constitutional reform of 1991.

The most contentious issue peasants of Chiapas have with the Mexican state is the non-implementation of the land reforms enshrined in the Constitution of 1917, which stated that land that had been illegally taken away from the Indians would be returned to them. In addition to prohibition on the sale, rent or use of *ejido* land as collateral, Article 27 of the Mexican Constitution also guaranteed Indians an 'equitable distribution of land'. However, only the poorest areas of land were given back to the peasants, the fertile slopes being given to coffee plantations and valuable land to petroleum prospecting. Adding insult to injury, the 1991 amendment allows for the sale of *ejido* lands into private hands as well as for joint ventures with private enterprise.

The list of demands of the Zapatista movement in Chiapas might seem modest, but the implications are far-reaching. The first demand is land distribution programmes, so that native people can exercise communal landholding in fertile lowland areas, with guarantees of secure tenure. The second demand is the strategy of control over means of production, including the use of land. On top of these demands is that of local-level democratic decision-making, which Zapatistas want in the hands of traditional leadership. They want the Mexican state to comprise multiple nationalities. In addition, there are demands to make available schools, health posts, and so on. Seen from the demands of the Zapatista movement, Mexico does not seem to be a poor country but, as novelist Carlos Fuentes suggests, an extremely 'unjust' one (Fuentes 1996).

In Mexico and beyond, the celebration of 1992 as Five Hundred Years of Resistance confirmed a special resiliency among the 12 million or so Indigenous peoples throughout the Americas. A recent report confirms the long-held claim by the Indigenous peoples that 'the more power a tribe or nation has to make its own decisions, the greater chance it has of thriving'. The formation of Nunavut, an enormous Arctic territory in Canada, as an autonomous territory for the Inuit in 1998 is only one example of how real and feasible the idea of autonomy is. There are other examples in the United States and Canada where groups have built their own institutions and bureaucracies (while displacing federal bureaucracies) and have succeeded in economic development. In many cases the 'tribal council governments' established under the Indian Reorganization Act (1934) have been incapable of handling the kinds of environmental racism faced by these communities. Such government councils are at odds with the emergent Native American environmentalism that seeks to stop the use of Native American lands for toxic landfills, mining or harvesting of timber (Wilmer 1993).

In India, the impending crisis of governance in tribal communities was finally acknowledged when the Indian government passed a law in December 1996 that extends a scheme of decentralization in the *adivasi* areas. The Act, entitled the Provision of the Panchayats Extension to Scheduled Areas Act (1996), states that 'Every *Gramsabha* (village assembly) shall be competent to safeguard and preserve the traditions and customs of the people, their cultural identity, community resources and the customary mode of dispute resolution.' This Act recommends a series of administrative units starting from *Gramsabha* at the hamlet/village level to *Gram Panchayat*, the intermediate *Panchayat*, and the autonomous district councils. Most importantly, this provision gives the *Gramsabha* an unprecedented power over the use and protection of resources under its reach.

This legal provision constitutes a victory for *adivasis* in their long-drawn-out struggle for political autonomy. This is only one of the recent manifestations of the *adivasis'* demand for various degrees of autonomy in governance. Some *adivasi* areas of the northeast have asserted autonomy in the form of independent states outside the Indian union. *Adivasis* of middle India have sought regional autonomy within the Indian union, and separate states of Jharkhand, Uttarakhand and Chhatisgarh have been created.

Since the Act was passed, there has developed a sense that a legal victory has been won. Now the overriding concern is, how can the new constitutional provision enshrined in the Panchayati rule be used and transformed for the benefit of *adivasis*? How can it be used to realize the programme, as they say in Madhya Pradesh: *Mave Mate Mave Raj*? In the early days, comments Pradeep Prabhu, coordinator of the Alliance for Tribal Self-Rule, it meant 'my village, my rule', but as consciousness and intervention in political space grew, it came to signify 'my village, me the ruler'.

During my recent visit to India in 2000–2001, I saw that many ethno-ecological movements have taken on grassroots governance as a new challenge and have used their networks to implement it fully. In March 2000, representatives of 2,000 villages came together to announce that from now on their villages would be self-ruled, and a bamboo altar was erected at the entrance of each village as a sign of that declaration.

Obviously, much of the future of *adivasi* self-governance is open to speculation. We do not yet know what actual form tribal governance will take. Assured is that the form of governance will be new but built on the customary law that all land, forest, water and other biotic resources are collectively owned by communities. The customary Indigenous leadership have mostly been responsible for the just and sustainable management of these resources within the community (Parajuli and Kothari 1998; Prabhu 2001). Will this continue when they face the tentacles of the market economy? How will they negotiate the communal traditions of governance with the spirit of individualism implied in electoral democracy? This is one of the most challenging aspects of grassroots governance.

I do not want to propose a unitary concept or organization to articulate the concerns or identities of the 500 million Indigenous people of the globe – the peasants, fisherfolk and forest-dwellers who in aggregate still constitute the majority of the world's population. It would be foolhardy to project a conceptual homogeneity onto the evident diversity of Indigenous peoples. Such a unifying projection is in fact unnecessary and goes against the very grain of ethno-ecological politics. Searching for a unifying ideology leads to 'incorporative politics', which is based upon the idea of the modern nation-state and global organizations (Wilmer 1993).

Rather, I propose that the ethno-ecological political organizations uphold two cardinal principles. First, that they be based upon 'democratic equivalence' between several groups. Second, that they be premissed upon self-management of human relations as well as the relations between humans and nature. What emerges is not another state, but a federation of self-managing communities. The central feature of emergent ethno-ecological politics is, then, self-management of resources and cultures. In essence, they aspire to a different social mode with a view to different development alternatives. In this sense, Indigenous politics seeks a plurality of ways to organize autonomous units without a central authority such as the nation-state or any other uniform model as such. That is why the nation-state, whether it is in Mexico or India, is so hesitant to offer autonomy to Indigenous peoples.

Indigenous peoples are experiencing a new degree of confidence in their own autonomous history and cultural domain. First, there exists, outside of the state system and political culture, a radically different culture – with unique notions of law and order, nation, 'people-nation' and peoplehood. In order to exemplify this, I make a distinction between state and nation, society and culture, citizenship within the state and membership on the basis of ecological ethnicity (Parajuli 2001b). Second, there is an increased level of acceptance of the fact that Indigenous people's political culture can be as valid as (if not more than) the Western and modern political culture upon which the nation-states base their international relations. Since the majority of nation-states are multiethnic or multicultural, the power derived from the image of the state is simply coercive and bureaucratic. Where Indigenous peoples are concerned, the state merely aspires to integrate and assimilate them without respecting their systems of difference. Frank Wilmer (1993) has pertinently observed that the denial of Indigenous peoples' self-determination represents the unfinished business of decolonization. Recent upsurges in ecological concerns suggest that the scale and scope of decolonization have actually been deepened and broadened over time.

Ironically, the chances of ecological ethnicities achieving political autonomy have increased today because globalization of the economy has undermined the autonomy and decision-making power of the national state. The free-market policy that permits the flow of any resources anywhere in the world has also altered the ways nation-states are able (if they wish) to protect those who are adversely affected through a variety of welfare policies and programmes. As the power of the state in the international arena is subject to the constraints of multilateralism in defence, foreign policy and global public policies, including the environment, three questions loom large. Will the nation-state take sides with the march of capital or with the survival and identity imperatives of local and regional economies? Can a liberal-democratic state such as India maintain the delicate balance between the drive for accumulation through participation in the global economy and protection of the survival needs of ecological ethnicities at home? Can such a state manage the crisis of its own legitimacy that comes from the failure to deliver justice, and the crisis in the reproduction of capital that requires it to open new areas for extraction of resources? This precarious yet 'conditioned' position of nation-states leads me to explore the viability of governance based on community built around ecological specificities expressed as bio-region, watershed or foodshed.

One of the reasons I privilege community as a potential site of governance is that in contemporary grassroots politics the idea has been not to confront the state or the global institutions of power head-on, but to weaken the system in question by creating countervailing structures of power. The aim is to strengthen the capacity of local communities for self-governance to such a degree that centralized power evaporates (Parajuli and Kothari 1998). As discussed above, the proposal of the Zapatista movement in Chiapas, for example, is not to capture the Mexican state, but to democratize civil society based upon three principles: strengthening community, respecting ethnic identity, and exercising autonomous governance at the community level. Neither does the Alliance for Tribal Self-Rule in India aim to take over the state; it aims to exercise a firm command over resources at the ecosystem level and reclaim customary institutions of governance. It could lead to what poet Gary Snyder hopes for: the creation of a different kind of citizenship, a citizenship 'to become members of the deep, old biological communities of the land' (Snyder 1993: 262).

Resurrecting Zapata and Gandhi

Just when the newly triumphant Bolshevik Revolution was undergoing the rapid liquidation of peasantry in Russia (recall how Stalin considered the trio of tractor, electrification and collectivization to be the hallmark of communism) and the United States was creating the first dust bowls in the Midwest prairies, Mahatma Gandhi in India and Emiliano Zapata in Mexico were formulating a peasant-based, agricentric perspective for the liberation of their downtrodden masses from industrial capitalism. Interestingly, neither Zapata nor Gandhi captured state power, perhaps because they believed in power at the local level. While for Zapata, land and liberty (*Tierra e Libertad*) was the key to peasant survival and dignity, for Mahatma Gandhi *Hind Swaraj*, or a free India, was where peasants had their own village economy and had the power to decide on how they wanted to run things on their own.

Let us look at Zapata first. He came from a village named Anenecuilco of Morelos, which elected him as council president in 1909, the year when Mahatma Gandhi wrote the book *Hind Swaraj*. Zapata's nemesis was that the land of the village was transferred to sugar mills and hacienda owners. This reality propelled Zapata and his village folk to demand massive agrarian reform so that they could take back the peasant land. The Zapata movement had two goals. The first was to seek recognition of communal rights to land, which in popular parlance meant 'down with haciendas'. Second, it sought the right of small farmers to control their own villages – in other words, 'long live pueblos', a vindication of the peasant lifestyle. A pueblo life meant that decisions about the use of land and water would be made by the direct vote of community members. Local municipal autonomy was a key demand for the Zapata movement. The Zapatista army of that time was known in Mexico as 'country people who did not want to move and therefore got into a revolution'.

As Morelos peasants were the forerunners of resistance to capitalist agriculture in Mexico that provided the foundation for Zapata's ideas and movement, the peasants of the Champaran district of India's Bihar gave Mahatma Gandhi the first bitter taste of rural Indian reality in 1917. There the peasants were forced to cultivate indigo (a dye for British textile industries) for British planters and factory owners in three-tenths of their land under what was known as the *tin-kathia* system. Gandhi, who had just returned to India from South Africa, was brought to the Champaran district to study peasant grievances. Thanks to the rebelling peasants, it was in Champaran that Gandhi first educated himself about the reality of a peasant society. Working closely with village peasants, Gandhi was able to compel British colonial authorities to abolish the infamous *tin-kathia* system. In Champaran, Gandhi first tested his skills as a lawyer, documenting reality and arbitrating between adversaries – in this case between the colonial authorities and the peasants. At the same time, he articulated the notion of peasant-raj and *Rama-Rajya* (the rule the Rama). Ranajit Guha, the subaltern historian of India, once told me that it was in Champaran that Gandhi saw the light of a peasant India.

As events unfolded in Mexico, a corporate-capitalist agenda was enhanced and peasants were neglected, or, when needed, patronized under the ruling party Partido Revolucionario Institucional (PRI). The Zapata legacy continues today throughout the 12,000 rural communities and, especially, very deeply among the Indigenous and rural peasant communities (Stephen 2002).

Contemporary mobilization by Zapatistas after 1994 reminds us of how Zapata himself had issued his *Plan of Ayala* for the whole Mexican nation. By 1914, peasant armies were almost ready to take over the state, but Zapata or Pancho Villa did not take over the Mexican state. Instead, Zapata had a strong village community base and his focus was on securing control over water and the rich lowlands of Morelos for the toiling peasantry. Following the same tradition, the modern Zapatistas come basically from the frontier of the Lacandon jungle, where they eke out a living in a new land, and face the same difficulties due to not having access to resources.

The urban–rural and the industry–agriculture divides in India are often portrayed as the legendary difference between late Prime Minister Pandit Nehru and Mahatma Gandhi. Although close as personal friends, Gandhi and Nehru nurtured very different visions for India, both in terms of what India was and what it could be. While Nehru became the architect of heavy industrialization in India under a somewhat Soviet model, Gandhian experiments of living a simple life in ashrams, giving preference to a rural peasant life and pursuing self-reliance, were pushed to the margins after his tragic death in 1948. But, as indicated above, it became starkly clear by the 1980s that an urban-oriented, industrial model had bypassed the majority of Indians. Consequently, many of the initiatives for grassroots governance in India – including the movement to save the Narmada Valley from the proposed 30 major, 135 medium and 3,000 minor dams; tribal self-rule; and seedkeepers – are inspired by Mahatma Gandhi's vision of self-reliant 'village republics' (Lal 2001; Parajuli 2002).

For Mahatma Gandhi, 'village republics' were an example of how self-reliant rural Indian communities could produce, feed, clothe and, most importantly, govern themselves. His notion of 'village republics' cannot be properly understood without the corresponding practice of self-reliance, a concept different from the notion of self-sufficiency. 'Gandhi's vision of free India', comments Satish Kumar,

> was not of a nation-state but a confederation of self-governing, self-reliant, self-employed people living in village communities, deriving their livelihood from the products of their homesteads. Maximum economic and political power – including the power to decide what could be imported into or exported from the village – would remain in the hands of village assemblies. (Kumar 1996: 419)

In the Gandhian scheme, self-reliance implies the reduction of dependence on other places, but does not deny the desirability or necessity of external trade relationships. It is worth digging into what Gandhi meant by self-rule for India and liberation from the colonial order. He extended the notion of self-rule from merely political to the cultural and economic realms. In his celebrated book *Hind Swaraj*, or Indian Self-Rule, Gandhi writes: 'Real home-rule is self-rule or self-control. The way to it is passive resistance: that is soul-force or love-force. In order to exert this force, Swadeshi (self-reliance) in every sense is necessary.' This is how he came to conclude that only a non-violent and self-sufficient village economy would liberate the Indian masses from the impact of colonial rule in its many facets: political, cultural and economic.

I derive two practical suggestions from Gandhian political philosophy and practice. First is the redefinition of economy and market. According to Gandhi, the idea is to produce for local consumption and give priority to buying things that are produced locally. By practising self-reliance, communities can maintain networks of sociality that define the ethics of relationships in terms of proximity rather than distance, locality and regionality rather than nationality and globality. It is on this basis that we can articulate a Gandhian ecologism. I recently explained:

> Gandhi's ecologism (if we can call it that) was about rural peasants eking out their subsistence and necessities from a piece of land. In short, he might not have theorized the mathematics of sustainability but he showed us how to pursue sustainable livelihoods.... I want to note that Gandhi did not talk much about the abstract notion of earth but he talked a lot about land and soil. To support that economy, he also emphasized artisan economy (spinning of clothes with *charkha*, repairing of agricultural tools, arts and crafts) that made these rural peasant communities free from depending on machine-made and mass-produced industrial goods and tools. As is happening in India today, he did not want the village cobbler to be replaced by the Bata Shoe factory or the village blacksmith to be rendered obsolete by the Tata Iron and Steel Company. (Parajuli 2002: 61)

The second suggestion is the redefinition of politics by the devolution of centralized power in favour of a decentralized power that permeates to the bottom. As discussed above, distance, mobility, impermanence and velocity are the engines of globalization. At the other pole remain the virtues of ecology and localism, in which the role of the human is to assume stewardship of the land. Moreover, while the impulse of globalization of the economy has a tendency to homogenize cultures and spaces, localization is a strategy to foster the 'multiverse of differences'.

Foodsheds and the Legacy of Gandhi and Zapata

The appeal of the notion of foodsheds, writes Kloppenburg, is 'the graphic imagery it evokes; streams of foodstuffs running into a particular locality, their flow mediated by the features of both natural and social geography' (Kloppenburg et al. 1996). As Gandhi and Zapata might have liked to see, in North America farmers within a foodshed are engaged in what Kloppenburg and his colleagues call 'secession' – a strategic preference for withdrawing from and creating alternatives to the global food system. Participants within a foodshed want slowly to 'hollow out' from the structures of the global food system and reorganize their own social and productive capacities (Kloppenburg et al. 1996: 14). Akin to Zapata's *ejido* communities and Gandhi's village republics, a foodshed is based upon the idea of proximity, locality and regionality, flexibly built around boundaries set by plant communities, soil types, ethnicities, regional markets and exchange networks. Food is key in this new social organizing because what we are eating determines how we relate to the earth, and how we relate to each other. There are some inspiring examples to take into account. The Hartford Food System in the US northeast links farmers directly to low-income consumers by issuing food stamps at local farmers' markets. The Hudson Valley Watershed Group draws members all the way from the farmers of the Catskill Mountains to the residents of Manhattan. Their concerns range from the groundwater pollution of agricultural residue to the health of fish populations in the Hudson river, to the marketing arrangements for food produced in the foodshed to be sold in the restaurants of New York City. By now, there are thousands of such silent initiatives, and consumers are directly linked with producers through what is known as the CSAs, community supported agriculture.

In Portland, Oregon, where I live today, there is a new awareness among various growers, food merchants, consumers and certain sections of Portland City Council that food is a question of significance to the economy. Students, faculty and neighbouring farmers have even started a café at Portland State University where we want to experiment in growing, eating and thinking locally. Aptly named Food for Thought Café (www.fftcafe.org), our vision is to inculcate among college-age young people an appreciation for local soil, food, food growers and the seasonal diet. What has emerged from a series of discussions is that in order to ensure a local food policy, a number of factors have to be considered. First, farmers (especially the younger generation of farmers) need access to land and incentives to remain on the land. Second, public institutions such as city offices, universities, schools and soup kitchens should subscribe to organic food and sustainable agricultural products within their premises. Only time will tell whether we can really bring about some fundamental shifts in the way food is imported and exported in and out of

Portland. But it is a good beginning that the public is engaged in discussing the issue of food in a serious way.

Perhaps the tide is turning, and maybe ecological ethnicities will reclaim what Vandana Shiva calls the 'stolen harvest', as well as their stolen histories. Ecological ethnicities do not appear merely as the victim of the last 500 years' onslaught. They are actually endowed with a combination of historical and cultural repertoires that are in their favour. For example, their territorial claims are still active and are increasingly recognized. They also have the power of language as a bridge to the past. They have customary institutions of governance still operating that can be the basis of new democracy. They also have the technologies of sustainable living in a period when the need to fine-tune human technologies to earth's technologies is apparent. Today, they demonstrate the unique blend of bio-cultural diversity that enables them not only to uphold self-identity but also to seek civilizing proposals.

References

Altvater, Elmar (1994) 'Ecological and economic modalities of time and space', in Martin O'Connor (ed.), *Is Capitalism Sustainable?* New York: Guilford Press.

Bullard, Robert (ed.) (1994) *Confronting Environmental Racism*, Boston, MA: South End Press.

Collier, George and E. Quarantiello (1994) *Basta! Land and Zapata Rebellion in Chiapas*, Oakland, CA: Food First.

Daly, Herman (1996) *Beyond Growth*, Boston, MA: Beacon Press.

De Certeau, Michel (1986) *Heterologies: Discourse on the Other*, Minneapolis: University of Minnesota Press.

Esteva, Gustavo and Madhu Prakash (1998) *Grassroots Postmodernism: Remaking the Soil of Cultures*, London: Zed Books.

Fuentes, Carlos (1996) *A New Time for Mexico*, New York: Farrar, Straus & Giroux.

Gadgil, M. and R. Guha (1995) *Ecology and Equity: The Use and Abuse of Nature in India*, London: Routledge.

Guha, Ramchandra and Juan Martinez-Alier (1997) *Varieties of Environmentalism: Essays North and South*, London: Earthscan.

Hardin, Garrett (1968) 'The tragedy of the commons', *Science* 162, pp. 1243–8.

Harvey, David (1996) *Justice, Nature and the Politics of Difference*, Oxford: Blackwell.

Kloppenburg, Jack, et al. (1996) 'Coming in to the foodshed', in William Vitek and Wes Jackson (eds), *Rooted in the Land: Essays on Community and Place*, New Haven, CT: Yale University Press.

Kothari, Smitu (2001) 'Sovereignty and swaraj: Adivasi encounter with modernity and majority', in John Grim (ed.), *Indigenous Traditions and Ecology*, Cambridge, MA: Harvard University Press, pp. 453–64.

——— and Pramod Parajuli (1993) 'No nature without social justice: a plea for cultural and ecological pluralism in India', in Wolfgang Sachs (ed.), *Global Ecology: A New Arena of Political Conflict*, London: Zed Books, pp. 224–39.

Kumar, Satish (1996) 'Gandhi's swadeshi: the economics of permanence', in Jerry Mander and Edward T. Goldsmith (eds), *The Case Against the Global Economy*, San Francisco: Sierra Club Books, pp. 418–24.

Kurien, J. (1993) 'Ruining the commons: overfishing and fisherworkers' action in South India', *The Ecologist*, vol. 23, no. 1, pp. 5–12.

Lal, Vinay (2001) 'Too deep for deep ecology: Gandhi and the ecological vision of life', in Christopher Chapple and Mary Evelyn Tucker (eds), *Hinduism and Ecology*, Cambridge, MA: Harvard University Press, pp. 183–212.

Lokayan Bulletin (1996) 'Desh Bachao: Kisan MahaPanchayat' [Save the nation: Statement of Peasant Grand Assembly], *Struggle Notes*, vol. 13, no. 1, pp. 67–70.

Maffi, Luisa (ed.) (2001) *Biocultural Diversity: Linking Language, Knowledge and the Environment*, Washington, DC: Smithsonian Institution Press.

Nabhan, Gary Paul (1987) *Cultures of Habitat: On Culture, Nature and Story*, Washington, DC: Counterpoint Press.

Navadanya (1995) *Seedkeepers*, New Delhi: Indraprastha Press.

Parajuli, Pramod (1998) 'Beyond capitalized nature: ecological ethnicity as a new arena of conflict in the global capitalist regime', *Ecumene: A Journal of Environment, Culture, and Meaning*, vol. 5, no. 2, pp. 186–217.

——— (2001a) 'How can four trees make a jungle? Ecological ethnicities and the sociality of nature', in David Rothenberg and Marta Ulvaes (eds), *The World and the Wild*, Tucsan, AZ: University of Arizona Press, pp. 3–20. Formerly appeared in *Terra Nova* (special issue on *The World and the Wild*), vol. 3, no. 3, 1998, pp. 15–31.

——— (2001b) 'Learning from ecological ethnicities: towards a plural political ecology of knowledge', in John Grim (ed.), *Indigenous Traditions and Ecology*, Cambridge, MA: Harvard University Press, pp. 559–89.

——— (2002) 'Towards an environmentalism of the global south: a playful conversation around Mahatma Gandhi', *Encounter* (special Gandhi issue), vol. 15, no. 2, pp. 56–70.

——— and Frédérique Apffel-Marglin (1998), 'Geographies of difference and the resilience of ecological ethnicities: knowledge claims under globalization', *Development: Seeds of Change*, vol. 41, no. 2, pp. 14–21.

——— and Smitu Kothari (1998), 'Struggling for autonomy: the lessons from local governance', *Development: Seeds of Change*, vol. 41, no. 3, pp. 18–29.

Posey, Darrell A. (ed.) (1999) *Cultural and Spiritual Values of Biodiversity*, London: Intermediate Technology Publications.

Prabhu, Pradeep (2001) 'In the eye of a storm: tribal peoples of India', in John Grim (ed.), *Indigenous Traditions and Ecology*, Cambridge, MA: Harvard University Press, pp. 47–70.

Pulido, Laura (1997) *Environmentalism and Economic Justice*, Tucsan, AZ: University of Arizona Press.

Scott, James (1999) *Seeing Like a State: How Certain Schemes to Improve the Human Condition Have Failed*, New Haven, CT: Yale University Press.

Sharma, B.D. (1996) *Globalization and Tribal Encounter*, Delhi: Har-Ananda Publications.

Shiva, Vandana (2000) 'The significance of Seattle', FoodFirst website (www.foodfirst.org). See also www.vshiva.net for her various works and publications.

Snyder, Gary (1993) 'Coming in to the watershed', in Scott Walker (ed.), *Changing Community: The Graywolf Annual Ten*, St Paul, MN: Graywolf Press.

Stephen, Lynn (2002) *Zapata Lives: Histories and Cultural Politics in Southern Mexico*, Berkeley: University of California Press.

Wilmer, Frank (1993) *The Indigenous Voice in World Politics*, London: Sage Publications.

15

A Dream of Democracy
in the Russian Far East

PETRA RETHMANN

Petra Rethmann is Associate Professor in the Department of Anthropology at McMaster University. Her current work focuses on the intersection between history and political imagination, with particular attention to issues of violence, power and struggle. She is author of *Tundra Passages: Gender and History in the Russian Far East* (Penn State University Press, 2001).

How does a globally circulating social category such as 'democracy', as a corollary of the almost equally ubiquitous term 'civil society', come to mean something in a particular political context? Can it mean anything at all? Anna Tsing (1999: 159) describes such globally circulating categories as 'dream machines' that can offer promising possibilities for social projects while at the same time being practical tools that help put such projects into place. I, too, argue that dreams can be powerful tools for considering social possibilities. They may open up ways of thinking about local practices and social actions in circumstances that seem desolate and devoid of hope. The dreams I have in mind are not personal dreams that one pictures in one's private room. They are configurations of social practices and ideas that assume at least a tentative political power through their sharedness and collective enactment. They are dreams with social and material effects. This chapter puts such a dream at its centre. It seeks to analyse and describe how one group of Native activists in the Chukotka Peninsula in the Russian Far East endeavours to build an Indigenous community and movement, Ionto, that stands in the way of various regional and economic developments. But, equally important, Native activists try to find ways to imagine regional initiatives on their own terms. The doubled relatedness of the phrase 'in the way' involves techniques of both resistance and defiant challenge, and the creative ability to think about alternative political styles. It is, then, in this sense that this essay contributes to discussions on the creation and composition of Indigenous social movements, political possibility, and self-determined schemes of development. While it does not situate itself within frameworks of development in any direct way, it builds on and works against them as they insinuate themselves into regional and Indigenous relations.

The exploration of social dreams is unusual terrain in the formation of development and democracy. In Russia, as elsewhere, social scientists are expected to build their analyses on data that help to build models, paradigms and identifiable patterns. Hardly ever do researchers build their analyses on social visions and ideas whose promise has not yet been redeemed. In the northern Russian context there is a growing literature on Indigenous land claims and environmental degradation, identity and place, traditional knowledge, property, and identity (Anderson 2000; Fondahl 1998). For the specific Chukotka context, Patty Gray's (1998) research on the difficulties of Indigenous organizing has shown how Chukchi political aspirations and desires have been systematically suppressed since the country's democratic transition. Precisely because the conditions of everyday living are so terrible in the Russian Far East, scholars and activists interpellate Chukchi as the quintessential subject of 'endangerment' and risk (Schweitzer and Gray 2000; see also Pika, Dahl and Larson 1996). It is certainly true that since the beginning of the 1990s Chukotka's Native residents have experienced dramatic rises in poverty, violence, drinking, disease, jealousy and inequality (see, e.g., Abriutina 1999; Pika 1993). Yet when analysts imagine Indigenous residents in ways that stress their inability to think and act self-consciously, representations emerge that easily, although unintentionally, overlook the political possibilities that Chukchi women and men try to create for themselves. This chapter argues for the importance of a critical anthropology, including the study of political possibilities and creative imaginations. Given the current disenchanted state of public and intellectual debate, such analyses seem all the more urgent. Instead of succumbing to a politics of cynicism and the real (realpolitik), I argue that we must begin with the question of how particular social visions and dreams come to mean something to people caught in particular dilemmas. It may be that in these alternatives − creative innovations rather than 'old' forms of contestation − just futures are to be found.

My focus on Ionto's hopes and dreams seeks to facilitate such a discussion. Since the end of the 1990s, the movement has worked hard to create a space for political initiative and debate. In its efforts to build the conditions for thinking about social alternatives and action, Ionto draws on elements that are understood, albeit appreciated in different degrees, by most Indigenous residents in the peninsula. Reindeer and the cultural practices associated with them are Ionto's guide to what Tsing (1999: 160) calls a 'field of attraction', a space in which Indigenous women and men are able to imagine themselves as agents capable of envisioning the conditions of their own existence. True, not all Indigenous residents in the Chukotka region have lived or live by reindeer herding. Whale, walrus and seal hunting, fishing, collecting mussels, seaweed, birds' eggs, various kinds of berries and tundra herbs, too, constitute forms of the Chukchi livelihood and help to extend Chukchi knowledge beyond the land to the sea. In the ethnographic imagination, the Chukchi are known as the people who herd *chauchu* (reindeer) (Bogoraz 1909: 11). Reindeer, and the land, endow people with a deep sense of who they are, and they continue to define the responsibilities and obligations, along with the enjoyments, people can and do have.[1] Dislocation, collectivization of traditional economies, environmental disasters, 'newcomers' (*priezhie*) and the problems they bring, unemployment and, more currently, the botched politics of economic privatization are all part of Chukchi knowledge of the contemporary world. And although people have lived in government settlements for about the last sixty years, reindeer and the cultural and economic practices associated with them remain a focal point of the Chukchi identity. They provide the means – hides, meat and cultural meaning – through and by which people can live. They are at the centre of Chukchi autonomy and independence.

In focusing on animals and the products they yield as principal components for achieving justice and a social movement, it is Ionto's tactics and style that sets it apart from most other Indigenous and social justice movements in the region. In Chukotka, as elsewhere in the Russian Federation, RAIPON (Russian Association of Indigenous Peoples of the North) is currently both the voice and framework through which most Indigenous organizing in Russia occurs.[2] Founded at a convention on 20–23 March 1990 in Moscow, RAIPON is an outflow of Russia's civil society movements, during the era of perestroika, that also comprised Indigenous activists. Originally created at Russia's federal level, the association has been quick to institute itself at the district and village levels to (1) create regional and local venues for an Indigenous voice, (2) channel information concerning Indigenous issues and rights into villages and regions, (3) dispense monetary aid and funding for Indigenous projects, and (4) guarantee the flow of knowledge and advice between the centre (Moscow) and the regions, and among the regions. The movement has created much excitement at both international (for example, at the United Nations and Arctic Council) and Russia's federal levels, but it has also generated much scepticism in Russia's regions.

In the main, criticisms revolve around the failure of RAIPON representatives to address the interests and concerns of local people. Since the inception of the association, foreign monetary support has been generous, and projects that flow from foreign funding currently operate throughout the Russian North – with some regions being better served than others. So far, Chukotka's Indigenous constituencies have received comparably little funding, and there is a growing awareness that most funding models are not designed by community members but favour rather standardized strategies to train local communities in a range of political and legal fields. At the same time, the complex vulnerability of those who seek political power at administrative levels frequently prevents Indigenous representatives from speaking out against political and economic inequality. As one result, in Chukotka RAIPON representatives are either not well known or associated with forms of political exclusiveness or co-optation. This is certainly part of the reason why people often keep a distance from politics. This distance, too, stems from deep-seated distrust regarding many aspects of public power, as well as its institutional forms and rhetorics.

Ionto is working within these contexts and confinements. The movement's approximately fifty members (as of 13 November 2002) form an eclectic group of community workers, elders, and young and independent leaders. Although many of Ionto's key initiators, including Anton Tynel', intellectual architect of the movement, are Chukchi, other Indigenous residents in the region – Evenk, Even, and Iukaghir – have joined in. Indeed, the fact that Ionto's membership is based not on ethnicity but on articulations of cultural empathy and sharing is one of the reasons that it is able to attract divergent constituencies. Although Ionto was thought up and founded in Anadyr', Chukotka's administrative centre, most meetings are held in Tavaivaam, a government-created village in close proximity to Anadyr'. In the mid-1990s, Tavaivaam became the organizing centre for bold, in-your-face tradition-oriented practices, and flagrant demonstrations of Native cultural consciousness vis-à-vis Chukotka's authoritarian government. In Tavaivaam, reindeer-hide-covered tents (*iarangas*) stand side by side with dilapidated buildings within this still largely Soviet-era space. Many of Ionto's members have actively developed their own interpretation and practice of culture, a memory work by which people consult neighbours, kin, elders and their own memory to learn about *obychie* (traditions) that are overwhelmingly experienced as a site of loss. Although this practice may not be too surprising, and certainly does find its parallels elsewhere, in Russia it is less than self-evident. It is part of Ionto's provocation.

Several layers of historical and cultural context are necessary for the force of Ionto's challenge to emerge. I begin with the processes of Russia's current economic transformations and their effects on contemporary Indigenous cultural politics. Most frequently, Russia's economic restructuring and 'transition' are looked at from the perspective of domestic or market relations. Soviet nationality politics, however, changed too as the country began to unravel. Recent historical analyses argue (Brubakers 1989; Slezkine 1994b) that the Soviet state created 'nations' to promote systematically the national consciousness of non-Russian cultural minorities.[3] As Francine Hirsch (2000) has shown, in the Soviet Union the 'nation' was a construction of history, not its description. By granting nationhood the Soviet state sought to split above-class national alliances that were based on cultural identity and forms of historical consciousness associated with them. By eroding the conditions for the continuation of strong identity formations – so the argument goes – class divisions would automatically emerge, which would allow the Soviet government to recruit proletarian and peasant support for their own agenda. The resultant politics are torn and contradictory.

More than an antiquated relic of the Soviet Union, nation-building was and is part of the political consciousness that informs a great deal of Indigenous organizing at Russia's federal and regional levels. In Chukotka and elsewhere, there is an implicit criticism that institutional Indigenous organizing is steeped in the history of elite-making, and that there are too many urban-based and institutionally affiliated professionals that do not connect with the country's very different regional cultures and peoples. In implicit criticism of Indigenous representatives associated with Chukotka's local administration, Ionto argues that ways need to be found to make political initiative look like a possible and worthwhile project for regional women and men. One consequence of 'market reform' was the descent of Chukotka's Indigenous residents, and many of their non-Indigenous neighbours, into entrenched poverty and destitution. In Chukotka this situation is aggravated by structuring economic logics that keep Indigenous residents in conditions of perpetual dependence. As a challenge, Ionto poses its own vision of the market, turning democratization from a process of disempowerment into one of promise in which people craft their own political practices and futures.

The power of Ionto's dream is not to be content to identify what is. It is to show the possibilities that might become.

Democracy

In Russia at the beginning of the 1990s, democracy became one of the political key sites around which the country's hopes and economic aspirations rallied. The new democratic regime sought to put an end to the trappings of the old regime – the Communist command economy, one-party rule, non-elected political representatives, and the strong influence of the military (as expressed in strong criticisms of the unpopular Afghan war at that time) – to move towards democratic media representations and elections. Yet as political possibilities seemingly opened, it quickly became clear that they were short-lived. The astonishing energy that had led to the emergence of a variety of civil society movements in Eastern European countries and the Soviet Union was quickly curtailed when, on 6 December 1991, the

Soviet Union officially dissolved. Superpower political status no longer translated unambiguously into economic status. With the end of the Cold War, the new post-socialist regimes found themselves at the mercy of IMF debt-rescheduling guidelines developed for the economic restructuring of countries like Mexico and Brazil. The social impact of being considered economically a Third World country was humbling. Democratic issues were relegated to the sidelines while economic issues became dominant.

Translated into a programme for the transition from a planned to a market economy, the overriding Western (chiefly US) policy concern was not whether incorporation into global capitalism should occur, but how quickly and on what terms. For Russia's post-Soviet citizens, the word 'shock' (*udarnik*) – a historical term in the former Soviet Union which implies jolting an economic system into gear through rapid acceleration of the transformation process – returned in a new context, as the 'shock therapy' economic programme designed by Harvard economist Jeffrey Sachs rose to hegemonic prominence.[4] Speed of implementation became paramount in order to prevent political debate about the social desirability of such trans-formation. Yet if speed is necessary to avoid political debate, political debate needs to be avoided because it slows down the speed of implementation. Circularity was the epistemological essence of both kinds of 'shock therapy'. But, even more significant for the argument here, recent reform-driven shock therapy separated decisively two projects that at first appeared to be inextricably linked: the economic project of free markets and the political project of democratic rule. In this separation, it was democracy that was ex-pendable. The goal of instituting capitalism had clear priority. The tragedy of this separation was not the destruction of the old socialist economy, but the fact that Westernizers in post-socialist governments no longer identified the elimination of socialism with the establishment of principles of democracy. In the case of Russia, it meant that Yeltsin (as currently Putin) did not feel himself necessarily burdened by putting democracy into practice.

The national restructuring of the Soviet economy had several consequences that fundamentally changed the political relationship between Indigenous and non-Indigenous representatives in governmental and administrative bodies. In April 1932, roughly two years after the inception on 10 December 1930 of the *Chukotskii natsionalniy okrug* (Chukotka National District), the First Chukotka Okrug Congress of Soviets decided to inaugurate a parallel political system which was to grant both Indigenous and non-Indigenous CPSU (Communist Party of the Soviet Union) members equity and po-litically balanced shares of power. At the regional level, the chairperson of the Worker's Deputies was invariably Russian, while the chairperson of the Executive Committee of the Soviet of Workers' Deputies was invariably a Chukchi woman or man. In highly formalistic implementation of this rule, from 1932 until 1991, Chukchi women or men served as chairpersons of the Executive Committee or *ispolkom*. To the astonishment of Chukotka's residents, in 1991 this rule was reversed when Chukchi politician Vladimir Mikhailovich Etylin was elected chairperson of the Soviet of Workers' Deputies, while a Russian 'newcomer' (*priezshie*), Aleksandr Viktorovich Nazarov, was chosen as chairperson of the *ispolkom*.

To outsiders, the fairly high status and power of Indigenous representatives at government levels since the inception of the Soviet Union may be surprising, but recently historians have argued that Soviet nationality policies were one important step in creating what Terry Martin (2001) has labelled the 'affirmative-action empire'. The 'affirmative-action empire' may have been the Soviet Union's own unique historic response to a problem that has troubled, and still troubles, many multinational states and federations: how to integrate cultural multiplicity within larger governmental configurations by maintaining, at least in appearance, justice and equality among them?[5] The answer to this question, the 'nation-builders' (as represented by Lenin and Stalin) among the Bolsheviks argued, lay in the implementation of affirmative action (*polozhitel'naia deiatel'nost'*) policy in the name of *korenizatsiia*, loosely translated as 'indigenization'. After many debates at previous party meetings, at the Twelfth Party Congress in April 1923, *korenizatsiia* matured into an idiom for Indigenous affirmation and decolonization.

Scholars of social policies and history tend to study *korenizatsiia* as an institution (Brubakers 1996: 38), analysed for its structure and mode of legitimation, and for the way it took part in both the establishment and disavowal of Soviet imperial power (Slezkine 1994b; Martin 2001; Suny 1993). But, more importantly to the Chukchi men and women and the analysis here, *korenizatsiia* is also a persistent part of the social context within which a great deal of popular Indigenous organizing and its political articulations occur. More than an antiquated relic of the nation-building process that was to make the Soviet Union, it is also part of the political consciousness that informs a great deal of Indigenous organizing on Russia's federal and the international scene. Perhaps more than anywhere else, in Russia questions of recognition and cultural rights are entangled with the history of the state and its forms of institutionalized power: a history of social advancement and prestige through and by allegiance to the Party and more than seven decades of well-calculated government rhetoric that posited the state as the nexus of political possibility, progress, justice and cultural rights.

The termination of the policy in 1993 as a consequence of economic power struggles in Moscow distressed Russia's Indigenous residents because there no longer existed a guaranteed institutional basis for their voice. In December 1992 a fist fight broke out in parliament over the nomination of the pro-Sachs 'Westerner' Egor Gaidar for the position of prime minister. In May 1993 over 500 people were wounded in a Moscow May Day riot. In October 1993, tanks ordered by president Boris Yeltsin moved onto Russia's Parliament building. In the ensuing violence, between the elected Members of Parliament who opposed Yeltsin on several accounts and the 'new' democratic government that was unanimously backed by all member states of NATO, 187 people died, Russia plunged into a deep economic crisis, and the president won almost tsar-like powers for himself. Never mind that Yeltsin, in opposition to the communist Gorbachev, was one of the founding members of the democratic party Nash Dom – Rossiia ('Our House is Russia'), by the end of October the outcome of all this upheaval was enacted in true authoritarian style. Fearing for the continuation of his leadership and political survival, Yeltsin called for the dissolution of all Soviets of Workers' Deputies. Their chairpersons were replaced by carefully chosen members of Nash Dom – Rossiia and the Yeltsin clan. In Chukotka, Vladimir Etylin, who from 1991 to 1993 had served as chairperson of this Soviet, was summarily dismissed, and Aleksandr Nazarov advanced speedily to the position of governor.

Thus, in the perception of many Chukchi, seven decades of affirmative action ended. Effectively barred from all positions of decision-making power and struck – like the rest of the country – by dramatic increases in poverty, unemployment and inflation, the Chukchi communities sank into a state of despondency and despair. At the same time, Aleksandr Nazarov, the new 'governor', ruled by harassment, intimidation and authoritarian decree. Departmental divisions that exclusively dealt with Indigenous affairs were closed. In 1996 the *iaranga* (the Chukchi term for the traditional reindeer-fur-covered tent that was used by reindeer-herding Chukchi), a meeting place for various Chukchi cultural and political groups, was disbanded and, in the same year, the Chukchi section *Murgin Nutenut* ('Our Homeland') of the regional newspaper was terminated. Demonstrations and public protests led to more dismissals, and in lieu of activists and independent leaders Indigenous staff loyal to and financed by the governor were offered positions within governmental institutions. Among the Chukchi, these *budzhetniki* (Indigenous representatives whose work is included in the budget of the government) are simultaneously disrespected and feared. On extra-regional trips and on the international Indigenous stage, they endorse the regime of the governor, saying what he wants them to say.

The reason why RAIPON representatives in Chukotka are so often distrusted needs to be understood in the context of these constellations. But to argue that in Chukotka the efforts of institutionalized Indigenous movements have often been in vain is not simply to dismiss their organizations, or to disagree with those who see them as the single most important way to a political voice. To relate regional politics in such a way is not to deny what many have argued, namely that the self-conscious articulation of an Indigenous movement in challenge to the Communist regime created an important political space in which Indigenous issues could be heard (Gray 1998). One problem is that most of these organizations were produced within the logics of the old regime, rather than being the consequence of their defeat. As one consequence, in Russia RAIPON's Indigenous critics charge that representatives situated on institutional levels produce rather standardized political demands and forms that mirror bureaucratic limitations rather than peoples' wishes and needs.

The implications are that Indigenous politicians are rarely trusted by their own constituencies, partly because of the legacy of the Soviet Union itself, partly because of their manoeuvrings and rhetoric that put governmental aid at their nexus, thus actively asking for protection, making appeals for dependency, albeit by implication. This is a politics that cannot enliven the imagination or inspire. What is needed here are new modes of producing consciousness and awareness, modes steeped in a different kind of morality and – to evoke a rarely used term – integrity. Modes that can rally citizens and community, and make political activists work look like an identifiable and worthwhile object for Chukchi women and men. This is precisely the project on which Ionto has embarked: how can we meet the needs of the present without submission to state governance and the forms of the governing mentality that come along with it? For a start, consider a fragment from an interview with Anton Tynel, one of Ionto's founding members and key leaders.

Initiative

> The fair [iarmarkt] is the foundation of our independence. If we start now, in the beginning, only two or three people will come. Let them bring meat, and nothing more; let them bring animal hides, and nothing more. But this will be the beginning of our trade activism. We will do it ourselves and not through some government. This is what we will do for ourselves; we will do it how it was for a long time.

Trade fairs? What is happening here? Is this fragment part of a tradition-oriented but politically eccentric dream of empowerment and self-determination? Is this a fetishizing of origins summoned in opposition to governmental credos? Or does this statement offer evidence of a withdrawal, a retreat into the certitude of tradition, of what once was, of an unrivalled past in which many things Chukotka's Indigenous residents now lack were a given? Through this statement I can ask about Ionto's attempts to motivate and inspire Chukchi women and men, while at the same time being limited by the same discursive, institutional and political constraints as other leaders. I can ask about Chukchi fantasies, imaginings and hopes, and the possibility of their realization.

The segment of Ionto's vision as related above must be read in light of, but not reduced to, the commitments, significance and love Chukchi and their Indigenous neighbours attach to animals and reindeer herding as a meaningful form of making a living. There is a tendency in northern Russia studies to emphasize the material utility and worth of animals, including reindeer. But the significance of reindeer stretches well beyond considerations of diet (intestines, meat and marrow) and utility (shelter and clothes). If whaling, fishing and sealing are important to the economic and cultural livelihood of Chukchi women and men, reindeer are also cultural media for expanding and connecting their identities. Precisely because people herded and thus travelled with these animals, they were able to establish meaningful and enduring bonds between themselves and animals, as well as within and between communities.[6] Reindeer were the medium through which the Chukchi formed and form ontologies of social and spiritual relations (Rethmann 2001). Even at the beginning of this millennium, after disease and the effects of national and international economic policies, including collectivization and privatization have undermined the material bases of reindeer herding, reindeer remain a sign of social identity and wealth, albeit in a radically transformed cultural and political environment.

The significance of animals for producing connections gains importance, too, in the economic realm. In Chukchi communities, women and men actively remember trade fairs and the mobility associated with them as important and constitutive aspects of their livelihood. In Chukchi memory and in the native country, trade fairs (dense networks of economic transaction and exchange) were important places of *biznis* (business) and commerce, connecting different Indigenous constituencies – Chukchi, Koriak, Even, Inupiat (Kotzebue 1821, I: 228) – and non-Indigenous constituencies – Russian, Japanese, and American – into the bargain (Burch 1988). Fairs enter the ethnographic record as early as 1789 (Bogoraz 1904: 56) and were then held in the area of Ostrovnye and Anui at irregular intervals. Eventually the latter location prevailed and Fort Anuisk was built. The Anui fair grew rapidly in importance, and around the 1880s financial turnover amounted to 200,000 roubles a year.[7] Older Chukchi men and women confirm the reports of scholars that there must have been fairs in villages as remote as Naukan or Uelen, to which people travelled, again, fully armed, offering their wares to each other on spear points (Bogoraz 1904: 53). Their mobility and autonomy allowed Chukchi herders to establish far-reaching trade relations in the region, and stretch out – across the ocean – throughout the entire Bering region.

Historic changes at the turn of the century, however, forced the Chukchi to shift the emphasis in trade from intraregional to interregional relations, resulting in the intensification of trade among Chukotka's Indigenous and non-Indigenous constituencies. The Chukchi recall some of the specificities of such exchange in great detail (Krupnik 2000: 224–31). Cultural memories of this trade continue to enthral younger Chukchi as sites of enchanting action; communication between generations becomes possible. Younger people ask about the prizes for knives and rifles (how many reindeer hides did you 'sell' to buy a gun?), and older people consult each other and their memory to answer these questions as accurately as they can. To the Chukchi women and men I know, interregional trade identifies them as wide-travelling and knowledgeable people: trading people are people who can manage their own affairs.

In fashioning its own vision of autonomy, Ionto works hard to create political meanings that may resonate with a position 'from below'. It is not a statement that addresses the desires and hopes of the Chukchi in the name of transcendent abstractions: Indigenous justice, democracy, sustainability and human rights, as if such articles were invariably the property of states, development agencies or international political bodies. Precisely because the statement deploys Chukchi history, memory and knowledge to inspire the Chukchi people is Ionto able to attract attention. Promising openings have been created. In 1998 Chukchi women and men from the western Chukotka territory of Bilibino thought of organizing such a fair to protest against the radiation and emissions from Bilibino's nuclear power station which kills animals, humans and plants. At that time, the Chukchi let the idea of trade pass so as not to direct attention away from the goals they pursued then. To the excitement of everybody involved, the idea was a success. Bilibino's resident Chukchi were there, but many more arrived from far away to participate. 'There was even a couple that travelled on reindeer sledge for three days with their newborn.' Elders came. People danced, played the drum, and drank less. Everybody seemed to have a good time. A 'field of attraction' had been created and cleared within a social landscape of desire and hope, granting Chukchi agency within the imaginations of their own making.

Government Tradition

In Ionto's statement, tradition is turned to its own unexpected ends. Not all tradition is licensed to empower, as its dramatization on the governmental stage of cultural recognition makes clear. One of its key aims is appeasement and accommodation, whether we refer to Soviet-era ritualizations or to the dawning of Russia's post-Soviet, 'new' democratic epoch. Theatrical representations of the commonwealth's cultural multiplicity and that of its 'cultures' sprang up all across the Soviet Union in the 1920s (Rolf 2000). In the name of 'allying' (*smychka*) and, again, the 'Friendship of the Peoples', ritualized stagings of 'everyday life' (*byt*) turned into dramatizations of life as song and dance, a highly routinized catalogue of artistic movements and gestures contrived to pass the phantasm of culture as its own factuality and truth. In this highly socialist economy of signs, tradition as the concrete stuff of Chukchi everyday life turned into a simulacrum of itself, a mirror that reflects meaning as image alone. Following the Soviet creed that 'culture' should be 'nationalist in form, [but] socialist in content', the traditions of 'the people' metamorphosed into fetishized articulations of the regime's good intentions and will, duplicates without – and this is what concerns the Chukchi most – genuine matter. '[They] perform (*tantzuem*) traditions, but their meaning is gone.' I have previously claimed that the Chukchi, in search of political possibility, invoke tradition not so much in the spirit of the authentic but of the fantastic. In this section, I turn to the question of tradition as governmental ritual to show (1) how rituals which are enacted in the name of Indigenous rights actually help to maintain authoritarian government, and (2) how these rituals in their very simplified and compressed forms open spaces for the very reversal of their own code.

The ideals of the Bolsheviks may be gone, but the legacy of the Soviet Union lives on. In the Chukotka Autonomous Region this is nowhere more evident than in the ritualized forms of public recognition, including cultural difference and rights. On 9 August 2000, the newly democratic government of Chukotka celebrated the 'International Day of Indigenous Peoples' (*Mezhdunarodnykh den' korennykh narodov*) in Anadyr'.[8] The celebration, conducted under the auspices of the regional government, assumed a grandly theatrical form. In keeping with the theme of the day, the elevated stage engulfed almost one-third of the plaza that stretches out in front of Anadyr''s House of Culture (*dom kul'tury*), with the municipal administration doing its best to approximate some sort of original of Chukchi culture. Indeed, there was nothing particularly spectacular in Anadyr''s rendition. An open and wide *iaranga*, with all the trappings of exemplary Chukchi life, furnished the background and the illusion of cultural simplicity and authenticity. Reindeer-hide-covered drums were hanging from cords along the side of the tent; boots, mattresses and coats sewn from reindeer fur either lay or hung down on the ground; antlers, bows and the odd spear stuck out everywhere; and, finally, a rounded plate manifesting a quintessential Chukchi sign of life, the sun, shone over the entire charade. Walrus tusks and simulations of Chukchi petroglyphic imagery of sea mammals, including whales and seals, *baidars* (boats), and hunting scenes had been painted on pieces of cardboard, each of which was attached to the stage.

Under the slogan 'our way, our pride', difference not collectivity took centre stage. Alongside the governor and the Russian administrative elite stood Chukchi representatives, their amplified voices overpowering the everyday sounds of Anadyr''s life. Aleksander Nazarov spoke of economic achievements ('We now have 500 Indigenous students studying here'), of justice ('I want to tell you that the law concerning the Indigenous Peoples of the North, Siberia and the Far North was passed.... And this fact gives grounds to the growth of Indigenous self-consciousness. Today, we also work for other laws.... And we also prepared a series of laws which are presently under review in the Federal Duma. That is The Law of the Arctic. The respective committee should work and give this law to the people'), and of debt, with the inkling of an apology ('Ahead of us, there is a task. Together with preservation of the ethnic and cultural uniqueness [*samobytnost'*] of the Indigenous peoples of the North, we will also need to elevate them to the level of a modern civilization.... Our debt today: the continuous, harmonious, and, most importantly, compassionate (*dobrovol'noe*) introduction of our Indigenous people to a modern level of life'). Indigenous representatives avowed the governor's claims in their own speeches, only to be interrupted – but always in carefully staged intervals – by the dancers and drummers of Ergyron, the 'Chukchi-Eskimo' national dance ensemble founded in 1968 to the general edification of Chuktoka's Indigenous and non-Indigenous residents. Amidst the cries that Eryron's dancers emitted in imitation of the seagull, official Chukchi leaders, too, spoke in enthusiastic, albeit very general, ways of the accomplishments and kindheartedness of the governor. The few Chukchi who were there observed this newly democratic but also terribly familiar scene with their own air of practised detachment.

It will be remembered that in the political culture of the Soviet Union the recognition of Russia's non-Russian constituencies was situated at the threshold between negation and affirmation, between the denial of 'culture' as a site of difference and its avowal as folkloric aestheticization. This was a dialectics that created its own particular form of exclusion by purportedly empowering that which it sought to keep out of its political realm. As Chukchi women and men are well aware, the logics of this system have not been abandoned but live on: in the creation of new political vocabularies and legal language, rhetorics of patronage masquerading as kindness, dependencies disguised as guardianship and care through which the spectre not of communism but of democratization rises. No one but the governor himself makes this more clear. That day, in an act of singular and magnanimous ostentation, Aleksandr Nazarov had allowed himself the pleasure of a special gesture. Piles and piles of pinkish-grey layers of bowhead whale fat (*makhtak*) were heaped up on long wooden boards alongside the *iaranga*. The adjoining banner read: From the Governor (*Ot gubernatora*)!

Aid

Ionto's concerns grow directly out of these perplexities, provoked by a democracy driven by cunning and deceit rather than by, as much current political philosophy would have it, virtue and sincerity (e.g., Tully 1995; Kymlicka 1995). This is the context in which Ionto works to turn the fantasy of tradition to its own unexpected ends. Yet there is one more aspect that I need to explore before the ingenuity of Ionto's project can come fully into view. What about the explicitly economized aspect of Ionto's vision, the market? Does not the statement maintain, albeit by implication, that 'tradition' acquires its antithetical value in the very process of its marketization, its trafficking and exchange? How can the 'tradition' that must find its commodified (if not always monetized) 'other' be useful in granting political possibility or, indeed, in fulfilling sovereignty and self-determination? My concern with the possibility of imagination as a site of hope turns here to the possibility of subjugation and enslavement in the context of gift-giving in its particular form of 'humanitarian aid' (*guminitarnaia pomosh*'). Since 24 December 2000, the Chukotka Autonomous Region has been run under the auspices of a new governor, Roman Abramovich, whose allegedly altruistically given help has compelled Chukchi women and men to think even more deeply about political styles and innovations than during the authoritarian rule of Aleksandr Nazarov. In the following I work to understand Chukotka's own logics of promise and debt in which Chukotka's Indigenous residents have recently become ensnared. Although I follow Roman Abramovich's efforts closely, my argument extends beyond the political ambitions of one particular politician to understand the underlying logics and effects of regional developments in the form of the ostensibly altruistic gift.

Who is Roman Abramovich? There are at least two totally different incarnations behind this name. First, Roman Abramovich is Chukotka's latest manifestation of self-aggrandizing benevolence and care. In the words of one of his closest advisors, however, he is just part of a 'bunch of young men from Moscow who came to Chukotka to do good'.[9] Recall that in the recent ethnographic imagination Chukotka is always a region of immense poverty, a state-of-being in which the Chukchi hover incessantly at the brink of extinction. This is a situation that cannot fail to evoke empathy and compassion, and one that 'merits attention on humanitarian grounds alone' (Carnegie Foundation 2000: 69). Abramovich actualizes, in the flesh, what Russia – according to many international observers – so bitterly lacks: (our) commiseration, sympathy and sharing. Roman Abramovich comprises all these qualities in abundance. In summer 2000 he paid for hundreds of Chukchi children to spend the two summer months of their school vacation in well-staffed camps on the Black Sea. Jet planes flew back and forth between Anadyr´ and Sochi, covering thousands of miles, financed by Abramovich's own wealth, promoted by his own propaganda machine. Pictures of healthy-looking and, for once, non-starving children were published in his own weekly paper, *Polius Nadezhdy* ('Pole of Hope'). As if to underscore all of this 'assistance', the new governor, too, sends 'humanitarian aid' in the form of food, clothes and shoes, but also candles and fishing rods, to Chukchi villages in Chukotka. Yet there is one article that Roman Abramovich will not give: 'aid' in its rawest form, money. Yet it is the latter, Chukchi argue, that they so urgently need. Money not only buys products and food. Money also buys technical tools and mechanical devices that might aid them in their own endeavours.

Considering Roman Abramovich's almost frantic giving, there is one obvious question that emerges here: why is he providing all of this 'assistance'? What are his intentions, his motivations? A look at Roman Abramovich's second incarnation might provide the answer. In Russia, Abramovich is better known as one of Russia's oligarchs (if not the 'most powerful [and] wealthy' [Lloyd 2000: 91]) – key beneficiaries of the economic reign of the few (the 'oligarchic period') who have decided Russia's economic fate since the beginning of the 1990s. Trading a career in the Komsomol (Kommunisticheskii soiuz molodezhi, 'Communist Youth Organization') for a risky future in Russia's emerging private sector in the late 1980s, Abramovich enjoyed the distinct advantage of growing up under the strong tutelage of Berezovskii within the Kremlin 'family'. Together with other members of this economic elite he entered his apogee in 1996 when 'the oligarchs' received important slices of state property at extraordinarily low prices (the so-called 'loans for share' deal) in return for their collective decision to underwrite and finance Yeltsin's re-election campaign. The move guaranteed Abramovich's apotheosis as an 'oil baron'. He currently holds a significant percentage of the shares of Sibneft (Siberian Oil), one of Russia's most powerful corporations, and a considerable portion of Rossisskii Aluminy. Yet in Russia speculations persist that the 'oligarchic period' may soon come to an end.

Such tentative assumptions have everything to do with another significant change on Russia's contemporary political scene: the tough-fisted regime of Russia's president, Vladimir Putin, who wishes to curtail both freedom of the press and the oligarchs' sway. Abramovich and his accomplices may all be very rich, but for most of them it is an uneasy, robber-baron kind of wealth that may be snatched away at any time. Since their ascendancy to economic wealth and power, Putin, then chief of the KGB, has been keeping *kompromat* on them, material gathered by the security agencies on their rise to wealth. Putin's decision to employ this material in his interests depends on whether Russia's top businessmen can throw off a decade of corruption, strong-arm tactics, private feuds and cheating foreigners to emerge as credible financial leaders.[10] So far, membership of the Federation Council by virtue of his position as governor has guaranteed Abramovich immunity from prosecution, but he may want a safer bet. What better way, then, to show the *noblesse* of a kindred spirit in economic hard times and donate, bestow, present?

As a result, the humanitarian aid given by Roman Abramovich may be largely conceited, although some of it may be sincere. Yet if it carries traces of altruism and care, it summons them with enormous ambiguity – an ambiguity, indeed, that marks the very disruption of Abramovich's wished-for goodwill. In its most severe form, the doubled intent of all this gifting expresses itself in the very continuation of the conditions that bring about the economy of the gift in the first place. In this context, Ionto's vision emerges as one of disruption, of unexpected challenge that confronts the conditions of dependency in the gestalt of kindness through the conception of a market based on the rejection of the economy of the good deed by replacing it with – as a vision – an economy of equivalence. The market of Ionto's imagining outlaws indignity and exploitation by reclaiming autonomy and sovereignty. It does this through a vision of production based not on distancing and alienation but on local history, interests and loyalties. The entrepreneurial activities of Ionto's market are build on parochial experience, yet they are capable of its transcendence by involving always larger, far-flung constituencies in the bargain. Such trade does not necessarily involve the conditions of its own corruption. It holds the promise of possibility precisely because it is based on a morality whose standards and rules the Chukchi create themselves *for* themselves.

It is too early to say how Ionto's project will evolve. On the one hand, there is little to suggest that Ionto's vision of exchange and trade will grow into a powerful initiative, fulfilling its own promise by dissolving the spirit of the economy of dependency and debt. But on the other hand, there are grounds that dispute the certainty of governmental giving through the self-conscious refusal of accepting Abramovich's 'help'. 'We are fed up [*nadoeli*] with all his humanitarian help', Ionto states. This is a rejection that contains the rejection of enslavement that set the conditions of 'humanitarian aid' in the first place. Kindness and protection are the idioms in Chukotka in which democracy is spoken, but they are also the idioms of governance. Danger continues to loom for Indigenous peoples: if nobody will take care of them, they will become the victims of all this democratic modernization. Only under the guidance of outsiders will the Chukchi be able to solve their problems. The double-edged sword of that danger is clear to the Chukchi. Only if they escape the guidance of outsiders and think about their own models do they stand a chance of gaining autonomy and independence. This is the spirit of Ionto's own project. It refuses the dialectical logics of domination and enslavement. The conditions for self-determined independence are set.

Development

The importance of this point for the Chukchi communities cannot be overstated; a last example will make this clear. In October 2001, Chukotka and Alaskan regional officials, scholars, Indigenous representatives, and environmentalists convened for a two-day meeting in Anchorage to discuss the creation of an international Beringia Heritage Park – 'bridge of friendship' (*Beringia – most druzhby*) between the US and Russian governments, and a link to unite the lands and peoples of the Bering Straits in exchanges of culture, conservation ethics and scientific findings, and natural and cultural resource management technologies. Amidst the upbeat atmosphere of the convention, the Alaska assistant governor pointed out that the meeting's focus on joint action and intergovernmental cooperation was a testimony to the serious commitments to improve relations and bring about change in this one-time Cold War zone. Speakers commented on the ecological and economic challenges especially in the Chukotka peninsula, and an attentive audience listened. Many scheduled Chukchi, however, drew attention not because of the acumen of their presentations but due to their absence. Rumours had it that poor weather conditions had made it impossible for them to board the plane from Anadyr´ to Anchorage. However, official representatives of Chukotka's government had managed to get to the meetings. One of them was Chukotka's official spokesperson on economic affairs; another was the governor's official and Native assistant on Indigenous affairs.

On the first day, the governor's representative on economic affairs spoke of the wonderful commercial possibilities in the region. Due to the work of the new government, he explained, Chukotka had finally a fair chance of riches. The industrial exploitation of the oilfields in the peninsula's north would open up the region to the influx of international capital and investments, help Chukotka to become a powerful player on the global financial scene, and dramatically improve living conditions for all residents. The possibilities were limitless. But to the astonishment of the speakers, a few Indigenous representatives in attendance were not so easily won over. A Yupik man from Alaska stood up, demanding to know if the people he considers culturally his kin had been informed 'of all of this development?' Had there been public consultations with Native peoples about the government's plans? What did Chukotka's Indigenous residents think about the environmental impact of oil activity on reindeer herding and tundra lands?

Among Chukotka's spokespeople, evidently, the question caused some commotion. In response, the government representative stepped gallantly aside while the governor's Native advisor stepped forcefully in. Chukotka's government had done nothing wrong, he explained. The recent drillings involved no violations of Chukchi customary rights. Besides, he continued, isn't it up to the involved communities rather than the government to inform themselves about what is going on? 'Native people, you have to understand, cry (*plachut*) all the time. They are passive and lethargic. They are not prepared to do anything on their own but always wait, with their hands open.'

Having most certainly awaited a different kind of answer, the Yupik man sat down in stunned silence. Someone else from the audience tried to be helpful. One might want to consider the creation of Native parks, protected areas in which no industrial activity can be pursued without a referendum by the Native inhabitants, was the speaker's suggestion.[11] That way, Native communities would not run the danger of being swallowed up by all this new and inevitable development. Better still, the Chukchi would be able to retain certain parts of their land, their subsistence, and their traditions. The parks, of course, would be free of non-Native residents. Native peoples could pursue their own subsistence-maintaining activities; non-Indigenous residents could proceed in their endeavours. The region would profit. Everybody's interests would be served.

Within the context of economic restructuring, aid giving and regional openings to developmental interests it is, of course, self-evident that not everybody's interests will be served. Within the capitalist economy, it proves incomparably easier to segregate the Chukchi than it is to discuss issues of justice and land rights. The settling of Chukchi in parks has the effect of encapsulating them in history, denying them the possibility of active participation in the future of the region.[12] Precisely because such suggestions are based within frameworks of cultural stasis and not debate or dialogical exchange, they support the argument that only in isolation can Indigenous peoples maintain their assumed authenticity. Even if we grant the suggestion's best intentions, it forestalls the possibility for self-determined futures.

Challenges and Dreams

Democratization in Chukotka has been largely an ambiguous process for Russia's Indigenous constituencies, having led simultaneously to the improvement and aggravation of their situation. Precisely because a great deal of democratization meant not the creation of a public culture of discussion and careful examination but economic reform at enormous speed, debates about the desirability of the transformation and Russia's political future shape were missed. At the same time, openings have been created. During the Gorbachev-inspired era of perestroika, 'friendship visits' between Alaska and Chukotka became possible, and there was even a USSR agreement on visa-free travel between Chukotka and Alaska for Chukotka's Indigenous peoples. In spite of the many difficulties they face, Chukotka's Indigenous residents have since the beginning of the 1990s travelled, attended conferences, and communicated their political desires and concerns to larger audiences. And although Chukotka's familiar authoritarian logics quell Indigenous initiatives and rights, the recent processes of democratization have enabled Ionto and other Indigenous women and men to debate openly their aspirations and hopes. For these reasons, democracy needs to be criticized in the name of the hope to which it gave rise, not as a rejection of it.

The challenges that flow from all these issues and concerns are numerous and complicated. They are steeped in both Soviet and Russian cultural politics and in the transition from a planned to a market economy. As Russia emerges out of the crucible of Soviet politics, Indigenous peoples have begun to pursue projects for cultural recognition, land rights and self-determination in Russia's chronic climate of political uncertainty. At the same time, political strategies are often contested, and differences in political background and tactics frequently put activists at odds with each other. Spearheaded by RAIPON, Indigenous organizations press for Russia's ratification of International Labour Organization (ILO) Convention 169, which supports the strengthening of Indigenous cultural rights, languages, schools and autonomy. The creation of a draft law on *obshchinas* – tradition-oriented and voluntary communities of families and kin who wish to use and govern their own traditional lands, as well as protect these lands from uses that conflict with those supported by and supporting Indigenous peoples – has been considered a breakthrough for Indigenous justice. (More recently, the draft law has turned into a site of intense conflict. *Obshchinas* have the right to petition for land and its exclusive use; however, land title remains with the state.) Yet ongoing tensions and debates over the legitimacy, tasks and responsibilities of the institutionalized movement have led to internal critiques that focus on issues of funding, centre–regional relations, and differences in political outlook and culture. Recently, RAIPON publicly acknowledged for the first time that more concentrated work and a better rapport with Indigenous communities in the region are needed.

At the same time as Indigenous associations in Russia have found ways to ride the current wave of global funding, impoverishment in the regions has set in. Rising unemployment, declining wages, cutbacks in social welfare, drastic increases in poverty, deteriorating health and education – in short, a massive decline in the standard of living of the majority of a country's citizens – are now an all-pervasive reality. When post-socialist government leaders took up the discourse of 'shock therapy' and endorsed its principles, they acquired certain political benefits, and tapped into the legitimating aura of Western expertise. They spoke the language of private property and liberalization that has garnered sympathy from the IMF, the World Bank, and other international pro-capitalist agencies. And, perhaps, they could cover their own helplessness in the face of persistent economic decline by saying they were 'letting markets work'. But at the same time, Chukotka's Indigenous residents endure new forms of humiliation in economic forms. Market reforms and liberalization did not have the desired effects. Rather than establishing new industries that could create a global niche for Russian products, 'free trade' encouraged the practice, immediately profitable, of selling raw materials and other non-renewable valuables in exchange for manufactured imports.

This is the pivotal point around which Ionto's efforts revolve. In order to be meaningful and effective, economic projects must resonate with Indigenous desires and needs. As long as Chuktoka's structuring economic logic is based on projects envisioned solely by non-local peoples and outsiders, such imaginings will remain dreams. Their political promise appears greatest when they are able to involve and rally people and communities. Rather than working within government-inspired structures of identity, they draw on materials – affinities with animals, community-making and fairs – that are already there and are meaningful to Chukchi women and men. Then it might become possible to think about communal political initiative.

Critics might argue that I am too sanguine about Ionto's project and the politics of tradition in the Russian context. In introducing this analysis, I am aware that dreams are not the most powerful constellations around. There is perhaps the charge that dreams take us back to an earlier era marked by an intellectual romanticism that many of us hope to have left behind. But such an interpretation might miss the challenges particular people face. Thus, instead of beginning with our own scholarly common sense and conventional rejections, I have argued that we must begin with the question of how the extraordinary but down-to-earth aspects of Ionto's dream come to mean something to people caught in particular dilemmas.

It is easy to read Ionto's social vision as part of a tradition-oriented but politically eccentric dream of empowerment and self-determination – a dream of unwarranted ideals. But such an interpretation would not even begin to understand the challenges people face. The dream is part of the Chukchi refusal to be crushed by the exercise of daily patronage; it is part of the endeavour, in however exceptional a form, to work towards autonomy and independence. Ionto's dream helps to create a context in which struggle and commitment are not meaningless articulations.

Notes

1. Chukchi knowledge that the land needs to be treated with respect sits together with much work on Indigenous human–animal–land relations. My own insights into the emotional, spiritual and symbolic significance of Chukchi animal–human–land relations

stem from my earlier work in tundra reindeer herding camps (Rethmann 2001), and from my many conversations with Chukchi women and men. A point of entry was frequently the insight that animals and the land 'feel', 'hear' and 'can be offended', and thus need to be treated with respect. Chukchi women and men make this abundantly clear when, for example, they entertain the spirit of killed animals and present offerings to sacred sites. To those who care, the land gives. Chukchi pointed this out to me upon my arrival in summer 2000 in Anadyr´, when the local government refused me permission to leave the airport (the airport is separated from the land by the ocean) and set foot in the region. After having filled out an endless array of paperwork (although I had all necessary documents), after a personal audience with the governor (who wanted to know what I was doing), and after polite yet insistent inquiries of Chukchi friends (who waited patiently in front of doors behind which I disappeared), I was finally handed the document permitting me to stay for several months in the region. Chukchi friends, however, explained that I was only authorized to live, at least for a while, in the Chukotka peninsula because I had thought 'good thoughts about the land'. In return I needed to 'feed' the land. The point, here, is not one of ethnographic sensitivity. The point is about the sensibility of the land.

2. On 30–31 March 1989, representatives of more than twenty-eight Indigenous groups of the then-Union of Soviet Socialist Republics met in the Kremlin to discuss issues of political domination. Not altogether breaking with seventy years of Soviet logics, at that meeting – which was supported and attended by then-communist Party leaders Mikhail Gorbachev and Nikolai Ryshkov – representatives formed the 'Association of the Small Peoples of the North'. Soviet interpretations of Indigenous peoples as 'small' did not necessarily carry, as one might readily assume, aspects of belittlement and depreciation – although the term certainly carries such traces. Although sheer demographics and numbers certainly played their part, the term 'small' ascertained also the position of Indigenous peoples as 'non-chauvinistic' nationalities within the context of the Soviet Union. RAIPON is the successor of the 'Association of the Small Peoples of the North', and the voice and framework through which most Indigenous organizing in Russia occurs.

   In Russia, RAIPON is mostly referred to by its foreign name. The proper Russian term is AKMNCCiDV RF (Associatsiia korennykh malochislennykh narodov Severa, Sibiri, i Dal´nego Vostoka Rossiiskoi Federatsii).

3. A consequence of Soviet nation-building is the fact that the notion of the 'nation' in Indigenous politics is used somewhat differently than in, for example, Canada. While in Canada Indigenous nationhood – which has a long and well-documented history – is a powerful political force, in Russia it is often used to homogenize Indigenous diversity and peoples.

4. During the first and second Five-Year Plan in Soviet Russia, construction work became one of the most significant labour activities to aid socialist advance. Construction was performed in rushes or 'storms', a style of work that was called 'shock work' (*udarnyi trud*). Predicated on the assumption that high production levels could be achieved through a combination of labour exploits and systematic work organization, shock work was carried out in brigades. Shock work (analogous to the West's 'shock therapy') became synonymous with a highly aggressive, competitive and unpitying economic style and climate.

5. Or, in the more concrete terms of Russia's revolutionary government in 1917: how to avoid discontent, overthrow and failure (and thus the fate of the Habsburg empire that the Soviets inherited) by taming the terrifying forces of nationalist loyalties and aspirations?

6. They were also able to arrange marriages and reproductive rights and labour, and also to forge relations of inequality.

7. Bogoraz (1909: 56) states that at that time 1 rouble was equivalent to 50 cents. Converting roubles into US cents, this means that the traffic at the Anui Fair amounted to about US$100,000.

8. The date marks the day of the first convention of the United Nations Working Group on Indigenous Peoples of the Sub-Commission on the Promotion and Protection of Human Rights in 1992.

9. Personal statement by one of Roman Abramovich's advisors at the Beringia Conference on 12 October 2001, Anchorage.

10. And Putin may well be serious, as the arrest of Vladimir Gusinskii in June 2000 showed.

11. The argument has a long-standing history in Russian anthropology (see Bogoraz 1922; Slezkine 1994a: 148–9, 154). As early as 1923, the ethnographer Bogoraz maintained that the creation of territorial reservations and parks would be the only way to protect Chukchi from the destructive influences of state encroachment and Russian culture. In 1924 Bogoraz's suggestion was rejected by the People's Commissariat on Nationalities (Narkomnats) in Moscow, which directed Native affairs in Siberia until 1924. The idea, it turned out, found itself in insurmountable contradiction with Marxist–Leninist teachings on the non-capitalist development of backward peoples and their passage to socialism through the active assistance of the revolutionary proletariat.

12. The impetus for the creation of parks emanates often from outside sources, with academic participation involving urban scholars from distant Russian and non-Russian institutions.

References

Abriutina, Larissa I. (1999) *Narody Severa Rossii: Pravo na Zdorov'e* [The Peoples of the Russian North: The Right to Health], Moscow: MacArthur Foundation.

Anderson, David (2000) *Identity and Ecology in Arctic Siberia*, Oxford: Oxford University Press.

Bogoraz [Bogoras], Vladimir [Waldemar] G. (1904) *The Chukchee*, The Jesup North Pacific Expedition 7, *Memoirs of the American Museum of Natural History*, Leiden and New York: G.E. Stewart.

——— (1922) 'O pervobytnykh plemenakh [About primitive tribes]', *Zhizn' natsional'nostei*, vol. 1, p. 130.

——— (1923) 'Ob izuchenii i okhrane okrainnykh narodov [About the study and protection of marginalized peoples]', *Zhizn' natsional'nostei*, vol. 3, no. 4, pp. 168–80.

Brubakers, Rogers (1989) *Nationalism Reframed: Nationhood and the National Question in the New Europe*, Cambridge: Cambridge University Press.

Burch, Ernest (1988) 'War and Trade', in William W. Fitzhugh and Aron Crowell (eds), *Crossroads of Continents: Cultures of Siberia and Alaska*, Washington, DC: Smithsonian Institution Press, pp. 227–41.

Carnegie Foundation (2000) *An Agenda for Renewal: A Report*, Washington, DC: Carnegie Endowment for International Peace.

Fondahl, Gail A. (1998) *Gaining Ground? Evenkis, Land, and Reform in Southeastern Siberia. Cultural Survival Studies in Ethnicity and Change*, Boston and London: Alleyn & Bacon.

Gray, Patty (1998) 'Pursuing a Native moment in a Russian space: the predicament of Indigenous peoples in post-Soviet Chukotka', Ph.D. thesis, University of Madison – Wisconsin.

Hirsch, Francine (2000) 'Toward an Empire of Nations: Border-making and the Formation of Soviet National Identities', *The Russian Review*, vol. 59, pp. 201–26.

Kotzebue, O.V. (1821) *A Voyage of the Discovery into the South and Bering Straits, for the Purpose of Exploring a North-East Passage, Undertaken in the Years 1815–1818*, London: Longman.

Krupnik, Igor I. (2000) *Pust' govoriat nashi stariki. Rasskazy asiatskikh-eskimosov-iupik. Zapici 1977–1987 gg* [Let our elders speak. Stories of the Asian Iupik. Recordings from 1977–1987], Moscow: Ob-vo 'IUPIK'.

Kymlicka, Will (1995) *Multicultural Citizenship: A Liberal Theory of Minority Rights*, Oxford: Oxford University Press.

Lloyd, John (2000) 'The autumn of the oligarchs', *New York Sunday Times Magazine*, 8 October, pp. 88–94.

Martin, Terry (2001) *The Affirmative Action Empire: Nations and Nationalism in the Soviet Union, 1923–1939*, Ithaca: Cornell University Press.

Pika, Aleksandr [Alexander] (1993) 'The spatial–temporal dynamic of violent death among the Native peoples of northern Russia', *Arctic Anthropology*, vol. 30, no. 2, pp. 61–76.

———— Jens Dahl and Inge Larsen (eds) (1996) *Anxious North: Indigenous Peoples in Soviet and Post-Soviet Russia*, Selected Documents, Letters, and Articles, International Work Group for Indigenous Affairs (IWGIA) Document 82, Copenhagen.

Rethmann, Petra (2001) *Tundra Passages: History and Gender in the Russian Far East*, University Park, PA: Pennsylvania State University Press.

Rolf, Malte (2000) 'Constructing Soviet time: Bolshevik festivals and their rituals during the first Five-Year Plan: a study of the Central Black Earth Region', *Kritika*, vol. 1, no. 3, pp. 447–79.

Slezkine, Yuri (1994a) *Arctic Mirrors: Russia and the Small Peoples of the North*, Ithaca: Cornell University Press.

———— (1994b) 'The USSR as a communal apartment, or how a socialist state promoted ethnic particularism', *Slavic Review*, vol. 53, no. 2, pp. 414–52.

Suny, Ronald G. (1993) *The Revenge of the Past: Nationalism, Revolution, and the Collapse of the Soviet Union*, Stanford: Stanford University Press.

Tsing, Anna (1999) 'Becoming a tribal elder, and other Green development fantasies', in Tania Li (ed.), *Transforming the Indonesian Uplands: Marginality, Power, and Production*, Amsterdam: Harwood Academic, pp. 159–201.

Tully, James (1995) *Strange Multiplicity: Constitutionalism in an Age of Diversity*, Cambridge: Cambridge University Press.

16

The 'Risk Society':
Tradition, Ecological Order and
Time–Space Acceleration

PETER HARRIES-JONES

Peter Harries-Jones is Emeritus Professor in the Department of Anthropology at York University, Canada. His recent work has been on the joint themes of social movements (the environmental movement in particular) and the epistemology of ecology. His most recent book is *A Recursive Vision: Ecological Understanding and Gregory Bateson* (University of Toronto Press, 1995).

Let me begin this chapter with a metaphor, 'wild globalization'. Following the Earth Summit in Rio de Janeiro in June 1992, the United States, supported by other countries including Canada, attempted to create an international consensus on environmental issues through extension of 'free market' principles. The first phase of attempted consensus culminated in the Kyoto Protocol of 1997, which aimed at cutting emissions of greenhouse gases through international exchange of carbon credits. From Rio to Kyoto, the global oil industry and other transnational enterprises questioned the validity of the proposition that human activity is an integral part of global climate warming. Kyoto was significant in that world leaders, for the very first time, acknowledged that human industrial activity increased the release of carbon dioxide and other greenhouse gases into the atmosphere and is, therefore, a contributor to climate warming – a point on which scientists had become convinced even before the Rio conference. The Kyoto Protocol was only mildly ameliorative, but had the global cut in emissions standards been accepted, the cuts would not have halted global warming, though they might have affected the rate of change and validated an international framework with which to confront its inevitability. As it turned out, a meeting held at the Hague in December 2000 failed to ratify the Kyoto proposals. This failure was dramatically enhanced by the decision of George W. Bush, president of the United States, on 29 March 2001 not to send the Kyoto Protocol to the US Senate for ratification. The president stated at the time that he believed that the costs of Kyoto would cripple the US economy. The result is a political vacuum at the centre, filled only by nongovernmental agencies, each with a segmented approach to global warming, but no central agency through which overall policy can emerge – in short, 'wild globalization' (Gray 2000: 9).

'Wild globalization' brings strongly to mind an image of runaway capital-intensive production without proper assessment of cost, either social or environmental, the very opposite of sustaining better health and better economic opportunity for all. Some environmental critics claim, with good reason, that the prospect of 'wild globalization', whatever its dangers, is no worse than the centrally managed approach that immediately preceded 'wild globalization': that is to say, a 'top-down' neoliberal economic approach based on 'free market' principles led by supra-governmental agencies such as the World Bank, the World Trade Organization and the International Monetary Fund. In their opinion these institutions' rigid application of 'free market' principles has led to repeated disasters for the economic performance of some LDCs (less developed countries), in both the former Soviet Union and the countries of the South.

In any event, both 'wild globalization' and the neoliberalism of its immediate predecessor are useful contexts for juxtaposing the two terms in the title of this chapter, the 'risk society' and 'tradition', discussed below. The 'risk society' is both a contributor to and a product of 'top-down' neoliberal economic globalization. The 'risk society' threatens the integrity of the biosphere, while at the same time loosening the political framework of the nation-state. 'Life-politics' is a concept that arises from an alternative project of society, that which expresses a 'bottom-up' approach to political control, and the emergence of a multilateralism grounded in civil society. The agenda of 'bottom-up' multilateralism is that of much greater protection of the biosphere, a greater diffusion of power among social groups and institutions of the state, the pursuit of social equity, and nonviolent means for dealing with conflict (Schechter 1999: 1). The first step towards bottom-up multilateralism is much greater protection of the biosphere, policies through which knowledge of ecological effects are given the same or greater importance in 'development' than conventional market indicators. An additional feature of multilateralism is acknowledgement of the cultural visions of Indigenous peoples as they, too, contest the ravages of the 'risk society' in their own lands.

The 'Risk Society'

The 'risk society' is a cultural thesis about the effects of wild globalization. According to its primary author, Ulrich Beck, 'risk society' stands for a type of thought and action not perceived by nineteenth-century sociologists. In that era both government and industry were able to calculate risks and relate solutions to unambiguous outcomes. They were able to do so because the premises of social order in the society of that time were relatively unambiguous. A century or so later a quite different situation has emerged. Risk is omnipresent and is no longer calculable in the same way. Risk is an automatic outcome of goods production and the set of material conditions necessary to bring them into production. The most noticeable risks emerge from nuclear or chemical mega-technology, and most recently from genetic research. Other aspects of risk include arms sales and increased carbon emissions from industrial production and use of automobiles. Today one cannot choose or reject risk. In Beck's view, exposure to risk is an outcome of industrial and political processes that are blind and deaf to their own effects and threats. Risks accumulate because they are automatic side effects of the whole industrial process and are infinitely reproducible. Industrialism in its advanced stage, from the second half of the twentieth century, has increasingly produced effects that can no longer be encompassed or covered by the calculus of risk and insurance. Rather, these latter confront the technical and social institutions of the 'precaution state' with threats that nullify, devalue and undermine all calculations at their very foundations (Beck et al. 1994: 181–2).

As risks increase, the instruments of rational control in industrial society – more technology, more government, more market opportunities – no longer seem able to cope. The side effects of industrial success have already undermined the foundations of the society out of which it has emerged.[1] Social, political and economic risks increasingly escape the institutional monitoring of risk in industrial society, and threats far exceed the social ideas of safety. The inability to calculate risk has made institutional monitors blind to this transformation of the pattern of risk in industrial society, but such blindness is no mere happenstance. The loose coalition of business firms, policymakers and experts who comment on and/or devise policies about risk in contemporary society have constructed a discourse of euphemisms as a means for disavowing their responsibilities. Nevertheless, the dangers of the present situation have led to a new form of politics, 'life-politics'. This follows from the belief that minimizing environmental hazards is the key to ameliorating a general feeling of insecurity, 'ontological insecurity', that pervades current Western society. Beck states that 'life-politics' are an evident part of a number of new social movements, each of which strives to introduce new sources of meaning to life itself, as collective disenchantment exhausts other sources of meaning, like faith in technical progress and class consciousness.

'Life-politics' and the new meanings it sustains have to be rooted in localism and in the political thrust of civil society in order to reshape society from below, argues Beck. His analysis is no longer simply academic talk. As risks increase so also do the combination of NGOs, support for 'life-poli-tics' and the ideas of a multilateral approach towards altering instruments of rational control in industrial society. Nevertheless, Beck's analysis of 'life-politics' sticks almost entirely to a discussion of conditions in Western society. Beck's portrayal of 'life-politics' in Western industrial settings is a concerted reflection upon the concept of 'reflexive modernization', or how the activities of life-politics result reflexively in 'modernization *undercut[ting]* moderniza-tion'. Beck assumes that 'life-politics' is highly individual, a feature typical of Western industrial societies but not one that is repeated on a global scale. He argues that the new 'life-politics' will enable individuals to stage their own biographies through social networks, in their 'compulsion to find and invent new certainties' contra those of the 'risk society'. Something along these lines seems to have occurred with the European protest against the acceptance of genetically modified food from 1999 to the present.

Yet Beck confines himself to situations where human rights, rights of dis-sidence and protest are in many ways respected – though protestors may be beaten and jailed. He does not consider typical situations of environmental protest in the non-industrial world where the pervasive epistemology of individualism is either absent or diminished, and where organized protest takes on very different characteristics. Nation-states are often 'rights-aversive' rather than rights-supportive, and in rights-aversive societies international conceptions of human rights are constantly buried in military or other direct action against minority populations. The issues that give rise to protest about 'life-politics' are matters of life and death.

Social Process and Time–Space Acceleration

The concern with 'life-politics' as a heightened expression of individualism against the state and industrial practices is supported by Anthony Giddens, a co-author of the concept 'reflexive modernization'. However, Giddens im-agines that with the coming of 'reflexive modernity' we in the West would, for the first time, be living in a 'post-traditional society'. In a pointed refer-ence to anthropology's concern with tradition, Giddens argues that reflexive modernization will take us away from 'a way of life to which we can no longer bear witness' (Beck et al. 1994: 100). In other words, the anthropologi-cal concept of tradition is dead. Giddens interprets reflexive modernization as an argument about historical transition – away from traditional ways of thinking to a new form of cognitive reflection arising from globalization.[2] Associated with this is a change in the form that risk manifests itself, from natural hazards to socially created risk. In addition, 'A phenomenology of modernity has to probe the experience of living in created environments in which pre-existing ties between trust, security, risk and danger have become substantially transmuted' (Giddens 1989: 279)

Giddens's statements about the supposed disappearance of tradition are welded to his well-known thesis that globalization is concerned with the organization of time and space. Likewise, he declares, tradition is about the organization of time and therefore also space. Whereas tradition controls space through its control of time, giving emphasis to the value of past practice and the continuation of past order to present time, globalization fosters the marking of time–space the other way around, through time–space acceleration. Globalization is essentially 'action at distance'; and, unlike in colonialism, which required the physical presence of managers of capital, their physical absence in global control of capital flows predominates over their physical presence. The disembedding consequences of abstract systems of capital flows are so forceful that globalization excavates traditional contexts of action (Beck et al. 1994: 96). No longer is social thinking controlled in the sedimentation of time, as in traditional society, says Giddens; instead, financial globalization with its time–space acceleration has far-reaching ramifications (a point supported by Marcus; cf. Marcus 1995).

If Giddens's analysis refers to global politics, then the disembedding consequences of abstract systems have led to a number of dangerous political crises in recent years in which self-ascribed parties of modernity have been challenged by traditionalists. Politically speaking, the forces of traditionalism have not disappeared but rather have become resurgent. The resurgent forces of tradition in the Middle East over the last twenty years have left the West puzzled as to how to deal with them; the same political polarities have appeared and reappeared in the post-colonial politics of many countries in Africa like Chad, Sudan and Nigeria. As I write, the latest area of conflict is Turkey, and the outcome may well affect the entrance of Turkey into the European Union. So it is evident at the political level that Giddens is mistaken. Yet I wish to disagree with Giddens not so much on political grounds as on his epistemology: that is, on how ideas of time–space affect our understanding of persistence and change. Giddens has shown, more than any other recent sociologist, how concepts of time and space are central to social theory. He also shows how time and space, though abstract concepts, are linked to repetitive day-to-day social activities. Face-to-face interaction typically takes place in a definite setting for a definite period with other persons present both in time and in space. Moreover, the routine ways this day-to-day activity occurs is bound recursively to rules and resources in macro-level dispositions in society (structuration). So far, so good. Giddens is one of the very few authors in sociology or anthropology to discuss abstract concepts like 'structure' in terms of the recursive characteristics of social interaction; doing so he makes a remarkable contribution to social theory.

Giddens goes on to argue that technology extends social interaction in time and space in such a way that 'the other' in face-to-face interaction is no longer immediately present. As this occurs 'the locality' no longer has the same significance as the boundary within which routinized activities occur, and this time–space distancing (or 'distanciation', as he calls it) in turn brings a change in the generation of control by nation-states. Giddens argues that his notions of time–space acceleration of global capitalism and time–space distanciation in social interaction are much better concepts than others used in sociology's repertoire to denote the countervailing tendencies of persistence and change. These latter, he says, nearly always draw their notions from the concepts of Western physics and provide limited opportunity to match social theory to meanings and experience. Yet Giddens himself is not entirely free from the framework of physics, for behind his exposition lies a fundamental belief that the commodification of time–space relations in Western culture, integrated with its sophisticated measurement techniques, has indeed produced 'acceleration' in time–space that affects both monitoring and control over peoples. Also, Giddens borrows many of his ideas from the time-geography networks of Hägerstrand, who portrays a social system as a series of time–space paths flowing through a set of stations. To my mind Giddens is still far too close to a natural science or physics-based account, instead of an ecological account, of the response of human beings or any other living system to the interaction of other human beings or organisms in time and space.

Somewhere in all his analysis of time–space relations, both *knowledge-ability* and *agency* of human beings become attached to the activities of the modern sector, while tradition, including tradition understood 'as a mode of routinization by means of which practices are ordered across time and space', becomes displaced. Although Giddens acknowledges that tradition is always open to reinterpretation, he argues that the controls of tradition, rooted as they are in 'how things are always done' and ensuring that the highest degree of stability is attached to 'how things are always done', become displaced by rationally defensible purposes, the hallmark of modernity (Giddens 1989: 277). A major problem with all this is that Giddens's version of tradition always seems to stem from conditions which he categorizes as being 'pre-modern' – as if tradition, like the notion of the pre-modern, is lodged in a past stage of events, and is not an important concomitant of the present conditions of modernity. This mistake has affected much anthropological analysis as well as sociological theory, as Johannes Fabian has pointed out (Fabian 1991: 113–29). In making this mistake Giddens brings his arguments within the orbit of older sociological conventions – of social process proceeding in a stage-like manner. It could be argued that such an approach is, in itself, a side effect of the blindness of industrial capitalism, namely an 'internment' of all alternatives, unreflectively burying them out of sight and out of mind (Escobar 1995: 204).

There is nothing in Giddens's discourse about the relationship of time–space acceleration to ecological order, despite the fact that one would expect such a provocative notion as time–space acceleration to include reference to global climate change. That a thesis on the 'risk society' should ignore responses of traditional societies to this threat created by rampant globalization seems unreasonable. Another important point not addressed is the relation of tradition to the conventional political ideas of liberalism and conservatism. In North America the politics of conservatism and liberalism are wrapped in the perceived historical transition from traditional society to modernity. Conservatism in a conventional political sense expresses a strong political interest in tradition as an exemplar of stability and in maintaining 'how things are always done'; but the very opposite of stability will occur by simply maintaining 'how things are always done' in the context of global climate change. At the same time, progressive use of science and technology, the hallmark of liberal thinking, is no guarantee of remediation since the progressive use of technology unlimited by the awareness of deleterious ecological effects has produced the current alarming growth in natural hazards. Nor can the command and control systems of socialism adequately deal with global change unless and until people in Western industrial states willingly give up much of their profligate lifestyle. Stripped from the conventional politics of conservatism, liberalism and socialism, but deeply embedded in the prevailing conditions of ecological change, wherein lies the 'life-politics' of traditional societies? At the very minimum I would argue that where 'risk' and culture and ecology conjoin, a new understanding of their conjunction changes discourse about Western understanding of both 'tradition' and 'reflexive modernization', from the way that both Beck and Giddens have understood it.

'Life-Politics' and Tradition

The response of traditional orders to global climate change has been varied, and a complete discussion would require detailed comparative evidence that I do not have available. Here I will outline three trends. The first is a matter of survival, of life and death and outright rejection of global practices of industrialism. The second may be described as a resurgence of tradition based on a notion of 'reflexive traditionalism'. The third is an attempt to combine traditional values with the modern science of conservation in order to enhance the planned response to known environmental change stemming from global climate change. It is a politics of shared experience, in which cultural forms of understanding in traditional societies, or traditional sectors of industrial society, find common ground with the investigations of environmental planners and scientists. The common ground is not necessarily agreement about common perspectives; in fact perspectives are likely to differ. There is, nevertheless, an overriding attempt to make perspectives, experiences and actions *fit* each other. For various reasons, including the enormity of the risk and the fact that environmental science has to proceed within large measures of uncertainty, it has come to accept – reluctantly perhaps – that the perspectives of traditional order are not merely anecdotal, and that the prospect of *fittedness* between science and traditional ecological knowledge may be fruitful.

Trend 1: matters of life and death

The U'wa who live in the foothills of the Andes of Colombia gave a categorical reply to Shell and Occidental Petroleum in 1998 when they were told that these transnational oil companies would begin extensive exploration in the Samoré area of Colombia, a sizeable part of the U'wa existing territorial area and ancestral lands. They told Shell and Occidental that the U'wa will throw themselves off a high cliff called the Cliff of Death in an act of mass ritual suicide when the transnationals moved into their territory. The Cliff of Death is sacred territory to the U'wa, and ritual suicide a part of U'wa culture (*Guardian Weekly*, 12 October 1997, p. 8). The U'wa then secured a court injunction against further oil exploration. The oil companies contested this ruling. In April 2001 they began exploration once again in U'wa territory, estimating that there were 1.5 billion barrels of oil in the area. The U'wa then declared a National Day of Action and Prayer. In July 2001, Occidental Petroleum announced that its first exploratory well on U'wa land had turned up dry. At its annual shareholder meeting in May 2002, it announced that it would return its oil block to the Colombian government

The response of the U'wa is evidently an extreme example of the outright rejection of traditional societies to the intrusions of oil, gas, mineral and other exploitation of Indigenous peoples' environment, but many local populations beside the U'wa have no means to resist development programmes. The vulnerability of marginal populations is nearly always structurally reinforced through government action at the national or international level (Aaragon 1997). Some populations are more vulnerable than others. Governments tend to view environmental protest as threatening the status quo and respond by denying the protestors' rights and resources in their own land, in the name of economic growth, national security or national debt. With little alternative for peaceful protest, local groups may then move from local protest to political rupture, and finally resort to armed conflict.

In rights-abusive states there is no national arena in which a local environmental movement can advocate alternatives, hence no local arenas for the sort of 'life-politics' to which Beck refers. In fact, the overall evidence suggests an alternative view: despite international accords and conventions establishing inalienable human rights for all peoples, violent protest occurs most frequently in rights-abusive settings – that is, where the hopes of having peaceful advocacy of land claims and territorial governance are minimal (Johnston 1997: 15). For example, the World Commission on Dams recently acknowledged the shoddy economics and human rights violations that attend large dam construction. Up to 80 million people have been physically dispossessed of their land and millions more impoverished as a result of these dams. In addition, the destruction of species in flooded areas affects the food supply and livelihood of millions more. In the past the global dam industry largely ignored the social protests of those it would deprive of their lands and livelihoods, even though many of these protests were violent and resulted in loss of life. Now the World Commission agrees that dams should be built only if developers can gain the 'demonstrable public acceptance' of affected communities at each key stage of the decision-making process. It recommends that developers negotiate binding agreements, enabling communities to hold developers accountable to their promises of resettlement and compensation (McCully 1996; McCully and Williams 2000: 26).

Trend 2: reflexive traditionalism

My second example is that of the Inuit of the new Territory of Nunavut in the Canadian Arctic. They have taken it upon themselves to foster traditional ecological knowledge (TEK) as part of ongoing government practice. In this case the fostering of TEK is a direct counter to the activity of societies to their south that has created massive chemical pollution of Arctic waters, affecting fisheries, wildlife and human diet. The argument put forward within various Nunavut government departments is that TEK ought not to be cast in traditional notions of 'the traditional' – that is, tradition as its own time-warp vis-à-vis the temporal expression of modernity. TEK is much more than it has been defined as the continuation of traditional practices (berry-picking, hunting, preparing seal skins, listening to the elders, and the like). These are only small parts of a very much larger story. Arnakak and others are reconceptualizing 'the traditional' in TEK as 'healthy, sustainable communities regaining their rights to a say in the governance of their lives using principles and values they regard as integral to who and what they are' (Arnakak 2000).

This version of TEK has undergone extensive discussion in the Nunavut Social Development Council, the Department of Sustainable Development, and in curriculum planning for schools. TEK is defined as the knowledge of country that covers weather patterns, seasonal cycles, wildlife, use of resources. It includes the interrelationships of these elements; and of practical truisms about society, human nature and experience passed on orally, from one generation to the next, that one can learn best through observing, doing and experience. Such a broad approach to TEK releases the traditional from the time warp in which it has been impressed for so long a period of time. In the context of this chapter the Nunavut version of TEK seems more akin to time–space expansion of tradition than space–time acceleration. The relationship of TEK to Avatimik Kamattiarniq ('environmental stewardship') is best represented by Paul Okalik, premier of Nunavut, in August 2002 when attending a conference of Canadian provincial leaders. He defended the federal government's position in approving the Kyoto Protocol, stating: 'our goal is to be self-reliant and to be as prosperous as Alberta [an oil-rich province] and to rely on our resources.... Our custom is to pass on our knowledge, our traditional knowledge, to our children and you can't put a price tag on that.'

The Inuit concept of self-reliance through environmental stewardship is one of the fundamental sets of ideas embedded in the notion of *Inuit Qaujimajatuqangit*, IQ for short. IQ is interpreted as 'healthy, sustainable communities' and affirms Inuit intentions to regain their rights to a say in the governance of their lives using principles and values they regard as integral to who they are. Certainly there is a strong lobby in Nunavut to develop IQ as an epistemology that can be taught in the primary school system through the concomitant expansion of Inuit language learning there (Martin 2000). This reinterpreted concept of 'traditional' strips away the more ineffable aspects of culture and presents IQ with its concomitant principles of TEK as a means of organizing tasks and resources which has ramifications for organizing family and society into coherent wholes (Arnakak 2000).[3]

This whole process could be described as 'inverse anthropology'. Instead of outside anthropologists providing analysis of how family–kinship relations underpin the structure of Inuit life, and in so doing provide the fundamentals of an Inuit tradition, the Inuit take it upon themselves to teach other societies how their family–kinship model is an appropriate management model whose roles and relationships provide profound insights into stewardship of the environment. Another way of looking at this process is as 'reflexive traditionalism'. If modernity is, as Giddens and Beck argue, characterized by reflexivity, so too the Inuit example introduces 'reflexive traditionalism' in the sense of appraising Inuit traditions in light of the failing of industrial modernity to take into account appropriate stewardship of the Arctic environment.

In short, far from heralding the passing of traditional thought, the traditional order with its intense localism can appeal to a radical contemporaneity among its subjects. The key difference between this revamped version of tradition and the more usual versions of 'traditional' is the way in which modern scientific discourse, including social science, places 'tradition' in opposition to 'modernity' as a process of continuous change, but conveniently forgets to include *the risks generated by modernity including wild globalization* when it comes to pass judgement on this process of change. Thus it turns 'tradition', something that is profound, enriching and alive, 'into something that is meaningless, sterile, and awkwardly exclusionary', as Arnakak notes (Arnakak 2000).

Trend 3: a question of fit

The third example is the growing trend, since 1994, of constructing a Vulnerability Index for less developed countries. As their title suggests, the various Vulnerability Indices are an important recognition of the vulnerability of small nations to ecological impacts of global warming and have been put together by NGOs, United Nations agencies and small island governments. They are particularly evident in the planning documents of forty-two countries that are all members of the Alliance of Small Island States (AOSIS), but today other nations that are not small islands and are not necessarily designated as 'Third World' countries are compiling this approach to global ecological change. AOSIS members feel their Vulnerability Index will soon replace such standard economic indices as gross national product (GNP) and gross domestic product (GDP).

AOSIS members state that not only does calculation of per capita income through standard procedures of GNP or GDP make the world's smallest nations look more prosperous than they are, but, more significantly, these statistics fail to deal with the phenomenon of the increasing rate of natural disasters visited upon them. The statistical relationship between increased per capita income and quality of life has become severely warped through recurrent disasters in the small island states. Disasters include more frequent tropical cyclones, damage to fishing stocks, and loss of land as a result of rising sea levels – events that one way or another are attributed to global warming. Some of the small island states in Micronesia and the Maldives already know they will lose a significant proportion of their land through rising global ocean levels within this coming century.

The compilation of Vulnerability Indices is a major move away from Western nations' valuation of wealth and prosperity. By identifying increased vulnerability to disaster as a primary handicap to increasing quality of life, the various indices are altering perspectives about the linkage of risk to ecological events, which, in turn, has altered perspectives about the benefits of development in the less-developed countries as a whole.[4] As Herman

Daly has pointed out, conventional economics does not usually admit to the importance of 'exogenous factors', such as ecological fluctuation or natural disaster, as a limitation on economic activity. Development is predicated on quantifiable technical variables of growth and expansion – that is, the continuing expansion of goods and services as a means to procuring a better quality of life for the population as a whole (Daly 1996). This conventional attitude affected the first batch of indices. The Commonwealth Vulnerability Index completed in 1999, for example, concluded that the impact of 'external shocks' was only one of a number of determinants affecting the volatility of income in small island economies. However, researchers soon began to appreciate that ecological fragilities themselves were a primary threat to the implementation of any developmental strategy, and furthermore that ecological frailties covered a very broad base of activity. Research emphasis began to shift more specifically towards constructing an EVI, an Environmental Vulnerability Index, assessing both the relative susceptibility to natural disasters and the relative susceptibility of the ecology of countries to damage by anthropogenic activity (Howarth 1999; Pacific Islands Development Program/East-West Center 2000).

Meanwhile, putting together EVIs had revealed how top-down development, bad economic planning, and sheer ignorance on the part of development planners can accelerate risk and vulnerability in fragile economies. If development planning could heighten risk of vulnerability, then the usual responses – even more development to counter such risk – might not apply. Thus, the compilers of EVI began to consider all appropriate responses to mitigation of repeated disaster by examining all possible avenues of anthropogenic (human-caused) hazards associated with an increased rate of natural disasters and plan alternatives (Vermeiren 1993). At this point they began to incorporate traditional ecological knowledge in their planning documents as one avenue through which anthropogenic (human-caused) hazards might be lessened.

In some areas the compilers found, to their surprise, that the evidence of the efficacy of traditional ecological knowledge had been undervalued even by ethnographers. For example, one survey of TEK in New Caledonia, a small island state, concluded that while the religious aspects of societies were well reported, it was evident that 'context and importance [of the practical activities of villagers] have not even been understood'. References to TEK are dispersed and anecdotal in these anthropologists' writing, the survey stated, because ethnographic research had concentrated on agriculture.[5] The growing of crops of yams and taro was well documented, as was the use of terracing, spill ways and other water management devices. On the other hand, documentation on traditional medicine was 'almost non-existent', as was evidence of traditional controls of pests and disease. Above all, detailed evidence about the agricultural calendar was missing, as were questions of decisions about timing, although 'such timing was one of the most important aspects of Melanesian life'. The research survey concluded that while New Caledonians' (Kanak) knowledge of nature and the environment was very large indeed, little of that rich heritage had been recorded. Only a hint of the former existence of practice or knowledge that might have been useful as a guide to solving current resource management problems was available, and what was evident in New Caledonia is repeated and has much wider implications for the whole of the Pacific Islands.

Researchers compiling EVIs soon found they had to transform the standard terminology of GDP in order to accommodate their focus on risk, vulnerability and its alternatives. A key idea that emerged was the necessity to build up 'intrinsic resilience' in these small island states, a non-economic concept which approximates the health and integrity of the environment. The concept of resilience will be dealt with in more detail below, but it can be noted that the concept is non-economic and refers to the health and integrity of ecosystems, rather than the quantitative physical and material utilities of ecosystems as a type of natural resource. While 'resilience' does not necessarily translate Indigenous peoples' conceptions of risk and misfortune – since these are often expressed through sacramental or religious belief systems – 'resilience' has provided a means by which TEK can be brought into the planning documents not only among AOSIS members but elsewhere.

For example, evidence from Greenland suggests that while ecologists and Inuit have their own rationales that are differently thought out and phrased, they may and often do agree on common conservation policy and issues. Ethnographic material from Nunavut and Greenland Inuit demonstrates that people regard animals as 'non-human persons' who are able to build up knowledge about their environment. This enables skilled hunters and fishers to rely not only on their own interpretation of the environment but also upon the understanding and interpretations of animals about animal interaction with the environment. The behaviour of fish and seals not only gives signs about the location of fish and seals to Inuit hunters in Greenland but indicates the behaviour of whales, glaciers, winds, water temperature and other physical aspects of the environment. Animals may be disturbed by what people are doing in ways rarely mentioned in the conventional ecological literature. Greenland Inuit are able to observe and account for animal movements and other aspects of behaviour in a systematic way because they believe that animals have their own semiotic interpretation of the environment. This evident information, at least evident to Inuit, enters directly into Inuit discourse about environmental change (Roepstorff 2001). Berkes (1999) and Ingold (2000), following Feit (1994 and Chapter 6 in this volume), discuss similar issues in the environmental thinking of the Crees of Northern Quebec.

Resilience, then, is a concept that permits *fittedness*, a concordance between the science of ecology and the 'life-politics' of embodied tradition, the one perspective different from, but not unrelated to, the other. Those ecologists accepting resilience as a valid scientific approach to an understanding of ecological order are impelled by their own knowledge of ecosystem change and impermanence to listen to the evidence of how traditional peoples have helped maintain flexibility and resilience in their own habitat over so many years.

Time–Space Events and Temporal Recursion

Initially, the response to EVI research was sceptical, even United Nations economists doubting whether it would be possible to gather sufficient information about how human activity relates to ecological fragility. Yet once ecological ideas like 'resilience' became accepted into research discourse, the collection of EVI data proved to be much easier than originally expected. The notion of resilience owes a great debt to the work of the Canadian ecologist C.S. Holling. In the early 1970s Holling began to use this idea, or similar ideas, to explain the formal dynamics of spruce budworm outbreaks in New Brunswick, Canada, treating the budworms as predator and the trees as prey. Holling's stated intention in developing the concept of resilience was to transform classical notions of equilibrium in ecosystems, based on physical determinants of time and space, to account for uncertainty and surprise in ecological events (Holling 1998: 1–5). That is to say, ecosystems tend to 'flip-flop' from one set of conditions to another in a manner not represented in linear continua. His idea was to elaborate the methodology of 'flip-flop' and build a bridge between analytical science and policy that takes these conditions into account. Unlike prior analytical perspectives of biotic interactions drawn from the physical representation of space and time, resilience embodies inherent unpredictability and unknown outcomes of the interaction between ecosystems and the human societies with which they are linked. Note resiliency is not the same as stability – stability refers to how resistant a system is to change, whereas *resilience refers to the conservation of opportunities for ecosystem renewal*, the absorptive ability to respond to change.

The concept of resilience can be traced back to the qualitative mathematics of René Thom and his 'catastrophe theory' of the late 1960s, a qualitative account, in mathematical terms, of how a set of continuous events can undergo a sudden transition, or threshold jump, into a different dynamics. Resilience also draws, in more recent work, on sophisticated models of the 'layering' of ecological order according to ecological temporal rhythms. In this respect, the work of Allen and Hoekstra (1992) is a landmark study.

Unlike most ecologists, who concentrate their attention on the physical and energy components of biomass, Allen and Hoekstra are distinctive in the way they define ecological order. They argue that living systems escape the constraints of the physical world through the way in which they are able to recycle their resources over time.

Like Holling's notion of 'resilience', Allen and Hoekstra's notion of 'recursion' in temporal cycles enables a shift of focus from material dimensions of ecosystems conceived as biomass – with all its quantitative thermodynamic properties – and pays attention instead to the ways in which constraints in ecosystems derive from their temporal layering. Obviously their work does not deny that a movement of an organism and its interactions with other organisms are material events. Yet any organism can be a part of many cycles; an organism has its own life cycle – further, in its life cycle the organism passes through the life cycles of many other organisms with very different temporal cycles, all of these organisms together constituting a field of living systems. If material structures are only some of the components of ecological order, then material components ought not to be the sole focus of connecting social and ecological order; nor should the physics of temporal transformations – that is, transformation in time–space continua – be the sole model of social transformation borrowed by the social sciences from natural science – a point evidently missed by Giddens.

Most important in Allen and Hoekstra's model is the way they incorporate the analysis of time sequences in temporal cycles to build up an understanding of the 'logic' of recursive constraints. In any ecological system there are different levels of cycling whose order is strongly correlated with the frequency of the return time of its recycling processes. This *recursive characteristic* of recycling engenders critical behaviour of the 'level' in question. Higher 'levels' of an ecological order have a longer return time – that is, their critical behaviour occurs at a lower frequency; while lower 'levels' of an ecological order have a relatively quick return time – that is, their critical behaviour occurs at a higher frequency. All recursions at any 'level' can be related to relative frequency in this way.[6]

Recursions among levels are of utmost importance because some recursions are more important to observers than others. Critical pathways of recursive recycling create a 'context' for observers to monitor. Knowing critical constraints leads, in turn, to a better understanding of the buffering capacity of an ecosystem; that is, whether it can withstand perturbation and continue to oscillate around existing recursive cycles, or whether the perturbation is sufficient to result in those cycles changing their pattern of oscillation. Overall, the buffering capacity of an ecosystem determines if it will withstand change or if it will cross a threshold of oscillation and become a different form of ecosystem, as with the cutting and burning of trees in the wet tropical forests of the Amazon. The buffering capacity helps define ecosystem 'resilience', the same notion of intrinsic resilience incorporated into the Vulnerability Indices discussed above.

Allen and Hoekstra also argue that since ecological order is multi-levelled, it is always necessary for observers to examine several scales or levels at the same time. Consider the cycling of nitrogen. Nitrogen occurs at many levels, from those inside the organism up to the level of nitrogen formed by electrical discharges in the atmosphere. Each particular cycle relates to a particular level of observation. In fact Allen and Hoekstra suggest that because all ecological phenomena are multi-levelled, it is always necessary to consider at least three levels at once if one wishes to obtain robust prediction – that is, three 'contexts' in which the cycle appears most cohesive, explicable and predictable. The three levels of ecological hierarchy are: (1) the level in question; (2) the level below that in order to reveal physical mechanisms; and (3) the level above that, which gives context or significance to the level in question. The requirement for a three-level check, as they point out in their analysis, results in maps compiled by using different criteria at each level, each representing different perspectives among observers, and each observer generating different focal analyses in his or her depiction of ecological order.[7]

Here comes the beauty of their model, for Allen and Hoekstra's multi-perspective, contextual model of temporal cycles breaks the deterministic criterion that has pervaded the disciplines of social sciences[8] and biology and ecology. This enables not only a more unified approach to *fittedness* in eco-social links, but also enables a procedure of cross-scaling. Cross-scaling places data dealing with social effects on ecological resources – a relatively quick time recursion – in conjunction with biophysical data in ecosystems, and with relatively longer time recursive loops of the biosphere as a whole. The idea of cross-level, or cross-scale, interactions in which differing recursive temporal loops interact with each other at different levels of observation brings new insights to the pervasive problem of persistence and change in ecological order. For social scientists, better understanding of cross-scaling of the social and the ecological (Little 1999) avoids the sort of mistake that Giddens made in presupposing that time–space acceleration in the social order would have a single level and thus a totally dramatic effect on the framework of tradition and traditional culture. Though cultures are in many respects a material manifestation of social order, they, like the ecosystems of which they are a part, are also strongly associated with temporal repetition and oscillation in the manner of ecosystems. And, as with transitions in the whole biophysical realm, cultures are highly non-lineal yet resilient through their capacity to reorganize their responses to perturbation, more so than the concepts of physical stability would suggest.

Conclusion

I would argue that Allen and Hoekstra's field theory can be extended to many situations where human activity is considered from a more loosely defined 'ecological' perspective. Though their intention, like that of all good scientists, was to improve both predictability and control of ecological systems, what they have released is a very flexible methodology for examining 'risk'. The topological mapping of ecosystems based on concepts of recursion, together with Holling's notion of resilience, provides a more useful methodology for an alternative expression of global market expansion and its promiscuous utilitarianism than that of Giddens. Other authors, both ethnographers and ecologists, have also found these ideas useful in making the link between social and ecological systems, though with less emphasis on 'vulnerability' and the 'risk society' (Berkes and Folke 1998).

Finally, taking into account the recursive form of ecological events evokes the broadest issues of human attempts at mega-intervention in nature. As Gregory Bateson has pointed out, in all biological phenomena the field of immanent order consists of events and relations between events which recursively draw on the other. Human beings and their cultures are no different in this respect from the rest of nature. All are in temporal fields, and patterns of change are always complex because they never fall into a single temporal dimension. A primary requirement is to understand how humanity is itself within or outside the recursive events that it tries to control. Only then does evidence that change in pattern is coming too fast for a culture or an ecosystem's capacity to meet change give rise to a viable response, one in which flexible adaptation to recursive transformation has much chance of success (Harries-Jones 1995). 'Life-politics' in traditional order is associated with this understanding.

Notes

1. The major institutions of modern society are addicted to treadmill expansion because they feel they have a common interest in sharing the fruits of the treadmill, which in turn induces them to collaborate in accelerating the treadmill of economic growth. Schnaiberg and Gould (1994: 160ff.) make the case that grassroots environmental organizations have not been able to confront their opponents successfully because even they have a close attachment to elite aspirations and lifestyles. Meanwhile, Munich Re, the world's largest re-insurer, noted that in 1998 total losses from storms, floods, droughts and fires for the first eleven months of the year were far ahead of the C$85 billion in losses for the entire decade of the 1980s, even when adjusted for inflation. Commenting on Munich Re's report, the World Watch Institute said: 'More and more, there's a human fingerprint in natural disasters, in that we're making them more frequent and more intense and we're also making them more destructive' (*Saturday Star* (Toronto), 28 November 1998, p. A2).

2. The actual context of Giddens's statement is provocative, at least to an anthropologist: 'The anthropological monograph preserves, in much the same way as a protected relic does, a testament to a way of life to which we can no longer bear witness' (Beck et al. 1994: 98). Today, 'anthropology is directly embroiled in the institutional reflexivity of modernity, and anthropology thus becomes indistinguishable from sociology' (1994: 100). The point here is not to justify anthropology but to contest the notion that there is a global historical two-step: the first step involving 'from traditional to industrial', and the second step 'from industrial to reflexive modernization'.

3. I am indebted to Ian Martin for bringing this discussion to my attention based on his experience as consultant to the Nunavut government.

4. They derived from an increasing realization during the 1990s that the usual mechanism for reducing economic risk from natural disaster, property insurance, was no longer as available and affordable in small island states of the Mediterranean, Caribbean and South Pacific.

5. The report refers to anthropologists such as Maurice Leenhardt, Jean Guiart and André Haudricourt. It notes that while these and others had recorded reasonably well some areas of traditional knowledge, other aspects entirely escaped their interest. But a practical approach to risk reduction required that every opportunity for natural hazard mitigation should be assessed (Dahl 1989).

6. Such knowledge is the hallmark of TEK. The Dene (North Athapascan people who occupy the subarctic land from Manitoba to Alaska) have become great experts on the caribou through sophisticated understanding of temporal recycling processes that enter into caribou migration. Their very social organization can be explained in terms of their knowledge of the cycling of caribou movements over a long period of time (Berkes 1999: 99). What Allen and Hoekstra add to TEK is understanding of the complex feedback relations that recycling engenders together with an understanding of critical constraints to ecological resilence.

7. Recall that in this version of ecological hierarchy, a hierarchy has nothing to do with the concept as used in models of political control. In an ecological hierarchy upper levels constrain lower levels, but they may constrain by doing nothing. A constraint is always related to the time-frames of that which is constrained, so that a time frame for lower levels indicates a higher frequency of recursion. The critical aspect of an upper level context is that the upper level is observed to be spatially larger or more constant over time than the lower level for which it is a context.

8. Anthropologists, for example, have often taken 'landscape' as the central ecological criterion. Focal criteria in the 'landscape level' may seem obvious and predictable, because they are so tangible and because they have been so well depicted by geographers and naturalists since the nineteenth century. On the other hand, criteria for ecosystem mapping are far less tangible. An ecosystem represents a conceptual map of sequences of temporal events. Those events can be described as transformations of matter and energy travelling along recursive pathways in time, but these criteria are by no means as visual as those of landscape. Hence scaling landscape to ecosystem involves a match of the tangible material features of landscape to the conceptual temporal features of ecosystems, and of the differences in recursive patterning at each level.

References

Aaragon, Lorraine V. (1997) 'Distant processes: the global economy and Outer Island development in Indonesia', in Barbara R. Johnston (ed.), *Life and Death Matters: Human Rights and the Environment at the End of the Millenium*, Walnut Creek, CA: Altamira Press, pp. 26–42.

Allen, T.F.H. and Thomas W. Hoekstra (1992) *Toward a Unified Ecology*, New York: Columbia University Press.

Arnakak, Jaypetee (2000) 'Using Inuit family and kinship relationships to apply IQ, Inuit Qaujimajatuqangit', *Nunatsiaq News*, 25 August.

Beck, Ulrich, Anthony Giddens and Scott Lash (1994) *Reflexive Modernization: Politics and Tradition and Aesthetics in the Modern Social Order*, Stanford: Stanford University Press.

Berkes, Fikret (1999) *Sacred Ecology: Traditional Ecological Knowledge and Resource Management*, Philadelphia and London: Taylor & Francis.

—————— and Carl Folke (eds) (1998) *Linking Social and Ecological Systems: Management Practices and Social Mechanisms for Building Resilience*, Cambridge: Cambridge University Press.

Dahl, Arthur L. (1989) 'Traditional environmental knowledge and resource management in New Caledonia', in R.E. Johannes (ed.), *Traditional Ecological Knowledge: a Collection of Essays*, Gland, Switzerland, and Cambridge: IUCN, The World Conservation Union, pp. 45–53. Revised version online at http://www.unep.ch/islands/dtradknc.htm.

Daly, Herman (1996) *Beyond Growth: The Economics of Sustainable Development*, Boston, MA: Beacon Press.

Escobar, Arturo (1995) *Encountering Development: the Making and the Unmaking of the Third World*, Princeton, NJ: Princeton University Press.

Fabian, Johannes (1991) *Time and the Work of Anthropology: Critical Essays 1971–1991*. Chur, Switzerland: Harwood Academic.

Feit, Harvey (1994) 'Dreaming of animals: the Waswanipi Cree shaking tent ceremony in relation to environment, hunting and missionisation', in T. Irimoto and T. Yamada (eds), *Circumpolar Religion and Ecology: an Anthropology of the North*, Tokyo: University of Tokyo Press.

Giddens, Anthony (1989) 'A reply to my critics', in David Held and John B. Thompson (eds), *Social Theory of Modern Societies: Anthony Giddens and His Critics*, Cambridge: Cambridge University Press, pp. 249–301.

Gray, John (2000) 'Wild globalization: how politicians' failures usher in a bleak environmental future', *Guardian Weekly*, 28 December, p. 9.

Guardian Weekly (1997) 'A tribe's suicide pact', 12 October 1997, pp. 8–9.

Harries-Jones, Peter (1995) *A Recursive Vision: Ecological Understanding and Gregory Bateson*, Toronto: University of Toronto Press.

Harvey, David (1996) *Justice, Nature and the Geography of Difference*, Oxford: Blackwell.

Held, David and John B. Thompson (eds) (1989) *Social Theory of Modern Societies: Anthony Giddens and His Critics*, Cambridge: Cambridge University Press.

Holling, C.S. (1998) 'Two cultures of ecology', *Conservation Ecology*, vol. 2, no. 2, pp. 1–5.

Howarth, Russell (1999) Environmental Vulnerability Index (EVI). Online at http://pidp.ewc.hawaii.edu/pireport/1999/March/03–22–20.html.

Ingold, Tim (2000) *The Perception of the Environment: Essays in Livelihood, Dwelling and Skill*, London and New York: Routledge.

Johnston, Barbara R. (1997) 'Introduction', in B.R. Johnston (ed.), *Life and Death Matters: Human Rights and the Environment at the End of the Millennium*, Walnut Creek, CA: Altamira Press, pp. 9–21.

Little, Paul E. (1999) 'Environments and environmentalism in anthropological research: facing a new millennium', *Annual Review of Anthropology* 28, pp. 253–84.

Marcus, George (1995) 'Notes on ideologies of reflexivity in contemporary efforts to remake the human sciences', in K. Geuijen, D. Raven and J. de Wolf (eds), *Post-Modernism and Anthropology*, The Hague: Van Gorcum.

Martin, Ian (2000) 'Discussion paper on language of instruction in Nunavut schools', Department of Education, Nunavut, unpublished.

McCully, Patrick (1996) *Silenced Rivers: the Ecology and Politics of Large Dams*, London: Zed Books.

——— and Phil Williams (2000) 'Guidelines give protesters hope, and poor are sold down the river: campaigners feel the World Commission on Dams has evaded the real issues', *Guardian Weekly*, 7–13 December, p. 26.

Pacific Islands Development Program/East–West Center for Pacific Islands Studies, University of Hawaii at Manoa (2000) 'Pioneering environmental work assesses vulnerability of Pacific Islands'. Online at www.pidp.ewc.hawaii.edu/pireport/August/08–08–20.htm.

Roepstorff, Andreas (2001) 'Thinking with animals', paper presented to First Gatherings in Biosemiotics, Copenhagen, 24–27 May, unpublished.

Saturday Star (Toronto), 28 November 1998, p. A2.

Schechter, Michael G. (ed.) (1999) *Future Multilateralism: The Political and Social Framework*, London and New York: Macmillan and St Martin's Press for the United Nations University.

Schnaiberg, Allan, and Kenneth Alan Gould (1994) *Environment and Society: The Enduring Conflict*, New York: St Martin's Press.

Vermeiren, Jan C. (1993) 'Disaster risk reduction as a development strategy'. Online at www.oss.org/en/edmp/document/lossredn.htm.

17

Conflicting Discourses of Property, Governance and Development in the Indigenous North

COLIN SCOTT

Colin Scott is Associate Professor of Anthropology at McGill University. He has worked with James Bay Crees in Canada for twenty years, and recently with Torres Strait Islanders in Australia. He recently edited *Aboriginal Autonomy and Development* (UBC Press, 2001).

Contested rights of property and governance are at the core of structural reform vis-à-vis Aboriginal peoples, as debated from left and right in contemporary politics. This chapter is an effort to map the general contours of conflicting political discourses on Aboriginal entitlement to lands, waters and resources; and to scrutinize the assumptions, values and positions that underlie alternative policy prescriptions. These assumptions and values are rooted in long-standing European notions about civilization and progress, race, freedom and equality. I am interested in the effects of these notions for ideologies of state governance, property and market organization, and their insinuation into disagreements over options for Aboriginal self-determination and development, as liberal democratic 'settler' states attempt to come to terms with their colonial origins and legacies.

At one level, then, this chapter is an effort at Euro–North American self-examination, at a particular moment of 'our own' cultural history. At another level, it critiques claims from the political right about certain practical necessities and inevitabilities stemming from Indigenous peoples' involvement in contemporary civil society and market organization that are allegedly antithetical to collective entitlement to property and self-government. I am especially interested in the circumstances of Arctic and subarctic regions, where the entrenched doctrine of 'public' lands and resources competes with – and has historically overshadowed – Indigenous property systems and authority structures. Although private title to land in these regions is very limited, substantial alienation of Indigenous lands, waters and resources has occurred and persists, principally through the licensing by state-level governments of large-scale resource extraction. Against this loss, Aboriginal politicians seek innovative arrangements of resource tenure and governance to reduce dependency and promote self-sustaining northern economies. The struggle focuses on the questions: to whom do territories and resources rightfully belong, and according to what regimes of tenure and authority should they be developed and managed?

Recognition of Aboriginal rights and titles to lands, waters and resources is one approach to rebalancing the distribution of rights in property, and to implementing certain self-government forms of territorial jurisdiction (including co-management) that retain or restore a degree of Indigenous control over homelands and waters. These measures are important elements in an approach that Thomas Flanagan (2000b) has termed the 'new aboriginal orthodoxy'. As one of the more closely reasoned positions on the political right – a rare one from a person with scholarly expertise on Indigenous topics (see Flanagan 1991, 1996, 2000a) – his arguments are a useful foil for considering the advantages of developing northern Indigenous homelands through stronger recognition of Aboriginal title and territorial jurisdiction.

The Royal Commission on Aboriginal Peoples: Harbinger of a 'New Orthodoxy'?

The principal tenets of a widespread (though by no means homogeneous) view among Aboriginal and non-Aboriginal intellectuals from left of centre are in fact reasonably well summarized in Flanagan's (2000b) portrayal of the 'new orthodoxy', though he overstates the extent to which these tenets have penetrated state policy, or found expression in institutional reform. Their espousal by the Royal Commission on Aboriginal Peoples (RCAP 1996) is indicative, for Flanagan, of their growing policy influence.

RCAP was noteworthy both for its timing and its composition. It was convened by the Canadian federal government in 1991, in no small measure as a response to the deepening political impasse in relations with Aboriginal peoples. The 1990 'Oka Crisis', involving armed stand-offs between Mohawks of the Montreal area and provincial police, and culminating in extraordinary recourse to intervention by the Canadian armed forces, was the most costly, widely publicized and internationally visible manifestation of this impasse. But blockades and protests had erupted in many parts of the country, helping to focus the minds of Canadians on unfinished business in relation to Aboriginal people, whose patience had been stretched thin by nearly a decade of largely stalled constitutional negotiations and proposals for self-government reform, and nearly two decades of snail's-pace progress on land claims. The litany of bad news about Aboriginal poverty, suicide and domestic violence was a daily background reminder on the pages of newspapers and the screens of televisions.

A roughly balanced number of Aboriginal and non-Aboriginal commissioners, public figures in their respective institutional and policy spheres, headed up the Commission. They sought advice from dozens of scholars and researchers whose careers had been devoted to an understanding of Aboriginal issues, including many who prepared studies and reports. Public hearings were held throughout the country, on every dimension of Aboriginal life. The RCAP reports, it is fair to say, reflect views that are broadly based in Aboriginal communities, the ranks of engaged professionals, and the interested public. To be sure, the positions adopted by RCAP are within a stream of thinking whose impact on policy, court decisions, and institutional arrangements over the past three or four decades has been significant.

But it is noteworthy that state authorities remain resistant to several of the Commission's key recommendations. Their reluctance is particularly evident in relation to recommendations concerning the ownership and control of territory and resources: for example, (1) that nation-to-nation relations be pursued on the basis of Aboriginal consent; (2) that Indigenous territorial and civil jurisdictions be established as a third order of constitutionally empowered self-government, including jurisdictional sharing with federal and provincial governments in areas of overlap; (3) that First Nations be assured an enhanced share of territory, resources, and resource development revenues – together with compensation for past and present resource exploitation and social disruption, and provision of economic development funding; (4) that treaty-making (past, present and future) not be understood to extinguish rights and titles, and that existing treaties be renewed in a manner appropriate to contemporary conditions (RCAP: Appendix A).

Official resistance to these recommendations takes two forms. First, there is opposition in principle. Federal and provincial governments, and the courts, have generally rejected the idea that nation-to-nation arrangements require the consent of First Nations. Resource co-management regimes, for example, typically reserve ultimate veto power to a provincial or federal government minister. Second, official acceptance of other principles is in many cases not accompanied by expeditious implementation. Federal and provincial governments are engaged in comprehensive claims and treaty negotiations over lands and self-government, but their terms for settlement are sufficiently restrictive that final agreements are rare and elusive. At the current pace of concluded agreements, it will require at the very least many more decades to address the comprehensive and specific claims now in queue.

RCAP recommended institutional innovations to ease existing bottlenecks, several of which have gone largely unheeded: (1) a proclamation affirming bilateral nation-to-nation relations, and setting forth principles for the process of treaty-making, implementation and renewal; (2) federal, provincial and territorial treaty commissions together with an Aboriginal Lands and Treaties Tribunal to provide monitoring, support and adjudication; (3) a Canada-wide legislated framework for self-government treaties; and (4) an Aboriginal Peoples Review Commission to assess progress in the fulfilment of treaties, the implementation of self-government, the provision of adequate lands and resources for Aboriginal peoples, and the improvement of social and economic well-being. Even where central governments have ostensibly embraced selected tenets of the 'new orthodoxy', budgetary caution and delays in process may have a greater impact on actual outcomes, and be more reflective of true policy commitments, than the tenets themselves.

One suspects, in fact, that the old orthodoxy, nicely articulated by Flanagan in his rebuttal of RCAP recommendations, is well entrenched among federal and provincial politicians, and remains powerfully influential in the worldview of the Canadian public. The old orthodoxy is often latent and unspoken because it is the common sense of established ideology, not because it has become a minority view. For this reason, if no other, it is well worth probing Flanagan's arguments.

At stake are visions of Canada's future. Flanagan (2000b: 5) fears that RCAP recommendations entail a Canada that is

> redefined as a multinational state embracing an archipelago of aboriginal nations that own a third of Canada's land mass, are immune from federal and provincial taxation, are supported by transfer payments from citizens who do pay taxes, are able to opt out of federal and provincial legislation, and engage in 'nation-to-nation' diplomacy with whatever is left of Canada.

The cost to Canada would not even be offset by improvement in the lives of ordinary Aboriginal people, who unlike their political leadership 'would remain poor and dependent, marginalized on reserves and other territorial enclaves' (Flanagan 2000b: 5). This bleak forecast hinges on several notions, some having to do with the conception of rights, and others having to do with the practicalities of economic and political development. The latter category will be dealt with in a later section. For the moment, let us turn to the issue of rights.

The Rejection of 'Special' Rights

The premiss of Aboriginal rights is, in Flanagan's view, inherently flawed. Being here first should confer no unique rights on First Nations. 'Aboriginal peoples contested with each other vigorously for control of land, resulting in conquest, assimilation, displacement, and extermination', Flanagan (2000b: 23) tells us, and 'Europeans are, in effect, a new immigrant wave, taking control of land just as earlier Aboriginal settlers did. To differentiate the rights of earlier and later immigrants is a form of racism' (2000b: 6). One problem with this line of argument is that the vanquished in the course of colonial history were commonly denied rights precisely along lines of race, to the calculated advantage of the newcomers who seized property and control. It is cruel irony indeed to suggest that Aboriginal people should now be denied differential rights on grounds that this would be racist, in most cases forcing them to assimilate to the lowest socio-economic denominator with nothing more than the cold comfort of assurances that they enjoy rights 'equal' to those of other Canadian citizens. It is hard to escape a sense of double standard.

Flanagan's opposition to unique Aboriginal rights is also predicated on a particular view of human freedom. Society is 'a spontaneous order that emerges from the choices of individual human beings', wherein government makes and enforces the 'rules that allow society to function. Individuals naturally congregate in families and other associations, but these must be voluntary if society is to be free and prosperous' (2000b: 8–9). Sorting people into categories with differential legal rights, based on 'immutable character-istics such as race and sex … interferes with social processes based on free association' (2000b: 9).

Many problems are raised with this position, not least of which are ethno-centric conceptions of the individual and of freedom. But we needn't get into an extended discourse on cultural relativism to point out that Aboriginal rights are neither race-based nor racist. They are, more accurately, inherited, not unlike the well-accepted European tradition of rights inherited along family lines. It is a sociological commonplace that most of the wealth in the hands of mainstream wealthy classes is inherited rather than earned (unearned, that is, by present-day holders of that wealth). A small subset of Euro-Canadians are disproportionately represented in the ranks of the super-wealthy – a situation that tends to perpetuate itself through inherit-ance – but this may be an insufficient basis for regarding their wealth as a racist institution per se. Aboriginal ownership of a disproportionate land base on the basis of inherited rights, similarly, is not inherently racist. Aboriginals frequently marry non-Aboriginals, and their children inherit as members of rights-holding Aboriginal collectivities, notwithstanding steadily diversifying racial origins. By definition, Aboriginal title began with people who were Indigenous and not European, not because of *race*, but because they were the people who possessed the land when Europeans arrived, according to customary orders of ownership and governance.

As with property rights, so with rights of self-government. 'At bottom', Flanagan tells us, 'the assertion of an inherent right of Aboriginal self-government is a kind of racism' (2000b: 25). But again, just as Canadian citizenship is heritable, so is First Nation membership, and in both cases this is a matter of descent, not of race. Furthermore, First Nations formerly had means, and many still find ways, to incorporate non-Aboriginals into their social orders, even though the definitions of the Indian Act, and scarce resources, have severely hampered autonomy in this realm. This conceivably could change if First Nations gain more power to develop citizenship rules within their own jurisdictions. We have seen, furthermore, with the examples of Nunavut and Nunavik (Hicks and White 2000; Jull 2000; Nunavik Commission 2001), that these Indigenous polities are not inherently opposed to the inclusion of people of other ethnicities in institutions of government within their respective territories. Nunavut, a new federal territory created through the division of the former Northwest Territories, and Nunavik (a regional territory corresponding roughly to the Arctic portion of the province of Quebec), are populated by clear majorities of Inuit who are comfortable with a 'public' model of government in which non-Inuit have full participation in voting and the holding of office. The pressure to define its enfranchised polity more strictly along inherited 'ethnic' lines comes when an Indigenous nation is threatened with political minority status in its territory.

A further difficulty with Flanagan's position, apart from the misnomer of race, is the contradictory manner in which the principle of free association is applied. If society is to be based on free choice and voluntary association, how does the nation-state exempt its own constitutional order from this standard? Is the 'spontaneous order of society' not compromised when peoples are incorporated against their will, on terms without their consent? But contradictions and double standards are apparently excusable, and forgettable, in the name of civilization, progress and their historical inevitability.

Social Evolution and Progress

Flanagan acknowledges that First Nations enjoyed a kind of sovereignty, using the term in a 'relaxed' sense, while they were 'free from outside control', living 'according to their own customary laws without being ruled by other tribes or imperial states' (2000b: 49). He believes that this historical fact does not give rise, however, to inherent rights of self-government, in either domestic or international law. Because 'sovereignty in the strict sense exists only in the organized states characteristic of civilized societies' (2000b: 59), European states were able to extinguish the sovereign rights of stateless peoples by subjugating them and claiming their territories under the international law doctrine of *terra nullius*. This doctrine 'was never concerned with property rights, only with sovereignty' (2000b: 57). As Flanagan also points out, however, 'the assertion of sovereignty involved creating and protecting property rights in order to make intensive agriculture possible' (2000b: 59). In other words, the *terra nullius* doctrine *was* readily converted into a rationale for stripping Indigenous inhabitants of much of the property they possessed and occupied.

European civilization, in Flanagan's understanding, 'was several thousand years more advanced than the Aboriginal cultures of North America' (2000b: 6) so that colonization of the latter by the former was inevitable, and 'if we accept the philosophical analysis of John Locke and Emer de Vattel [as Flanagan appears to do], justifiable' (2000b: 6). Because Aboriginal people in Canada lacked states, they lacked sovereignty in the strict sense. If they were nations in a kin-linked and cultural-linguistic sense, they were not nations in the modern political sense. They were subjugated relatively early in contact history, and today their only real option is to exist as ethnic groups subordinate to the nation-state.

All of this rests on the common view of progress that gathered force during the Enlightenment, and achieved full momentum in nineteenth-century evolutionist thinking. With civilization came superior science, technology, mastery over nature, and institutionally more complex social orders, which 'led to increases in human numbers and longevity, the flowering of the arts and sciences, and a refinement of human relationships, manifest in the abolition of slavery, democratic control over government, and legal equality between women and men' (2000b: 9). The free market emerges triumphant as 'the only economic system that has brought a high standard of living to a complex society' (2000b: 9).

One might question the achievement in regard to 'standard of living' of a system in which the wealth and power of a few nations have contributed so heavily to the poverty of much larger segments of the world's population. Other conceptual, practical and ethical conundrums are apparent. If acts of dispossession and subjugation were justified in the past, is the invasion of smaller, weaker, less developed countries by more complex, scientifically advanced, and materially powerful states any less acceptable today? If *complexity* is an index of progress, was the reduction of political complexity of European empires as they withdrew from former colonies in Africa, Asia, Oceania and Latin America a retrograde movement? If growth in interstate institutional complexity compensated for the loss of intrastate complexity, why is the political decolonization of Indigenous peoples in countries like Canada so threatening? Would decentralized political rights for Indigenous peoples represent a loss or an increase in the complexity of transnational orders?

The historical absorption and replacement of 'earlier forms of society' (2000b: 35) by societies exercising 'greater technical mastery over nature and increasing size and complexity of social organization' (2000b: 33), contrary to what Flanagan seems to believe, is widely recognized by many social scientists sympathetic to Aboriginal rights, few of whom would assume 'that native American cultures did not differ fundamentally from European cultures' (2000b: 35). It is, after all, possible to acknowledge historical patterns and tendencies of social evolution, and yet recognize existing and potential diversity in institutional and cultural orders. If complexity is a positive value, is it best realized through the whole world subscribing to a uniform set of economic and political institutions? Might there be greater complexity, not to mention adaptive flexibility, through diversity? Or is the only complexity that matters of the kind that can be orchestrated by dominant capitalist states?

So firm is the conviction of political conservatives and liberals in the capitalist recipe for progress, and in the ability of progress to be maintained, that they underestimate the adaptive and evolutionary significance of diversity; and they lose sight of the reality that there are always more ways than one to organize economies and polities, whether 'simple' or 'complex'. Shibboleths are made of the free market, and of the sovereign democratic state, eyes of needles through which all the world must uniformly pass on the road to progress. The ploy of ideology has ever been to represent as natural and necessary arrangements that are in fact merely conventional and contingent.

Agriculture displaces hunting, as states displace 'small-scale, stateless' societies, processes 'so prominent in human history that it seems almost beside the point to raise questions about morality' (2000b: 39). Yet Flanagan himself is not entirely untroubled by the ethics at stake. Hunters need the lands regarded by agriculturalists as 'surplus', if the former 'are to live as they have always done'; and he 'can see no moral justification for telling the hunters that they must give up one way of life and adopt another. On the other hand, [he] cannot see a moral justification for telling the agriculturalists that they cannot make use of land that, from their point of view, is not being used' (2000b: 43–4). This is an ethical dilemma, to which Flanagan later returns: 'By what right', he asks, 'do the civilized require the uncivilized to renounce their ancient way of life?' (2000b: 60). His answer circles back to the historical inevitability of much more powerful civilized societies dominating uncivilized ones, and to the recognition by other states of 'prescriptive' title established through sustained possession and control of claimed territory. In short, the dilemma is unanswerable for Flanagan in ethical terms. Since he rejects as 'racist' the recognition of Aboriginal rights, there is no remedy, in effect, for the patent injustice of a situation in which I may take something of value to you, simply because I am strong enough to do so, and because I value my way of life above yours.

Aboriginal Title and Prospects for the
Development of Northern Homelands

The Royal Commission on Aboriginal Peoples placed considerable emphasis on Aboriginal control of lands and resources which, together with the monetary component of land claims settlements, would provide the means for self-governing First Nations to develop economies within their territories. Flanagan applauds the pro-capitalist enterprise orientation of RCAP recommendations, as well as their insistence on finding ways to break the welfare cycle. Nonetheless, he argues, 'RCAP's economic vision is unlikely to succeed in practice' (2000b: 183) because public spending cannot be expected to increase sufficiently to implement RCAP's proposals, and, even if it did, the emphasis on Aboriginal control of lands and resources is flawed. The cyclical nature of natural resource-based economies, the long-term trend for commodity prices to fall in the world marketplace, and the technological and organizational conditions for profitability mean that 'ownership of resources, in and of itself, is of diminishing importance' (2000b: 184). More fundamentally, Aboriginal title is an inappropriate institutional vehicle for economic development.

Flanagan articulates two commonly heard reasons. The first is that Aboriginal title fosters a rentier mentality, inimical to authentic productivity and growth: 'Ownership of resources may produce some royalty flow, which allows the recipients to purchase consumer goods as long as the flow lasts; but unless the rentiers acquire the skills and attitudes – the human capital – needed in a modern economy, the royalties will quickly be dissipated' (2000b: 184). The judgement is that Aboriginal people as rentiers are unlikely to deploy rents in ways that effectively address their own economic difficulties, let alone benefit the broader economy. The second objection is that judicial definition of Aboriginal title as collective and inalienable precludes the effective use of Aboriginal title in a modern economy. Involvement of Aboriginal political leadership in the development corporations would invite the corruption and inefficiencies generally associated by political conservatives with government-run enterprise. And even if this problem could be solved through arms-length arrangements, the inability to mortgage, sell or individualize property is an inflexibility that fatally reduces the competitive standing of Aboriginal development corporations.

In short, the strategy of Aboriginal self-sufficiency through enlarged self-governed land bases – where they would seek prosperity at home through a combination of transfer payments, resource revenues, employment and entrepreneurship – is in Flanagan's view headed for failure. 'Implementation of RCAP's economic vision would actually increase unemployment, welfare dependency, and human misery in Aboriginal communities' (2000b: 187), though an entrepreneurial and professional Aboriginal elite can do well out of rents and transfers. But the attempt to stimulate general economic growth in regions and sectors to which capital investment is not spontaneously drawn will be no more successful in First Nations territories than it has been in the Atlantic region of Canada. Aboriginal people who remain on reserves or in rural and remote homelands will be a growing burden on the general taxpayer; it would be better if they could be induced to assimilate to the mainstream, mainly urban-oriented labour market: 'prosperity and self-sufficiency in the modern economy require a willingness to integrate into the economy, which means, among other things, a willingness to move to where jobs and investment opportunities exist' (2000b: 7).

Experience with broad-spectrum implementation of RCAP-style strategies for development is so shallow in historical terms that it is difficult to respond empirically to Flanagan's prognosis. We can confidently say that peoples such as the James Bay Crees and Inuit of northern Quebec, who have gained a relatively strong measure of control over lands and resources, and greater monetary benefits from the development of those resources, have suffered less 'unemployment, welfare dependency, and human misery' than many of their Indigenous neighbours. While statistical indicators of social well-being among these peoples are not always enviable in comparison with the Canadian mainstream, they suggest significantly less traumatic conditions than those characterizing the majority of Aboriginal communities who have *not* benefited from comprehensive claims settlements. Qualitative studies reinforce this conclusion (Scott 2001).

Flanagan's prediction that development predicated on First Nations jurisdiction will fail, to the cost of us all, runs into empirical difficulties elsewhere on the continent. The Harvard Project on American Indian Economic Development, based on a decade of research throughout the United States, concludes that the success of Indian sovereignty, nation-building and economic development are tightly interdependent; that nation-building and 'de facto' sovereignty have indeed been the most important preconditions for successful economic development in 'Indian country' (whether in the lower forty-eight states or in Alaska); and that 'tribal sovereignty' generates substantial net economic benefits for surrounding non-Indian economies (Cornell and Kalt 1998: 2).

Still, Flanagan's prognosis highlights a series of challenges to which First Nations governments must find practical responses as they seek to enhance entrepreneurial and employment opportunities through strategic investment in their homeland areas. It will indeed be extremely difficult politically for many First Nations to generate either a sufficient share of lands and resources, or sufficient monetary capital, reasonably to test the potential of the RCAP strategy. Scarce resources could aggravate the risk of kin-based factional rivalries, nepotism and corruption that Flanagan fears are endemic. To clear the starting blocks – leaving aside for the moment the hurdles enumerated by Flanagan – the RCAP strategy depends on a major shift in resources available to Aboriginal governments.

The legal basis for such a shift was seemingly strengthened by the Supreme Court of Canada's (1997) *Delgamuukw* decision. This decision is regarded as a watershed in Canadian jurisprudence, committing as it does to broadly applicable principles and procedures for the recognition and definition of Aboriginal title. A succession of Supreme Court judgments over the prior quarter-century had concluded that Aboriginal title endures where not explicitly extinguished by valid treaty, but these judgments remained either vague or selectively and guardedly specific about the content of the right. *Delgamuukw* at last offered a relatively inclusive definition of Aboriginal title, affirming the Aboriginal right to use lands and resources for a diversity of purposes, uses not necessarily confined to Indigenous traditions and practices. Chief Justice Lamer did, however, limit the scope of this right in two ways. First, the land cannot be used in a way that undermines the connection to the land upon which the group's claim to Aboriginal title is based. Second, although Aboriginal title-holders have the right to develop homeland re-sources, the Crown also has the right to authorize such developments as forestry, mining and hydroelectricity, and to create new human settlements. The Crown may only take such action after consultation with Aboriginal title-holders and compensation for losses; indeed, in most cases (unspecified) Lamer declares that the Crown's obligation runs much deeper than mere consultation (implying that Aboriginal consent may actually be required). The net effect of the judgment is to increase pressure on central govern-ments to negotiate in earnest any Crown-authorized use of lands under Aboriginal title, and to proceed on the basis of genuine (i.e. consent-based) co-management arrangements; but much still depends on the political will of governments to do so.

There is, in some provincial jurisdictions at least, growing policy receptive-ness to such reform. A recent agreement with the James Bay Crees of northern Quebec (Anonymous 2002; Scott 2002), a fifty-year, C\$3.5 billion dollar settlement with the provincial government enabling a further hydro-electric project on Cree territory, is instructive in a number of ways. First, it suggests that margins of profitability in some resource sectors, at least, are sufficient to pay Indigenous owners a share of resource rents that is signifi-cantly greater than any past settlement. Second, it shows that a provincial government can approach large-scale resource development with the prin-ciple that Aboriginal consent is required, and reach a mutually satisfactory agreement. Third, it shows that even though Aboriginal title may ostensibly have been subject to 'blanket extinguishment' (in this regard, the James Bay and Northern Agreement, 1975, did not differ greatly from the treaties of the late nineteenth and early twentieth centuries), the Crees' self-government structures were able to generate sufficient political control of their territories to be dealt with on a nation-to-nation basis.

Conclusions

The old orthodoxy misrepresents collective entitlements for Indigenous peoples as race-based attacks on the equality of individuals and their freedom of association. In the same breath it denies the freedom of Indigenous people to associate with one another or with encapsulating settler states on their own socio-territorial terms. Hence, property and jurisdiction over northern 'public lands' are claimed in the name of the general citizenry of the state and wrested from Aboriginal control. The result has been profound social inequality, manifest in the poverty of the majority of northern Aboriginal communities, in sharp contrast to the wealth of non-Aboriginal corporate elites granted licences to exploit the resources of the 'public lands'/expropriated homelands in question. If the process is unjust, it is nevertheless accepted as the historically inevitable course of evolutionary progress.

The 'new orthodoxy', in response, favours the reinforcement and enlargement of collective, inalienable title to Aboriginal homelands, and a leading role for Aboriginal governments in the economic development of their homeland territories. The application of these measures in state policy to date has been limited and selective, not to say experimental and politically opportunistic. These newer measures, in fact, have not achieved the status of 'orthodoxy' in the routine practices of the state, but rather comprise a political current that is, at best, only slowly undermining the deeply embedded old orthodoxy.

Apart from the organizational and developmental advantages of self-governed jurisdictions, the nature of subarctic and Arctic resources relevant to the contemporary industrial economy makes it difficult to see how Aboriginal entitlement could be equitably and effectively implemented except collectively. Hunting, trapping, small-scale commercial fishing, and tourism in some areas could perhaps function on the basis of more individualized tenure regimes, and individual private capital. But hydroelectricity, forestry, petroleum and mining are capital-intensive sectors requiring large investments and, often, blocks of territory that exceed what could (or should, in terms of social equity) be owned on an individual basis.

Lands and resources could be held by Aboriginal governments on behalf of their constituencies, analogous to the manner in which provincial governments have historically held Crown lands on behalf of their citizenries,

or they could be vested as the property of Aboriginal business corporations, whose role would be more narrowly proprietary and entrepreneurial.
Reliance on the latter option imposes unacceptable risks and liabilities, however, as the Alaskan experience has shown (Berger 1995). Where Aboriginal
control of lands and resources hinges solely on the commercial success of
development corporations, other Aboriginal and environmental interests are
readily compromised, and the land itself may be forfeit. Aboriginal governments, on the other hand, constituted on a regional scale, can engage in
strategic and coordinated economic development across multiple sectors, in
a way that an Aboriginal business corporation cannot. First Nations governments are also more likely than Aboriginal corporations to be able politically
to address and balance the wider spectrum of interests, from 'traditional' to
industrial, of their constituencies in subarctic and Arctic homelands. In short,
the self-governing, jurisdictional dimension of title cannot be divorced from
the proprietary dimension.

We do not yet know the extent to which northern First Nations' control
of homeland territories, together with adequate shares of resource development revenues, can build regional economies adequate to the support of
growing populations. Left solely to mainstream patterns of capital investment
and labour supply-and-demand, subarctic and Arctic regions might indeed be
even more scantily populated than they currently are. On the other hand,
there is sufficient variability in the level and diversity of economic activity in ecologically similar regions to suggest that not just existing external
markets, but endogenous features of northern social, political and cultural
organization, will determine outcomes.

Success is not guaranteed, but the alternative offered by the political right
is that northern Aboriginals would have extremely limited ownership rights
to lands and resources within their traditional territories, and only to those
that are feasible to hold on an individual basis. It would be left to provincial
governments to continue the management of Crown lands, divvying up resource licences and concessions to private corporations, with most Aboriginal
people driven by economic pressures to employment or unemployment in
the cities, or (since presumably the welfare system is not to be entirely dismantled) left to languish in northern reserves and villages in circumstances
of economic stagnation. Issues of equity and justice, however, will not be
satisfied in this fashion. And the way ahead will not be decided as a matter
of presumed evolutionary or institutional inevitability. Paths of development
are, in fact, more experimental in character, and can only be decided as visions of possible futures, anchored in cultural values and political action, are
brought to the testing ground of experience.

References

Anonymous (2002) *Agreement Concerning a New Relationship between Le Gouvernement du Québec and the Crees of Québec*, Nemaska/Quebec: Cree Regional Authority/Le Gouvernement du Québec.

Berger, T. (1995) [1985] *Village Journey: the Report of the Alaska Native Review Commission*, New York: Hill & Wang.

Cornell, S. and J. Kalt (1998) 'Sovereignty and nation-building: the development challenge in Indian country today', *American Indian Culture and Research Journal*, vol. 22, no. 4.

Flanagan, T. (1991) *Metis Lands in Manitoba*, Calgary: University of Calgary Press.

——— (1996) *Louis 'David' Riel: Prophet of the New World*, Toronto: University of Toronto Press.

——— (2000a) *Riel and the Rebellion: 1885 Reconsidered*, Toronto: University of Toronto Press.

——— (2000b) *First Nations? Second Thoughts*, Montreal and Kingston: McGill-Queen's University Press.

Hicks, J. and G. White (2000) 'Nunavut: Inuit self-determination through a land claim and public government?' in J. Dahl, J. Hicks and P. Jull (eds), *Nunavut – Inuit Regain Control of their Lands and their Lives*, Copenhagen: International Work Group for Indigenous Affairs, pp. 30–115.

Jull, P. (2000) 'Inuit and Nunavut: renewing the New World', in J. Dahl, J. Hicks and P. Jull (eds), *Nunavut – Inuit Regain Control of their Lands and their Lives*, Copenhagen: International Work Group for Indigenous Affairs, pp. 118–36.

Nunavik Commission (2001) *Amiqqaaluta – Let Us Share: Mapping the Road Toward a Government for Nunavik (Report of the Nunavik Commission)*, Ottawa: Indian and Northern Affairs Canada.

RCAP (Royal Commission on Aboriginal Peoples) (1996) *Report of the Royal Commission on Aboriginal Peoples,* 5 vols., Ottawa: Canada Communication Group.

Scott, C. (2002) 'Co-management and the politics of Aboriginal consent to resource development', paper presented at the conference 'Reconfiguring Aboriginal-State Relations/Canada: The State of the Federation 2003', School of Policy Studies, Queen's University, Kingston, 1–2 November.

——— (ed.) (2001) *Aboriginal Autonomy and Development in Northern Quebec and Labrador*, Vancouver: University of British Columbia Press.

Supreme Court of Canada (1997) *Delgamuukw* v. *British Columbia* [1997], 3 S.C.R.

18

Resistance, Determination and Perseverance
of the Lubicon Cree Women

DAWN MARTIN-HILL

Dawn Martin-Hill is Mohawk, Wolf Clan, from Six Nations of the Grand River. She is Academic Director of the Indigenous Studies Program at McMaster University. Interested in cross-cultural comparisons of Indigenous peoples, in particular Indigenous knowledge, Dawn Martin-Hill works increasingly in the area of Indigenous health-related issues.

Indigenous Knowledge and Power

In this chapter my intention is to contribute to the growing body of Indigenous theory and method that makes space for Indigenous women, and in the process to contribute to the struggles of the Lubicon Cree women of northern Alberta, Canada. The impact of development and colonial domination is evident in women's life stories. So are the forms of survival and resistance of their communities.

There is a great deal of confusion and dysfunction within our communities. We are in the process of reconstructing, rebuilding, reinventing and revitalizing our nations. To continue to try to validate ourselves to the very people who almost destroyed us is to remain in a colonial mind-set. This is contrary to our goals. From an Indigenous knowledge framework it is meaningless to demonstrate precisely the impact of development on people's social reality through a scientific, objective or quantitative methodology. We must position ourselves in the centre of our own knowledge, not speak from others' margins to try to tell them about ourselves.

While the appalling statistics on the conditions in which Indigenous women live in Canada have been well documented by social science researchers and provide a measure of the human costs of colonization (see Frideres 1993, 1998), as a Mohawk woman I can say along with many

Lubicon women that we are intimate with the experiences of these costs. In academia, as well as in policy circles, what Indigenous women experience and do is often viewed as insignificant. It is not enough to objectify. What is relevant is not so much comprehending where I or the Lubicon women are in socio-demographic terms, but where we are coming from in human terms – spiritual, emotional, psychological, social and physical. The fact that we are here, continuing to do what we do, is testimony to our strength, resilience and beauty as Indigenous women. By acknowledging the realities of Aboriginal women, by hearing our own voices, the Lubicon women and I are positioned not as victims but as survivors.

The challenge as a researcher is to provide an opportunity to learn from Indigenous women's experience as we remain active participants with them in dismantling colonialism in real terms. I seek to contribute to this kind of Indigenous knowledge/practice by presenting life stories from the women of the Lubicon Cree Nation, and by supporting them in achieving justice. Their stories express and embody the collective and personal human costs of colonization, of resource exploitation, of their long land-claim struggle, and of government betrayal. It is through their experiences that the social impact of the dominant society's oppression can best be demonstrated.

My Lubicon women's-centred discourse evolves within a larger Indigenous knowledge framework. The Chair of the United Nations Report on the Protection of Heritage of Indigenous People, Dr Daes, states:

> Indigenous knowledge is a complete knowledge system with its own concepts of epistemology, philosophy, and scientific and logical validity … [which] can only be fully learned and understood by means of pedagogy traditionally employed by these people themselves. (Cited in Battiste and Henderson-Youngblood 2000: 41)

The processes that seek to devalue this knowledge involve a systematic rhetorical strategy developed to justify the oppression and genocide of Native 'others' (Churchill 1997: 1–19; Jaimes 1992: 1–13). Maori scholar Linda Tuhiwai Smith writes,

> to a large extent, [Western] theories about research are underpinned by a cultural system of classification and representation, by views about human nature, human morality and virtue, by conceptions of space and time, by conceptions of gender and race. Ideas about these things help determine what is real. Systems of classification and representation enable different traditions or fragments of traditions to then be played out in systems of power and domination, with real material consequences for colonized peoples. (Smith 1999: 44)

In contrast to 'Western' traditions, Indigenous methodology approaches a community as a network of kinship systems, as family. This network is not, however, limited to human society; it extends out and is inclusive of all living things. This approach is profoundly rooted in an Indigenous epistemology. The Indigenous societies of North America hold specific knowledge about their relationship to the universe. Their 'awareness' is complex in that it not only accounts for this world, but for the principles governing the spirit world as well. These ways of knowing involve a *developed* sense of the connection of kinship and cosmos that can inform behaviour and influence social action. The earth is positioned as mother, the moon as grandmother, and the sun as father or uncle. This makes kinship a general epistemological foundation that in turn demands the acknowledgement of reciprocal responsibilities and obligations between Indigenous people and their environment. This includes an understanding that human beings are not endowed with the right either to dominate others or to destroy that which is around them. This is not 'mythology', or even religion; it is an assumption, or truth, which is at the core of Indigenous knowledge and consciousness.

Overview of the 'Histories' of the Lubicon Struggle for Their Land

Histories of the Lubicon Cree struggle for recognition and for control of their land have appeared repeatedly in recent years, written by journalists, social scientists, and sometimes independent commissions, and each has documented the series of ignored Lubicon initiatives, bureaucratic duplicities, betrayed agreements, and the century-long denial of recognition of Lubicon lands and rights.

The Lubicon Cree are a hunting society from northern Alberta. They have traditionally lived around Lubicon Lake, hunting and trapping within a 70-mile radius. Although their contact with outsiders was minimal at the end of the nineteenth century, because of their isolated territory, the Lubicon elders of the time were aware that it was important to secure their lands from the encroachment by white settlers then going on elsewhere in the territory (Smith 1988; Richardson 1989; Goddard 1991; Martin-Hill 1992). Thus in 1899, with the help of visiting missionaries, they wrote a letter to the government and sent delegates to Whitefish Lake to speak with government representatives concerning their signing a treaty. The treaty with the Lubicon never materialized. The Lubicon continued to lobby for official agreements with the government for several decades. In 1939 they were successful in gaining legal recognition as a Indian 'band' under federal law (Smith 1987; Lennerson 1989; Goddard 1991; Mandelbaum 1979). C.P. Schmidt, an Indian agent, visited them that year and calculated that the band was entitled to 25 square miles of land as a reserve. An aerial survey took place and by 1940 the reserve boundaries had been drawn up (Goddard 1991). However, due to World War II, there was a shortage of ground surveyors and an actual ground survey never took place. In 1942, an official of the Department of Indian Affairs removed Lubicon from registered lists and then moved to reduce the recognition of the Lubicon as a band.

In response to these failures to get recognition, the elders decided the youth should learn English in order to pursue their land claim. Several men, including Walter Whitehead and Bernard and Larry Ominayak were persuaded by the elders to attend high school. Walter was elected chief in the early 1970s and began to lay the legal groundwork for the land claim just as oil exploration began in the area.

The provincial government began to build an all-weather road into the area to facilitate oil exploitation, and by 1980 there were at least ten major oil companies with over 400 wells within the territory of the Lubicon (Goddard 1991). One consequence of the resource development activities in the region was that between 1974 and 1985 the Lubicon became a welfare-dependent community (Fulton 1986; Goddard 1991).

In 1980, the members of the Lubicon band filed an action in the Federal Court of Canada, requesting a declaratory judgment concerning their rights to their land, its use, and the benefits of its natural resources. The claim was dismissed against the provincial government and all energy corporations except one (Petro-Canada) on jurisdictional grounds. The claim with the federal government and Petro-Canada as defendants was allowed to stand, and it dragged on for years. In 1988, after Lubicon band members erected a road blockade, Alberta Premier Donald Getty agreed to meet with them, and they arrived at a mutual agreement, now known as the Grimshaw Accord. The agreement allowed for 79 square miles to be transferred to the federal government for the purpose of establishing a Lubicon reserve and another sixteen square miles would be under the jurisdiction of Lubicon. The 79 square miles included sub-surface and surface rights, as at other reserves in Alberta, while the sixteen only included surface rights (Goddard 1991). The federal government agreed to accept the 79-square mile reserve, plus 16 miles, but was only prepared to provide services to members it designated as 'Indians', the 235 of the approximately 500 Lubicon members who were descended from the reduced band list of five decades earlier (Lennerson 1989; Goddard 1991). The Lubicon were not prepared to allow Ottawa to split their members (into those who had a federally recognized Indian status and those who were 'non-status'), and they rejected the offer. In 1990, the United Nations Human Rights Committee found Canada to be 'in violation of article 27 so long as historical inequities ... and certain more recent developments [continue] to threaten the way of life and culture of Lubicon people' (United Nations 1990).

An independent non-partisan commission was formalized in 1991 to seek a resolution to the Lubicon land claims. This Lubicon Settlement

Commission of Review's final report, published in 1993, after a year-long investigation, stated: 'Our principal finding is that the governments have not acted in good faith' (Lubicon Settlement Commission of Review 1993: 4).

Thus the Lubicon Cree have been victims both of globalizing corporate resource interests and of long-standing national and provincial governmental pressures that have become complicit with those corporate interests. The Lubicon Cree's struggle for their land base and rights demonstrates clearly Canada's unwillingness to exercise its own laws and apply them to all citizens (Churchill 1999: 208–22; Martin-Hill 1995; Dickason 1992: 390–92; York 1989: 253–7).

The well-publicized land-claims agreements in Canada, which effectively force Aboriginal people to barter away their rights in order to have the opportunity to achieve basic social justice, are thus just one way in which the governments exploit and violate Indigenous rights. Another way is by actively seeking to break communities apart, while alternatively ignoring, silencing and betraying Indigenous peoples' attempts to seek justice. This is particularly the case with the Lubicon Cree.

What is lost in all of these Lubicon 'histories' is the human costs of the land claims and resistance, and this is reflected in the collective and private struggles of the Lubicon women.

The Women's Circle Reaches Out

Within an Indigenous epistemological framework everyone's experiences and insights are seen as critical to the whole community.[1] Everyone is considered to have important experiences and insights to share with others. Social realities are shaped through experience in different ways, and for that reason it is critical to include the diverse voices of the Lubicon. Women's knowledge shapes and directs our understanding of their history and contemporary situation.

I first visited the Lubicon community at Little Buffalo in Alberta in the fall of 1989. I spent only a week there, but the relationship grew when Chief Bernard Ominayak visited my community, Six Nations, between Toronto and Buffalo, the following month to discuss his issues with the traditional governing body of the Haudenosaunee. The following December, I found myself on a plane with elder, chief and faithkeeper, Hubert Buck, on our way to assist the Lubicon chief and council in a ceremony. After that we traveled a dozen times back and forth to answer their calls for spiritual help and moral support. I decided to continue my work with the Lubicon, which meant continuing with the education that sponsored many of the trips. The Lubicon were the reason I continued my Ph.D. education.

In the early summer of 1992, and in the wider context of the Lubicon's intention to restructure their community in non-Western, 'traditional' ways, Chief Ominayak requested that I help the women who had expressed their desire to stay involved with legal and social proceedings relating to the land claim and the well-being of the community. The women were also concerned about what would happen if the government arrested the male leaders. The Lubicon Lake Nation Women's Circle began to meet bi-weekly, attending political meetings, assisting with speaking engagements, developing a community-oriented social service programme, sponsoring healing circles, cultural survival workshops (crafts and bush skills), teen dances, and many other community events including ceremonies. I was involved in this process, and it was often after events, especially ceremonies, when we shared our deepest thoughts, fears, and feelings, that I would write down our collective ideas and statements.

Yet the process began at our first meeting when there were expectations that we could draft a statement for the Alberta Commission of Review, which was preparing a report on the treatment of the Lubicon for the Alberta government (see above), and which was going to visit the community. When the women gathered I asked them what they would like to say to the public. The ideas started rolling in like thunder. Two and a half hours later, we had more than enough to edit into a statement. I was shocked by their anger, frustration, and outspokenness. These women had a lot to say, and, as one put it, 'We have been silent too long. Now we will be heard and we will make them hear us!' (Lillian Whitehead, June 1992).[2]

The written statement is overwhelming, a condensed version of all of their pain. They read the statement and quietly signed their names. Over twenty Lubicon women composed the statement that was to be read in public. They chose a young woman by the name of Rose Ominayak to read the statement. Several days later, we gathered at the Longhouse for the hearing. There were reporters from as far away as Germany. The presence of so many white people made the women nervous, this was entirely new to the community. Bernard Ominayak asked the women to speak first. Rose quietly moved towards the front table. Head down, she was shaking as she read the statement. She was only able to read half before she finally broke down in tears. Everyone sat in silence while she composed herself to finish the statement:

> We, the Lubicon Lake Nation, are tired. We are frustrated and angry. We feel we cannot wait another minute to have our land claim settled. Fifty years is too long. In those fifty years we have watched our land and lives be destroyed by Canadian governments and corporations. Our children are sick from drinking water that oil has spilled in. They are sick from breathing the poisoned and polluted air the pulp mill has made. We are sick from eating animals, animals that are sick from

disease from poisoned plants and water. Our children have nothing – they can't breathe – even that has been taken. Their culture, the bush life, has been destroyed by development. When we were young we lived in the bush – it was a good life. Now, we have no traplines, nothing to hunt. There are no jobs, no money to live a decent life. We see ourselves, our men and our children falling into despair, hopelessness, low self-esteem and drinking. Families are broken like never before. Drinking and violence rise as our spirits fall.

We live our lives in constant danger. Since the blockade we have been afraid to go certain places in town. Our sons have been beaten by white men when they say they are Lubicon. We are even afraid to say that we are what we are! The roads are dusty and dangerous to travel. The logging and oil trucks run us off sometimes. We have lost many young ones because of the horrible roads. We are not even safe in the bush. We are afraid to go into the bush because the white sports-hunters shoot at anything that moves.

We ask why? Why us? What have we done to deserve such treatment? Why can't the government settle with the Lubicon? Why have they spent so much time and energy trying to destroy us rather than deal fairly with us? What have we done, our children, our people? What wrong have we done to the outside?

We are not dogs, but we are treated like dogs. We are people just like you. We are equal. We have every right to be here. The Creator put us here in this place. We are important – our future. We have lost more than you can imagine: our way of life that we loved, our culture, our beautiful land, our health and our happiness. What else can we lose?

The Lubicon women demand an end to the physical, emotional, economic, cultural and spiritual destruction. We demand an end to the invasion and devasta-tion to our lives. We demand an end to the government and corporation warfare with our lands and lives. We demand an end to the mockery of our Nation! We demand an end to the genocide. Hear our voice and our message – we don't know if we'll be here tomorrow. (Martin-Hill 1992, read for the Lubicon Lake Nation Women's Circle by Rose Ominayak, August 1992)

There were men and women alike with their heads down and eyes watering. The Lubicon women had broken the silence, and powerful it was.

The local media's response to their statement was interesting, in that it was suggested that the Lubicon women wanted a settlement out of desperation and that they would accept anything. The federal government responded by trying to establish, in their communications with the media, that they sympathized with the women and hoped they would tell their chief to stop stonewalling the federal government's offer.

The women held several meetings after the Alberta Commission of Review hearings. The women were outraged that the federal government was trying to blame the chief for the impasse. They requested copies of the latest Lubicon offer Siddon had given to the chief and Band Council. They read it through and saw that issues of membership, compensation and community development were unsatisfactory, and they requested a meeting with Federal Minister of Indian Affairs Tom Siddon. The Honourable Tom Siddon did not respond.

During a gathering at the opening of the Longhouse in August 1992, the women decided they wanted to attend the next meeting between the chief and Tom Siddon. Two elders, Louisa Ominayak and Josephine Laboucon, three delegates, Maggie Auger, Rose Ominayak and Jennifer Ominayak, and I, were appointed to attend. The women also requested that five women elders from a nearby Aboriginal nation, Hobbema, attend to offer support and direction. In September, I drove Louisa, her daughter Rose and Josephine to Edmonton. On the way there Louisa said, 'This is really good, we have not been helping as much as we could. I think this should go on and the women should not quit once you are gone' (Louisa Ominayak, September 1992). The two elders occupied themselves watching for a moose. It was not a good sign if you did not see at least one animal on the way to Edmonton; it was best if you saw a moose. Josephine spotted several foxes, which she believed to be a sign of Siddon. She said that he was going to 'be sneaky, like a fox' (Josephine Laboucon, September 1992). We agreed. Louisa decided, upon the second sighting of a fox, that we were going to have to 'outfox the fox'. Josephine wanted to see a bear, but we never did.

Meeting the Minister of Indian Affairs

As the meeting with the minister began, Maggie Auger asked Siddon why he never responded directly to the women's letter, choosing instead to send his response to the media. He responded that he thought he had sent a letter to them. Maggie stated:

> In the letter to the media you say you feel bad for us and that you will do everything in your power to help. You try to blame our Chief for us not having a land-claim deal. We don't like you trying to say it is our Chief that is the problem. We have read the offer you gave us in August. It is not good. Was there not an agreement between the band and your government to hire independent cost estimators to evaluate how much a new community would cost? (Maggie Auger, September 1992)

Siddon responded, 'Yes, we had agreed to have independent cost estimators determine the amount of building a new village at Lubicon Lake.' Maggie then responded:

> Then, Mr Siddon, if there was an agreement to wait for the independent cost estimators to determine the amount, how did you come up with C$73 million

in this deal you offered a few weeks ago when the cost estimators have yet to complete their estimation? Isn't that in itself breaking the initial agreement with the chief?

Siddon replied: 'I think C$73 million is a large sum. In fact, it is one of the most generous offers the Lubicon ever received. You have to realize how much money that is that we are offering you. You women have said yourselves how poor you are and your living conditions.' Louisa Ominayak interjected,

> You have made billions off our land. Don't tell us that you are being generous with our own money! We are sick of playing games. You never answered Maggie! Why did you offer a deal when those men that were supposed to come up with the amount, you didn't wait, you went ahead and put this in the media just to make it look like we are bad people. You are the ones not being fair!

Jennifer Ominayak then added:

> That is our land, you need to get that one straight first. Our land! You are trying to make it look like we keep turning offers down, but you had an agreement with my Dad to go with the independent cost estimators and, instead, before they even finish, you are on TV saying you have a new deal for us. Now, you know who is wrong here. You're just trying to make us look bad, and we know better. Besides, you also agreed to drop the membership issue, that we would determine who is a member. Now I read this new offer and you bring up membership again, there again. You are breaking your promises. What do you have to say? Tell the truth.

Siddon responded, 'Now wait just one damn minute here. You are making me angry. There is no need to tell me to tell the truth! I came here of good will and agreed to meet with you for five minutes, and they're up!' Louisa Ominayak told him he was going nowhere without a deal. Maggie said:

> You need to show respect to us if in turn you want to receive it, and you are not showing us respect. You are lying to us. Now, I will ask you again and I want an answer, not to change the subject, but an answer to my question, did you agree with the Chief to have an independent cost estimator determine the amount of the land claim settlement for building a new village, yes or no?

Siddon responded,

> I realize the cost of a new village is more than even what the Lubicon's proposal suggested because of the inflation rates and so on. We took this into account. Now you must realize the C$73 million is a whole lot more than the $45 million you were offered. It is quite fair and you should talk to your Chief and tell him how fair it is. We cannot give you more, especially since your band has lost many members. Even taking this into account we are giving you a lot of money.

Siddon only evaded the questions and the discussion led nowhere. The meeting lasted for over three hours. Over the course of this time, tensions rose and Siddon practically shouted at the women. Louisa Ominayak warned him once again. He evaded all of their questions and left visibly shaken. The media immediately questioned the women. Maggie wearily responded: 'He swore at us, he shouted and he lied. He is not a man of honour and we are disappointed with his answers. He talked in circles. Maybe the Chief will have more luck' (Maggie Auger, September 1992). Siddon went to met with the chief, and we gathered at the restaurant for dinner. When Bernard arrived he told us that Siddon was shaking when he came in to meet with him. He said that Siddon asked, 'Who the hell is that Mohawk woman, and what is she doing with your women?' Bernard said he told him, 'She is a researcher, and it's not her you have to worry about. You met the Lubicon women and now you know what I have to face each time I come home and report "No deal!"'

The meeting with the Minister of Indian Affairs galvanized the Lubicon women into formalizing their association. The women decided that they would continue to support the land-claims struggle and their leadership, but would also focus on improving the community's social well-being. The women expressed concern about the 'human condition'. They felt the community had been torn apart through years of struggle, which had created social breakdown and collective community stress.

The Women's Circle began work to establish a 'collective spirit' critical to the healing of the community. Continuing in this direction is of utmost importance to them. As the head of the Women's Circle, Maggie Auger stated in November 1992:

> As a woman I am aware of all the problems here, the miscarriages, the babies that die. We know better than anyone how this development has hurt us, that the outside never sees or hears about. But we don't normally talk of our personal tragedies, that's not our way. But truthfully, the government has done quite the job on us. Letting us hang in the air like this. Creating new bands. Tearing families apart. This has taken a toll on us and we never let anyone know how much suffering really goes on here. The Women's Circle maybe can ease our pain. Keep us together, support for one another. We must stay together and keep our ways strong. That is what I believe will get us through this. (Maggie Auger, November 1992)

Forgotten Voices of the Lubicon Lake Nation Women

It is the Lubicon women who have suffered most significantly because of the development in their territory and government colonial policies. They have much to add to the story of the Lubicon. During one of the women's meetings, Lillian Whitehead told me: 'We want you to tell our story, what we have been through, what we are fighting for' (Lillian Whitehead, August 1992). I promised the women that I would tell their story.

One of the first women I met in the community of Little Buffalo near Lubicon Lake was Louise Ominayak. In December 1989, she was grieving the loss of her mother. Sensing her pain, I opted to stay with her instead of visiting with the chief and band council. It was during this visit that she agreed to give me an interview.

I have been raising kids ever since I can remember. My mother was sick and I had to look after eight of them. We lived in the bush. It was a hard life but a good one. I miss that, even though it was hard. I went to school for a while. Not very good at it. Bernard and I were always scrapping with other kids at school. We used to like to fight, even then [laughs]. I had to stop to look after the kids. He went on, he was smart. Me, I just know the bush.... I was only about fourteen or fifteen. But we had fun. Somehow we had fun. Can't explain it. We laughed, went places on horseback, it was my best memories. We raised all of them.

Now, everything is upside down, nothing has been right. This land claim. He never goes to the bush anymore. I miss the bush. Out there it is so peaceful and quiet, good. It was not bad when we first lived here [Little Buffalo]. Then, one day he asked me about becoming the Chief. I said, 'OK, I stay home and raise the kids while you do what you have to.' I did not realize I was agreeing to give him up. I've been on my own ever since. The children miss their father so much. It was hard, especially when they were sick. Our boy Lou, we almost lost him as a baby. His lungs, he was so sick and Bernard had to go to [New York] that time. That was real hard on all of us. People just don't realize how this has torn us up inside. And him, he has changed. Worried all the time, quiet. I don't know what goes on out there, where all he has been, or seen, but he thinks a lot. Me, I don't like to go on the outside. I went to Edmonton once and wanted to go home right away, too many white people. Then my home, we always have reporters, strangers in and out all the time. I just feed them and don't say much, but I listen to what they are saying. They take pictures of how the land is being torn up and all the trucks and then they leave. I often wonder what happens to all these pictures, if anyone out there is listening or seeing what is going on up here. But things just keep getting worse.

The hardest part is my family being torn up. I don't understand how that happened. One by one, my brothers and then sisters left to go to the new band, Woodland Cree. I just can't figure that out. Why? After we raised them and helped them, now they are against us. My father has a lot to do with that. After leaving us he got jealous that Bernard raised them. But all those years ... now no one talking to one another (shaking her head slowly). I miss my mother so much. If she were here I would ask her what to do.

Sometimes I ask God, what is He taking everything away for? I wonder if I was bad or something, losing everything that I know and really love. Bernard says don't worry so much, just look after the kids. So I do, just keep them out of trouble. Kids wander around in the dark around here, drinking and getting into no good. Sometimes their parents are drinking and their kids are hungry; they come to the door for food. I don't let mine out after dark. It's hard, people changing, drinking and fighting. Sometimes the young people come here, a girl is hit or something. I try to help them, tell them to stay with it. That's what I am trying to do. Sometimes the drunks come here when he is gone away. One time this man, I beat him with my broom, I got him out of here. But this is not good, I miss being in the bush. My kids, they are not learning the way I wanted them to. I wish my mother was here. She could tell me what to do. (Louise Ominayak, December 1989)

The next time I was able to visit Louise was over a year later, in the summer of 1991. She had moved to Codotte and was living in a Woodland Band-owned trailer. She appeared even less happy than the last visit. She said she had left Little Buffalo because it was 'getting to her', but she was not joining with the Woodland Cree. Her brother was now the Chief of the Woodland Cree and was pressuring her to sign with them. She refused. Edmonton reporters were seeking her out to find out if the Lubicon Chief's wife had left to sign up with the Woodland Cree. The Woodland Cree were about to vote on a plebiscite for a land claim deal. Louise informed me that the Woodland band was paying up to C$1,000 for people to sign with them. She also told me that 'They are fools. Their welfare money will be taken away' (Louise Ominayak, June 1991).

In July of 1992 Louise stopped by Bernard's and gave me a beaded belt, barrettes and necklaces she had been working on. We attended the round dance at the 'steel building' that evening and she was looking well. We had more of a chance to visit. She told me:

I am staying in Trout now. I get to the bush a lot. I don't like it in Codotte, too much drinking. They are always after me to drink or give them money. I miss Little Buffalo. My kids want to stay here too. I needed time to sort things out in my head. Everyone is trying to get me to turn against Bernard, but I won't. People must not realize how we shared everything all these years, grew up together. They forget, I don't. They can't buy me. The white man is trying, but they can't give me anything I want. They took all that away and they are still taking everything. Maybe I will move back here. Not right away, but I still visit him. I can stay there if I want. He let me take whatever I wanted. I stayed for a while last winter. We are just too different now, but I can stay there if I want to help with the kids and the house.

But I need to get my life going, my own life. My brothers are nice to me now, too. I missed them and my father is not well. I tried to help him out. Boy, things are crazy. They were after me to sign up with the Woodland, but you never do that, you stay with him on that one. They just want to have me sign up so that will make headlines. After all this, why would I do what the [white man] wants? They must think I am stupid. When I wouldn't sign they wanted me out of the trailer. If I signed I would have been promised new things and money. I am Lubicon and I am going to stay Lubicon, so I had to get out of there too!

That's why Trout was good. I was left alone up there, just stayed in the bush, tanned hides and beaded. You and I, we will stay friends no matter what, right? People around here are making all kinds of rumours, but we know, don't we? (Louise Ominayak, July 1992)

I told her that I understood and didn't listen to the rumours. If anything, I admired her for the way she had held up under the circumstances. I felt anger over what this woman was being put through. It was through Louise's experiences that I was beginning to comprehend the human cost of this ordeal. The government capitalized on the human pain of individual Lubicon members, sparing no one in its attempts to undermine the Lubicon land claim.

The following spring of 1993, we spoke again. This time Louise had moved back to Little Buffalo and was living at home again. She was upset because a very young baby had died in the village, and she was the first to arrive. She did not want to talk about it and said she was trying to forget what she saw. I spoke with her again that spring. She was feeling better and was about to begin a new job.

It is good, this Women's Circle, having people doing things together again. I hope that it goes on. Maybe I will go to a few meetings and see what is going on. They have asked me to help the younger girls to bead and tan hides. Maybe, if I have time, I will. I should teach you, you don't know anything of the bush but then I can't write books either, so don't feel bad [she laughs]. (Louise Ominayak, May 1993)

Over the years I also grew close to Bernard and Louise's daughter, Jennifer Ominayak. When I first met her in 1989 she was 18 years old and had completed high school. She was also very pretty and carrying a child. She did not seem to be thrilled about her condition so I left her alone most of the time. When my family stayed at the house during the summer of 1991, she had a beautiful little girl, Lennett, and was carrying a second child.

It wasn't until the fall of 1992 that she opened up and discussed her feelings. I feared the tragic consequences that could be associated with someone young and intelligent living in a community that had very few resources at its disposal, and little opportunity to offer an energetic person. Jennifer frequently expressed how 'bored' she was and how little there is to look forward to in Little Buffalo. She agreed to be interviewed:

I remember, too, or, my mom told me about my fingers. See them? The nails don't grow on this hand. I always hide this hand. But I guess they were in the bush and it was real cold, like a blizzard. My father had left the camp and got stuck somewhere, we were running out of food and everything. So my mom carried me in the blizzard for maybe ten miles! I guess my hand got frostbite. So this old couple that my mom had went to see for food, the old man fixed my hand with our medicine. But can you imagine carrying a baby that far in the cold? Holy, my mom is tough, not like us, we are spoiled.

But I wish I could do things like her. She can bead and everything. I remember being in the bush when we were young. Man, we had a good time riding our horses and our cousins were with us. That's when things were fun. We were like a family more then…. That's one thing I am good at, riding horses, but I don't ride as much with the kids being so small.

Melissa [her younger sister] is lucky, she doesn't have to go to school the way I did. Dad is teaching them how to do things. She can ride good! And she goes to the cabin more with him. Erwin, too, he is a good hunter. Lou doesn't have to go to school either. I wish that would have happened with me, but they wanted me to finish school. It was hard catching up all the time because I was sick. Finally, Dad and Fred took me somewhere far away to this special doctor and ever since then I haven't been so sick. But I missed a lot of learning, being sick and away from them.

Now I am educated but don't have a damn thing to do, no work, nothing. What good was it? Maybe that is what my father figures, what good did it do me? So he is teaching the others everything. I like to write but don't know what to write about. I want to help in the land claim but don't know how to. I see my father, so tired, running all over the place and he doesn't eat right. I worry that he will get in a car accident because he is on the road all the time. What would we all do if anything ever happens to him? I can't help worrying and I am worried until I see him pull in. Then I can sleep OK. But everyone around here is calling, worried too. It's crazy, eh, checking to see he is alright.

I know he was mad because I was going out and partying a little bit, but it is so boring around here. I am sick of it. I get up and clean, get the babies dressed and then what? Maybe go for a visit, but that gets tiresome after awhile. No one has any money to go to the show or anything. All of us are bored and we don't know how to go in the bush. So that's why we drink. Nothing else to do here and we all know it's wrong but it's hard to have nothing to do day after day. Everyone is just waiting for the land claim because nothing will really happen around here until we get that. So, it's really the waiting and the sadness of all this. We were involved more when we were younger. Even the principal of the school was involved and let us go to blockade and write about it. But the province got rid of him and now we have this woman that is not very good at all. Lots of kids don't want to go to her school and she is driving everyone away. They don't teach anything about our people there or nothing! It was better when I went there and the principal was more involved. It was fun to learn, so I don't blame all these ones for dropping out. But then look at what they are doing instead, drinking. I wonder if anything will get better around here?'

I am really glad that you[r] people keep coming here. That is the only action around, the round dances and those people from the Sacred Run. I miss that old man Hubert, he teased everyone. When he was here it seemed as if everything was going to be all right, but when he would go it would seem as if everything was bad again. People over the years have dropped off. It seems like when I open up to someone and get to really like them they have to leave and go to their own lives, and we are left here, just lonesome. That's why I don't bother trying to get to know anyone anymore. I am afraid to lose them again and be lonely. Like you, I am getting real used to you being here and talking with you, but you will go home and I will miss you and be bored again. I miss your girls running around here already. But you already have a reserve with lots to do there. You are lucky, I don't blame you for leaving this place. I will try not to drink anymore, stay out of trouble. Maybe I will ask my father what I can do to help with the land claim again, maybe help the Women's Circle, eh, like last summer?

That was really good when we told that guy, what's his name? Siddon, Tom Siddon, yeah, when we told him.… He thought he was going to treat us women like dummies, like we don't know what he is up to. Oh man, I will never forget that guy's face, it was all red! He looked like he wanted to hit you, if he would of, well, we would hit him. That's when I got upset. He had no right to treat you in that way, like scolded you because you had a tape recorder. I told him, didn't I? He was trying to make it look like Daddy was a liar too. We should all be mad at Daddy. What did he think, we never read the paper he sent? It must be hard on Daddy to meet with guys like that all the time. I know they lie, but he sat there and lied to us and that's why I think we all got so upset. I got him on the membership question, didn't I? I remember asking you and the lawyers over and over again, I knew I had it straight. Then he said membership wasn't an issue, when he stated right in that paper it was! That felt so good, to tell him what we know. I wonder if they will ever meet with us women again? Maybe not, but I still wonder why they are putting us through all of this when it is ours, our land, everyone so poor, nothing to do. Why are they doing it, do you think?' (Jennifer Ominayak, November 1992)

I explained to Jennifer that I wasn't all that sure either. I also explained to her that I believed the government did not want to settle fairly with a land claim because that would set a precedent in the north. She failed to understand why being fair is a precedent.

Louisa Ominayak, who died a short two months after I interviewed her, was an outspoken elder and almost 60 – she was not really sure. She was born around Marten Lake. I had been lucky enough to meet her in the summer of 1992. She was active in the Women's Circle, and we traveled to Edmonton for the meeting with the Minister of Indian Affairs. I miss her robust laughter and outspokenness.

Louisa spoke fairly good English. She went to school with the priest and nuns at Marten Lake. She figured there were around seventeen families at the time she lived there. She married Jim Ominayak and together they raised their children. They built a cabin at Marten Lake because of the school and the availability of game. This is her story.

Ya, we were poor, had nothing. But we had wild meat, ducks, grouse, rabbit, moose and berries. We ate, the children were poor, clothes, not much. We built that cabin, it cost us C$11.00 for the logs and we had to get a permit to build there. Then they served us papers, but we were not there, like most other families. We came back from the bush just in time. We had only been given four day's notice to get out of our house, they were gonna run everything out of there. We had to borrow a team from Whitefish to get our stove and everything out. Then, some didn't even know.

Boy, they came in and bulldozed the whole place. We had no home. They never did pay us for our home we lost. We felt so bad. That was our home! It was nice there, quiet, no drinking, had a little school there. In Codotte there was drinking, but not there. The government never talk about that day we all lost our homes. I never see that on the news. They never know how we felt there, watching our nice place being bulldozed. I'm still mad about that.

I went to a convent from the time I was seven until I was fourteen. It was good there, lots to eat. They treated us nice there. That is how I can talk and write.... I got out of school and got married, moved to Marten River. All my kids were born in the bush except two, Mike and Martha. I lost three, one as a baby, one in that accident.

Joseph Laboucon used to be the Chief in the '50s. He died now. I have been waiting a long time for our reserve. I wait and wait, but never nothing. They think we don't know all the oil that was at Marten where they bulldozed our homes. We know it has oil all over there. They kicked us out. They don't want to give us a damn cent for what we know is ours. They don't know how tough we are. We'll fight right to the very end. And we will tell everyone what they did to us up here. Someday they will have to own up to what they have done.

They cry about the money, but who has all the money? Not us. I want my children to have a nice home, nice jobs and a nice place to grow up. Not welfare and drinking and no animals. We won't settle for that. What will there be for our grandchildren if we accept that deal they want us to? Welfare, poor houses, beg them for everything, that's what they want. We lived on our own and we know what is ours and what is not. They have gotten rich off our lands. What we got? Bulldozed homes, TB [tuberculosis] and welfare. Nope, I am gonna fight along with the Chief. He's smart and he won't let them rip us off, that's why we made him that, Chief. So, next time I see that Siddon, I ain't gonna be so nice as I was in Edmonton. I don't have long, so I'm gonna give him a good one. They still owe me that C$11.00, I'm gonna get it, too! (Louisa Ominayak, December 1992)

When I returned to visit Louisa, she had been taken to the hospital. At the time, we heard it was an abscessed tooth. The following month Maggie Auger received a call that she was very ill; I was at the house at the time. Louisa wanted Maggie and me to know that she had cancer and not long to live, but not to tell anyone. My visit was cut short because my elder, Hubert Buck, had passed away. I tried to visit her on the way to the airport, but we ran into a blizzard and barely made my flight on time. She died only a few weeks later. She was another elder that never lived to see what she wanted most, a settlement.

There are many, many more stories that the grandmothers before them and the ones living today have to tell. The themes are similar: the loss of a way of life they loved, loss of loved ones, and finding strength to continue the battle. Few have visited a community that has been torn apart on every level as the Lubicon have. Yet as a Haudenosaunee elder who visited the community stated, 'As long as the women hold together, the Nation will survive no matter what. When the women fall, so do all the people, the Nation' (Chief Hubert Buck, 1991).

Epilogue

The Women's Circle lost momentum not long after I left the community. The strain of funerals, wakes, conflict and continued struggle left little energy for the women to organize. I visited the community in the winter of 1997. The elders interviewed had all since passed away. The land claim was not settled. There was now a sour gas plant located near the land set aside for the Lubicon community near Lubicon Lake. Logging, oil exploitation and other development projects continue as the Lubicon struggle to hang in there. I meet up with Jennifer Ominayak and others in Edmonton at least once a year. She tells me of the many miscarriages, the family violence, alcohol abuse, illnesses and depression many young women are experiencing. The community is on hold; schools, homes, health centres – life on hold. I understand why the only control some young women feel is to take their own lives: then no one can hold them hostage or put their lives on hold anymore. I have talked several young Lubicon women out of suicide, but I am running out of words of encouragement. The Lubicon women know they are under attack in a silent war of wills between their people and corporate interests and the governments. Their main goal in telling their stories is for Canadians, the people, to know how it feels to be a Lubicon woman.

The Lubicon women are testimony to the sheer strength of Indigenous women, who hang in there no matter what.

Notes

This chapter, the Lubicon research, and the analyses cited here are all collective efforts, and therefore ownership of the work cannot be claimed by one person. Elders from Lubicon, Six Nations and the western prairies have touched the thinking, the patterns and the work in ways both big and small.

1. The dynamics of this Indigenous knowledge encourage an adherence to the Creator's law, which is manifested and revealed through ceremony, song, dance and prayer. They are the glue which unites Indigenous consciousness (Mieli 1991; Dumont 1990; Die et al. 2000).

2. All unpublished passages quoted in this chapter were tape-recorded and transcribed

from interviews, meetings and events during my field research (see Martin-Hill 1995 and in press).

References

Battiste, Marie and James Henderson-Youngblood (2000) *Protecting Indigenous Knowledge and Heritage: A Global Challenge*, Purich's Aboriginal Issues Series, Saskatoon, Saskatchewan: Purich.

Churchill, Ward (1997) *A Little Matter of Genocide: Holocaust and Denial in the Americas 1492 to the Present*, San Francisco: City Lights Books, 1997.

––––––– (1999) *Struggle for the Land: Native North American Resistance to Genocide, Ecocide and Colonization*, Winnipeg: Arbeiter Ring.

Dei, Sefa, Budd L. Hall, and Dorothy Goldin Rosenberg (eds) (2000) *Indigenous Knowledges in Global Contexts: Multiple Readings of Our World*, Toronto: University of Toronto Press.

Dickason, Olive Patricia (1992) *Canada's First Nations: A History of Founding Peoples from Earliest Times*, Toronto: McClelland & Stewart.

Dumont, James (1990) 'Journey to daylight land', unpublished MS, University of Sudbury, Ontario.

Frideres, James S. (1993) with Lilianne Ernestine Krosenbrink-Gelissen, *Native Peoples in Canada: Contemporary Conflicts*, 4th edn, Scarborough: Prentice-Hall.

––––––– (1998) with Lilianne Ernestine Krosenbrink-Gelissen, *Aboriginal Peoples in Canada: Contemporary Conflicts*, 5th edn, Scarborough: Prentice-Hall, Allyn & Bacon.

Fulton, David (1986) 'Fulton discussion paper', February, unpublished.

Goddard, John (1991) *Last Stand of the Lubicon Cree*, Vancouver and Toronto: Douglas & McIntyre.

Jaimes, M. Annette (ed.) (1992) *The State of Native America: Genocide, Colonization, and Resistance*, Boston, MA: South End Press.

Lennerson, Fred (1989) 'The Lubicon Lake Nation Cree', unpublished paper, Edmonton, Alberta.

Lubicon Settlement Commission of Review (1993) 'Final report', Edmonton: Lubicon Settlement Commission of Review.

Mandelbaum, David G. (1979) *The Plains Cree: An Ethnographic, Historical, and Comparative Study*, Regina: Canadian Plains Research Centre.

Martin-Hill, Dawn (1995) 'Lubicon Lake Nation: spirit of resistance', Ph.D. thesis, Dept of Anthropology, McMaster University.

––––––– (in press) *Indigenous Knowledge and Power: The Lubicon Lake Nation*, Toronto: University of Toronto Press.

––––––– (ed.) (1992) 'Statement from the Lubicon Lake Nation Women's Circle'.

Meili, Dianne (1991) *Those Who Know: Profiles of Alberta's Native Elders*, Edmonton, Alberta: NeWest Press.

Richardson, Boyce (1989) *Drumbeat: Anger and Renewal in Indian Country*, Toronto: Summerhill Press.

Smith, James G.E. (1987) 'The Western Woods Cree: anthropological myth and historical reality', *American Ethnologist*, vol. 14, no. 3, pp. 434–48.

––––––– (1988) 'Canada – the Lubicon Lake Cree', *Cultural Survival Quarterly*, vol. 11, no. 3, pp. 61–2.

Smith, Linda Tuhiwai (1999) *Decolonizing Methodologies: Research and Indigenous Peoples*, London: Zed Books.

United Nations (1990) 'United Nations: International Covenant on Civil and Political Rights', Human Rights Committee: 38th session, CCPR/C/38/D/167/1984, 28 March.

York, Geoffrey (1989) *The Dispossessed: Life and Death in Native Canada*, Toronto: Lester & Orpen Dennys.

Power dam and industries affecting the Mohawk Nation at Akwesasne

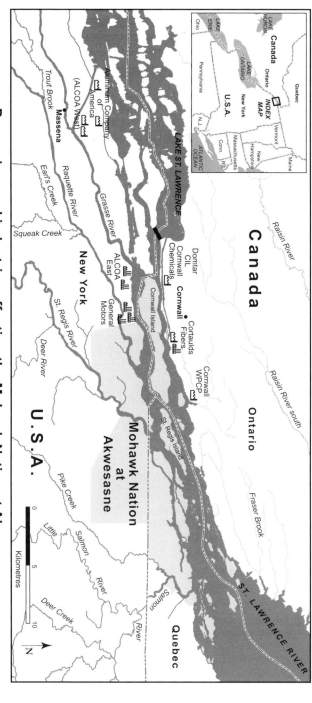

Source: Akwesasne Task force on the Environment.

NOTE: This map indicates the location of the Mohawk Nation
of Akwesasne and not the extent of the Territory of Akwesasne.
The map was prepared under the direction of the book editors,
and it is not an official document of the Mohawk Nation at
Akwesasne or any of its organizations.
Industries and their locations are indicated up to 2000.

©Map by Glenn B. Garner 2003, glennbgarner@yahoo.ca

Legend:

- Canadian or U.S. city
- Moses-Saunders power dam
- River
- State or provincial boundaries
- Water intake / outfall
- Water outfall
- Mohawk Nation at Akwesasne

19

Restoring Our Relationships for the Future

MARY ARQUETTE, MAXINE COLE AND THE

AKWESASNE TASK FORCE ON THE ENVIRONMENT

Mary Arquette is a Mohawk of the Wolf Clan and resides in Akwesasne. She is an environmental toxicologist and Doctor of Veterinary Medicine and has been a member of the Akwesasne Task Force on the Environment (ATFE) since 1986. She currently serves as the chairperson of the Research Advisory Committee for ATFE.

Maxine Cole is Bear Clan from the Mohawk Nation at Akwesasne and mother to one daughter, Kahentawaks. She is working on an M.Sc. in Epidemiology at the University of Ottawa. A member of ATFE since 1998, Maxine Cole was the principal investigator for the cultural resource study regarding the socio-cultural effects of the St Lawrence–FDR Power Project on the Mohawks of Akwesasne.

In 1953 the Federal Power Commission of the United States issued a fifty-year licence for the St Lawrence–FDR Power Project to the New York Power Authority (NYPA). The power project is a hydroelectric development on the St Lawrence River and connects the United States and Canada near the towns of Massena, New York, and Cornwall, Ontario. The dam was completed in 1958 and included development of the Seaway, which required excavation of the St Lawrence river bed to facilitate the passage of cargo ships from the Atlantic Ocean to the Great Lakes. The Great Lakes–St Lawrence River waterway provided a route from the Atlantic Ocean to the interior of the USA and Canada for cheaper and more massive import and export of both natural resources and manufactured goods between North America and global markets.

The NYPA began the relicensing process in 1995. In 1997 the Mohawks of Akwesasne began a parallel process with the NYPA to bring attention to the unresolved issues of the construction of the hydroelectric facility and excavation of the St Lawrence River. As part of the relicensing process, the NYPA is mandated under US federal legislation, the National Historic

Preservation Act, Section 106, to define and identify traditional cultural properties within specific areas of the dam. Consequently, the traditional government and the two elected governments of Akwesasne formed the Mohawk Working Group and in 1999 secured a contract from the NYPA to identify the traditional cultural properties of the Mohawks of Akwesasne. The Mohawk Working Group delegated the work to the Akwesasne Task Force on the Environment (ATFE), which is a community-based organization founded to conserve, preserve, protect and restore the natural and cultural resources within the territory of Akwesasne. The ATFE works to fulfil the responsibilities that we as Onkwehon:we (Original People) have to the natural world to promote the health and survival of the sacred web of life for the next seven generations. The ATFE works with the traditional government and the elected governments of Akwesasne and with individuals to resolve environment issues.

First Words, on Respect and Responsibility

As Rotinonshonni or Haudenosaunee (People of the Longhouse), our perspective on the river and the relationships of respect and responsibility that should exist among all parts of creation are contained in the words of our *Ohen:ton Karihwatehkwen* (Thanksgiving Address). This teaching instructs us to believe in the interrelatedness and interdependency of all parts of the natural world. We believe that in order to gain a true understanding of any aspect of the natural world, respect must be shown for the entire web of relationships that exist and form our natural environment.

We strongly believe that the *Ohen:ton Karihwatehkwen* provides the only appropriate basis for reconciling the disruption of the natural state of the Kaniatarowanenne (St Lawrence River) and our larger environment and for charting a recovery from the changes caused by the St Lawrence–FDR Power Project. It places human beings firmly in an interdependent coequal relationship with what we know as other 'nations' – these being the various elements of creation that others think of as separate species, natural forces and phenomena. Importantly, it places a burden of responsibility upon each nation to ensure the proper functioning of creation. The special set of responsibilities it places on the shoulders of human beings and the lessons it teaches about the fulfilment of our responsibility to the rest of creation make it a crucial teaching in the struggle to understand environmental and social justice. For this reason, and because the *Ohen:ton Karihwatehkwen* reflects the elegance and power of our narrative tradition, its substance and structure will be the foundation of our approach to addressing the problems before us and in working with the NYPA.

Two-Row Wampum

As told by our elders and other knowledge-keepers, when the Dutch first came to Turtle Island, the Rotinonshonni welcomed them as friends. As the two peoples lived side by side in peace and harmony, they decided to continue their friendship – a relationship based on respect for each other and a commitment to peace. The two peoples came to an agreement about the terms of the relationship, and to ensure that this agreement would pass on to succeeding generations, the Kahswenhtha (Two-Row Wampum) was created. The principles reflected in the Kahswenhtha have always guided the Rotinonshonni in the conduct of their relations with other nations, but the Kahswenhtha was especially created to govern the brotherly relations between the Rotinonshonni and the newcomers – a kinship that would provide mutual aid when necessary. These living principles, if respected, are still capable of ensuring just and peaceable relations between our peoples into the future. They will also ensure a respectful coexistence in the river of life for the Rotinonshonni and the newcomers, as was the original intent.

As a physical object, the Kahswenhtha is a belt of two purple rows of wampum (beads which are made from quohag shells) on a background of white wampum. In its design and colouring, the three white rows of wampum signify peace, friendship and respect between the parties to the agreement. The two rows of purple wampum symbolize a canoe and a sailing ship moving parallel to each other in the river of life, with the understanding that neither nation is to interfere with the other's culture.

In essence, the canoe and the ship symbolize two distinct nations. This concept of a relationship reflects a deep spiritual commitment to the integrity of all peoples' identity and right of self-determination. The Kahswenhtha instructs that we must not attempt to steer each other's vessel. These ideas continue to be a fundamental principle in the Rotinonshonni's negotiations with the newcomer nations. Any restoration and protection of the Kaniatarowanenne and its surroundings must consider the principles of the Kahswenhtha. If respected, the Kahswenhtha will help to establish a sustainable relationship, thus ensuring that restoration and protection of the environment will occur.

The issues before us present a complex web of problems. But the heart of the matter is simple: the Kahniakehaka (Mohawk or People of the Flint) have a special relationship with the Kaniatarowanenne, and this relationship has been undermined. The recent damming of the river has seriously altered the fabric of our community and all of the other nations in the natural world of this area and is in direct violation of the Kahswenhtha. As Kahniakehaka, along with our Rotinonshonni sisters and brothers, our identity is constituted in the values, principles and beliefs embedded in our ancient and living culture. For Rotinonshonni, the Kaniatarowanenne and the other waters in our territory are the bloodlines of Mother Earth: they are sacred and very much alive. The river, and all that it relates to, feeds and shelters, are part of our culture and our identity.

Robert Moses and the St Lawrence Seaway

Sadly, during the 1950s, the damming and industrialization of the Kaniatarowanenne dramatically altered our long-standing relation with the river. The master plan for this development included the construction of the St Lawrence River–FDR Power Project and the St Lawrence Seaway and the industrialization of the region. The people of Akwesasne named the power project and development of the Seaway 'the Project'. In addition, it was understandable that the people would view the Project holistically because its proponents explained all the components of the development as a package deal. Robert Moses, chairman of the NYPA and an astute politician, engineer and the Project developer, expressed very clearly the 'need' to 'develop' the river. Also clear was Moses' determination to see the Project completed in New York State.

> Moses' ideas for economic and energy development were the keys to his master plan and were to have the most impact on Mohawk life along the St Lawrence River.... By developing public hydroelectric power along the St Lawrence River ... he would stimulate heavy industry and at the same time, seaway transport. By constructing a series of parks and parkways for tourism and recreational purposes, while providing special low rates for St Lawrence residents, he would counter any local opposition to the project. By improving the state's total economic picture, he would satisfy the utility companies' quest for increased profit margins. By sacrificing Indian land or those that were claimed by Indians, who were small powerless racial minority largely outside the American electoral process, he would not alienate white voters and their political representatives, especially in the economically depressed North Country.... Dams, reservoirs, and power development were part of the 1950s idea of progress and were seen as more important than Indians and the protection of their treaty rights. (Hauptman 1986: 141)

Incentives for Development

As part of the package deal, Project proponents encouraged several industries to move to the region, attracting them with the promise of cheap hydroelectric power provided by the dam. The General Motors Corporation – Central Foundry Division (now Powertrain Division), Reynolds Metals, and the Aluminum Company of America (ALCOA) have utilized this inexpensive electricity for more than forty years to operate facilities in Massena, New York. Currently, the three industries receive an allocation of 57 per cent of the total hydro power generated from the St Lawrence–FDR Power Project. The power of Kaniatarowanenne has been used to import raw products for these industries and export processed materials, commodities and goods to global markets. As a result of this industrial activity, toxic-laden waste was dumped in and adjacent to the river. In effect, the power dam, owned by the NYPA, a public utility, has served to subsidize the environmental contamination of the St Lawrence, Racquette and Grasse rivers and their ecosystems.

As understood by Kahniakehaka, once the energies of the many nations of the ecosystem had been altered and harmed by dams – due to flooding; continual changes in water levels, nutrient levels, and flow rates; the loss of spawning grounds; entrainment; and now pollution – they could no longer fulfil the responsibilities given to them by the Creator. The scientific view is that specific forms of damage have resulted from the accumulated harm caused by the damming of the river and its resulting industrialization. Our view is that as a consequence of these actions, the reciprocal relationships between human beings and non-human nations have been negatively affected. By the mid-1980s numerous scientific studies reflected what our people noticed years before. Undeniable evidence showed that the damming of the river and industrial activity located along it were endangering the well-being of humans, land, plants, water, animals, fish and the skyworld.

> The Kahniakehaka people believe that it is our responsibility to speak on behalf of the other nations whose lives are as inextricably tied to the health of the Kaniatarowanenneh, as they are for us. For that reason, the expressions of concern presented here today are not only on behalf of the people, but on behalf of all the elements of creation who are directly and indirectly impacted by the New York Power Authority power-generating facility on the Kaniatarowanenneh. (Joyce Mitchell-King, Kahniakehaka Nation Council of Chiefs 1997)[1]

It is this profound sense of responsibility and the sincere desire to preserve our culture that motivate our people in the actions they have taken. It is our strong belief that we must turn away from the attitudes and practices that have brought such harm to the natural world and to our relationships with creation. We continue to demonstrate respect for all nations by defending them. It is clear that the construction of the St Lawrence–FDR Power Project has affected the natural world, including the people.

In this spirit and with this commitment, we take up our responsibility to demand respect for the environmental philosophy of the Haudenosaunee. The foundation of our environmental philosophy lays out a path to maintaining and restoring relations between all nations and people. When relations with all nations are restored, we people regain our balance and harmony with the natural world and are better able to fulfil our responsibilities. This chapter concludes with a set of recommendations that we believe could serve as the basis for restoring the natural world that has been disrupted by the damming of the Kaniatarowanenne.

The Kahniakehaka and the NYPA come from two very different cultures, and we do not expect the NYPA readily to understand our relationship with or attachment to the environment. However, any misunderstanding can be cleared up with the NYPA's cooperation and with meaningful consultation with the Kahniakehaka, which can be established over time. Each successful consultation can form the basis of an ongoing relationship that is built on trust. As trust continues to be built, it will become inherent, and meaningful negotiations will take place.

In the dialogue that will evolve from this chapter, we invite the NYPA and the relevant governments of the United States to extend their vision into the future and to see things as we do – from a position of love, respect and concern for other people, the land, the water, the animals and fish, the plants and trees and our relatives in the skyworld. We firmly believe that it is possible to coexist peacefully and with justice for all. By striving to achieve *kanikonri:io* (the good mind) and by acting on the principles of the Rotinoshonni environmental philosophy, it is possible to transcend history and restore balance and harmony in our world. We pray that NYPA members will take up their responsibility as human beings, so that we can welcome them as brothers and sisters sharing the path of righteousness and reason into the future.

Issues of Concern to the Natural World

We offer these words with respect for the inherent wisdom of the *Ohen:ton Karihwatehkwen*, both as a teaching tool and as a way of understanding the proper relations among the nations in the natural world. In effect, these words are a reading of the *Ohen:ton Karihwatehkwen* for the time and place we live in today. Because of the substance of the issues we face as a community, these words will go beyond a thanksgiving to include a lament for the injuries that have been done to the nations and to our relations with them.

The people

> Today we have gathered and we see that the cycle of life continues. We have been given the duty to live in balance and harmony with each other and all living things. So now, we bring our minds together as one as we give greetings and thanks to each other as people.

The Creator has given us the duty of maintaining peaceable relations between the other nations of the natural world and ourselves. People are not superior to the natural world; we are interrelated with the nations and celebrate their diversity, which sustains balance and harmony. Our primary responsibility is to listen to the other nations and to share our interpretations of their messages with our fellow human beings. People have a concomitant responsibility to strive for and preserve the well-being of other nations to enable them to carry out their duties. We are able to communicate with other nations through the land- and water-based activities that we carry out and by continuously acknowledging the gifts provided by these relationships through our language, ceremonies, dances, songs and medicine societies.

Our responsibility as human beings in creation is to strive for balance and to live in harmony with each other and with all living things. The duties we have as human beings and the balance and harmony we seek as an ideal are reflected in our relationship to the Kaniatarowanenneh. When we are fulfilling our duties, we enjoy the fruits of balance and harmony in the health, happiness and prosperity of our people. When we neglect or are prevented from fulfilling our duties, we suffer the consequences in many different ways.

Our people maintained balance and harmony in our natural environment since time immemorial. The river also fulfilled its responsibility to the other nations by sustaining them with water, cleansing the land, and providing spawning grounds, breeding sanctuaries, staging areas, feeding grounds and wintering areas, migration paths and corridors, and habitat for plants, fish, birds, mammals and other creatures. Previously, the river had provided the Kahniakehaka with food to eat or barter for other goods, a means of transportation, places for recreation for meditation, a source of power to heal and physical and spiritual sustenance. The creation of the Project interrupted the Kaniatarowanenne's natural flow. Our peace was disrupted and our relationship with the river forcibly severed in very real ways by the actions of the newcomers.

People in Akwesasne were never consulted; nor were they ever offered substantial compensation for their lost property. Furthermore, since the 1820s, the ownership of traditional territory for Akwesasne has been an issue between the US federal government and New York State. The NYPA was well informed of the land claims, but no consideration was given to the people of Akwesasne to discuss this issue. Mistrust and anger resulted.

Cultural and dietary changes

The Project created a dramatic transformation in the community. From a traditional society rooted in the culture and values of the Rotinoshonni, we were forced into the mainstream economy and found ourselves pressured by the values of that competitive, materialistic culture. Our traditional economy was disrupted as a result of not being able to rely upon farming, fishing, trapping, hunting and gathering as a means of living. Lost to our people were the opportunities to engage in important traditional cultural practices. A large number of our men worked on the Project as construction specialists for the short term. When it altered the land and river, these men were not able to return to their traditional land-and water-based practices. Consequently, they maintained non-traditional jobs, which eventually led them to leave the community. Family life suffered. Aside from the deep social disruption this caused, our community began to suffer culturally from the effects of having the core of our traditional political and social system, the family, ripped apart, as well as having English supplant Kahniakeha, the Mohawk language. We view the building of the Project as a major disruption of our social and cultural continuity.

With the disappearance of certain species of freshwater fish – the American eel, for example – our ability to communicate with that particular fish has diminished, hence our language has suffered. The impact is also reflected in the loss of protein in our diets, which has resulted in higher incidence of diabetes. (This was confirmed by a health study conducted by physicians from the Mount Sinai School of Medicine, Selikoff 1980.)

The Project has endangered our previous peaceful coexistence – the entire network of responsibility and interdependency among all these nations has been undermined. Interdependence and self-sufficiency are intricately linked; once one is broken the other is affected as well. Our strength as a people has been threatened by the Project and our self-sufficiency has been undermined. The Project and the dangers it brought physically prevented the people from achieving the three main cultural requirements for human fulfilment in our tradition: *sken:nen, kahsahstenhsera tanon kanikonri:io* (peace, power and righteousness).

The Earth

> We are all thankful to our Mother, the Earth, for she gives us all that we need for life. She supports our feet as we walk about upon her. It gives us joy that she continues to care for us as she has from the beginning of time. To our Mother, we send greetings and thanks.

When the Creator gave the Kahniakehaka the *Ohen:ton Karihwatehkwen*, he instructed the people to give thanks and greetings for all of creation. Each day we are to give recognition to the importance of the earth as our mother and to give thanks for all her gifts. Without fail since time immemorial,

Mother Earth has provided us with food and the essentials necessary for life. As Kahniakehaka we know that our survival depends upon Mother Earth fulfilling her responsibilities. When damage is done to the earth, such as that caused by the Project, it is our responsibility to correct that damaging force and to restore balance to our relationships with the earth. As the sustainer of life, the earth provides for all the nations and the people. As part of our responsibility, we must work hard to care for, protect and repair any damages that occur to Mother Earth. This is of primary importance in fulfilling our duties as Kahniakehaka.

Through our culture, in the form of stories and myths, spiritual beliefs, ceremonial activities and the practices of sharing and providing mutual aid, we have defined appropriate and necessary modes of behaviour in harvesting the gifts from the earth. Our culture also affirms and reinforces our relationship to the earth and other nations. These behaviours, which are land-based practices and activities, have evolved over time to reflect the changes to the land as well as the necessity to adapt to our changing world to sustain our relationship with the earth. Our culture is built on learning, which ultimately includes sharing of traditional knowledge generation to generation. It is the intergenerational teaching and learning about the importance of the land that secure a future for the Kahniakehaka.

The transference of naturalized knowledge systems involves activities that provide a foundation for our social and cultural values and beliefs. The family is the basis of the social organization, and in turn fishing, hunting, trapping, gathering, gardening and farming reinforce these kinship relations. These activities are part of a dynamic process that involves observational, experiential, theoretical and interactive learning that is acquired over a lifetime. It is through our continued relations with all the nations of the natural world that we will derive sustenance. Once we gain this nourishment from our relationships, we are able to share the nourishment and knowledge of everyday activities that gives strength to the individual, the family, the community, the nation, and thus the Rotinoshonni. The Kahniakehaka who settled in Akwesasne learned through generations of family and friends what the maintenance of a positive and healthy relationship with this land entailed. The relationship was such that the people knew when and how the earth would provide physical, mental, spiritual and emotional sustenance. What we had learned to do was to listen to the land and observe the signs that tell us that the time was right for planting and harvesting. We became part of the land and therefore known as Akwesasronon (People of Akwesasne).

Akwesasne is part of Kahniake, the traditional Kahniakehaka territory, which our people have inhabited since time immemorial. Kahniakehaka made a sacred wampum belt known as the Ohkwaho Kaionwi ne Akwesasne, or the Akwesasne Wolf Belt.

The Akwesasne Wolf Belt [says that] The Land and the People are One. Akwesasronon have a very special relationship with the Land and Territory that they call home. Notice of their ownership is conveyed through their Ohkwaho Kaionwi ne Akwesasne … [Akwesasne Wolf Belt]. It records the Community Charter created by the Mohawks who formed the Akwesasne Community, within the Traditional Kahniakehaka Territory at Akwesasne. (Salli Benedict, Akwesasronon, 1999)

Our attachment to the land is sealed in the fact that generations of our ancestors are buried throughout the territory.

Burial sites are not only found in cemeteries. When I had a miscarriage and we lost our first child, we returned her to the embrace of her earth mother, here in Akwesasne. Only my husband and I know the exact location. It is not for any-one else to know. What I will tell my other children is that their sister is buried here on this land and they must always be respectful of our earth mother and her children. This respect is something very old. It goes all the way back to the creation of our people. When [our child] was placed in the earth, all of this land was considered sacred. Not only does our earth mother embrace the bodies of our human relatives, both past and present, but also she holds the coming faces of the future. All the land is a burial site for someone – a plant, an animal, a bird, and a child. It is for this reason that we must be very careful and respectful of all the earth that makes up our territory. (Akwesasne mother, 1996)

Today this issue of the remains of our dead and their belongings is still unresolved; other people hold many of our 'artefacts', cultural properties and other material pieces of our heritage.

The land is knowledge

In addition to what our teachings communicate to us, we have intimate knowledge of the land. This relationship developed between the people and the land is derived from naturalized knowledge systems, which have been learned. When man-made structures and developments such as the Project do not consider the knowledge acquired over lifetimes and through intergen-erational teaching, artificial barriers are erected which impede the fulfilment of the natural world's essential responsibilities and duties.

The inability to carry out the Creator's instructions results in subtle but profound effects on the people. For most of us, these effects are only noticed when relationships cannot provide the gifts that we take for granted, such as the good, clean earth that nurtures us and supports all life. As a resident of Akwesasne stated: 'We lost more than land when the Seaway and Power Project came through Akwesasne' (Akwesasne Elder, 1990).

The plants and trees

> The plants, trees, fruits and medicines are honoured for their part in this world. They offer nourishment for the well-being of all creation as well as a strong spiritual foundation. The People were instructed to respect the values of the elements contained in the plants, trees, fruits and medicines for their spiritual well-being and their role in creation, and for that we give thanks.

These forms of life are precious gifts from the Creator and are essential to our physical and spiritual survival. It is important to consider the diversity and responsibility of each one of these gifts in the maintenance of harmonious coexistence of all the nations.

All plants, including trees, have energy and power that can be prepared as medicines to help people maintain their well-being. It was common for families to go out and pick certain plants to treat their ailments. 'When I was about fifteen years old, was the first time I went to see a "doctor" when I was sick. All the time before that my grandmother would go outside and come back with plants and fix a medicine for me. Everything we needed was outside' (Akwesasne Elder, 1999). To this day the well-being of many families is dependent on the knowledge of healing plants. Gathering plants for healing is very common throughout Kahniake, including on lands that the NYPA claims as part of the Project.

Other small plants and grasses, which grow throughout the seasons and in various habitats, are special gifts in themselves. They are valuable to us because they filter toxins out of the air, thus providing clean air for the natural world. Some grasses, such as sweetgrass, can be found along rivers and in wetlands and other habitats that have moist soil. Sweetgrass and black-ash splints are used to make baskets. Previously, basket-making was one way the people within Akwesasne would barter for food and other necessities of life. An Elder remembers people bringing in baskets to sell at his grandfather's store and how important they were to the families' survival.

> They made baskets, pounded logs, splints, and pack baskets mostly. Wasn't fancy. Just plain pack baskets. Sold them to stores, lumber camps, hunters brought them and used them. Made them by [the] dozen. Nothing for them to work all winter. No jobs. Make them all winter and sell them in summertime. That was their income. No jobs anywhere. (Akwesasne Elder, 1999)

Today basket-making continues as a means of economy and expressing artistic talent. Exhibitions of contemporary Native artists continue to display baskets alongside paintings, sculpture, photography and other expressive media. Since the construction of the Project there are very few areas left where sweetgrass grows in Kahniake. The NYPA must negotiate with the Kahniakehaka to protect those areas that remain and sustain and restore them to their natural ecosystems. There are many trees that we honour for their gifts, such as the maple for syrup, hickory for lacrosse sticks and axe handles, and black-ash for splints. Countless hardwood trees are used as firewood to heat homes. Ashes from these trees are considered medicine and are important in cooking traditional foods. The trees are acknowledged for the protection from the wind and hot sun that they provide to the nations, including the people and small plants.

The Project continues to harm plants and trees by changing water levels and ice flows, which erodes islands and affects wetlands; promoting poor land-use practices such as spraying pesticides and herbicides; creating tourist areas and buildings; and replacing indigenous plants and trees with foreign horticultural species. The dam has created a physical barrier separating the people from the plants and trees they depend on for survival. The effects on trees and plants have caused alterations in their relations with the other elements of the natural world, including the people. Following the damage to the plants and trees, we have experienced spiritual disruption, interference in economic trade, loss of the Mohawk language, loss of habitat for plants and disruptions to intergenerational teaching.

The waters

> We are thankful to the Waters of the World for quenching our thirst and providing us with strength. Water is life. We know its power in many forms: waterfalls and rain, mists and streams, rivers and oceans. With one mind, we send greetings and thanks to the Spirit of Water.

The responsibilities of the waters are to provide sustenance to all beings, to quench our thirst and to give us strength. Consequently, the waters are the bloodlines of our Mother Earth; they connect, nourish, cleanse and purify all nations. *Tsi Kiontonhwentsison* (the Creation Story) describes the important relationship that we have with the waters. It teaches about the water world existing prior to the creation of the earth. Water animals and waterfowl assisted Sky Woman's landing on the giant sea turtle's back, and thus began the creation of the earth.

The waters have provided spiritual, ceremonial, social and functional gifts to the nations, including the people. Water's energy and power for disciplining and educating children is reflected in stories and legends that speak about water being used to encourage more positive behaviour. They also show our spiritual dependence on the powerful flow of the river and clean water. It is important for the water to be clean, but spiritual, ceremonial and functional uses also require the unrestricted, moving flow of the current.

I remember as a young boy, swimming under the water with a real fast current, really listening to the water. It had a language. You'd see the weeds and the different colour rocks as you're going underwater. And it speaks to you of being free. Our philosophy talks about being free, as an Indian people. (Akwesasne Elder, 1988)

When the waters were healthy, it was common to harvest fish from this clean environment, which was evident from the clarity of the waters.

I used to go fishing with my father; I'd drink water right out of the river. The river was clean then. It was bluish blue, blue and clean colour. You could see, on a calm day, 20–50 feet deep. River bottom, you see fish at the bottom, fish that eat at the bottom.... We use to go spearing. It was a lot of fun.... We caught fish we could eat. (Akwesasne Elder, 1994)

Uses of the waters

In addition to providing gifts of fish for sustenance, the waters provided transportation for the Kahniakehaka throughout the traditional territory. Islands west of the present day St Lawrence–FDR Power Project were reached by boat during the spring and summer months. During winter months people travelled over ice roads on foot or by horse and sleigh. Elders who were familiar with the river and its currents before the Project knew the safest routes to cross the ice. Day trips to socialize with family and friends; to trap, hunt, fish and gather; and to go to the nearby towns to trade goods for food and other necessities were well planned, and access to these areas was never restricted.

When the Project was constructed and the river bed was dredged, it altered the flow of Kaniatarowanenne. As the water level was regulated, the strength and thickness of the ice became unpredictable. While Kahniakehaka were relearning the river, people drowned.

Once the Project was constructed, it severely restricted access to the territory west of the dam. Kahniakehaka say that the dam is also a barrier to the fishermen, hunters, gatherers and other Kahniakehaka. This has caused a serious disruption to our people and has diminished our knowledge and intimacy with the traditional territory. The dam and regulation of the water level prevent the natural cleansing of the river bed and adjacent lands, including the tributaries.

When I moved here in the spring the ice would break up and hit the shore and the land. The ice jams cleaned the bottom of the river. It was so powerful and made such a thunderous noise you could hear it coming. It would take several weeks to go through. You don't see that anymore. The ice jams used to break the shorelines away, but it cleaned everything, it was nature's way of cleaning. (Akwesasne Elder, 1995)

The effects of the Project went far beyond restriction of access to traditional territory. The dam also interfered with bartering for the necessities of life; disrupted family relations; changed relations with the animals and other nations; rendered water unfit for animals, plants and people; and threatened the transference of inter-generational learning. Our minds and souls are linked intricately to the waters and their ability to carry out their responsibilities and duties.

> There was a whole culture of a river. You could talk about the culture of the Cajuns, if you went to Louisiana. Well, among our Mohawks there was a river culture, there was a river language, there were feelings, there were songs, there were stories, and the Seaway just amputated that. (Akwesasne Elder, 1988)

The animals and fish

> We gather our Minds together to send greetings and thanks to all the Animal Life in the World. They have many things to teach us as People. We see them near our homes in the deep forests. They provide us with many essentials. When we are hungry, they become our food. They provide us with furs for warmth and tools for protection and survival. Their stories teach us about life, and for that, we are thankful.
>
> We turn our minds to all the Fish in the Water. They were instructed to cleanse and purify the Water. They also give themselves to us as food to nourish us. We are grateful that we can still find pure Water in this World. We turn to the Fish and send our greetings and thanks to them.

The animals and fish are acknowledged and given thanks for their gifts to all the nations, and in their continued existence they are fulfilling their roles and responsibilities as instructed in the *Ohen:ton Karihwatehkwen*. We acknowledge them and their gifts in our language, ceremonies and songs. In the *Tsi Kiontonhwentsison* a time existed when only the water world was present. It was the water animals and waterfowl that assisted Sky Woman in creating the earth. It was the water animals that made several attempts to grasp dirt from the bottom of the water world, so that Sky Woman could place it on the turtle's back to create the earth. They were the first inhabitants of the earth and were critical in preparing for the coming of human beings.

In many ways we are very much dependent on the life of animals. From a practical aspect we are dependent upon them for our food, clothing, shelter and medicines. They have taught us about medicine. We have learned how to hunt, store food and survive from them. We also rely on them for our emotional and spiritual strength. In many ways, animals remind us of our humanity. They teach us to share, to take care of our children, to protect our territory, to look out for others and to love our families. Our kinship with the natural world is a very real thing. Animals are relatives, and as such they deserve to be treated with respect.

The clan structure that binds our families, communities and nations together is based on the animals, fish and birds from the eastern forest. The animal families have certain distinct characteristics, and we have learned many things from observing their behaviour. The *ronathahion:ni* (wolves) have taught us how to be loyal, how to work together and how to love and take care of our children and community. The *rotiskare:wake* (bears) taught us how to live in the forests by showing us which species of plants, berries and roots are good to eat and which are good for medicine. The *rotiniahton* (turtles) have taught us how to be tough and resilient. The deer, snipe, eel and others have taught us how to live together peacefully as a community.

The construction and ongoing operation of the Project have affected the animals, birds and fish we depend upon, in many ways. If we do not have those other nations in the natural world, critical relationships in Kahniakehaka culture are endangered. Actual contact, observation and reflection are essential parts of the dynamic of how the Kahniakehaka culture is learned. The culture, therefore, is dependent on our ability to interact with healthy populations of animals, birds and fish.

Numerous and various fish habitats have been altered or destroyed by the Project due to altered water flows, changing water chemistry, erosion, loss of wetlands and pollution. The long-term effects on the fish, including the eel, have been noticed by the Elders of Akwesasne. People have witnessed numerous fish and eel sliced or cut up since the Seaway was completed. The Elders believe it is the passage through the turbines of the dam that is the source of these injuries to the fish and eel. Approximately 25 per cent of the eels do not pass through the turbines intact. The Elders are concerned that the adult eel and fish are being destroyed, resulting in fewer reproductive-age fish to replenish the population. The lack of an adequate fish passage at the Project (both upstream and downstream) has been detrimental to the fish and eel nations. This is unacceptable to the Elders.

The disrupted relationship with the turtle is a good example of how threatened our culture is because of the Seaway. Kahniakehaka have many stories and legends that describe the behaviour and characteristics of the turtle. We know that turtle is very old, strong, and resilient and we are reminded of his role every time a turtle rattle is used in our ceremonies. The earth was created on the back of a giant turtle, so any harm to the turtle reflects harm done to the earth. Profound changes have occurred in the turtle's habitat, consequently having dramatic effects on the turtle. The *a'nowara* (snapping turtle) maintains residency in the same area throughout its life. In several areas of Akwesasne, the turtle's habitat is very highly contaminated due to PCBs. For the Kahniakehaka, contamination of the snapping turtle is a warning to all the nations, including the people, that toxins are quickly poisoning our relations with the animals, and there is more to come. It is our responsibility to let other human beings know when the animals are being injured so that we may take appropriate action to regain the coexistence that we have been instructed to strive for.

The skyworld

> The Creator has given the responsibility to the Grandfather Thunderers to put fresh water into the rivers, lakes and springs to quench the thirst of life. Our Eldest Brother the Sun has the responsibility to shine the light so we may see and radiates warmth that all life may grow. Our Grandmother the Moon has been instructed to take charge of the birth of all things and [the Creator] made her the leader of all female life. All babies are born by her orchestration. Our Grandmother the Moon is in charge of the waters of the world and is responsible for the tides. The Stars provide direction in finding our way about the earth and let us know when ceremonies take place for continued thanksgiving for the cycles of life. Our Creator made all life with nothing lacking. As humans our responsibility is to not waste any life and be grateful and give thanks every day.

We have been warned of the implication of not upholding our responsibilities, which will result in effects to all nations including the people. The prophecies of the Rotinonshonni were delivered to the people generations ago. Today, Rotinoshonni Elders are concerned about the natural world and people because of the unfolding of the events that were prophesied. Community members have noted many of these events.

As instructed in the *Ohen:ton Karihwatehkwen*, we must give greetings and acknowledge the natural world we live in, and this should be done on a daily basis. If the other nations are not acknowledged and shown respect, they will leave this earth and travel back to the Creator's world. We have seen the disappearances of many four-legged animals, birds, plants, trees and their habitats as a result of the Project. We can not simply focus our attention on protecting and restoring individual species but must also focus on protecting and restoring sacred spaces that all nations depend on for survival. The lands claimed by the NYPA as within the Project boundaries meet Kahniakehaka definitions of sacred spaces.

For the Kahniakehaka, living with the impacts of the Project has created many obstacles to maintaining peaceful and healthy relations with creation and spiritual beings. As we pray in our traditional and customary ways, our communications with the Creator may not be clear, for even relations with the Skyworld have been altered to some degree. The knowledge of our people and the other nations has been supported by scientific studies that tell us the Skyworld beings have had to work harder to fulfil their responsibilities.

We have continued, however, to carry out our responsibilities of acknowledgement for all nations and the Skyworld, as instructed.

Prophesies instruct us

As we were told in our prophesies, the natural world has begun to unravel, and the Project has been a ruinous force. Our prophesies were told to us because we needed to make conscious decisions about our future, and the future of generations yet to come. Kahniakehaka firmly believe that, in co-operation with the NYPA, we must reflect upon the past and take action not to repeat our mistakes – collectively think about how to protect and restore the natural world to build healthy and sustainable relationships.

The Path of Righteousness and Reason

Sken:nen, Kanikonri:io tanon Kahsahstenhsera

Since the beginning of time, our Creator has told our people to strive for peace: as individuals, communities and nations, we must constantly strive to talk, work and live in peace and to be at peace. Also, we must strive for peace with the nations of the natural world. *Sken:nen* (peace) is more than just the absence of conflict or war; it has spiritual, social and political foundations. *Sken:nen* is the active striving of humans for the purpose of establishing universal justice and is the product of a unified people on the path of righteousness and reason. That means the ability to enact the principles of peace through education, public opinion and political unity. It is the product of a spiritually conscious society using its rational abilities. When we work for *sken:nen*, we develop a *kanikonri:io* (good mind), or a good way of thinking. *Kanikonri:io* means the achievement of a shared sense and mentality of the people using their purest and most unselfish minds. It occurs when people put their minds and emotions in harmony with the flow of the universe and the intentions of the Creator. The principle of this righteousness demands that all thoughts of prejudice, privilege or superiority be swept away and that recognition be given to the reality that creation is intended for the benefit of all beings equally. Reason is seen as the skill that humans must be encouraged to acquire so that the objectives of a good mind may be attained and other nation's rights are not abused. When we work for *sken:nen* and *kanikonri:io*, we develop *kahsahstenhsera*. Strength flows from the power of the good mind to use rational thinking and persuasion to channel the inherent good will of humans to work toward peace, a good mind and unity to prevent the abuse of human beings and Mother Earth.

Using the Kahniakehaka environmental philosophy to think about traditional cultural property and environmental issues in our territory, we are compelled to refocus on restoration. The answers to our problems exist and have existed in the teachings given to us by the Creator. Collectively, all we need to do is to focus our thinking on these teachings and bring our actions in line with the basic teachings that have been part of our culture since time immemorial. The basic problem we face is that we human beings are unable to fulfil our responsibilities to creation properly because of the Project's impact on our culture.

Most importantly, because of the damage to our communities and traditional lifestyles and economies, which resulted in our inability to participate in traditional cultural practices and thus fulfil our duties, our language, our existence as Kahniakehaka, and the existence of other nations of the natural world have been endangered.

We offer the Kahniakehaka environmental and political philosophy to the NYPA as a foundation to the creation of a just and harmonious future relationship with our people. The environmental philosophy as instructed by the *Ohen:ton Karihwatehkwen* and the political philosophy as governed by the Kahswenhtha would establish a relationship based upon peace, power and righteousness and would restore harmony, strength and balance to our natural world and to the Kaniatarowanenne. Based on Kahniakehaka philosophy we have made recommendations to the NYPA.

We have a great opportunity to learn from the past, reorient our relations, and build a relationship based on mutual respect and partnership in the sharing of responsibility in this land and natural world. To achieve this, we must transcend our individualistic motivations and move away from thinking in material terms. It is possible to use the resources of the Kaniatarowanenne in a beneficial and responsible way. It simply means thinking of accountability in a different way. Accountability should mean that we uphold our responsibilities and strive to achieve balance not only of the 'books' but in much broader terms. We call on the NYPA to reconsider its commitment and sense of responsibility and to adopt the approach of a triple bottom line: *sken:nen, kanikonri:io tanon kahsahstenhsera*. In a very real sense, we are asking the NYPA to join us as we reflect, and then to proceed as partners with us in the restoration of balance and harmony in the world that we now share.

Notes

This chapter was made possible because of the work undertaken by the Akwesasne Task Force on the Environment, including the staff, Elders, volunteers, Community and Academic Advisory Committees and many others who assisted. Mary Arquette and Maxine Cole have served as compilers and editors of this text. The chapter is a condensed version of the Cultural Resource Study undertaken by the ATFE to identify the traditional cultural properties of the Mohawks of Akwesasne.

  1. All quotations not from a cited source are from materials shared by community members with the AFTE.

References

Akwesasne (1997) 'Kaniatarowanen:ne: one river, many nations', public scoping hearing held 9 September 1997, Akwesasne Mohawk Nation (64 Mohawk presentations), Akwesasne Mohawk Nation: ATFE.

Akwesasne Task Force on the Environment (1997) 'Superfund clean-up at Akwesasne: a case study in environmental injustice', *International Journal of Contemporary Sociology*, vol. 34, no. 2, pp. 267–90.

———— (2001) 'Cultural resources study', Akwesasne Mohawk Nation: ATFE.

Bilharz, J. (1998) *The Allegany Senecas and Kinzua Dam: Forced Relocation Through Two Generations*, Lincoln: University of Nebraska Press.

Gefell, A. (1988) 'River recollections: portraits of life along the St Lawrence river in the 20th century', *Northeast Indian Quarterly*, Fall 1988, pp. 4–15.

Hauptman, L. (1986) *The Iroquois Struggle for Survival*, Syracuse: Syracuse University Press.

International St Lawrence River Board of Control (1982) 'A report to the International Joint Commission on concerns of the St Regis Band regarding impacts from the St Lawrence Seaway and Power Development', unpublished report.

Parker, P. and T. King (1988) 'Guidelines for evaluating and documenting traditional cultural properties', *National Register Bulletin* 38, Washington, DC: National Park Service.

Patch, S. and W. Busch (1984) *The St Lawrence River – Past and Present*, Cortland, NY: US Fish and Wildlife Service.

Recht, M. (1995) 'The role of fishing in the Iroquois economy, 1600–1792', *New York History* 16, pp. 5–14.

Selikoff, I. (1980) 'Effects of environmental contaminants on the health of the people of the St Regis Indian Reserve', New York City: Mt. Sinai School of Medicine.

Tarbell, A. and M. Arquette (2000) 'Akwesasne: a Native American community's resistance to cultural and environmental harm', in R. Hofrichter (ed.), *Reclaiming the Environmental Debate: The Politics of Health in a Toxic Culture*, Cambridge, MA: MIT Press.

20

In Memoriam

CHIEF HARVEY LONGBOAT (1936–2001)

Haudenosaunee (Iroquois) Confederacy Chief Harvey Longboat (Deskaheh) represented the Confederacy as external affairs officer. A Cayuga Chief for the Bear Clan (Teskahe), he was involved in the 1990 Oka negotiations for the Confederacy. His contributions to developing respectful, heartfelt and insightful communication and friendship echoed a lifelong commitment to enhancing the sovereignty of his people, to education and to mutual understanding. He deeply touched and affected all those who were fortunate enough to know and work with him. He graduated from Wilfred Laurier University and was Superintendant of Education at Six Nations for ten years. Chief Longboat was a central contributor to the development of this project. He encouraged the development of this volume, and prepared a manuscript paper. Unfortunately he passed away before this project, or his paper, were finalized. In Memoriam presents some selections from his paper and from his talk at our meetings. The title and the italic selections are from the talk, the roman from the paper. Words in brackets were supplied by us.

Development: The Beginning to the End

Life in the modern world is one of spectacular scientific, technological and electronic achievement resulting in abundant material prosperity and waste. The cost has been inexorably high. This phenomenon is slowly creeping into all parts of the world, generated by the [North] Americans' vision of progress as based on consumerism and development. These people came to North America to start anew and quickly saw a land of material abundance. They set about taking everything that the land could provide and turning it into wealth, all in the name of progress. This abundant material prosperity has come at the expense of unprecedented exploitation of human and material resources and the degradation of the environment. This vision of development comes from a people who have yet to envision an identity and a cosmological connection with the natural world. The vision is generated by an image without substance, technique without soul, and knowledge without context. The crisis we as peoples of this world face may ultimately lead to a social, cultural, and ecological catastrophe. The people of the Americas must come to grips with who they are, develop a spiritual connection with the natural world, and learn to associate with others in a multicultural surrounding.

When I look at development and the environment and what it means to Indigenous people I find that probably one of the biggest difficulties we have is one of understanding. I think ... that we really do not understand each other....

[I will try] to convey to you what I mean by the beginning and what I mean by the end.... And hopefully ... how we see development, or how we see development so far, and how we see development into the future.

In the beginning, after the Creator completed the natural world with all the plants, insects and animals, he decided to create human life.... Following creation the people drifted aimlessly over time without a purpose that could bring them together and create a cohesiveness. During the history of the Haudenosaunee people the Creator has sent messages to the people when he sees that they face a crisis. This has happened three times. The first message established a formal yearly set of four thanksgiving ceremonies that the people are to perform to show the Creator that they are thankful for everything that they receive to ensure their survival.... This sequence of ceremonies around the natural calendar gives purpose and meaning, helping the people put soul into their relationship with the Creator and the natural world as they struggle to survive....

As time passed our people wandered from these teachings and wars started among groups who had banded together for protection. The Creator again looked down and saw how these wars were destroying his people and sent a messenger to bring peace. The Peacemaker went to these warring groups with a message based on caring, on using a good mind to come to one mind, and on realizing the strength that comes from unity.

The coming of non-Indians brought tremendous change. At first they depended on Native people for their survival, but as time passed mere survival changed to development.... This concept was foreign to people who lived and revered nature.... The Creator again looked at his people, saw the predicament that they were in and sent them another message through Handsome Lake, about 1810. The message is filled with adaptations for ensuring the survival of the culture.... [But also] Handsome Lake makes a number of predictions of what life will be like in the future [predicting environmental damages and wars]....

These predictions colour the entire message, and the warning it leaves us is scary. Throughout, his message is presented in such a way that cultural and environmental survival depends on the actions of the people. So we are the architects of our future.... I would like to end with a plea for understanding other peoples of the world and the environment as we face the crisis of the new millennium.

Index